"A major, highly readable contribution to Canadian legal history."

MICHAEL BLISS, *Toronto, historian and author*

"A fascinating account of one of the greatest and oddest judges in Canadian legal history, Patrick Boyer's vast research has resulted in an important book."

JUNE CALLWOOD, *author and social reformer*

"A powerful, straightforward, superb biography on one of the more influential individuals in the history of Canadian law. Boyer vividly presents, in a highly readable fashion, a fascinating record of an extremely complex Canadian personality ... Thanks to Patrick Boyer, we can all appreciate and understand the human dimension, the flaws of character, and the greatness of a very important, common sense jurist. I recommend this book to everyone interested in Canadian history, law, or letters."

EDWARD L. GREENSPAN, Q.C., *Toronto*

"This book ruined my sleep. I stayed up virtually all night and spent countless hours on planes doing nothing but reading *A Passion for Justice*."

W. LAIRD HUNTER, Q.C., *Edmonton*

"In this engaging study of an outstanding jurist, Patrick Boyer demonstrates that McRuer's legacy derived as much from his famous inquiry into civil rights and his pioneering work as a law reformer as from his accomplishments on the bench."

HON. R. ROY MCMURTRY, Q.C., *former Canadian High Commissioner to the United Kingdom, Attorney General of Ontario, and Chief Justice of Ontario*

"Boyer finally explains what turns someone whom the *Financial Post* once described as 'a decent competent, quiet Toronto lawyer who made an excellent Sunday school teacher,' into a jurist of uncommon distinction with a lasting influence on the legal system of his country.

"Patrick Boyer's masterly biography of James McRuer is far more than a recital of the numerous positions held by McRuer or a listing of his considerable accomplishments. The author investigates the sources of McRuer's views of the law, society and life: family origins, class, relation to the land, ardent political opinions and, in particular, McRuer's deep religious convictions. He also examines how these origins combined with the evolving influences in McRuer's life in forming the lawyer, the judge, and eventually the law reformer. The most significant motivation in McRuer's career is described as his outrage at injustice. This sentiment led him to conceive of the law not only as a set of rules for civil society, but as an expression of personal and collective ethics.

"Patrick Boyer's work is thoroughly researched and informative. While the author is an obvious admirer of McRuer, his treatment of McRuer is entirely balanced."

GREGORY TARDI, *legislative counsel, Ottawa*

"Boyer has done a top-flight job! He's dedicated thousands of hours to this 'labour of love' and and it shows. Patrick even read through McRuer's personal books of account to obtain insights from what he spent his money on. The work from original documents is outstanding, and the interviews Patrick conducted give amazing depth to this story. His gift of many hours of pleasurable reading is a significant contribution to Canadian legal history.

"I only knew Chief Justice McRuer through a small group seminar in my third year of law school but I found him a fascinating individual. *A Passion for Justice* documents his intriguing life, complete with many contradictions. Indeed, Patrick has explained the rationale for many of those contradictions."

HON. JUSTICE RANDALL SCOTT ECHLIN, *Superior Court of Justice (Ontario)*

"Patrick Boyer spent 17 years researching and writing a biography that displays deep admiration for its subject ... an exhaustively researched account of McRuer's long and immensely productive life. His was the life of an idealistic realist—dedicated to fighting injustice, to protecting individual rights and to defending the best of our political and legal traditions, while still welcoming reform."

PETER CALAMAI, *Ottawa journalist*

"*A Passion for Justice*, which is about Canada's greatest law reformer, James Chalmers McRuer, has surprising connections to the United States, from fraud prosecutions and Prohibition era justice to McCarthy era Cold War espionage and the United Nations Charter signed in San Francisco.

"With an engaging grasp of both legal issues and political pressures, author Patrick Boyer, himself a lawyer and former Member of Parliament in Canada, helps Americans see that despite differences in the judicial and political systems of our two countries, we share a deeper connection across issues of law reform, women's rights, protection of the environment, the interests of children under the law, stock frauds, Cold War investigations, grisly murders and far-reaching civil rights issues.

"I cannot imagine how Boyer amassed so many fascinating details."

JUDGE JOAN ZELDON, *Washington, D.C.*

"Donald Creighton with his splendid two-volume study of John A. Macdonald clearly established that biography can enrich history. Patrick Boyer has now revealed that biography can enliven the study of law. Lawyers and law students owe a great debt of gratitude to Boyer for painstakingly producing this outstanding portrait of a great jurist and law reformer."

GORDON BALE, *Emeritus Professor of Law, Queen's University, Kingston*

"McRuer was a splendid lawyer and also a great judge, often a royal commissioner, and a law reformer across the board, from the constitution to monopoly-busting to crime and the police. Patrick Boyer as McRuer's biographer had so much on his plate: more than half a century of accomplishments by a marvel of brainpower, energy and dedication. The image of a shy, austere, puritanical, busy, incisive, polymath does break through the long train of deeds. McRuer was so capable that time and again Tory politicians gave him big jobs though he was a keen, open Liberal.

"It's unlikely that any other Canadian lawyer has ever done so much so well and so often for public good. So Boyer had much to chop and compress. One gets almost a synopsis of legal issues from the 1920s to the 1980s ... revealing of our courts, our judges, and the law a fascinating and very political panorama."

DOUGLAS FISHER, *Ottawa, Parliamentary Press Gallery*

"Whatever the place of that 'passion for justice' in the makeup of this complex, contradictory, and perhaps unknowable man, McRuer undoubtedly reflected and influenced the nature and practice of law in his day. He is well served by this widely researched and fluently argued study."

CHRISTOPHER ENGLISH, *St. John's, Newfoundland, historian*

"Boyer's opus is hardly a dry, historical tome. Far from that, it is a highly readable account of an industrious man who believed that law should be used to improve the lot of ordinary human beings. Of particular interest is Boyer's description of Canada's seven penitentiaries, the scene of 16 full-scale riots between 1932 and 1937. Boyer has done a remarkable job in making McRuer more understandable, if not necessarily more likeable."

HAROLD LEVY, Toronto Star *courts and law writer*

"This great piece of Canadiana traces the life and delineates the complex character of a man who was born and raised on a farm near Ayr, Ontario in the latter part of the 19th century and who died in Toronto in 1985—a veteran of the First World War, active in the work of his church and his political party, a prison reformer, busy counsel, president of the Canadian Bar Association, justice of the Court of Appeal for Ontario, chief justice of High Court for Ontario, sole commissioner of the Royal Commission Inquiry into Civil Rights, first Chair of the Ontario Law Reform Commission—a true public servant whose work throughout, as the title indicates, was informed a passion for justice."

HON. JOHN W. MORDEN, *Counsel to the Royal Commission Inquiry into Civil Rights, 1964–71*

A PASSION FOR JUSTICE

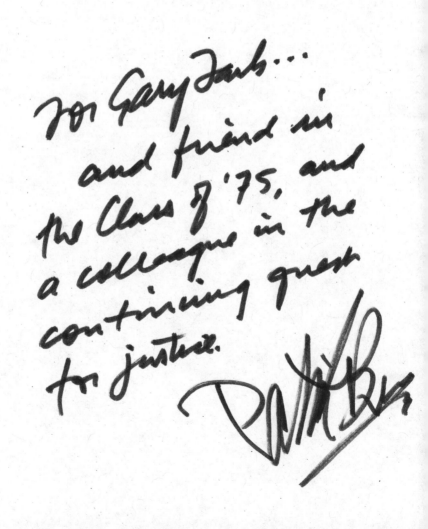

For Gary Jarls...
and friend in
the Class of '75, and
a colleague in the
continuing quest
for justice.

A PASSION FOR JUSTICE

*How "Vinegar Jim" McRuer Became
Canada's Greatest Law Reformer*

J. PATRICK BOYER, Q.C.

Foreword by

Hon. R. Roy McMurtry, Q.C.

*President, Osgoode Society
for Canadian Legal History*

Blue Butterfly Books
THINK FREE, BE FREE

Blue Butterfly Book Publishing Inc.
2583 Lakeshore Boulevard West, Toronto, Ontario, Canada M8V 1G3
Tel 416-255-3930   Fax 416-252-8291   www.bluebutterflybooks.ca

Complete ordering information for Blue Butterfly titles is available at:
www.bluebutterflybooks.ca

First publication of paperback edition: 2008.
Hardcover edition published by The Osgoode Society for Canadian Legal History
ISBN 0-8020-0656-6   www.osgoodesociety.ca

LIBRARY AND ARCHIVES CANADA CATALOGUING IN PUBLICATION

Boyer, J. Patrick
A passion for justice : how "Vinegar Jim" McRuer became Canada's greatest
law reformer / J. Patrick Boyer ; foreword by R. Roy McMurtry.

Includes bibliographical references and index.
ISBN 978-0-9781600-0-5

1. McRuer, J.C. (James Chalmers), 1890–1985. 2. Ontario Law Reform
Commission. 3. Ontario. Royal Commission Inquiry into Civil Rights.
4. Canada. Royal Commission to Investigate the Penal System of Canada.
5. Law reform—Ontario—History. 6. Judges—Ontario—Biography. I. Title.

KE416.M37B69 2008   347.713'014092   C2008-903169-5
KF345.Z9M37B69 2008

Typeset in Minion by Fox Meadow Creations
Printed and bound in Canada by Transcontinental-Métrolitho
Text paper (except picture section) contains 100% post-consumer fibre,
was processed chlorine-free, and manufactured using bio-gas energy.

PHOTOGRAPHS: *Front cover*—Ashley and Crippen, from the McRuer family collection. *Interior*—Unless otherwise indicated, all photographs are from the McRuer family or the author's collection.

No government grants were sought nor any public subsidies received for publication of this book. Blue Butterfly Books thanks book buyers for their support in the marketplace.

This book is dedicated
to the memory of

Catherine Helen MacLean

MANY LIVES TOUCHED *and were touched by James McRuer's.*
Catherine MacLean's was one. Yet this was different, rare to the
point of uniqueness, because she also touched him.

Catherine first met the Great Man in 1974 as a legal research
officer joining the Ontario Law Reform Commission McRuer
chaired. He was 84. She was 24.

To most of his colleagues and acquaintances, the pre-emi-
nent jurist J.C. McRuer was an austere man. Rather than being
intimidated by him, however, Catherine acted as naturally as

she might have with any other older and special person like a grandfather or great uncle. As one of her fellow students and friends at the University of Toronto Law School, I'd got to know Catherine as a bundle of life, always laughing, ever intelligent. At the Law Reform Commission, McRuer got to know her as someone who would actually tease him—and he loved it, chuckling, his eyes twinkling.

When I talked with him about Catherine, he'd suddenly get an easy smile on his face. He'd relax, recalling her on a different channel of memory. It was a beautiful thing.

McRuer delighted in Catherine's lack of formality. She would just walk into his office and comment on something, or engage in quick-witted banter that challenged him and instantly broke the legendary McRuer ice. Yet she was always respectful of him and would never cross that invisible line. Somehow she simply recognized that behind the mask of formality lived a shy and sensitive man. Jim McRuer was, in fact, a lonely man. He hid behind the positions he was in. Catherine went around behind the mask to where the human was. They became close friends.

Twenty-five years later, Catherine was living in Ottawa, a popular part-time professor at University of Ottawa and, as the Law Times *put it, "one of the country's top labour lawyers." She represented public service workers and air traffic controllers in long-running disputes with the government, and in 1989 won a landmark case forcing the government to offer retraining to laid-off federal workers to fill job vacancies. "She loved her clients," said colleague Janice Payne. "The notion of helping people in their workplaces appealed to her tremendously." She was happily planning her wedding.*

On Saturday afternoon, January 27, 2001, Catherine and a friend walked her dog along a sidewalk in the quiet Rockcliffe neighbourhood near Rideau Hall. A car careened out of control and killed her.

The heavily intoxicated driver, Andrei Knyazev, the third-ranked diplomat at the Russian Embassy in charge of political information, claimed diplomatic immunity, just as he had in three previous drunken automobile accidents in the prior two years. Public outrage and the Government of Canada's efforts to have 45-year-old Knyazev stand trial for the five charges that included impaired driving causing death and refusal to provide a breath sample were rebuffed by Russian officials. Catherine's tragic death, the massive injuries to the legs and face of her companion, Catherine Doré, the badly maimed pet dog that had to be put down, and the impunity and indifference of the culprit sparked a national debate over claims for diplomatic immunity under the 1961 Vienna Convention.

Recalled to Moscow, Andrei Knyazev was tried and sentenced to three years. He served four months, then was released.

CONTENTS

FIVE FACES OF LAW REFORM: *R. Roy McMurtry, J.C. McRuer, Derek Mendes da Costa, Arthur A. Wishart, and H. Allan Leal. Each pursued numerous roles in the administration of justice and law reform including, for Roy McMurtry and Arthur Wishart, significant terms as attorneys general of Ontario implementing reforms in law and policy. McRuer, Mendes da Costa, and Leal each served as chairman of the Ontario Law Reform Commission.*

THE TRIUMPH OF HUMAN CHARACTER

by Hon. R. Roy McMurtry, Q.C.

SOMETIMES A LIFE STANDS OUT more sharply the further removed in time that person becomes and the more the individual's impact endures into our own life and times. This is certainly the case with James Chalmers McRuer.

Even in his own day Jim McRuer loomed larger than life in many ways, a character imprinted on his times, a man not only reflecting changing tides in history and Canadian society but also doing something tangible about them. Now in retrospect this jurist, educator, law reformer and advocate stands even taller on the historical landscape for his role in rendering laws and institutions more effective in serving the ends of justice and the needs of the people.

With a life spanning nearly a century of upheaval and change from 1890 to 1985, J.C. McRuer embodied much that was in transition throughout the twentieth century and fulfilled his highest purpose in reforming the law so it kept up with society as society moved forward. This required deep understanding of the purpose of a law, its antecedents, and its future possibilities. It also called for an approach to law reform that was systemic, not sporadic or partial. We who inherit McRuer's legacy are fortunate that a man with these rare talents, and wisdom, also had such a passion for justice.

I recall how feelings about Mr. Justice McRuer were mixed. Some dubbed him "Hangin' Jim" because of the number of murder trials he presided over where the man convicted went to the gallows. Others found his ways prissy and sour and gave him a different moniker, "Vinegar Jim." One commentator, Claude Bissell, president of the University of Toronto, looked back on McRuer's career, focusing on early phases of his zealous activities during the Prohibition era and in church work, and described him as "the last great Puritan." As invariably happens, others then repeated those terms for years which often reflected the spark of battles waged. Certainly many other people in the same period saw Jim McRuer as heroic, inspirational, a man above and apart from his times.

Patrick Boyer's comprehensive perspective on J.C. McRuer, entwining the conditions of his life with the decades of his impact on Canadian society, show us that he was in fact a complex man.

His resolute focus on justice changed the lives of married women with no property rights, children without legal protection, aboriginals caught in the whipsaw of traditional hunting practices and government-imposed game laws, and prisoners locked away and forgotten. Environmental degradation and those causing it, murderers, stock fraud artists, and Cold War spies all came within the purview of J.C. McRuer's sharp legal mind and his profound passion for justice, and now emerge with new clarity on the pages of this remarkable book. As the author demonstrates in a variety of ways, Jim McRuer pushed the limits frequently in many ways.

As a formidable lawyer and distinguished chief justice of the High Court of Ontario, as law reformer and civil rights advocate, he left an indelible mark. For McRuer the law was an integral part of our democratic values and traditions, but nevertheless one that had to be constantly guarded and renewed.

When he stepped down as the chief justice of the High Court of Ontario on reaching age 73, his life did not slow down but shifted into overdrive, an example which has inspired many of us, including myself, who retired as chief justice of Ontario last year. Amazingly, it was then that James McRuer embarked on his most important work of all, namely pioneering contributions in the field of law reform and his famous 1960s Inquiry into Civil Rights. He acquired new energy in this productive fulfilment of his life, remaining active well into his 90s, even addressing legal issues of privacy in relation to spy satellites orbiting the earth. A measure of his impact was the steady pace at which the Ontario government of Premier John Robarts implemented a rigorous law reform agenda from McRuer's flood of recommendations in the 1960s and early 1970s that left virtually no corner of Ontario society untouched. When John Robarts stepped down as premier, a reporter asked him to name the most significant achievement of his government. He replied in a single word, "McRuer!"

Our legal history both enriches our understanding of present conditions and serves to inspire us by showing how a determined individual can work for justice and make a difference. As Patrick Boyer illustrates in this thorough and thoroughly engaging study of an outstanding Canadian jurist, bitter disappointments and deep uncertainties early in his life left Jim McRuer doubting that he would ever make any mark at all. This is therefore a story about the triumph of human character as much as it is about the law.

This particular book, I should also point out, itself has a unique story. Thirty years ago at my summer cottage in Muskoka I read a book by Ontario historian Peter N. Oliver entitled *Public and Private Persons* in which he lamented that Ontario, although Canada's most populous and wealthy province, was impoverished in one respect: it lacked a sophisticated description of its identity. A professor at York University, Peter wrote "one might expect a literature, both creative and historical, which would portray with strength and precision just what it has meant over the years to be an Ontarian. Curiously, such a literature does not exist."

About that time my friend Patrick Boyer arrived for dinner and we began discussing this subject at length into a Muskoka summer's night. Patrick, who holds degrees in both law and history and had already written several books dealing with law in its historical context, shared the concern I outlined, triggered by Peter Oliver's observation. I had long been concerned that many historically significant and colourful stories making up our legal history were disappearing into the mists of time. I was happy that my own father, Roland Roy McMurtry, Q.C., had written his book *Days in Court* before he died, but I knew he had many more important stories that had never been recorded.

As a history major at university, I believed strongly that it was important to record our history, in order to pass on a rich and accurate legacy to future generations. As the attorney general of Ontario at the time, I not only felt a personal responsibility but also believed that it was time to act. I learned that Patrick and Peter Oliver were friends who had worked together for Ontario's Oral History Project, conducting interviews of numerous figures about their earlier days in the public life of the province. He agreed to arrange a meeting. A few days later, on the morning of August 17, 1978, Patrick arrived with Professor Oliver for our first meeting in the attorney general's office on the eighteenth floor at 18 King Street East in Toronto. Suddenly everything began to come together.

With the enthusiastic support of the Law Society of Upper Canada, a new entity, The Osgoode Society for Legal History, was soon incorporated in 1979 to sponsor research, and the publishing of the books that would in turn create the distinguished legacy of The Osgoode Society. Peter Oliver served as editor-in-chief from 1978 until his death in 2006. Marilyn MacFarlane, who had worked with Peter and Patrick in the Oral History Project, joined The Osgoode Society and for three decades has successfully managed its operations. The Law Foundation of Ontario has supported The Osgoode Society financially from the beginning, and today it is supported by a number of generous donors and growing membership. The Osgoode Society has now published some seventy books covering a broad range of Canadian legal history and has significantly influenced the writing of legal history in other jurisdictions.

Peter Oliver recommended to J.C. McRuer that Patrick Boyer write the official biography and The Osgoode Society supported the project which extended over seventeen years. During that period, Patrick also served for nine years as a Member of Parliament and wrote six texts on election law in Canada. On one occasion I hosted a dinner party at which those familiar with McRuer could relate their anecdotes and describe the major events that they had shared with him. Patrick's note-taking that evening resulted in many important additions to his manuscript that are both highly entertaining and enhance the historical record.

Patrick Boyer's biography of James McRuer, first published in hardcover as one of those Osgoode Society titles, is now appearing for the first time in paperback. I am delighted because *A Passion for Justice* deserves the widest audience including individuals who have no direct connection to the legal profession.

Patrick's own experience as a journalist, lawyer, university professor, parliamentarian, and chair of public policy organizations has enabled him to capture J.C. McRuer's professional life with realistic balance. His singular accomplishment is bringing this fascinating story onto the pages of his biography which has led to many positive reviews in both the popular and scholarly journals when the hardback edition of *A Passion for Justice* appeared.

—*Hon. R. Roy McMurtry, O.Ont., Q.C.*

Toronto, Ontario
March 4, 2008

AUTHOR'S PREFACE

ONE DAY, ON SITTING DOWN TO LUNCH in the parliamentary restaurant, I found myself between two senators. When the conversation turned to what I was doing in my spare time, I replied, "Writing a biography of J.C. McRuer."

Senator Richard Doyle, former editor of the *Globe and Mail*, grew almost misty-eyed. "McRuer was the greatest law reformer this country has ever seen," he asserted conclusively. On hearing this, Senator David Walker, former Toronto lawyer and Diefenbaker confidant, could not contain himself. "McRuer! He was the meanest son-of-a-bitch I ever encountered."

Doyle and Walker were both right. Over seventeen years, while gathering the information for this book, I have heard hundreds of McRuer stories. Some of these portray McRuer as someone who was almost a saint; others describe a much different man, the mean, authoritarian "Vinegar Jim." Arthur Martin, who chose his words carefully, said "McRuer could be mean." Not that he was mean in nature, but could be when he became seized of an issue. John W. Morden, who worked closely with McRuer and knew him very well, believed "McRuer pushed beyond the limits of what a judge ought to have done" in the KVP river pollution case, the Evelyn Dick "torso murder" case, and the Mason case of a wife forced to sell her farm property. Everyone saw a part of Jim McRuer; no one saw him all. Many dimensions of his character were either hidden behind the mask of his austere judicial personage or obscured by his ceaseless compulsion to work. When his son John read an earlier draft of the manuscript, he was surprised to discover "how very little I know about Father. I feel closer to him as a result of your work, than I ever did, at any time." John Morden read this book and told me, "I learned things I didn't know, and I was very close to him." J.C. McRuer was a tower of strength—but a strength unto himself.

I first met McRuer in the 1960s when working as executive assistant to Ontario Attorney-General Arthur Wishart, who was busily engaged in implementing a vast array of legislation based on the ideas and recommendations that had poured forth steadily from McRuer's commissions on civil rights and law reform. He was referred to by most everyone at Queen's Park as "J.C."—a shorthand expression that some used respectfully, others less so (as if an abbreviation for "Jesus Christ"). I still remember the surprise I therefore felt one day when Rendall Dick, the deputy attorney-general, handed me a book with the comment, "You'll enjoy reading this." It was entitled *The Trial of Jesus*, and the author was J.C. McRuer.

The more I learned about McRuer the more I recognized that, whether people liked him or not, or whether they turned to him for support or from him in fear, everyone was in awe of his accomplishments. How did he do it? Why, when most people retire in their sixties, did this one-man industry keep running? He did some of his most significant work after age seventy, he was a regular and active participant in law reform through his eighties, and he was still engaged with public policy issues in his nineties. In time, I began to understand that the reasons for his amazing productivity lay in his self-discipline, his steely determination, and his unshakeable sense of mission. There was a passion in the man— a passion that expressed itself in a burning desire to root out injustice.

His record speaks for itself. Throughout a legal career that spanned more than half a century—from his call to the bar in 1914 to his work on the Ontario Law Reform Commission in the 1960s and 1970s—McRuer had a powerful concern for ones whose voices were often inaudible and whose interests were frequently ignored: the poor, women, children, and native people. Accompanying this concern was a conviction that the justice system should be made to serve the oppressed, regardless of their ability to pay. The intensity of McRuer's commitment to justice for all was evident in his career as a lawyer and in his involvement with the Archambault Royal Commission on Penal Reform from 1936 to 1938. It was to receive its most striking and sustained expression, however, following his appointments as judge on the Ontario Court of Appeal in

1944 and chief justice of the Ontario High Court in 1945. His judicial decisions in the 1940s and 1950s, his work as head of the Royal Commission Inquiry into Civil Rights (1964–71), his years as chairman and later vice-chairman of the Ontario Law Reform Commission (1964–77)—all demonstrated his profound belief that the legal and judicial systems were meant to right wrongs, not perpetuate them.

I spent countless hours with McRuer between 1977, when I started the research for this book, and 1985, the year of his death. He was aware of his place in history and wanted it recorded. More than that, however, he also had a sparkling excitement about the law that he wanted to share with others. Whether it was his injunction to the architects of the new courthouse in Toronto to revise their original drawings to include more public galleries, or his frequent suggestions to me to include some dramatic murder trials in the book so as to hold readers' attention to the workings of justice, Jim McRuer cared that the law be known and understood—not just by judges and lawyers, but by everyone.

So he pressed me as firmly as he dared, since we had agreed that I would finish my series of books on Canadian election law before writing his biography. In 1981 he agreed to write a foreword for one of my other books, and I can still recall him dictating his piece to me during a long-distance telephone call from Florida, where he was vacationing. There was a slight tremble in his voice—he was now in his nineties—but his meaning was resoundingly clear: "It is fundamental to the democratic idea that there be a social acknowledgment that not only must the source of power to govern lie with those subject to power, but they must have a right to define and limit its exercise." As he continued, and I kept writing, I saw him, in my mind's eye, in the inspiring procession of venerable warriors who never give up, who just keep driving on because their beliefs are so strong and their commitment so deep.

This book is the one Jim McRuer was waiting for, but never saw. It is an attempt to understand the essence of McRuer the man and the jurist, and also to assess his work as Canada's greatest law reformer. McRuer was a very private person who, like many of his generation, carried himself with an air of quiet dignity and seldom let his feelings show, even to his own family. He was also immensely complicated—the judge who was so committed to penal reform was known as "Hanging Jim" for his readiness to send people to the gallows, and his commitment to justice did not prevent him from sometimes displaying in his personal life a curious insensitivity to human feelings. In the pages that follow, I endeavour to delve behind McRuer's legendary reserve with the aim of exploring the complexity of his character and of explaining how that character shaped his career and the nature of his contribution to the law.

JAMES CHALMERS MCRUER died on 6 October 1985. On the 9th, family, friends, and colleagues gathered for his funeral in Bloor Street United Church, Toronto. The eulogy, delivered by the Reverend Clifford Elliott, was both eloquent and accurate. "If we were to think of a word that became flesh and dwelt among us in the person of J.C. McRuer, the word that would immediately spring to mind is 'justice.' In fact, if he had not been officially called 'Justice McRuer' we would have nick-named him that. For justice was the theme of his life." McRuer knew that justice by itself was meaningless, said Elliott, "unless it was translated into specific laws, actions and attitudes. He knew that justice had to be done." He also possessed in abundance the three elements that are necessary if justice is to be done: "First of all, a keen intellect—to discern injustices and to conceive of laws that would implement justice. Secondly, a strong discipline that does not allow for sentiment nor the attitude of others nor powerful opposition, nor least of all self-indulgence or sloth, to get in the way. But most of all for justice to be done we need someone with a passion for justice."

The next day, some sixty miles to the southwest of Toronto, the heavens opened and the rain came down. The pale yellow of the autumn foliage brightened the mood a little, and dark green spruces sheltered those of us waiting by the graveside. At half-past two that afternoon, a long black hearse pulled into the cemetery. Transporting Jim McRuer's coffin, it slowly came past the rows of grey tombstones and along the curving soft-earth road. We were standing upon a height of land overlooking the village of Ayr, the place where, almost a century before, McRuer's story had begun ...

1

AYR AND BEYOND

IN 1890, THE YEAR OF JIM McRUER'S BIRTH, the British empire was vast and still very much intact. The dominant culture of English-speaking Canada—white, Anglo-Saxon, Protestant—placed a high value on membership in that empire, and nowhere was this imperial sentiment more widespread or fervent than in Ontario. Even people with no family ties to the British Isles referred to "the Old Country," and their school-age children were intensively instructed in Shakespeare, Milton, Scott, and Dickens, in the heroics of the explorer Dr. David Livingstone and the anti-slavery crusader William Wilberforce, and in the major events of English constitutional history. These pupils in small and scattered schoolhouses gazed with respectful awe at the Mercator map of the world (provided courtesy of the Cadbury Chocolate Company) where they could see the colonies of the British empire—on which the sun never set—coloured a bright red.

Canada then counted for a wide expanse of British red on the world map, and most English-speaking Canadians connected with the rest of the world, both emotionally and intellectually, through their personal sense of belonging to this empire. The pervasive Britishness was a cradle of stability. One did not think or speak, in these times, about independence; that was the path the republican Yankees had erroneously taken. Whether in a city, the smallest village, or on the farm, one thought and spoke rather of the world-wide British community—united by common language, common law, parliamentary institutions, and a vibrant and inspiring cultural heritage. As in a dozen other countries, the red-white-and-blue Union Jack fluttered proudly over Canada from a thousand flag-poles.

This vision of Canada and its place in the world, although grand, was held by a small population. In the country as a whole, there were fewer than five million people scattered over a seemingly endless territory. Ontario, styling itself Canada's "Empire Province," had a population of 2,100,000.

Several hundred of these people lived in the village of Ayr and several hundred more resided on the surrounding farms which the village served. This small part of the British empire lay in Waterloo County, whose very name was an evocative reminder of the triumph over Napoleon earlier in the century. The village itself, boasting one of the world's rare place names of only three letters, had been founded by a transplanted Scot familiar not only with the village's namesake in the old country but also with the bard Robbie Burns's description of it: "Auld Ayr, whom ne'er a town surpasses/For honest men and bonnie lasses."

James Chalmers McRuer was born in the family farmhouse near Ayr on 23 August 1890. His undiluted Scottish bloodline flowed from both his father, John McRuer, and his mother, Mary Chalmers, each of Lowland Scottish origin. The name Chalmers derived from the old French phrase *de la chambre*, in the sense either of a chamber attendant or of a member of the treasury chamber (that is, a chamberlain).[1] The name McRuer, a rare one in Scotland, meant "son of three." The stories of its origin vary, but the one best known to the Canadian McRuers involved three brothers of the house of Loren, a sept of the clan McDonald. Two of the brothers fell in love with the same French girl, but when one captured her and carried her off to wed, the other pursued them and in a rage murdered his brother and fled. The girl later died in childbirth, and her infant boy was raised by his two uncles, thus becoming the "son of three" men.

On both his mother's and his father's side, Jim McRuer was born into a family where the struggle to survive, disciplined work, and a readiness to move elsewhere to improve one's lot had become long-standing traditions. His paternal great-grandfather, also named John, was a stone-mason from Doune, Perthshire, who could find no employment in Scotland during the depression that followed the Napoleonic Wars. Together with his wife, Mary Mcintyre, he immigrated to Canada in 1823 in the hope of obtaining work on canal-building projects. They settled first in Montreal, but, having little luck in finding work and with a slow succession of babies to feed, they soon moved on to Lachute, where John used the last of his money to buy 200 acres. With his own hands he hacked out a farm, hard up against the ancient Laurentians, faintly, tauntingly, reminiscent of Doune. Yet it was gloomy territory and the farm was described in a family letter as "rough, hilly, narrow … very poor, mixed farm and lumber, and wilder and rougher than Scotland." Then, too, it galled John McRuer that the land he acquired was still not fully his own—the deed said that he had to pay a levy to the seigneur "as long as the waters run and the mountains stand." By the time he died on his rocky property in 1863, still bitterly homesick for Scotland, the government had in fact made the land free of such charges, through the abolition of the seigneurial system in 1854.

The migratory nature, or restlessness, of the McRuers was borne of economic need, and of the sense that, elsewhere, conditions had to be better and hard work more satisfactorily rewarded. By the 1860s, several of John and Mary's children had already escaped from the Lachute farm. The eldest son, Duncan, the McRuers' pride and joy, was sent, at great family sacrifice, to Knox College in Toronto. He was ordained a Presbyterian minister and posted to Blenheim, Ontario, and then to nearby Ayr, in 1854. At Duncan's encouraging report of fine farmland in the flat and fertile townships of western Upper Canada, the second and fourth sons, John and William, followed him to Ayr in 1864, and bought farms on land west of the Grand River owned earlier by the Six Nations Indians. Duncan himself moved away in the 1870s to minister to some Scottish Canadians who had settled in Gentry County, Missouri. The third McRuer boy remained in Lachute; his two sons stayed there, too, and died in their seventies, two old bachelors rocking on the porch and watching the potatoes grow. The fifth son moved to Kenmore, near Ottawa, followed by the two daughters; and the eighth child, another son, moved to Manitoba to farm.

The John McRuer who brought his wife Jesse (née Drew) from Lachute to Ayr in 1864 had five children survive infancy, the eldest of whom was named, for a third generation in a row, John. This John, sixteen years old when the family moved from Quebec, was to become Jim's father. In 1873 he married Jane Patton, the very young daughter of a prominent local builder. The newlywed couple settled on a farm that had been acquired by John's father (he had purchased good land when arriving in Ayr in 1864 and soon prospered enough to buy two additional farms for his sons), in a house built for them by Elizabeth's father. Their farm was on the townline that ran out from Ayr along the boundary between South Dumfries and Blenheim townships.

The farmhouse built by father Patton was mostly completed by late spring 1874, being constructed with the kind of quality, albeit economical, workmanship one expected of a Scot. Located fifteen yards from the road, its lines softened by clusters of lilac and mountain ash, the house was clad in the warm yellow brick that was a distinguishing characteristic of architecture in southwestern Ontario. Using bricks hauled by wagon from the Muma Company brickworks at the village of Drumbo fourteen miles away, Patton, after laying a solid stone foundation, built the first-storey walls three bricks thick, reducing this to a two-brick width for the second storey. Better materials were used at the front and sides of the house, where they might be seen from the road, than at the rear, and where additions could be readily and inexpensively added as the family expanded.

All these hopes and plans soon shattered. On 14 August 1874 Jane, age seventeen, died in childbirth, and the unborn infant perished with her. Forlornly, John continued to live in the farmhouse. When he did finally remarry, some six years later, his new bride was a strong-willed but affectionate twenty-three-year-old woman named Mary Chalmers. John never spoke about his first wife again.

Mary was a tall, stoop-shouldered lass from Mornington Township, twelve miles north of Stratford. Her family, like John's, had come to Canada to escape the bleak prospects facing them in Scotland. Her grandfather, John Chalmers, and his family, Scottish weavers and paisley shawl makers thrown out of work by the introduction of mechanized looms in the woollen mills, had arrived in Hamilton in 1842 and then made their way to Perth County. They became the first settlers in Mornington Township, starting a farm on land so wild that herds of deer would come in to pasture with the cows. Mary's enterprising uncle Adam, elected a member of the first township council, established the Mornington Fall Fair, a horse and cattle market where participants showed off their home-made manufactures—flannel, tweed, boots, rag carpets, horseshoes—or piled up their cheeses and vegetables in a competition for prize ribbons. The Chalmers, a charter family in this southwestern district of the province, were especially proud of their budding young cousin, Alexander Mackenzie, the Scottish-born stonemason who in 1873 would become Canada's first Liberal prime minister.

The McRuers and the Chalmers rejoiced in the clear and free title to their land. Both families did well, taking advantage of the construction of railways and England's growing demand for wheat during the Crimean War. In 1867 Upper Canada became "Ontario," and, after a rocky decade of world depression, entered an era of steady—though not unbroken—economic growth. Although the Stratford and Huron Railway missed unfortunate Mornington by half a mile, the trains of the Credit Valley Railway puffed right through Ayr (a route not unrelated to the fact that the prosperous township had subsidized the railway to the tune of $110,000) and by 1880 sacks of Ayr wheat, from John McRuer's farm and those of his neighbours, were being shipped from the village straight to Toronto's docks and flour mills.

John McRuer's farm was the standard 100 Ontario acres, which was about the amount of land one man could manage in those days. Ten acres were planted in wheat, twenty acres in oats (or sometimes barley), and eight acres in peas. There was an orchard and an eight-acre woodlot, and the remainder of the land either lay fallow or provided hay for the five beef cattle and the five milkers. Horses were kept to help with the work.

John McRuer was a rugged, wiry man, the kind who was "never sick a day in his life." Mary, in contrast, was more fragile. As the eldest in a family of nine, she had borne a large share of the work on the family farm, and her health had been weakened by a bout of childhood tuberculosis. The couple's first child, a son born in 1885, was predictably named John. The second arrived two years later, a daughter christened Margaret. By the time Jim was born in 1890, Mary's hair was prematurely white and, though only thirty-three years old, she had the typical bowed-down look of a middle-aged farm wife.

Apart from family moments together, such as daily bible readings, trips into the village, or occasional visits to relatives, the McRuers' respite from daily chores was minimal. Most of the little relaxation they enjoyed was provided by infrequent letters fetched from the Ayr post office, chats with neighbours, and the local newspapers. Although the Ayr newspaper was a thin effort, the family also read other publications. The Woodstock *Sentinel Review* came to the Ayr post office weekly and brought with it some news of the world. The *Farmers' Advocate* magazine arrived as well, with regular instalments of Sherlock Holmes stories which young John would eagerly read to Jim.

At McCall's general store in Ayr, the McRuers used their token credit (the store issued "due bills") or bartered butter and eggs to obtain tea or trousers or tools. Sometimes the farmhouse would be visited by travelling salesmen promoting the latest in farm machinery or more humble merchandise. Jim was particularly entranced by one gentle, and elderly, itinerant pedlar who was quite happy to sleep overnight on the kitchen floor after displaying his wares for cash. Yet cash sales were rare in this economy of narrow margins and barter, and John McRuer Sr. once went for a full twelve months with just $2 in his pocket. He and Mary resolutely saved money, making sacrifices in doing so, for their children's education and with a hopeful eye to the future. The family never thought of itself as poor, but, as Jim realized, the arrival of anything new—a kitchen tool, a piece of farm machinery, or even an orange or some nuts in a Christmas stocking—was an "event."

Like other Scots in the area, the McRuers had high standards of morality and integrity, and they carefully brought up their children on a diet of oatmeal porridge and the *Shorter Catechism* of the Presbyterian Church. (From the latter came such question-and-answer exercises as: "What is the chief end of Man? To Glorify God and Enjoy Him Forever." Jim watched for laughter or frowns when he mixed up the response and said, "To Glorify God and enjoy yourself!") Again like their neighbours, the McRuers were profoundly isolated on their farm, and they yearned for community, intellectual challenge, and an escape from those bouts of loneliness and melancholy so common to the Celts. They had no electricity—Hydro lines would not reach the farm until 1936—and no telephone, although Alexander Graham Bell had made the world's first long-distance call from Brantford to nearby Paris in 1876. Life was simple, hard, and spartan; still, the McRuers considered themselves an above-average family and were proud of their reputation as good farmers. They also derived confidence, and perhaps just a bit of smugness, from the fact that they were Presbyterians.

Sunday was the high point of the week. Bouncing along the dusty concession road in the buggy, or carving through the snow drifts by cutter in winter, the family would never fail to drive the two and a half miles into Ayr to get to the Sunday school in Knox Church by 10 o'clock in the morning. A report card, which Jim proudly showed his mother after Sunday school when he, brother John, and sister Margaret joined their parents for the main service, recorded the verdict of his teacher, Miss Margaret McMillan: "Lessons very good. Also attendance."

The routine of Sunday school was always the same. Each week a new lesson was taught and small printed cards were handed out to each child. Printed illustrations in many colours from the presses of the Providence Lithography Company adorned these cards. Through 1898 and 1899 young Jim keenly studied his cards' dramatic lessons about "Ezekiel's Great Vision," "Daniel in the Den of Lions," "Encouraging the Builders," "Power Through the Spirit," "Rebuilding the Temple," "Returning From

Captivity," and "The New Heart." Printed on the back of each card was
a scriptural quotation, a few sentences of explanation, and a catechism
of nine or ten questions and correct answers on which Miss McMillan
drilled the youngster:

> Teacher: "Who are the lights of the world?"
> Pupil: "God's children."
> Teacher: "What do they need all the time?"
> Pupil: "God's help."
> Teacher: "How will He give help if you ask Him?"
> Pupil: "Freely all the time."

Jim treasured these little cards: they were something of his own. Each
one was dated for a different Sunday, and so his fine attendance meant
that he had virtually a complete set. Jim attentively studied the pictures
and the words. As it turned out, he kept these little cards all his life, and
he also kept the lessons he had learned from them close to his heart.
Throughout his adult life, Jim McRuer would be driven by the Christian
teachings he had absorbed as a boy. The need to do good deeds and great
works for the benefit of others was the indelible lesson of his Sunday
school classroom.

In the newly built Knox Church, a fairly grandiose structure for dour
Presbyterian Scots, the family sat together for the 11 o'clock service. As the
Reverend Dr. Thompson, successor to Uncle Duncan, earnestly preached
the weekly sermon, Jim's mother let him fall asleep, his head on her lap.
Occasionally, the McRuers would seek a change in their religious diet
and watch the itinerant Methodist circuit riders who sometimes set up
their tents in town or preached at the nearby Paris Plains Church. That
was great fun, although it meant that Jim's Sunday school attendance
record slipped a notch, which bothered him. He was extremely proud
of the virtually unbroken row of coloured stars behind his name, affixed
weekly, to the class attendance card on the classroom wall.

After church and the buggy ride home, the McRuer family sat in their
Sunday best in the formal front parlour, its sunless northern-exposure
windows casting cool light over the austere furniture and prickly horse-
hair-filled upholstery. John and Mary read bible passages to the children
or sometimes, as a treat, told them inspirational stories of famous men
such as Dr. Livingstone. Mary's tales, especially, prompted the eldest son,
John, to start dreaming about being a medical doctor some day, while
Jim, also stirred by the examples of great men that his mother held out

before him, would eventually begin entertaining thoughts of becoming a Presbyterian minister.

Mary, though sentimental and affectionate, was a no-nonsense woman, determined that her children would always follow the high road. One of her particular dislikes was the low life associated with playing cards, and once, when she caught John doing just that, she admonished him and called cards the "books of the devil." She was also a strong disciplinarian who believed in corporal punishment to keep her children on the straight and narrow. Young Jim periodically felt the raw sting of a fresh willow switch, ritually snapped across his hands for some immature impropriety or childhood naughtiness. Mary's approach to raising her children also included a strong measure of pride in the family's Scottish heritage. When Jim was four years old, she hustled all three children off to Paris for a formal portrait at the Bauslaugh Photographic Studio. Jim, dressed up for the occasion by his beaming mother in a Scottish kilt she loved, hated wearing this ancestral outfit "because it made me look like a girl." The next year she had the photographer come out to the farm and once more Jim reluctantly donned his Scottish skirt and frill-lace collar.

Along with religion, politics wove itself into the McRuers' life as a family. In fact, while John McRuer was a regular church-goer, as social custom demanded, he was vastly more interested in politics—and especially Liberal Party politics. In this respect, he was typical of the Scots in his part of the province. Committed to liberal principles in both political and economic life, the Scots of southwestern Ontario were steadfast supporters of the Reform cause and devoted followers of George Brown, the editor-publisher of the Toronto *Globe*. Together with the settlers of American origin in the region, they were, according to John A. Macdonald, the "most yeasty and unsafe of populations." It was the Scots of this part of Ontario who formed the bridgehead from which Liberals captured and kept control of the provincial legislature during the nineteenth century, and through most of the twentieth century they would serve as a solid core of Liberal strength in an otherwise rather hostile province.

John McRuer took second place to no one in his commitment to the Liberal cause. For political leadership, he and his fellow Liberals looked to the original Clear Grit himself, David Christie, whose gorgeous neoclassical home, "The Plains," graced the nearby fields of South Dumfries where grandfather John McRuer had himself entered the political arena on the municipal level and served as reeve. Christie kept John McRuer and his neighbours on the path of political righteousness, bitterly attacking those with "false hearts." "We want men who are only pure," Christie proclaimed, "and *clear grit*, without a particle of sand." Alongside Christie as McRuer's political heroes were Oliver Mowat, the Ontario premier who called himself a "Christian Statesman," and Prime Minister Wilfrid Laurier.

Laurier's word was gospel—a matter of belief, not argument—in turn-of-the-century Ayr; indeed, in Scottish settlements throughout southwestern Ontario, not to vote Liberal was to be outside civilized society. Grandfather McRuer, in the constituency of Waterloo South, took an active part in the election of 1896, campaigning vigorously on behalf of the local Liberal candidate and incumbent MP, a merchant by the name of James Livingston. Jim, still too young at age six to take part in such events, watched enviously as his father and older brother John drove the buggy into Ayr on election night to hear and cheer the glorious results at the Liberal committee rooms. Not only did the Liberals again capture Waterloo South, defeating Conservative businessman George Clare, but they won the country as a whole, taking 117 seats compared with 89 for the Conservatives. That night and for days following, there was much jubilation throughout Waterloo County and in the McRuer household especially. The forces of secular righteousness had triumphed.

Little Jim soaked up politics just as he did religion. Another fascination of his, again the result of his father's influence, was the mysterious and enthralling world of the law. Although John was taciturn and shy with his son, he still managed to communicate certain basic facts—and they weren't all about farming. He also spoke about the drama of the courtroom and the ways of British justice. Sometimes after supper he told his family about his experiences in jury duty, and on one occasion his appearance as a witness in a theft trial at Brantford became the focus of much family conversation. Reading to the family the newspaper accounts of the trial, he brought out all the excitement of the courtroom scene, and the impressionable Jim hung on every word. One day the boy was transfixed when his mother told him, "If your father had had a chance to get an education, he'd have liked to be a lawyer."

John McRuer knew he was well off in Ayr, certainly in comparison with the lot of his unemployed stonemason forbears in Scotland. Yet the hard farm life seemed increasingly to have little reward or bring any real satisfaction. He was a farmer in spite of himself. He longed to quit the farm and move to the city, where he could perhaps take up some role in law or politics. His discontent was reinforced by his Scot's brooding temperament, which had long hours to feed on itself while he worked in his fields alone, and by the McRuers' restless on-the-move nature.

Eventually, John would succeed in his ambition of leaving the farm behind for the easier life of the city. His dreams of becoming a professional, however, were destined to be realized only in the lives of his two sons. Their ambitions, and success, had their roots in John McRuer's unfulfilled longings for a life better than any the farm or the tiny village of Ayr could offer.

BOTH BECAUSE OF THEIR SCOTTISH HERITAGE and because of their isolation in the country, the McRuers valued their close family ties. Often the family visited the McRuer grandparents and Uncle William's family, a trip of three miles by horse and buggy. William was John's brother, and the five children of his household were good playmates for young Jim. Less frequently, because the trip was much longer, the McRuers visited grandfather Chalmers's farm in Mornington Township. The Chalmers family had established themselves in contiguous farms there, and so these visits afforded joyful reunions with a great many of Jim's cousins, as well as uncles, aunts, and maternal grandparents, in one fell swoop. For Jim, however, the visits were difficult. Skinny and frail—he was afflicted by a respiratory disease, perhaps tuberculosis—he was made fun of by his robust Chalmers cousins. Instead of calling him Jim, the cousins bruised his sensitive nature by sometimes taunting him with the "sissy" nickname "Jim-my"—hurled at him in whining voices.

At home, Jim McRuer had a rather lonely life. The neighbours across the road, George Muma and his wife, had children who went to the same Sunday school as Jim but they were too young for him to play with. Lacking friends, Jim grew close to his brother and sister. Yet John was older than Jim by five years, Margaret by two. This meant that for a couple of Jim's early years, between the ages of four and six, John and Margaret were away during the day at school and he was on his own. The long days lay heavy on him. He became a keen watcher, studiously following his mother and observing her perform chores or gazing for long periods at barnyard animals.

Jim's boredom and loneliness came to an end in September 1896, when he started school himself. He also got his first job. Because he lived just a few hundred yards up the road from the red brick schoolhouse his duty was to arrive by eight o'clock in the morning, start the fire in the box stove, and keep it going all day for the comfort of the teacher and the ten or twelve other students. For this chore he was paid the princely sum of five cents a day. His first purchase, when he had saved up $2.50, was his very own set of bed springs to replace the straw ticking—not perhaps a child's first choice, but he deferred to his mother, who wanted him to learn the importance of spending his money well on items of good quality that would last.

Jim's father put him in command of his own troop of white purebred Wyandotte chickens. The hens would nest anywhere, and it became a great game to find where they had laid their eggs. Jim successfully bred the chickens, showing the chicks in competition at the Drumbo Fall Fair. Eggs were one of the chief money-makers of the McRuer farm; the other was butter. Young Jim often helped his mother pour out the milk into pans in the cellar, down by the potato bin, skimming off the cream for churning as it gradually rose to the top.

Two years passed this way, with Jim making his way at school and doing odd jobs on the farm, when in 1898 his brother and sister were sent away from the nearby one-room schoolhouse into the village of Ayr to prepare for high school entrance. John and Mary McRuer had a Scottish faith in the benefits of a sound elementary education, and they knew that the teaching at the local school was not good enough for their children. Since they were still carefully putting aside money with the hope of being able to allow their children to go to high school and, in the boys' case, to university, they were determined to get their money's worth. Yet Jim was again lonely for John and Margaret, and, after returning from school, he waited at the window with all the yearning of an eight-year-old to see the horse and buggy come over the hill again at the end of each day with his brother and sister aboard.

While he was not a sickly boy, Jim, influenced by a mother who was pathologically afraid of "germs," was convinced that he was not cut out for farm work. His parents agreed, and in fact they had dreams of both Jim and his brother leaving the farm for the city, where they would become educated, important men. Such dreams, of course, reflected John's discontent with farm life, a discontent that was shared by the many farmers and children of farmers who were then leaving the countryside in droves for the towns and cities. Subconsciously, he and Mary may also have been looking for excuses to abandon the farm, and there was certainly no better excuse than the health of their children. Whatever the reason, however, Jim's father gave him only the small chores to do, nothing too strenuous.

Water for both household use and the livestock was drawn from a well powered by a windmill, behind the house. Storage tanks held the water, and Jim would have to watch the level of the water carefully, connecting the pump before it fell too low. When the water completely filled the tanks, he shut off the pump. Sometimes, distracted by more interesting spectacles in the barnyard, Jim returned to discover water overflowing and flooding the adjacent area. This was no calamity, however. The garden needed the water and it was only wind power that was being used.

Although his father never asked him to do the hard work of ploughing, by the age of twelve Jim was getting physically stronger and he spent much time driving the team and mowing hay. His closest friends were four enormous Clydesdale draught horses, whose different personalities he came to love. The road horse, "Charlie," who pulled the buggy (or in winter, the cutter), had now been succeeded by a mare named "Maude." As a project of his own, Jim dug out young cedars from the swamp three miles away, hauled them home on the wagon, and planted them in a row to extend the hedge his father had started to shelter the house from the dusty road in summer and the cold winds in winter.

The eight-acre woodlot on the farm was a place of adventure for Jim and his brother. Sometimes they went there squirrel hunting, and in the spring they had fun tapping the trees in some experimental maple-syrup making. These woods were also the source of household fuel. With increasing skill, Jim and John cut up the wood with a cross-cut saw and then split it with curved-handled axes before piling it in the woodshed. When he was twelve, Jim's father let him have all the apples from their orchard. He happily filled his barrels, hitched up "Maude," drove into Ayr, and sold them for $1 a barrel at McCall's general store.

Jim liked the community spirit in the village. He knew many of the people there, including the two leading families, the Goldies and the Watsons, and he had many enjoyable conversations. Occasionally, displaying an appreciation for fine things that he likely inherited from his mother, he visited Jim Fenn the jeweller just to look at the beautiful objects in his store. Invariably, his trips into town included a stop at the large trout-filled mill pond in the centre of the village, a major attraction created by Watson's dam, which emptied through a raceway right under the main street. From here he could see Watson's famous yellow-brick factory, handsomely rebuilt in 1882, which manufactured farm implements such as reapers and, as everyone with local knowledge could boast, the first automatic hay binders in Canada. Another of his stops was the stables, where he watched A.J. Anderson, the local blacksmith, shoe horses. Jim's eyes opened wide as the sweating, muscular Anderson pumped the bellows until the coals flared white hot, and then lifted out a glowing orange bar, bent it at the ends, and hammered it around the blackened anvil. Still red hot, the shoe was fitted onto the horse's foot with a hiss and a sharp smell of singed hoof, plunged into water with a pop, and hammered home.

Jim probably envied Anderson's strength, for his own life was a cycle of sickly periods and gradual recoveries. The first bout of illness came at age twelve and consisted of serious headaches. There was nothing much to be done for the pain, and his mother, who described his ailment as "tick de la rue," just held his head on her lap day after day, comforting him until he was better. Such episodes later led Jim to remember his mother as a "woman of great affection."

One glorious late winter morning in March 1904, a local farmer came by the school and dumped a load of firewood in the woodshed, without bothering to pile it. The teacher, young and inexperienced, told fourteen-year-old Jim and the other boys to put the wood in neat piles, and they agreed. At noon the weather was too beautiful for work, however, and they decided instead to play a lunch-time game of shinny (a Scottish version of hockey) on the rink they had flooded out back, and to put off the wood-piling chore until after school. At 4 o'clock, much to their outrage, the teacher dismissed the rest of the school, kept them behind, and, without asking for an explanation or even letting them speak in their own defence, thrashed them on their hands with a broadstrap. Injustice! Jim went home humiliated. He had never been in trouble at school or broken any laws. No McRuer ever had.

His father was furious. Raging at the injustice of the strapping like an Old Testament prophet, he insisted not only that the teacher had no right to thrash the students but also that she had no business asking them to pile the wood in the first place. True, the Ontario Department of Education had approved and issued standardized straps to every school in the province for disciplinary purposes, but Jim's alleged transgression, felt John McRuer, did not warrant such punishment. Vowing that his son would never return to the school, he briskly donned his winter coat, slammed the door, and went off in the cutter to lodge a complaint with the chairman of the school board. At a board meeting later that week he demanded, and got, an apology from the teacher.

This experience awakened a strong new sense of justice in Jim. He had learned personally the resentment that can come from injustice, and his father had taught him that everyone is entitled to a chance to explain his actions. The "wood-piling" incident was important in another way, too. The teacher's apology had not been enough so far as the McRuers were concerned—Jim would have to change schools. He was promptly transferred to the White schoolhouse near his grandfather's farm on the Paris-Ayr road, three miles away. In one of those wonderful twists of fate, at the White schoolhouse Jim came under the charge of Ida J. Tovell. His life would never be the same again.

This truly remarkable teacher, then in her late twenties, was fairly tall and slim, with dark hair and matching complexion. Attired in white blouse with tight collar and long black skirt, Tovell was a dynamic personality. Dedicated with complete selflessness to her students and her career as their teacher, she never married. When she spoke, it was with authority, and *she* certainly never needed to use the strap to ensure discipline. This was a school for learning, and for respecting the subtleties of human intelligence and motivation. Ida Tovell began to expand Jim's horizons. She taught him how to think. Through her, he learned to enjoy hard work, and to realize that he had some capacity for it. She inspired him to believe that to excel was worthy, and worthwhile.[2]

Within a month of his arrival at the White schoolhouse, Tovell had discovered how thin Jim's previous training had been, but also how bright he was under that humdrum, rustic, farm boy veneer. For a three-month stretch, she drilled him and another boy an extra hour every day after school, and Saturday morning as well. In that period she taught them to respect learning and to enjoy the game of "discovering what was there." Taking her cue from Jim's father, with whom she had discussed the state of the boy's education, Ida Tovell urged him to "amount to something, to succeed in life." "Amounting to something" became Jim McRuer's goal, and the phrase soon became one of his favourite expressions, used throughout his life when encouraging youngsters (his own or others) or when assessing someone's progress.

Every morning Jim now had to get up at 5 o'clock, study for two hours, drive two and a half miles to his grandfather's farm where he left his horse, and then walk another half-mile to school, where Ida Tovell would be there to greet him and keep up the pressure. She demanded much of her senior pupils, but it was nothing more than she was willing to give herself. It was hard work for Jim, but now at least he had goals. He wanted to achieve things.

Early in July 1904, Jim and ninety other boys and girls gathered in sweltering classrooms in the imposing Paris High School to write their high school entrance examinations. Each student, and especially Jim, was determined not to disappoint their parents or their teacher. The youngsters pored over the white printed paper from the Department of

Education, and then wrote until their aching hands cramped and the bell finally rang, releasing them for the summer and to await the results. On 14 July Jim drove into Ayr, bought a copy of the *Paris Review*, and happily found his name in the alphabetical list of those who had passed. Then, glancing across the page, he excitedly discovered that he had done what would have seemed impossible just a few months earlier. He had soared above all the other ninety students and come in first, even winning the coveted $25 Penman scholarship. Jim beamed, and his parents were even prouder. He could now move on to the next stage of his education.

The town of Paris, where Jim went to attend high school, was pictur-esquely situated downstream from Ayr where the Nith River flowed into the Grand. A hundred years earlier, in April 1793, government sur-veyors had been pressing a line through the bush and swamps west of Burlington Bay to the forks of the Thames, where Governor Simcoe first intended to establish his capital, when they reached the forks of the Grand. Across the river they spied a pinkish-white deposit of gypsum—which was valuable for fertilizer and which could be roasted to produce stucco and plaster of Paris—on the high eroded south bank of the Nith. Three decades later, at the same time as John and Mary McRuer were emigrating from Scotland, a Vermont-born entrepreneur, Hiram "King" Capron, began exploiting these gypsum deposits to make plaster in a settlement he naturally, and with a touch of whimsy, called Paris.

In 1904 Paris was a typical small Ontario industrial town, dominated by the spinning and knitting mill established by John Penman in the nineteenth century. As a boy, Jim had sometimes been taken into Paris by his parents, and he had always found the place exciting and slightly intimidating. Now, when he arrived in the town to begin his high school studies, his reaction was the same. In his eyes, Paris was colourful, vibrant, and astonishingly big, especially compared to the little village of Ayr with its two hundred souls. Along with the steady stream of farm boys stopping for a drink at the local hotels, the town's cast of characters included factory girls imported from Yorkshire, storekeepers, tavern-keepers, and other merchants, and King Capron's various descendants who now lived in splendid homes on a height of land (in fact a gypsum hill) above the town called King Street Hill. The summit of this street was crowned by the Paris High School, the new centre of Jim's life.

An imposing neo-classical structure that was a model of symme-try and balance, the school was fronted by four stone columns and by numerous harmoniously proportioned large windows with a dozen panes in each. It was a two-storey edifice of clean hard lines, with a modest cupola between the two central pillars and a large, detailed cornice capping the entire structure. Every morning Jim climbed the hill towards this temple of education, and for the final distance he mounted a long row of stone steps leading to the dual entrances (one for boys, one for girls) at the front, each overarched by smaller versions of the main cupola which towered directly above. As he climbed, Jim had to tilt his head backwards slightly to see the school, but once he was there the view was grand.

On leaving, at the end of the school day, the descent was easy and pleasant. At the foot of the hill, in a small grey stucco house located at 32 Burwell Street. Jim boarded for $2 a week with Annie and Minnie Forsyth, sharing a room with a sixteen-year-old student named Chester Robinson. A teacher lived upstairs.

The need to help support their families meant that many of Jim's fellow students soon dropped out to assume lifetime roles in the working world, generally at Penman's mill or back on the family farm. Enrolment in Jim's class at Paris High dwindled from eighty-five students in 1st form (grade nine) to nineteen in 2nd form (grade ten) and twelve in 3rd form (grade eleven). By 1907 only four or five students from his original class remained among the fourteen (nine boys, five girls) graduating from the 5th form. Given this rate of attrition, it was no sure thing that Jim would complete the distance. Yet, for several reasons, the odds were in his favour. His brother had blazed the trail and had already graduated to university studies, his parents expected and encouraged him to get the good education that farm life had denied them, the urging of Ida Tovell to "find out what's there" was always at the back of his mind, and his own determined nature was as strong as ever. Jim was an honours student all the way, never standing lower than third in his class exams, most often first or second. He obtained consistent "A" grades for class work. He rarely missed school, and the one and a half hours spent on homework in 1st form grew to three and four hours as he advanced. His best marks came in English grammar, Latin, botany, and mathematics. Next were science and history, while his marks in English composition, French, and drawing were invariably lower than the class average. Sometimes he became a little cocky. After a perfect score of 100 on his algebra exam in December 1905, he cruised into a near failure with a mark of 52 in the same subject the following March.

His education at Paris High was about as good as was available in the Ontario school system at the time. The man in charge of the entire enterprise, W.N. Bell, impressed the young McRuer as a "very fine" principal. Jim was an apt and hard-working student who liked school, and he was led to believe that he had a promising future. Yet not all the lessons he learned were academic. One afternoon early in his first year, Jim's algebra teacher challenged him to solve a problem. He worked all evening on the problem and, to his great delight, cracked it. The next day, bursting with pride, he showed his teacher the results, only to hear his teacher scoff, "Oh, you room with a third-year student"—meaning that he must have been given the solution by Chester Robinson. Jim deeply resented this cruel comment and again felt the sting of injustice. His teacher had not only failed to reward his hard work with some recognition and encouragement, but she had, by implication, accused him of cheating.

Track and field day was the big event of the school year at Paris High and lanky Jim, now more athletic and an avid pole vaulter, was anxious to take part. Friday was the day for the competition, but when heavy rains came, the school board decreed that the event should take place on Saturday. This was a great blow to Jim and other farm boys who went home on weekends to help out. They formed a delegation and went to see the chairman of the school board, Franklin K. Smoke, hoping to have him stage the event on a regular school day the following week. Jim, as spokesman for the delegation, presented their arguments carefully and politely. Chairman Smoke was unmoved. No further delay would be allowed, he decreed. McRuer "never quite liked the man after that"[3] and quietly nursed his resentment for a quarter-century until in 1930 he gleefully found an opportunity to speak at a political rally on behalf of Smoke's election opponent.

Jim McRuer created a small new world for himself in Paris, but he still felt the pull of the farm and his parents. During his first winter in Paris, Mary McRuer learned from a phone message that her son would be remaining in Paris for the weekend to watch a big hockey game on Saturday morning—an act of filial independence that was assuredly not well received. How could you keep a boy down on the farm, she must have wondered, once he has seen Paris? Most weekends, however, the old magnetism of family and farm worked, and Jim climbed aboard a buggy with a satchel of homework and dirty laundry and went home, eager to talk with his parents about the future. Those conversations made it clear that Jim's boyhood dream of becoming a minister had begun to fade, replaced by new dreams of himself as a lawyer. Sparked by his father's influence, Jim's thoughts of a legal career were encouraged by talks with Donald Cowan, from the farm five miles west, who was already at university preparing for legal studies. Jim looked up to Cowan, and became determined to follow his example.

In his years on the farm, and even during his time in Paris, the rigid rules and social customs of the Victorian age provided a framework within which Jim McRuer lived his life. And he was not alone. Sunday after Sunday throughout the English-speaking, Protestant world, church-going people, who were seriousness and sobriety personified, left the packed pews to return home for the same kind of sessions the McRuers had, the father of the family questioning his offspring on the theological points of the morning sermon. Suffusing this kind of society, as vital to it as air is to life, were widely shared assumptions and values. Jim McRuer's inheritance included these assumptions and values, and he had no real basis or need to challenge them. While the years to come would bring considerable change in his life, he always bore the indelible imprint of his upbringing. His Christian faith and commitment to family, his inter-est in politics and the law, his belief in the value of work and education, his Presbyterian adherence to a strict moral code, and his propensity to keep his emotions locked up inside—all these character traits had their roots in his earliest years.

While the Victorian era was an age of authority and conformity, it was also a period of growing uncertainty and ferment. New inventions, new scientific and theological ideas, industrial expansion, and urban growth challenged and changed the way people saw the world around them and their relationships with one another. These developments were long in the making and would not reach their culmination until the violent insanity of the First World War shattered forever the old imperial order. Yet, like a brewer's yeast, they were slowly fermenting even in the 1890s. In rural southwestern Ontario, the leading edge of social change was the mechanization of agriculture and rural de-population as people moved from the farm into the growing and industrializing towns and cities. An agrarian movement arose in response to this threat to the stability of the rural way of life, and by 1919 it had grown strong enough politically to form a provincial government with the support of organized labour.[4]

Amid these cross-currents, Jim's outlook on the world gradually began to take shape. Partly the result of the values he had absorbed as a youth, and partly a response to signs of social and intellectual change, that outlook was characterized above all by a thorough-going liberal-ism. Its other elements were a socially progressive brand of Christianity, a sense of justice rooted in the rights of the individual, a closeness to nature, and a view of life as a "game" and an "adventure." These elements would crystallize to a greater extent as his life took its unusual course over the decades ahead, just as their consequences would become clearer. Yet they were all present, or forming, in his early years on the farm and in the classroom.

He may have left Ayr for Paris, and soon he would leave Paris for Toronto, but he never forgot the lessons of either place.

2

THE MAKING OF A LAWYER

IN THE EARLY TWENTIETH CENTURY, there were two choices for an aspiring lawyer in Ontario. A young man—this was a solidly male enterprise—could spend two years articling with a law firm, followed by three years at Osgoode Hall Law School in Toronto with concurrent articling (two hours a day of lectures and the rest of the day working in the law office). A law student wanting to enter this five-year program required senior matriculation (graduation from the five years of high school). The second option was to take a university degree in arts, medicine, or engineering, followed by three years at Osgoode Hall with concurrent articling. Donald Cowan, Jim's friend back home in Ayr, recommended attending university, his own chosen course. Jim readily accepted his advice.

Jim's father next took him to Woodstock to meet a lawyer named W.T. McMullan, with whom they discussed a career in law. Eager that his son realize the dream that he had secretly cherished for himself, John McRuer also treated Jim to a day trip by train to Toronto, where they inspected the University of Toronto under the guidance of brother John, by now a medical student on campus, and the Ontario legislative buildings at adjacent Queen's Park. The day culminated when the three McRuer men wound up at the Canadian National Exhibition, where they marvelled at the prize-winning livestock and produce.

In the fall of 1907 young "James" McRuer, as the earnest seventeen-year-old now signed all his papers, having passed his junior matriculation with honours from Paris High School, entered the four-year honours political science program at University College in the University of Toronto. Lodged at a boarding house at 14 St. Mary Street, where his rent was $3 a week plus $2.50 for board, Jim found himself so poor that he threw a pauper's party and raised several contributions in the 45¢ to 50¢ bracket. Jim was self-conscious about the financial sacrifices of his parents, who provided money every few weeks (in instalments of $11 or $20 or so at a time). He dutifully recorded each contribution in his narrow black account book, including on one occasion the transfer of $10 to his brother.

Jim supplemented his boarding-house meals with food he would buy and keep in his room, such as peanuts (usually 5¢ worth at a time), bananas (10¢ or 25¢ bunches), and grapes (20¢ or 30¢ a bunch). He also bought milk for 5¢, beef tea for 10¢, and some spoons for 5¢. He kept up appearances (shoe blackening 10¢, collars 25¢, shoes $4.75, haircut 10¢, and laundry, about 22¢ a week), sought to be punctual (alarm clock, $1.25), and kept warm and dry as the autumn weather changed (raincoat $1.50, umbrella 75¢, pants $2.50, sweater $2, gloves $1). He kept in touch with his parents (long-distance telephone 60¢, stamps 10¢) and enjoyed some non-academic activities (skates $4.13, ticket to hockey game 25¢, skating 15¢). His weekly church collection started at 5¢ but gradually rose to 15¢. Once he lapsed into hedonism and spent 1¢ on chewing gum. All this, of course, was in addition to his purchases of books and supplies for university.

Jim signed on as a member of the University of Toronto soccer team in the fall of 1907; he was not the most forceful player on the squad, but his long legs and speed were an asset and he enjoyed the camaraderie of the game. As it turned out, however, the year 1907–8 was to be Jim's first and last at the University of Toronto. Late in the fall of 1907 he became ill. At first he seemed to be suffering from just a bad cold, but the sickness dragged on for months. By the late winter of 1908 it was clear that he was very ill indeed. In fact, he had contracted tuberculosis but did not realize it. Evidence of his deteriorating health even began creeping into his account book, as he recorded spending 30¢ for liniment, then 15¢ for a thermometer, and finally $6 for a doctor's visit. Dizziness and fever enervated him, forcing him to miss noon lectures in order to get extra sleep and eventually driving him into the three-year general program, where even here he could only barely keep up.

Angered by his physical weakness and determined to overcome it, Jim pushed himself even harder. This only made matters worse. Bitterly disappointed that his dream of a legal career seemed to be crumbling, he grew despondent. Back home, his parents were deeply worried. They resolved that their son should come home for a year to recover his health, and then, if all went as they hoped, Jim could try the non-university option of qualifying as a lawyer. Bowing to his parents' wishes, Jim spent long months, once again, on the farm, and he dejectedly began to doubt that he would ever leave the place.

Just when Jim's academic career and the prospects of his becoming a lawyer seemed in ruins, brother John came to the rescue. Now graduated from university and qualified as a doctor, John had recently set up medical practice in the town of Huntsville, from where he wrote letters full of praise about the Muskoka district's healthy climate. He also told Jim that one of his Huntsville friends, Albert Hutchison, was a lawyer who needed an articling student. On 6 February 1909, still fighting off exhaustion, Jim signed articles with Hutchison, even though he did not actually begin work until the fall, when he felt somewhat stronger. As the leaves of Muskoka took on their autumn colours, Jim arrived in Huntsville, moving in with John and his new wife, Edythe, at their home on Main Street.

Jim quickly came to love this fast-growing northern Muskoka town of about 2,000 residents and its surrounding lakes and pine forests. A leather tannery, saw mills, and tourism provided the basis for Huntsville's growing economy. Activity abounded everywhere. Main Street, a wide dirt road, was constantly busy with horse-drawn wagons and carriages, its elevated wooden sidewalks providing a dry and clean pathway for the women in their full-length dresses who moved from one store to another. Late in the previous century, on 18 April 1894, nearly all the wooden buildings on Main Street had been consumed in a fire, but by 1909 the centre of town had been completely rebuilt. Jim learned with interest about this local calamity, but he also captured the town's confident new spirit. The brick buildings along Main Street—which had replaced the earlier frame structures that had been burnt in the fire—stood two or even three storeys high, many with canvas awnings extending over the boardwalk in front of the shops and offices located on the ground floors. From several of these buildings flew the Union Jack, on flag poles jutting out at an angle over the street. Advertisements for hardware and livery services painted on the side brick walls of several buildings, as well as wide canvas banners with such messages as "Get Your Photographs Here" stretching across the street from one utility pole to another, conveyed an unmistakeable impression of prosperity.

About the only place to which this boom-town activity did not extend was Bert Hutchison's Main Street law office. Two other lawyers practised in town, and there seemed to be barely enough work to go around. Hutchison himself got on well with Jim—a common bond was their Scottish heritage—and the two sometimes had serious discussions about the law when Jim finished drafting a deed or reading the office's law books. Fundamentally, however, articling in Huntsville proved to be a disaster in terms of legal education, and McRuer spent most of his time chatting with Hutchison's pleasant secretary. Nevertheless, the Huntsville experience accomplished its purpose in another sense. Not only did Jim have a glorious winter holiday, but his spirits and health improved. The town surged with young people, and Jim met many of them at St. Andrew's Presbyterian Church, a fine new brick church built just twelve years earlier after a grass fire had ignited and destroyed the original frame church located across the river. The young Presbyterians at St. Andrew's had good bible study classes, many socials, and fine sleighing parties out to Lake of Bays. Huntsville was a big hockey town, too, and Jim found himself enjoying one of Huntsville's main winter pleasures. Gradually shaking off his illness, he sometimes travelled with his brother to see patients in lonely country farms or cabins in the woods, a few times journeying all night along frozen moonlit lakes to handle emergencies.

For Christmas that year Jim received a vest-pocket, leather-bound diary, with the date "1910" embossed in gold. He carried it with him everywhere, recording such information as memoranda of payments made for title searches, the cases being heard in magistrate Denison's court, his fluctuating monthly income ($10 in January, $20 in April), appointments, and names and addresses. Also tucked away between the covers of this constant companion was a worn clipping from a Toronto newspaper containing a poem entitled "Justice is Blind," which Jim frequently took out and read when he was alone. His fondness for this poem was significant, for it concerned a man imprisoned for selling substandard eggs while corrupt politicians and "plutocrats," guilty of far more serious crimes, "blithely go their way." Jim McRuer's view of justice was continuing to crystallize.

By the spring of 1910, Jim felt much better. The lanky (6-foot, 1-inch tall) nineteen-year-old now weighed a healthy 160 pounds, and his vigour was restored. Deciding to pull his life together, he wrote a letter to Sam Smoke, a Toronto lawyer with whom he felt some connection because Smoke's brother (the infamous schoolboard chairman who refused to change the date of the track and field meet) practised law in

Paris. Smoke replied that he had nothing to offer, but that the firm of Ross and Holmested, upstairs from his office, needed a student to search titles. An immigration boom was under way in Toronto in 1910, and plenty of petty real-estate speculation kept lawyers busy. Jim immediately made the trip to Toronto and sought out his prospective employer. When he arrived at the office of Ross and Holmested, Ross hired him on the spot— but without actually conveying this message in words. He simply took Jim over to the registry office, got down the proper abstract books, and showed him how to trace from one owner to another and make proper notes to establish the root of title. "Now you can carry on and finish off," said Ross, and he left.

Jim suffered the boring job of the registry office for a few months—it was, after all, a resumption of his legal training—but soon found that he was afflicted with a new fever: the love of the north country. Citing medical reasons, Jim asked to be let go for the summer, and Ross agreed. For the next three weeks, he relaxed in Huntsville, breathing deeply of the town's pine-scented July air. He was happy to be with his brother once more, looking up friends and dropping into Hutchison's law office. Memories of the Toronto registry office began to recede.

One evening Jim met the young artist Tom Thomson, who was a close friend of his brother and had been best man at his wedding. Thomson, destined to become a transforming influence in the world of Canadian art, had just spent a year in the woods around Huntsville, including Algonquin Park to the east, painting the forest, the rocks, and the lakes, and he was eager to show Jim some of the results. Taking him up to his room in the Dominion Hotel, he opened up his pack and excitedly spread out on the bed four feet of his brilliant sketches of Algonquin Park, which he intended making into large paintings in his studio back in the city. Telling Jim to "pick any two you like," the artist proudly stood by as Jim studied them in amazement. The air in the room was heady with the scent of oil paint.

"When I take these down to Toronto the big fellows will laugh and will ridicule them, but these are really the colours I saw," explained Thomson as he saw his new friend quietly studying the scenes. Jim did not laugh. He carefully chose two, which he would later frame and proudly hang on the walls of his successive residences.[1]

A few days later, on the weekend, Jim, John, Edythe, and Tom Thomson travelled north by train to Scotia Junction, ostensibly to scout locations for the artist but really just to enjoy an outing together. Thomson took photographs of the brothers—showing John by the train station at Scotia Junction, and Jim, the earnest young lawyer, wearing a formal hat in the middle of a field in northern Ontario. The photographs reveal the artist's instinct for balance and symmetry in composition, through the camera just as on the canvas. Yet they would not be seen by anyone for nearly sixty years. When Thomson died in a mysterious drowning accident in Algonquin Park in July 1917, the still undeveloped film was among his personal effects, and these were sent to the Thomson family home at Owen Sound, Ontario. Decades would pass before, in June 1971, the film was discovered and printed.

After the tonic of three weeks in Muskoka and a summer spent on the farm in Ayr, Jim McRuer returned to Toronto. At about the same time, his former employer, Bert Hutchison, made an important move in his own career. Bored with Huntsville and yearning for greener pastures, Hutchison packed his law books in several trunks and headed west. He started a practice in booming Swift Current, Saskatchewan, and became so busy that on 23 August 1910—Jim's twentieth birthday—he wrote asking his former articling student to join him. But Jim, constrained by his father's injunction to "finish your university," had resolved to stay in Toronto. He declined Hutchison's offer.

Instead of a move to Saskatchewan, Jim paid a short visit to Lachute, Quebec, to see the relatives still living on his grandfather's original Canadian farm. From the very first glance he understood the reason his ancestors had left the place—he had "never seen such a poor farm"—but he also made another discovery. Looking though the family bible in which names and dates for births, marriages, and deaths had been dutifully inscribed, Jim was startled to see beside his father's name the entry "Elizabeth Patton." "Oh," explained his cousin nonchalantly, "your father married a Patton." Jim now realized that he was not the only McRuer to keep things inside. It was the first time that he had ever heard of his father's first wife and her tragic death in childbirth.

Jim remained with Ross and Holmested until 15 August 1911, when, in the course of banging on the door of every law office in Confederation Life's swank new building at the corner of Yonge and Richmond streets, he discovered the firm of Proudfoot, Duncan, Grant, and Skeans. Hired on the spot for $10 a week, which was eight dollars more than most students were getting, Jim began looking forward to work more challenging than simple title-searching.

By now Jim had proven himself extremely tenacious and determined, particularly in his efforts to overcome illness and complete his legal education. His plodding away at title searches for Ross and Holmested, however much such work bored and frustrated him, had reinforced this aspect of his character. To his disappointment, the next stage of his legal education was to resemble the first, and again his patience and persistence would be tried. Fortunately, his life outside the law office and the classroom was to be more rewarding.

Jim's new firm, though rather narrow in its range of interests, had a fairly good reputation. William Proudfoot, the firm's stubborn and wily chief counsel, was simultaneously the member of the provincial legislature for the riding of Huron Centre. He also happened to be the closest friend and associate of Newton Wesley Rowell, then provincial Liberal leader, whom Proudfoot eventually succeeded as interim leader in 1917. As Rowell's confidant, Proudfoot was one of the toughest fighters against the Conservative provincial government of Premier James P. Whitney— digging up scandals, airing political pay-offs, and generally being the powerhouse of the Liberal opposition. Rowell himself was backed by a formidable galaxy of Toronto supporters that included stockbrokers A.E. Ames, E.R. Wood, J.H. Gundy, and F.H. Deacon as well as Joseph Atkinson of the *Toronto Star*.[2] Exposure to this world was an eye-opener for Jim and increased his interest in politics of the Liberal variety. Although Proudfoot's style of political attack was not one that Jim, more cerebral and civil, could readily duplicate, he relished the zeal with which Proudfoot fought his battles. He was especially intrigued by Proudfoot's ability to combine a law practice and a political career.

Among the other members of the firm, E.J.B. Duncan was a first-class, meticulous solicitor who enjoyed taking challenging hikes—Toronto to Hamilton being his favourite. Duncan always combed through legal documents on the lookout for McRuer's mistakes. W.H. Grant specialized in real estate transactions and was therefore someone whom McRuer, eager to put title searching behind him, sought to avoid. W.A. Skeans soon became a passionately loyal friend of the young McRuer, although he was a bit erratic and peculiar. Something of a religious fanatic, Skeans studied the scripture and loved to argue religion with his friends and clients, including several rabbis.

Jim was soon drowning in real estate practice again—tedious and exhausting work broken only by an hour in the morning (from 9 to 10 o'clock), an hour in the afternoon (from 4 to 5) for law classes at Osgoode Hall, and a lunch break every day in Simpson's dining-room where he would argue the law with his fellow students. Although interested in litigation—he adored poring over affidavits and pleadings—he had little time for it. Beginning to wonder whether he would ever see the inside of a courtroom, McRuer quipped to his friends that at least he had searched the title of every house in Toronto.

At this time, speculation in Toronto real estate was so fevered that sometimes Jim found himself handling twenty-five deals a day, mostly from three clients, Anshel Heller, Benjamin Olstein, and Barnet Moskowitz. These speculators would put $100 down on a $3,500 house and sell it a few days later for perhaps $3,800; the firm made about $25 per deal. Jim's experiences with this kind of legal work opened his eyes to a different way of making money, and his reaction to the practices of three Jews who had come to Canada from Russia and were now prospering was mixed. He was truly fascinated by them—they taught him that there was more to real estate than searching titles—but he also had some discomfort about the propriety of buying and selling property in this way.[3]

During his articling years Jim delighted in his rare visits to the family farm. In the 1911 election campaign, a bitter contest fought over the merits of a proposed reciprocity trade treaty with the United States, he even managed to get closer to the workings of politics by serving as a deputy returning officer in Oxford County. Although the county as usual elected its Liberal candidate, Ontario as a whole delivered a stinging rebuke to Laurier's Liberals—only thirteen Liberal MPs were elected compared to seventy-two for the Conservatives, led by Robert Borden. The spectacle of the Laurier government being replaced by a Conservative one was enough to send McRuer back, with renewed interest, to learning law.

In the evenings, Jim sometimes attended a public debate, run with correct parliamentary procedure, at the Ruskin Literary and Debating Society. The Ruskin Society brought Jim into renewed contact with University of Toronto students and the academic life he had been forced to abandon because of tuberculosis. The subjects discussed at the club's meetings often had more to do with issues and interests of the day than with John Ruskin, the English writer who had died just a decade earlier and after whom the group was named. Yet what Jim did come to learn about Ruskin himself struck a resonant chord. Ruskin had advocated an essentially religious aesthetic, in which the moral perception of beauty was superior to the merely sensuous and beauty itself revealed the attributes of God. His conviction that faith, morality, and education were prerequisites to the creation of fine art led Ruskin to take up the cause of social and economic reform in his writings. In many ways, this same insight would come increasingly to inform Jim McRuer's outlook, except that he spoke of "civilization" rather than art and addressed legal rather than economic reforms.

On other evenings, if he had neither the energy nor the inclination to go out, he returned to Mrs. Laidlaw's boarding house, where he shared a room with a young man who worked at Eaton's and made $17 a week. McRuer, so frugal with the $10 a week he earned at Ross and Holmested, often had to lend his friend money on the weekend. Mrs. Laidlaw, a widow from Huntsville with two daughters, kept a kindly eye on young Jim. One evening as he sat reading, she chatted with him about how he was getting on in the city, and suggested that he come to Frank Yeigh's bible class at Bloor Street Presbyterian Church. Jim gladly agreed. Bloor Street Presbyterian was a popular church with a fine choir and good rousing music, always packed to the rafters on Sunday. It was a place to meet other young people.

The bible classes of these times, reflecting the central place of religion in Ontario society, were like finishing schools for thousands of young and ardent Methodists and Presbyterians, and proved particularly helpful to young men and women from the country who needed an uplifting introduction to life in the city. They provided a mutual self-help society and encouraged young people to become involved in social welfare projects. In a prim and proper society that frowned on unchaperoned dancing and courting, they also gave young singles a nicely controlled, teetotalling environment in which sexual attraction could be channelled into moral uplift and the sound of wedding bells postponed until the suitable time. In this regard, the bible class at Bloor Street Presbyterian was certainly successful for the widowed Mrs. Laidlaw. She ended up marrying the Reverend Mr. Wallace, minister of the church for forty-two years, becoming his fourth wife. On her marriage, she could afford to give up the boarding house, forcing Jim to find lodgings elsewhere.

Frank Yeigh, leader of the bible class, had a profound influence on Jim. Apart from being a deeply committed Christian, Yeigh had gained renown as a travelling lecturer—Jim had once heard him speak on the topic of whales at a lantern-slide presentation in Paris. He was also one of the key backroom figures in Ontario Liberal Party politics, first as a close disciple of long-time Premier Oliver Mowat, and later as a friend and associate (secretary, publicist, speechwriter) of his successor, the fearless, quick-witted, and sharp-nosed Arthur Hardy, MPP for South Brant—the riding of David Christie and "The Big Thunder," Edmund Burke Wood. When Premier Hardy had to retire in 1899 because of ill health after only three years in office, Yeigh hustled off into a Queen's Park sinecure where he did writing and information work for the government. He wrote a Canadian travelogue, a biography of Mowat, and a centennial history of the legislative buildings of Ontario, and then took over publication of "5,000 Facts About Canada," a fine little booklet chock full of gently exorbitant boosterism. Yeigh, Hardy, Christie, and Wood were all Clear Grit crusaders of the Grand River valley, the kind of politicians of whom Jim McRuer, with his unquestioned Liberal sympathies, took special note.

Jim was truly impressed by all the different things Frank Yeigh had accomplished through his sheer industry. He came fully under Yeigh's spell. So did a whole generation of young people, all of whom had their education expanded, their ambitions nourished, and their consciences awakened in his bible class. Every Sunday afternoon Yeigh gave the class some interesting matter to discuss, or a project to organize, such as gathering up vegetables and supplies for people in drought-stricken areas. Sometimes a prominent businessman or lawyer would address the class on the importance of having goals—in short, the value of being ambitious. The class itself was well organized and conducted along business lines as an official meeting. The participants published a newsletter (to underscore the importance of communication), got training in committee work, and learned executive skills by serving as treasurer, secretary, or vice-president.

Recognizing a fellow son of southwestern Ontario, Yeigh took an early liking to Jim McRuer, saw his potential, and encouraged him to fill various executive positions. Jim became class president for a year and frequently acted as chairman for meetings. That both Yeigh and his protégé were Liberals further cemented the bond between them. One summer Yeigh obtained a job for Jim with the Grenfell Mission in Labrador, which they both hoped would lead him into a wider realm of service and experience, but at the last minute the arrangements fell through. For years afterward, right across Canada, Jim would meet men who had been involved in Yeigh's bible class and had subsequently risen to top positions in churches and corporations. The class had acted as a sort of young-boys network. Yet that was a secondary benefit; the main consequence for Jim was the impetus which Yeigh had given to a still uncertain young man.

While Yeigh's influence on McRuer flowed strong on Sundays, during the week he learned a great deal from his fellow students. To study for examinations, a group of five or six of them would meet in somebody's boarding house and grill each other with questions from past tests. These sessions were also a means of deepening friendships. One of Jim's colleagues in the study group was Norman Macdonell, who would rise to be an appeal judge. Another was Bill McCallum, the brightest student in the class, who later would be disbarred for his involvement in a stock promotion scheme. Nathan Phillips, who eventually became Toronto's "Mayor of all the People" in the 1950s, was another classmate of McRuer. Even though they stayed in touch all through life, McRuer and Phillips never became warm friends because Jim disliked being the butt of Phillips's jokes. Phillips frequently teased Jim about his thinness and his pallor, morbidly predicting that he would be the first in the class to die.

One of the most significant influences on all the law students in Toronto, and especially Jim, was Judge Monty Morson, the dragon of the Division Court (forerunner of the present-day Small Claims Court), where the students were allowed to plead. The last of Sir John A. Macdonald's appointments to the bench, Morson had a great sense of fairness—his court, he said, was a place of "equity and good conscience" where facts and justice were more important than case law. He was also colourful. Determined to move through his lists quickly—he customarily disposed of thirty to forty cases an hour—so that he could get to the racetrack by one o'clock, he was ruthless with students who entered his court with a pile of books ready to argue their cases interminably. At such times he would growl: "Don't pay any attention to those books; I dispense the law here." Rocking irritably back and forth in his chair if a student went on too long, or turning right around and kicking the wall or blowing his nose loudly—Morson gave Jim and the other law students a valuable perspective on both justice and longwindedness.

Jim certainly enjoyed these "lessons" better than one part of the formal curriculum at Osgoode Hall. His instructor in constitutional law, though striking McRuer as a pleasant young man, left the sinking impression that he did not know much about his subject. Years later, Jim still did not know how he managed to pass the exam, but he did. In fact, he survived all his courses. During the three years after he entered Osgoode, Jim studied assiduously, learned all he could, and was conscientious in reading the assigned cases and commentaries. He passed his examinations each year, but often only with average grades. Frail health was likely one reason he did not perform better; he had to spend much of his time resting. Another was the fact that the exams were heavily oriented towards practice, and Jim had received (apart from his training in title searching) an extremely shallow legal education while articling.

Ultimately, he was probably saved by the boarding-house drill sessions with fellow students.

In any case, Jim graduated in 1913. This was a moment for which he had been dreaming a long time, and much determination and hard work had gone into it. With good reason, he savoured his success. So did his parents, whose financial sacrifices on behalf of Jim's education had, in the end, proven a worthy investment.

Once Jim had graduated, John and Mary McRuer decided to make an important move in their own lives. Unlike some other Ontario farmers who bemoaned the departure of their sons to the cities, the McRuers not only celebrated it but were eager to follow. John sold the farm in 1914 and on the advice of his son Jim, who, after all, was most knowledge-able about the Toronto real estate market, bought a neat little house at 79 Gothic Avenue, a curving tree-lined street of trim, well-maintained residences just north of High Park. Daughter Margaret moved to Toronto to live with her parents, and Jim—after three years in Toronto boarding houses—was more than ready to move into the new family home.

There was, amid all this success and fulfilment, a cloud on the horizon. In 1913 Jim's brother, who had been ill the previous year, was diagnosed as having a seriously advanced case of tuberculosis, aggravated by overwork. Forced to abandon his medical practice in Huntsville, he travelled with his wife Edythe by train to the world-renowned sanatorium at Denver, Colorado. There was a sanatorium much closer to home, in Gravenhurst, but John had heard from other doctors that the mountain air of Colorado would prove even more effective in healing his lungs. Whereas his brother Jim had gone to Muskoka to recover from his case of tuberculosis, John now left Muskoka to try to overcome his.

FOR THE MCRUERS, 1913 HAD BEEN A REMARKABLE YEAR. Jim graduated from law school—fulfilling a goal that had been his father's as well—after uncertain beginnings and ill health. John McRuer Sr., in selling the family farm and retiring to Toronto, realized another dream that had taken shape over years of sweat and toil behind the plough, and he now was happily ensconced in urban comfort, with electricity. Jim was reunited in this new home with his family—a move that provided him with a more secure personal environment, although it also represented a step backward in his personal development as a mature adult. John's illness, finally, underlined for everyone in the family the vulnerability of human life.

Something else happened in 1913 that was quite a departure for Jim. After moving into his parents' new home in High Park, he changed congregations, transferring from Bloor Street Presbyterian to Victoria Church on Medland Avenue. Bloor Street Church had included, not only Frank Yeigh's bible class, but an active young people's group in which Jim had made many friends. Such an organization was important to him, and so his disappointment was great upon discovering that Victoria Church had no group whatsoever for young people. When he asked the minister why this was so, the latter perked up and said he thought it would be a great idea, and promptly put Jim to work organizing it.

In this new circle of friends that Jim pulled together at church was an attractive young woman named Mary Rowena Dow.[4] Meeting at one of the Monday night socials which Jim was keen to organize, they soon discovered just how much they had in common, from a deep interest in the bible to a love of skating. With such shared enthusiasms, it seemed ordained that the two should start going out together in 1913, and when spring turned to summer they spent much time on the tennis court, which, by coincidence, turned out to be yet another common interest. In 1914, after Jim had introduced Mary to his parents, they began discussing marriage. Mary shared the Dow family prejudice against premature commitments and whirlwind courtships, however, and so they decided to be patient, allowing Jim to concentrate on launching his legal career.

An important step in this direction was taken at the end of January 1914, a week before Jim was formally admitted to the bar. One of Proudfoot's clients had been sued for non-performance of a contract in a real estate case, and after consideration of the typed copy of the document, Proudfoot had glumly scrawled across it, "I see no glimmer of hope in this case." Within the law office Proudfoot's reaction meant that the matter fell to McRuer, the most junior person available. Jim eagerly met with the client, who told him under close questioning that the original contract he had agreed to sign was in longhand. Jim then subpoenaed the document and discovered that it was indeed different, just as the client had said. Delighted with his new junior associate, Proudfoot made his way to the courtroom of Justice William Edward Middleton, arriving just in time to hear the judge pronounce in favour of McRuer's client, giving him a victory in his very first case.

On 6 February 1914, five years after he had signed his articles, twenty-three-year-old James C. McRuer was called to the bar of Ontario. Staying on with Proudfoot, but now as a member of the firm rather than as a student, he saw nothing that could stand in his way. His health was sound,

and, as the weeks progressed, clients retained his services. He continued
to see Mary, regularly reporting to her on how well his law practice was
shaping up.

Then the "guns of August" opened fire, and the British empire of
which Canada was an integral part plunged into war. Soon Jim would be
forced to decide where he was needed most—in a Toronto law office or
in the trenches of France.

3

INTO EUROPE'S BLOODY MUD

IN LATE JULY 1914, JUST PRIOR TO THE OUTBREAK OF WAR, Jim and his sister travelled the long distance to Denver to see their brother. Although they were shocked by his failing health—over the previous year John's letters had had much to say about his fellow patients but little about his own condition—their visit was not unpleasant. Staying with John and his wife in a house they occupied at the sanatorium, Jim and Margaret were able to save on hotel costs, and the clean dry air was beneficial for Jim, too. While there, Jim celebrated his twenty-fourth birthday and, as he looked around at others waging their battles against tuberculosis, he said a silent prayer of thanksgiving that he had been cured of his own respiratory ailment.

At the end of August Jim and Margaret bid farewell to John and Edythe and headed home. Changing trains in Detroit, Jim bought a newspaper and read the dramatic news that Britain had declared war on Germany—an action that effectively committed all the empire, including Canada, to war as well. He was naturally concerned, but, like many others, did not think that Canada would be seriously affected by the war. Certainly he did not imagine that he himself would be involved in it in any way. The war seemed remote, a European matter. As they discussed it with others on the train back to Toronto, there was an almost unanimous view that the conflict would be fought by professional soldiers and that the mighty British navy would soon finish off Germany.

In the weeks following their return to Toronto, Jim discovered that some of his friends were already enlisting, anxious to get into the fighting before it was over. When he discussed the war with his father, who was a pacifist, John McRuer was adamant that his son not enlist. Having sacrificed so much to put Jim through school, and seen him overcome health problems and finally qualify as a lawyer, John would simply not allow his son to become a soldier and spill his blood in foreign fields. Besides, John McRuer thought that it would be beneath his son, now a respectable professional, to join the army. His father's iron determination settled the matter for Jim. He was content to devote himself to his fledgling practice of law, especially since he was now managing to get more litigation work. It was the courtroom battle that held most appeal for him, and because he remained convinced that the overseas military battles would shortly be concluded anyway, he saw no need to defy his father.

Fall turned to winter, winter to spring, and spring to summer, but the war still did not end. As Jim read the newspaper reports, Germany seemed even stronger while Britain, though far from collapse, no longer seemed the invincible power of his youth. Jim was comfortable in Toronto, with his growing law practice, his flowering romance with Mary, and his easy life with his parents at their new home in a lovely residential neighbourhood. Yet he began to be gnawed by doubt. Maybe, just maybe, he should be doing something more.

In August 1915 Jim again travelled to Denver, this time alone, to see his brother. He was glad to see him looking somewhat improved, but John was still far from ready to leave. Throughout their visit John spoke a lot about the war, their father's views on it, and the future, and as he spoke he seemed to grow stronger. Apparently forgetting about his condition, he continued talking even through coughing spells. But their reunion did not consist only of conversation. Taking Jim into the open country, John gave his younger brother rifle lessons and target practice with a .22 rifle. "Not that you should shoot Germans," John said evenly, his eyes meeting Jim's, "but you should know how to handle a gun." He had hit *his* mark. Jim now realized that there were divergent views in the McRuer family, and that his father's opinion about what an able-bodied young man should do at this time of the empire's greatest need might not be the final word on the subject. Was he his father's son, or was he his own man?

On his return to Toronto, Jim was determined to respond to his sense of duty, no matter what his father might think. As a start, he went to work for the Young Men's Christian Association (YMCA), which soon put him in charge of a large military canteen serving the army recruits camped in Exhibition Park. Yet Jim, like many of his un-enlisted friends, was still uneasy as he watched countless other young men preparing to go overseas on active military service. He felt almost naked in his civilian clothes while more and more of his contemporaries paraded around in handsome khaki uniforms. Living at home with his parents, the quiet moments with Mary, the courtroom pleadings in legal disputes between contentious clients—all this seemed trivial, even false, when armies were on the march.

While his parents were in the United States visiting John in April 1916, a restless Jim McRuer applied at the recruiting hall for a commission in the Canadian army, and he emerged as a lieutenant in the Toronto Field Artillery. When his father returned, his utter dismay over Jim's decision sparked a huge row. Seeing his son in uniform for the first time, John McRuer shouted, "I shall never forgive you." This was a crushing statement, and it tore Jim deeply. Yet his father's anger was understandable. Not only was his opposition to war heartfelt, but, with his eldest son's health continuing to decline, the haunting prospect now loomed that the family could lose both sons.

For months to come, Jim felt great anguish about the break with his father over military service. He knew the sacrifices both parents had made for his education, and the bright hopes they pinned on him. Yet he also believed that enlisting was the right thing to do. This decision to act against his father's wishes and in accordance with his own beliefs marked a major turning-point in his life. The influence of his father would now be measured, paradoxically, by the manner and the extent to which, in a clash of strong wills, Jim stood up to him.

LIEUTENANT JAMES McRUER spent his first two months in officers' training at the Royal School of Artillery in Kingston, Ontario, where he was shown how to groom horses and ride them. Jim was hounded, as were his fellow recruits, by a brutal Captain Ringwood, whose philosophy in training men was "Break them if you can; if not, they'll make good soldiers." Ringwood delighted in taking "softies" on twelve-mile runs, haranguing them all along the course, but he landed in hospital himself after collapsing in one race when one of the recruits actually outran him. McRuer then joined the 63rd Battery in London, Ontario, where, without equipment, he was forced to give his men "imaginative" make-believe gun drills. He also pushed them hard, in the Ringwood style.

The farm boy in him loved this life. The horseback riding was long and hard but out in the country. The rest of the training was intensive—in ammunition, artillery, and a half-dozen other areas—and exams were held each week. Jim wrote to Mary every day, describing his army life, the run he had scored in a baseball game, and "one of the most impressive moments" he had ever known—a Sunday evening church service for soldiers where, by giving witness to his faith, he touched the lives of forty-two other individuals who "came forward."

By August 1916 Jim was drafted for service overseas at Folkstone, England, where he spent a further eight weeks training at Ross Barracks, learning how to manage his men and, again, to ride horses. During this period of training, his fellow soldiers sometimes called him "Jimmy," which he disliked as much as ever, or, what was almost as bad, "Mac." But he was careful to hold his tongue, realizing that, army ways being what they were, he would never be called anything else if he dared to protest.

Once his training at Ross Barracks was concluded, McRuer joined the Second Division of the Canadian Field Artillery at Barlin, France, a unit that was then involved in some primitive but pioneering anti-aircraft battery work. This assignment was being given great importance since the Germans had a superb air force and were threatening to win mastery of the skies. Lieutenant McRuer and his group were the first Canadians to get involved in the questionable task, ridiculed by the regular troops, of trying to hit an enemy airplane with a truck-mounted eighteen-pounder gun, as if it were a flock of ducks. The technique involved firing a barrage of high-velocity shells with differently timed fuses that would burst in the air ahead of the German airplanes; the goal was to hit the planes or, failing that, scare them away.

After a few months' training north of Barlin, McRuer and his anti-aircraft battery moved to guard observation balloons at the village of Carency, behind and to the west of a long hill whose name still sends a cold chill down the spines of Canadians—Vimy Ridge. Flipping a coin with a fellow lieutenant to see who of the two would be second-in-command of No. 4 section, E Battery, Jim won. His friend went off to serve with the field guns, and was soon badly wounded.

McRuer's senior officer, Captain McLennan, knew nothing about gunnery, but this impediment was overcome when the Canadians of E Battery, No. 4 section, trained with a British battery through the fall and winter of 1916. The soldiers shivered in open barns while McRuer, as an officer, slept in a peasant's cottage. To pass the time, McRuer and his men, many of whom were Canadians of Scottish descent, often curled with brickbats on frozen French ponds.

The first Christmas overseas, away from family and traditional celebrations, was difficult for most of the men, McRuer included. Imagining his family on Christmas Day, Jim had pangs of nostalgia but he kept up a brave front. On Boxing Day, 1916, he wrote to his grandmother. "War is hardly what one expects," he told her. "It is horrible in the extreme at times but at others it is more like a big camping out party. We have good meals, not too much work and lots of sleep." Like most of the men writing home, he also sought to allay concerns about his well-being. "We feel quite indifferent" to the rain and mud since "we have lots of waterproof clothes and good boots."

On its very first time out, chilled to the marrow, McRuer's battery section got off a few shots at a German plane, forcing it to veer away from a British observation balloon. McRuer, in command of the operation, recalled how the German airman "treated our enthusiasm with the contempt that it deserved, and that was the utmost contempt. The pilot came right on toward the balloon and we continued to fire until not only were we firing at the German plane, but we were firing directly at the balloon … To show his contempt for everyone, without firing a shot at the balloon, the German airman turned tail and disappeared over Ablain St. Nazare to his own lines." During this intense activity McRuer had had his blinkers on, concentrating with single-minded determination on his main goal—hitting the German aircraft. He had been oblivious to side-effects, such as hitting the Allied balloon.

As the German airplane disappeared and the excitement of the first Canadian ground-to-air missile program died down, McRuer suddenly exclaimed to Sergeant Milne, who was standing beside him, "My God, I forgot that the balloon was in the sky!" In two or three minutes the military field telephone rang, and a trembling McRuer answered it. The voice on the phone said, "This is Captain Smith of Balloon Section 4 speaking." McRuer cringed, fearing that the word "court-martial" was bound to follow. He reasoned that one of two things had happened: either one of Captain Smith's observers had been hit with the shells, or the battery had shot a few holes in the balloon. Smith, however, was effusive. He "just wanted to congratulate" McRuer "on that shoot," adding, "it's the first time we have ever had any service from an anti-aircraft battery." With great relief, McRuer, now grinning at his men in relief while Smith talked on, gratefully accepted the captain's congratulations.

On 9 April, Easter Monday, 1917, the Canadian assault on Vimy Ridge began. Though out of the line of fire, Lieutenant McRuer and his platoon heard the deafening sound of the big guns ("Imagine the loudest clap of thunder you ever heard," Lieutenant A.G.L.M. Burns recalled, "multiplied by two and prolonged indefinitely"[1]) as the four Canadian divisions fought their way to the top of the strategic ridge, where solidly entrenched Germans troops had previously repelled several French assaults. The famous Canadian victory came at a costly price: of the 40,000 Canadian infantrymen involved in the assault, 3,598 died and 7,004 were wounded. On the morning of the 10th, while snow was falling heavily, McRuer's battery was ordered to advance onto the ridge. On reaching it, they found almost unimaginable horror. Bodies lay crucified, nailed to the earth by shrapnel, and the waters in the shell holes were stained a deep red. "Everyone who was there," McRuer recalled, "remembers the snow storm and the desolation of Vimy Ridge that morning."

Since their guns were mounted on trucks, E battery found it easier than those with fixed placements to evade German shelling, and eventually McRuer and his men made their way to some old trenches and dugouts just south of the village of Thelus. After making sure that his troops were safe and comfortable for the night, McRuer ordered Sergeant Milne to take a party of men to bury a dead and decomposing mule that was creating a horrible stench. While McRuer stood watching his men shovelling the earth over the stinking corpse, one poor lad named Ritchie suddenly struck an unexploded bomb buried in the earth. It detonated with a thunderous burst.

The blast killed Ritchie and seriously wounded three others, and McRuer was hit by three pieces of shrapnel whizzing through the air—one struck him in the groin, another in the hip, and a third in the arm. In this bizarre way, he and his men became a small statistical slice of the more than 10,000 Canadians killed and wounded at Vimy Ridge. "Wounds small feeling fine," Jim cockily telegraphed home on 10 June 1917 from England, where he had been invalided. He was one of many dozens of officers in the rows of iron beds with clean white linen in what had been a gay London dance hail but now served as a military hospital.

Shortly afterward, while still in hospital, Jim received word that his brother was dying in Denver. Since he was not serving the war effort where he was, he was prepared to suffer pain for the sake of trying to see John one last time. Given special convalescent leave, and sending word to his brother that he was on the way, Jim began the long journey by ship and train from the south of England to the west of the United States. During these weeks that his brother was travelling to him, John somehow held on. When Jim finally reached Denver and sat by his brother's bed, they talked quietly. Within the hour, John was dead.

Sadly closing up John's house in Denver that July 1917, Jim took charge of bringing his brother's body and his sister-in-law back to Canada. When switching trains in Detroit, Jim, still in discomfort from his wounds and preoccupied with caring for the widowed Edythe, had the added burden of arranging the transfer of John's body from one train to another and across an international boundary. Yet he was not too busy to remember that day when he was last here with his sister, Margaret, and they had learned that England had declared war on Germany—a war that they thought would be over by Christmas. When Jim reached Canada, he and the rest of the family returned to Ayr for John's funeral. After a service in Knox Church, John's body was laid to rest in the local cemetery, atop the hill overlooking the countryside where he had been born just thirty-three years earlier. Below, Ayr itself was quiet; virtually all the young men had left the village, either for the city or for the war in Europe.

Jim spent the rest of his leave in Toronto, happily getting to know Mary again, teaching a few lessons at the Victoria Church bible class, visiting his law office, even engaging in politics. Over the course of 1917 Prime Minister Robert Borden, with the aim of implementing military conscription and so ensuring a successful prosecution of the war effort, had remade his government into a coalition of Liberals and Conservatives. One of the most prominent recruits to the new "Unionist" government, as it was called, was Newton Wesley Rowell, who resigned as leader of the Ontario Liberal Party in October 1917 to become a member of the Borden cabinet. His successor as leader of the Ontario Liberals was none other than McRuer's law partner, William Proudfoot. At Proudfoot's request, Jim spoke on Rowell's behalf at a rally in the election held in December 1917—a bitter affair, fought over conscription, that pitted English Canadians against French Canadians. By now Jim had also come to believe in the necessity of conscription, and, as an officer in uniform home to recover from his wounds, he cut an impressive figure standing side by side with Rowell on a public platform. He enjoyed the experience and was encouraged by the election of Rowell and the victory of the Unionist government.

Not everyone, however, was pleased with Jim's action. Ontario Liberals were badly split by the issue of conscription, some remaining loyal to Laurier and rejecting it while others rallied to the Unionist banner to bring it about. In supporting the Unionists, Jim alienated many of his Liberal friends, who thought that he had left the fold. Certainly his father was quite disturbed by the spectacle of his son hobnobbing with a party that included Conservatives: he had not raised his son to be a Conservative, any more than he had raised him to be a soldier. This episode did nothing to improve feelings between the two, but Jim was now more determined than ever to do things his way. Whatever his father might think, Jim himself was convinced that partisan differences should not be allowed to obstruct the war effort.

By the time of the 1917 election, McRuer had taken up a post as instructor to the 71st Recruiting Battery in Exhibition Park, Toronto. His convalescence had been good and he now felt healthy, even though he was still light, carrying 150 pounds on his lanky frame. Restless, he longed to get back into the war, though his father was pressuring him to stay where he was. His impatience was reflected in caustic, sharp remarks, all of which increasingly irritated his superior, Major Burgoyne. To get rid of this thorn in his side, Burgoyne put McRuer in charge of a trainload of men who were travelling as part of the Royal Canadian Dragoons, bound for Halifax. McRuer had his hands full. Some of the men were American soldiers of fortune who had enlisted in Canada's armed forces prior to the United States's declaration of war in April 1917, the rest were conscripts, and all were wild and untrained. McRuer succeeded in putting them on the troopship with only a few defections, however, and soon he too was sailing from Halifax to England.

Reflecting on his relations with Mary during the return voyage across the Atlantic, Jim decided that the time had come to take the fateful step. Back in England, he purchased a ring from Tiffany's and sent it to Mary along with a letter proposing marriage. Then something odd happened. By the time Jim had mailed his letter, Mary herself was beginning to have second thoughts about their relationship. She was being courted by others (at least two Canadian men in uniform were corresponding with her at the same time as she was receiving Jim's almost daily love letters), but, more than that, she did not feel like getting married. At the outbreak of the war she had been studying towards a BA degree at the University of Toronto, but in 1916, in order to help support her family, she had given up her studies and taken a job as a secretary. Now, as the war neared its end, she was thinking more and more of returning to university and finishing her degree; she was not ready to settle down and become a homemaker. So, with great seriousness, she sent Jim a "dear John" letter. He never received it. The next letter she received from him was his offer of marriage, which, on reflection, she decided to accept. In this way she became, against her wishes, a "mail-order bride."

In the meantime, of course, Jim still had a war to fight. During the spring of 1918, after a six-week refresher course in field artillery at Whitley Camp, McRuer happily returned to his old anti-aircraft battery.[2] Stationed at Cambrai, the battery was involved in fierce fighting as the Germans made a desperate offensive push against the northern flank of the British army. There were new faces, fresh soldiers to replace those killed as the war dragged on and the death toll mounted. One of the casualties was Captain Ringwood, first encountered in the training camp at Kingston, who had been killed by a shell's direct hit; even though he never liked the captain, McRuer was sorry to hear that he had died. A far more devastating loss for Jim was the death of his close friend Bill Bright. Jim tried to console himself by writing to his mother a touching letter that talked about Bright and the meaning of his death.

Remembering his brother's advice, McRuer bought a revolver and practised endlessly in case the fighting ever became hand-to-hand. He found that he was a poor shot, however, and got rid of the gun. Perhaps it didn't matter. The German offensive was running out of steam as Germany ran out of oil, and the American troops at last arrived to join the conflict on what now appeared to be the winning side. At the beginning of November 1918, after shunting back and forth for months, McRuer and his unit found themselves fighting in France near the Belgian border, pursuing the retreating German army. Since this region showed little sign of devastation, the military activity occurred in a rather surreal atmosphere. The trees were undamaged and the countryside peaceful, except for the heavy traffic of artillery, trucks, and troops on the roads. It was a common thing to see civilians standing in the fields watching the guns firing. It seemed to McRuer that they had grown immune to shellfire. Once he saw an old man working on his land while the Germans were shelling no more than 300 yards away. His barn had received a direct hit only the day before, but this French peasant would not even look up when another shell came crashing in. The women were just the same, laughing and chattering away.

Given what these people had gone through, their stoicism was surprising. McRuer tried hard to understand. During the early days of November 1918, the civilians in this part of France first heard the sound of the Canadian guns approaching from the west, getting plainer every night. Then the German guns came back around their homes, then the Canadians' shells, then the German infantry, then Canadian infantry and German shells. Then Canadian guns came up and fired over their heads, then shot from their houses. The gunners slept in their houses and then moved on. The sound gradually died away in the east, and the war was over for them, except for the searing memories.

By 5 November the advancing Allied armies were moving briskly in pursuit of the Germans. McRuer and his unit had advanced the day before, and should have kept moving, but they were getting out of touch with headquarters and could not maintain their supply of rations without more transport. Frustrated, McRuer wrote of his superiors: "I could fill a letter with choice remarks about our HQ. They are at present at least 30 miles behind the line, and we have to get our rations from them. I went down there today to have a fight, but there was no one to fight with." Like every soldier who can see so plainly how a war should be conducted, he felt that it was insanity to be transporting rations over thirty miles of bad roads when headquarters could easily have been stationed much closer behind the advancing troops. "Too much whisky and fast life is responsible for it all," he huffed, adding for good measure, "it is nothing short of criminal."

In the face of the recently concluded peace with Austria and Turkey, McRuer was certain that Germany's surrender was imminent. Learning of the harsh terms meted out to the Austrians and Turks, he also concluded that, for Germany, "it won't be any shilly-shally armistice." Even at this stage, he and his men were enjoying all the features of an armistice. "The Germans have run away and we haven't caught up with them yet. However, we will probably meet up again tomorrow, and there will be some more war." Expecting the Germans to "kick in any day now" gave Jim and his men "a frightfully jumpy feeling." So they waited, always looking for surrendering Germans. No Germans appeared, but "the great day of peace cannot be far off," McRuer wrote. "The guns still tell that it hasn't come yet, but it's coming. Let us hope that it will come as a day of triumph for justice."

On 7 November it was officially announced that the terms of an armistice had been stated to Germany, and that plenipotentiaries had been dispatched to Paris to negotiate an end to hostilities. McRuer wrote that he and his men expected to "hear the great word" within twenty-four hours. Everyone was very quiet and thoughtful. That evening McRuer and the other Canadian soldiers in E Battery sat around a fire, playing a gramophone and talking of those back home. They were all on edge, McRuer said, but "we do feel we must play the game until then." With the war virtually won, these seasoned soldiers did not want to die now. "One doesn't feel like taking any risks for a day or two," McRuer confided to his diary. "Personally, I don't want to hear any more gunfire."

The next day they were on the move again. Everyone was. Crossing the border into Belgium, they set up camp in a small village. That night, McRuer and his men took shelter from the rain under a propped-up tarpaulin, with a wagon at the entrance to stop the wind. The Germans had given them the slip. The front had been quiet all day, and no one in fact knew any longer where the enemy line was. No word had come yet, but as he went to sleep under his tarpaulin, under the rain, McRuer once again expected an armistice to be concluded the next day.

The advance was then delayed for a couple of days by broken bridges. During the wait for bridges to be repaired, McRuer, pleased to learn that the work was going slowly, read some newspapers that had been brought up to the front. From them he learned that, although Germany was badly scarred, its leaders were insisting that they and their people would not agree to a humiliating peace. Angered by such an attitude, McRuer wrote, "They must be brought to know that freedom of thought and freedom of a government that recognizes the freedom of others is the only doctrine this world is going to tolerate." He also scorned the propaganda leaflets that German planes were then dropping on Allied troops. These leaflets announced that Germany had agreed to stop submarine attacks on passenger ships, stressed the need to end the destruction of Belgium, and deplored the prospect of further deaths among the brave Allied soldiers. McRuer judged this material "the poorest trash you ever saw." "They didn't say anything about the punishment of those to blame for it all. It's all right to blame the other fellow but they should be as much interested in seeing that he is punished as we are." To McRuer, the unfolding events had reached "such an interesting stage, and it is all history." German soldiers were now starting to surrender in large numbers.

From the brief messages that filtered through on the signals, McRuer and all the others felt confident that the war was over. Yet by 10 November the official word still had not been received. "It isn't ending with any great demonstration but is simply falling to pieces. Tonight we are a good many miles from the front, if in fact anyone knows where the front is. Fighting has practically ceased for over 24 hours. The Boche has cleared out and our troops are just marching." The news that did reach them that day, however, was that the kaiser had abdicated. "Rather a hard war on kings, isn't it?" gloated McRuer, wondering what all the ex-kings were going to do. He suggested that they should be given an island somewhere where they could fight or have peace, whatever they wished.

"Democracy," he wrote, expressing the sense that many had about the changing world order, "is certainly coming into its own."

The Germans had blown up every bridge and road for miles, and the repair work on the bridges still seemed no closer to completion. Rather than sit still any longer, McRuer decided on a new strategy. Instead of trying to advance from their present position, his unit would double-back and take the road from Valenciennes to Mons, using this round-about route to reach a point in the line from which they could more easily move forward. On the morning of 11 November, a cold grey Belgian dawn greeted Jim as he awoke, stiff but still impatient to get moving. The unit started out at 8 o'clock, and McRuer was quite depressed because he thought that the armistice was off. He had heard a gun firing and the air was full of Allied planes.

They had been marching for about a half-hour when a signals officer passed in a car and called out, pointing to E Battery's field gun, "Take it back. You won't need it." McRuer wrote later that the signals officer "and his companions were smiling so we knew what it meant." His account of this momentous day then continued: "As we came along, we met hundreds of civilians with all sorts of carts hauling their possessions back to the towns that they had vacated. All were wearing the Tricolore. The old women, girls and children shouted to us. The men raised their hats in a respectful *bonjour*. No one is happier today than the French and Belgian peasants returning home from bondage." Presently they came to some large towns that had not been shelled and in which the civilians had remained. French and Belgian flags were hanging everywhere and streamers had been hung across the streets. All the people were laughing, but there was no cheering. McRuer thought of taking up a position just south of Mons but, after hearing the news of the armistice, he decided to stop in a town about six miles from Mons to await further orders.

Those orders came on 13 November, when they were told that in four days' time they would be marching to the Rhine. "We will go through Belgium and into Germany as unquestioned victors," McRuer wrote. "I imagine we will sit very straight in our seats as we enter the first German town. We are not going in to retaliate for all the wrongs committed, but we will show them that the armies of justice can come with dignity. I hope that we go with flags flying and bands playing but no pomp, just dignity."

The next few weeks were spent on the march until, on the morning of 11 December, E Battery travelled for about three hundred yards along a road that divided Belgium and Germany, the border being marked simply by a post painted black and white in the same spiral manner as a barber's pole. McRuer and his troops were struck by the strange juxtaposition of friends on one side of the road and enemies on the other. A small Belgian flag hung from one of the houses on the right, but from the houses on the left—the German side—there was no sign of life except for some children peeking through the fence in the rear of one house. They marched a long time before they saw adults—a number of men of all ages working on the road. These Germans stood back and regarded the Canadian soldiers with curiosity. McRuer's men continued on their way. No bands played.

McRuer's unit, now in Germany as part of the Allied army of occupation, settled into an unusual role for soldiers: living with the enemy. Billeted in a suite of rooms once occupied by the kaiser, in the brooding Rhine castle of Baron von Deischmann, near Bonn, McRuer was amused to watch a fellow officer happily test the castle's wine stock and, to pass the time, fearlessly play contract bridge with their hostile host—"an oily sort," in McRuer's eyes, for whom the war would never be over. Once when his partner had stupidly led the wrong card, the baron stood up in a rage and shouted bitterly, "You're all conspiring against me!"

Down at the military camp near Bonn there was, in fact, a real conspiracy. McRuer had become suspicious that the profits of the canteen, which were supposed to be shared with the men, were being siphoned off by the sergeant-major and perhaps the base commander. Having worked at the YMCA canteen in Toronto, McRuer knew about these things, and the more he probed into the canteen's operation, the more indignant he became. Always loyal to his men, he told them of his suspicions, read them the relevant provisions of the army regulations, and stressed the injustice of what was taking place. Three days later a notice came, transferring McRuer out of the unit.

Sent to serve with the YMCA at Namur in the north of Belgium, McRuer managed two "Y" canteens there and played the military impresario, organizing and publicizing vaudeville shows, and billeting musical entertainers sent out from England. In his spare time he happily clattered about in the base's transport truck, burning up military gasoline, roaming the back roads of Belgium with his sergeant and an officer friend, John McNair (who later would become premier, and then chief justice, of New Brunswick). Much earlier in the war, while stationed in England, McRuer had started collecting fine china. At Namur, he continued his cultural indulgences, travelling east to Cologne to attend the opera.

With the war over, Jim thought more and more about the new life he hoped to make for himself and Mary back in Canada. He knew that he would have a struggle resuming his legal career; the only legal work he had done while in the army involved presiding over two courts-martial. Yet he was confident that he was up to the challenge. His health was good, and he would not be starting from scratch. He had a position with a good law firm to return to, and from which to build.

In the spring of 1919 Lieutenant James Chalmers McRuer received demobilization orders and shortly thereafter he was back in Canada, happily reunited with his family and Mary. His father was relieved that the war was over and Jim safely home, and the two men became reconciled. Soon Jim and Mary started planning their wedding, and their future. She and Jim now agreed that, after their marriage, she would give up her job. Yet Jim also had to promise Mary that she could resume her university studies as soon as they were financially established.

On 27 September 1919, after a six-year courtship which for half the time had been a wartime romance by mail, Victoria Church filled with McRuers and Dows, their friends and relatives, to witness the marriage of Jim and Mary. At the conclusion of the service, as the church organ swelled with the recessional hymn, a confident and healthy twenty-nine-year-old Jim McRuer escorted his bride down the aisle past their smiling guests and into the sunny autumn afternoon.

JIM MCRUER'S WARTIME DIARY AND LETTERS gave expression to his innermost feelings. It is clear that he had a sense of adventure, enjoyed mastering new skills, resented stupidity in his commanding officers, was very self-confident, and had poetic flashes.

War allowed McRuer to emerge from the lengthy shadow cast by his father. Jim's decision to enlist, and later his support of the Union government in the election of 1917, indicated that he was finally becoming his own person, still respectful of his father but no longer dominated by him. The war, in short, saw Jim McRuer mature as an adult. Another effect it had was to strengthen his relationship with Mary Dow. Jim would likely have married Mary whether the war had happened or not. Yet, in his case as in countless others, the war gave an added intensity to personal relationships and at the same time encouraged the making of formal commitments. Jim and Mary were too practical to marry while the war still raging, but they were not prepared to wait long once it was over. The war had been a terrible lesson to both of them, and to Jim in particular, on how short and precarious life truly was. In such an uncertain world, putting off until tomorrow what could be done today seemed to risk a precious opportunity.

McRuer's attachment to an anti-aircraft battery sheltered him somewhat from the worst carnage of the war. He witnessed horror, to be sure, but usually his exposure to death and destruction occurred in the wake of battle rather than in the midst of it. The fact that he was one step removed from the slaughter of the trenches, combined with his natural reticence, may explain why he had so little to say about the conflict's deeper meaning; in contrast to many others, McRuer emerged from the war essentially unchanged, his basic values and assumptions still intact. Indeed, McRuer in later years would tell his own son that "the happiest time of his life was overseas in the army. You had no worries. You might be dead tomorrow so you just made the best of today. People helped each other—nobody had ambition. You didn't need it to get ahead. A German bullet will make an opening for you—if you wanted it."

Yet the war did have subtle effects on McRuer's outlook. The references in his letters and diary to the cause of democracy and to German authoritarianism show that, for him as for others, the war confirmed cultural prejudices—the British empire and Germany symbolized the opposing forces of light and darkness, civilization and barbarism. The same references also offer a glimpse of a social and political philosophy that, while rooted in McRuer's upbringing, took clearer shape as a result of his wartime experiences. The fundamental elements of this philosophy were fairness and justice, principles that, in McRuer's mind, were just as important in the affairs of nations as in the lives of individuals. Another was a deep attachment to country.

In the cauldron years 1914–18, it has often been said, Canada became a nation. The old loyalty to the British empire still lingered, but increasingly it went hand in hand with a sense of Canadian identity that was focused on Canada itself. The stirrings of Canadian patriotism were reflected in several quarters during the war, and Jim McRuer gave expression to the same sentiment, though again in his characteristically understated fashion. In 1917 McRuer used a four-day leave to travel to Scotland. As if pulled like a compass to a lodestone, he found himself in the grassy, overgrown cemetery at Doon, near Stirlingshire, peering through the drizzle at old grey stones, pulling off the moss and reading the name of his family in all its archaic spellings—MacRuars, McRuars, MacRuers, and McRuers. He also visited his Chalmers relations in East Kilbride, near Glasgow, who in their gruff and simple way were enthusiastic to see him. The Chalmers made him feel welcome, for visits from North American relatives were rare events. For McRuer, an emotional circle had been completed—he had experienced "back home." Yet this visit to Scotland also helped Jim shed any illusions he might have had about "the Old Country." However proud he was of his Scottish heritage, Jim now realized that Canada was his home and he, to the very marrow of his bones, was a Canadian. In this respect, he had acquired an understanding of his identity that his future father-in-law, Dr. John Dow, did not reach until he was elderly. On his first visit to Scotland, in 1936, Dow had proclaimed, in a state of genuine culture shock, "This is not me!" Jim McRuer had reacted the same way on his visit in 1917. The experiences he had on the battlefield over the ensuing months only served to strengthen his sense of himself as a Canadian.

The war, finally, showed two sides of McRuer. One was brave, competent, and dedicated; the other was testy and difficult—not with his own men, to whom he was devoted and who respected him in return, but with his fellow officers. Many of these officers found McRuer prickly, and McRuer, for his part, considered many of them incompetent. This attitude had begun to take shape early in his military career, at the military camp in Kingston run by Captain Ringwood, and it became more and more pronounced over time. The fact that, as a plain-speaking puritan, he made no secret of his disdain for other officers probably accounts for his lack of promotion in the ranks: McRuer entered the war as a lieutenant, and he was still only a lieutenant when the conflict ended, a remarkable feat. Whatever its role in determining the course of his military career, however, McRuer's relationship with his officers showed him to be a person who did not suffer fools gladly, especially when they were in positions of authority and their incompetence could have fatal consequences. The war did not give rise to this frame of mind on McRuer's part—his early upbringing, with the stress it placed on the meaning of responsibility, probably did that—but his experiences during these years certainly sharpened his impatience with so-called leaders who seemed unable to lead, and especially with those who failed to see and accept responsibility for their actions and decisions. In later years, McRuer would again and again show this side of his character. There would be a few more Captain Ringwoods along the way as Jim McRuer pursued his career in the law.

4

ENFORCING THE LAW

AFTER THEIR MARRIAGE IN SEPTEMBER 1919, Jim and Mary McRuer, with the aid of Jim's $500 severance allowance from the army, settled down in a $40-per-month one-bedroom apartment in Parkview Mansions, in Toronto's west end. This first place of theirs had some fine touches—including Jim's own "dowry" of bone china teacups and elegant tablecloth (purchased in England during the war) and his two Tom Thomson paintings.

Professionally, Jim spent the first months after his return from the war rebuilding the legal career that had been interrupted by his enlistment, but he soon found that he was doing so on shifting ground. In December 1919 the old firm of Proudfoot, Duncan, Grant and Skeans broke up. With Proudfoot and Duncan parting company from Skeans, McRuer had to decide where to cast his lot. Eventually, he chose to remain with Skeans.

Some of McRuer's colleagues were puzzled by this decision, for Proudfoot and Duncan were good lawyers while Skeans was a mediocre one. But Jim had thought it through and knew what he was doing. For one thing, Proudfoot, as interim leader of the provincial Liberal Party, was now fully consumed by the political wars and had little time for his legal practice. Personal factors were also at work. Lawyers who practise law together in partnership, particularly in a small firm, need to work well together, to rely on and trust one another, and, ideally, to enjoy one another's company. McRuer was intelligent and meticulous as a lawyer, and he and Proudfoot shared a common interest in Liberal politics. Still, he had not been good at developing personal relationships and in fact struck both Proudfoot and Duncan as an austere loner. In short, they were not fussy about having him with them. On the other side, although Jim had learned a great deal from Duncan about being painstakingly attentive to legal documents, he came to feel constrained by the older man's finicky approach and wanted to work more on his own. Years later, in the middle of his career, McRuer's lone-wolf approach would get him into trouble with colleagues who were not amused by his unilateral decisions, and later still he would revel in his role on several occasions as a one-man royal commission. In 1919 this same desire for independence prompted him to go with Skeans into a firm where he would have more personal scope.[1]

Skeans was delighted to see Jim back, but such was not the response of Erell C. Ironside, the third lawyer in the firm. Skeans envisioned a firm in which Ironside would be in second spot and McRuer in third. McRuer himself, however, insisted on at least equal partnership with Ironside because of his military service. Skeans balked at this demand, as did Ironside, and relations between the three men—and especially between Ironside and McRuer—became tense. Matters came to a head after the trio moved their law office to the Imperial Bank Building, at the southeast corner of Queen and Yonge streets in downtown Toronto. Returning from court one day, Jim was outraged to discover that the freshly painted name on the door—Skeans, Ironside and McRuer—put him last. In the rows that ensued, McRuer refused to back off and eventually Ironside left the firm in a huff. The painter then returned to redo the name on the door, and the printer cranked out a new batch of letterhead. The firm's name was now simply "Skeans and McRuer."

This episode showed how determined, and stubborn, Jim McRuer could be in pursuing his goals. And he would not change. At times he was like a horse with blinkers on: he could only see one thing—the course ahead on which he had set himself. His determination led him to achieve many successes over the course of his life, but it also caused difficulties in his relationships with other people, Erell Ironside being only one of many he would antagonize. As for Ironside himself, he did well for a while after leaving Skeans and McRuer, buying his wife diamonds and driving a big car, but the Depression ruined him. In 1931 he was caught misappropriating a client's funds, and, before he could be disbarred by the Law Society, he committed suicide.

Meanwhile, in the two-man, trimmed down, relocated law firm, business was terribly slow and Skeans was able to pay McRuer only $1,500 a year. Remembering his days at Bert Hutchison's sleepy law office in Huntsville, days marked by pleasant conversations but precious little work, McRuer feared that he was faced with more of the same. One of his problems was that, however much they might praise the returned soldiers in public, the businessmen of Toronto preferred experienced legal veterans to glamorous military ones. Indeed, for a long stretch of time, McRuer had not one single client.

In the midst of these problems, Jim and Mary found a new home, a small cottage on Manitou Road, Centre Island. Both of them enjoyed the daily ferry ride across Toronto harbour to the mainland and back. Jim—a country boy at heart—felt closer to nature than he had since his boyhood on the farm, and the island isolation also allowed him to put some distance between his family life and work. Yet not even the pleasures of Toronto Island could make Jim forget his professional troubles. He began to worry, lost his appetite, and developed ulcers and intestinal trouble. He even began to think of giving up the practice of law. His family physician, Dr. Cavan, could do nothing to cure him. When McRuer suggested going south for his health, Cavan told him it would be a foolish thing to do. Then McRuer mentioned another possibility, a holiday in northern Ontario: memories of enchanting Muskoka were as fresh as ever in his mind. Cavan gave his assent to that idea, and so, with Mary's blessing and his last $60, Jim went north again in the late winter of 1920 to try to recover his health. His precise destination was the Highland Inn, deep in Algonquin Park.

This desperate excursion proved to be another turning-point in his life. At the Highland Inn, McRuer met two Conservative Party politicians, the shrewd, lugubrious Colonel W.H. "Billy" Price, MPP for Parkdale, and prominent Toronto lawyer Peter White. Price was on the opposition benches at that time, having held his Toronto constituency when most other members of the Conservative government were thrown out of office in the election of October 1919. Victims of the post-war mood for change, the Conservatives had forfeited the reins of power to a Farmer-Labour coalition headed by E.C. Drury of the United Farmers of Ontario. In fact, the strongman of the new government was Attorney-General W.E. Raney, and Price and White thought that McRuer might have a future in Raney's department.

A crusading Toronto lawyer, Raney was well connected. Not only was he a close friend of "Holy Joe" Atkinson of the *Toronto Star*, but he also had been a partner both of I.B. Lucas, the attorney-general in the preceding Conservative government, and of Hartley Dewart, who had just replaced Proudfoot as Liberal leader. Politically, he had had a chequered career, embracing first the Liberals, then the Conservatives, and then the Liberals again before finally joining the United Farmers of Ontario. Regarded as a bit of a fanatic and even as a bigot by many in his profession—Howard Ferguson, leader of the Conservatives, disdainfully called him a "little Napoleon who persecutes everybody"—Raney had served as counsel to the powerful Moral and Social Reform Council of Canada, a group of church and lay people who zealously preached against liquor and gambling. His special interest was tightening up the Temperance Act, a measure originally passed in 1916 and confirmed by Ontario voters in a referendum held simultaneously with the 1919 election. Having campaigned vigorously for the "drys" in the referendum campaign, Raney moved to add more teeth to the law. His amendments gave additional powers to the provincial Liquor Licence Board, doubled the fines under the Ontario Temperance Act, and prohibited anyone convicted of a liquor offence from keeping liquor in their home. With the same goal of enforcing the ban on liquor more effectively, he strengthened the crown attorney's office in the city of Toronto by expanding its jurisdiction to York County, which until then had been served by a separate office.[2]

Billy Price and Peter White suggested to McRuer that he approach Raney and apply for a position with the Toronto crown attorney. In offering this advice, Price and White probably believed that McRuer might prove a moderating influence in the enforcement of the Temperance Act. They undoubtedly realized, too, that his association with such good Liberals as Frank Yeigh and William Proudfoot, which had also come to light in their discussions at the Algonquin Park resort, might help him in Raney's eyes. McRuer himself was pessimistic about his chances of landing a job with Raney, citing his lack of contacts. To this, Price replied that he would put in a word for him.

McRuer doubted whether such a worldly partisan as Billy Price would have any influence with the upright, moralistic Raney, but he was proven wrong. After a few weeks at the Highland Inn, McRuer, his health much restored, returned to Toronto. Shortly afterwards he was summoned to a meeting with Raney, a neat little man with a goatee and rimless spectacles. This introductory session went well, and, in answer to Raney's request for references, McRuer obtained a strong letter from Peter White and a truly glowing testimonial from his minister at Victoria Church, the Reverend D.T.L. McCarroll. To his great delight and immense relief, he then learned that he was to be appointed assistant crown attorney for Toronto and York County. At a second meeting to confirm the arrangements, McRuer was asked by Raney what kind of salary he expected. He answered that all he wanted was a chance to work and a salary large enough to support him and his wife.

"Well," said Raney, blankly, lifting his bushy eyebrows, "would $4,000 be alright?"

Swallowing his astonishment and trying to appear composed, McRuer agreed on the spot. All his financial worries were now behind him; he would not have to abandon the law after all. The trip to Algonquin Park had not only restored his health but had also given him a second chance at a legal career. After so many false starts and so much uncertainty, Jim McRuer finally seemed to have a future.

ON 1 JUNE 1920 JIM MCRUER, regaining his self-respect after the difficulties of the last several months, moved eagerly into his quarters at the crown attorney's offices. He was fully ready to open another door in his legal career, and, as it turned out, he closed the one behind him just in time. Some months later Skeans was investigated by the Law Society for financial irregularities and debts to his clients, but, like Erell Ironside years later, he died before suffering the humiliation of disbarment. If McRuer had still been his partner, he would have been left with all the firm's obligations.

Most of McRuer's work in his new job involved cracking down on the illegal liquor traffic of the prohibition era. This was no easy task, and it became even more challenging when a second referendum campaign, held in April 1921, saw a majority of Ontarians vote to forbid liquor imports. That summer, Raney formed a special squad within the Ontario Provincial Police to enforce the ban on liquor. This squad concentrated on breaking up roadhouses and stills and pouncing on petty gangsters and outrageous rumrunners who prowled up and down the Detroit River—the United States had gone dry in 1920—smuggling alcohol. Armed with a blanket search warrant, the squad's commander in Windsor, a fiery young Methodist minister by the name of J.O.L. Spracklin, roamed the river at the bow of the government speedboat *Panther II*, or righteously roared up and down the dusty back roads in a police car, putting the fear of the law into transgressors. A bootleggers' vigilante group was soon formed to scare him off, and on one occasion his house was sprayed with a hail of bullets from a tommy gun—one slug narrowly missing his wife. Spracklin then began to carry a gun himself. One night, in a raid on a popular roadhouse, he shot and killed the owner, "Babe" Trumble, who had been a childhood friend.

A public outcry erupted over this tragic event, but Spracklin was supported by the crusading *Globe*, temperance societies, and the secretary of the Methodist General Conference, all of whom commended him for his zeal in enforcing the Temperance Act. The *Christian Guardian* expressed the tenor of the prohibitionist mentality when it stated that law enforcement was more important than "any merely sentimental feeling stirred up by the thought of the taking of human life."[3] In spite of the temperance groups closing ranks over the Trumble killing, there was a growing mood of contempt for the whole prohibition exercise, and Raney-baiting became a popular sport among "wets." *Saturday Night* magazine called the shooting of Trumble "the first act in a general campaign of bureaucratic terrorism authorized by the Attorney-General of Ontario and sanctioned by a great and influential religious denomination."[4] The law, and with it the whole apparatus of government, was being brought into disrepute, and Raney was increasingly attacked for maintaining an expensive army of spies or "spotters" as well as stool pigeons to help McRuer and other crown attorneys in prosecuting thirsty Ontarians. But Raney pressed on magisterially.

By 1922 Raney had even disallowed the sale of alcohol "for medicinal purposes" on a doctor's prescription. The law had become a joke. One doctor ordered 487 alcohol prescriptions in a single day, and drugstores were horribly crowded before holidays by people seeking "tonics." Parodying the situation, Stephen Leacock gleefully wrote that, in order to get a drink, it was only necessary "to go to a drugstore, and lean up against the counter and make a gurgling sound like apoplexy. One often sees these apoplexy cases lined up four deep."[5] Charges under the Ontario Temperance Act were laid against more than 300 Ontario physicians who played the game of circumventing prohibition, one of whom was the garrulous, hard-headed Tory MPP for West York, Dr. Forbes Godfrey. He furiously turned the tables on the government, taunting Chairman J.D. Flavelle and his Liquor Licence Board, which had been given new powers in 1920 to control the issuing of liquor prescriptions by the medical fraternity, as nothing more than a "soviet committee."[6] Yet, however controversial and unpopular these charges were, they had to be prosecuted in court, and Assistant Crown Attorney J.C. McRuer was in the thick of the action.

On his appointment to the crown attorney's office, McRuer, knowing nothing about criminal law, got a copy of *Crankshaw's Criminal Code* and launched himself on a two-week crash course of study. Learning on the job, he spent a great deal of time in the mornings sitting in court watching the fine and fair-minded Frank Hughes, part-time deputy crown attorney, who later became a noted civil litigation lawyer and justice of the Supreme Court of Canada. A master at his work, Hughes coached McRuer in the latter's prosecutions and was impressed by McRuer's quick grasp of criminal law procedure. Although McRuer's boss, Crown Attorney Eric Armour, was not enamoured of courtroom detail, Jim delighted in it—the methodical yet creative work of understanding and correctly applying procedural rules.

Most of Jim's prosecutions as an assistant crown attorney were violations of the Ontario Temperance Act. The courts were clogged with a whole new class of "criminals," and several magistrates appeared almost openly sympathetic to the needs of intemperate offenders. While minor bootleggers often could not afford to pay lawyers to defend them, the organized criminal element could and did hire the best in legal help—such as Toronto lawyer Jimmy Haverson. A great deal of money was being made in bootlegging and, as prohibition wore on, Haverson had grown accustomed to earning large fees from this branch of criminal activity. McRuer relished appearing in court against Haverson, partly because he found him very fair and partly because he liked his sense of humour. A good example of that latter occurred one day when Haverson took a McRuer prosecution to the Court of Appeal. Depending on how the court was constituted, it could be quite enthusiastic about enforcing the Ontario Temperance Act. On the day in question, however, McRuer and Haverson appeared before Chief Justice Mulock, no friend of prohibition. When Mulock enquired why Haverson had appealed the case, given that there were no legal points at issue, the defence counsel replied: "Well, my Lord, my client is an unrighteous man. When he appeared before the trial judge he got an unsympathetic hearing, so I thought he'd get a better hearing here."

With contempt for the law widespread, many policemen turning a blind eye to bootlegging, and growing evidence of the activities of organized crime, Raney tightened the screws of the law even further. He narrowed the grounds for appeal, prohibited the private importation of liquor from Quebec, and even tried to push through the Ontario legislature a dictatorial "Declaratory Act" to allow the government to set aside court judgments. Liberal leader Hartley Dewart criticized the last measure as a crime against Magna Carta.

Jim McRuer's personal views about prohibition—as well as the moral crusade he was waging in courtrooms—were influenced by his own tee-total habits. Raised not to drink, and going through his years in the army without touching a drop, McRuer thought that liquor was a great evil. He vividly remembered the day when, as a student, he stood on the sidewalk of University Avenue watching an exuberant procession of prohibition-ists marching up to Queen's Park with a four-foot-thick petition signed by countless thousands of Ontarians urging the legislature to pass the Ontario Temperance Act. A tremendous wave of support for prohibition of alcohol had washed across the whole continent, and McRuer believed that a permanent new order was in the making. In this transition to a better society, some attitudes and activities would need adjusting, and as a prosecutor he was simply "doing his duty" in this process.

Yet, as time passed, even McRuer began reflecting on the growing public resistance to the Temperance Act. He still was convinced of "the dreadful evils of bootlegging," but he also began to realize that the cure might be worse than the disease. More and more, the idea of government control and government sale of alcohol seemed a better approach. Moral absolutism enacted into laws simply lacked the balance that, in his view, was necessary if laws were to be respected and obeyed. His work, and that of others in the crown attorney's office in enforcing prohibition, began to appear counter-productive. As if to symbolize the absurdity and hypocrisy of it all, the provincial treasurer, Peter Smith of Stratford, was caught having a "Last Night Party"—with hard liquor and loose women—in his Queen's Park office to celebrate the end of the 1921 session.

Nevertheless, the crown attorney's office soldiered on, prosecuting breaches of the Temperance Act. In 1922 McRuer even published an annotated guide to the Ontario Temperance Act and its accompanying regulations for the benefit of those poor officers of the law required to enforce it. The Government of Ontario did not abandon its futile experi-ment in prohibition until 1927, and by that time McRuer was in private practice. For him, the failure of prohibition carried an important lesson about the dangers of moral extremism and the limits of the law. It was a lesson he would not forget.[7]

Something else Jim experienced, and would never forget, was the excitement he shared with Mary at the birth of their first child, whom they named Mary Louise, on 3 May 1921. The arrival of a new baby gave them great joy, but it also made life on Centre Island less practical. The cottage was too small for parents with an infant, it made more sense to be closer to other family members who could help out, and Jim's increasing workload meant that there was less time for commuting. So, moving up in the real estate market once again, Jim sold the cottage and used the proceeds to purchase a duplex at the corner of Tyndall and Springhurst avenues, just north of Lake Ontario in west Toronto. It was time, once again, to pack up the teacups and Tom Thomsons.

DESPITE MCRUER'S PREOCCUPATION with prohibition in the early 1920s, his heart actually lay in another legal area—stock fraud. As the thundering bull market of the 1920s gathered steam, every office boy dreamt of making a killing in the stock market, and stocks replaced sports as the topic of barbershop conversation. Unfortunately, the lack of proper securities regulations facilitated shady dealings in company shares and public stock offerings. For the crown attorney's office, the problem was impossible to ignore. McRuer spent his mornings in court prosecuting, but in the afternoons at his office he was swamped by public complaints about worthless stocks—"wallpaper," as they were called—of dead or vanished companies. Such scams, where honest citizens were being victimized by criminals, deeply offended McRuer's sense of justice. He was not prepared to let the challenge go unanswered. So, while the other two crown assistants, James McFadden and the professional Irishman Eddie Murphy, did police-court work, McRuer began to specialize in stock fraud.

In tracking down, sniffing out, and prosecuting crooked stock promoters, Jim experienced all the intense delight of the big-game hunter. Inspired by the Sherlock Holmes stories he had read as a boy, he revelled in the solving of stock-fraud cases through painstaking preparation and careful attention to procedural detail. Indeed, he was so successful at his work that the name McRuer became synonymous with stock-fraud busting. This development was greatly assisted by Joe Atkinson's *Toronto Star*, which gave the public a steady diet of stories about the young crown attorney who spent his time breaking down doors with a squad of Ontario's finest and a posse of accountants armed with red pencils and search warrants.[8]

McRuer's first stock-fraud case involved a swindle perpetrated in Winnipeg by a prominent Toronto operator named Gurofsky. After the accused was arrested in Toronto, his defence counsel, the aggressive Tom Agar, asked for bail. At this point, McRuer's instincts told him to get advice from an expert. Police Inspector George Guthrie pointed out to McRuer that bail was never allowed for someone arrested for extradition to another jurisdiction. When McRuer relayed this information to Agar, the latter became quite abusive towards the new upstart in the crown attorney's office. Failing to make any headway with McRuer's boss, Eric Armour, who preferred to let his assistant fight his own battles, Agar threatened to go to the newspapers. A determined McRuer told him to go right ahead. In the event, the newspapers ignored Agar and the controversy fizzled. Gurofsky was taken to Winnipeg to stand trial.

The first really big scam McRuer closed down concerned a fly-by-night firm called the New Coal Fuel Company, founded to process briquets from low-grade coal and coal dust. On the surface, it was an innovative scheme during a period of coal shortage and high energy prices, but appearances were deceiving. A lot of the people coming into McRuer's office had been sold New Coal shares and were left holding the bag. Instead of selling investors new shares, so that their money stayed in the company as working capital, the officers had stripped the company of these assets by selling their own shares—which previously had been awarded to them as consideration for the invention of the briquet-manufacturing process—and pocketing the investors' proceeds. The company's shares were now worthless, since they represented an interest in a virtually hollow shell.

Theft of this sort was hard to prove, but McRuer decided to act when investors complained that they were getting no answers from New Coal management. Taking a couple of detectives around with a search warrant, he seized the New Coal books, turning them over to a team of accountants led by Jay Howson of the firm Thorne, Mulholland, Howson and McPherson. Howson and McRuer, through this experience, became friends, and would continue to work well together on the bigger cases yet to come.

After meticulous preparation, McRuer took the case to court, and there found himself facing his friend from Algonquin Park, Peter White, and Arthur Slaght, who were, respectively, the toughest defence lawyer and the finest courtroom actor in the business. Slaght later confessed to McRuer that, since he was "such a frail looking customer," they had decided to try and simply wear him out physically by raising constant objections and challenging evidence. This tactic failed utterly. Their last stratagem was to have their own accountant mix up bonds and stocks to account for the lack of revenue in the New Coal treasury. In cross-examination, McRuer suggested that this was an unusual accounting procedure. When the accountant agreed, McRuer asked him where his instructions had come from. His reply—that the instructions had come from White and Slaght—was a fatal blow to the defence case.

McRuer soon repeated his success in the New Coal case by prosecuting an even more outrageous fraud. The Instantaneous Electric Heater Company of Toronto had quickly became famous for its startling new invention, which, according to its creator, McLaughlin, was able to heat water even as it ran out of a tap. To prove the point, the company showroom window on Victoria Street in downtown Toronto boasted a constantly steaming hot water tap. The demonstration attracted passers-by, who marvelled at the possibilities of the new scientific age. In fact, however, the real steam was being piped up from a regular boiler in the basement. Many hundreds of gullible investors bought shares in the Instantaneous Electric Heater Company. The money they lost could not be recouped; their only solace was that the crown, through the efforts of McRuer, took the company to court and won a conviction.

By far the largest stock-fraud case to fall into McRuer's hands was the notorious Jarvis-Smith affair, a freebooting conspiracy to defraud the public hatched at the highest levels of Toronto society. At its centre were Aemilius Jarvis, one of the leading members of the Ontario business elite, and Peter Smith, provincial treasurer in the Farmer-Labour government.[9]

During its period in power, from 1919 to 1923, the E.C. Drury government attempted in a variety of ways to destroy the political career of its leading opponent, Conservative leader Howard Ferguson. Yet all of its efforts—the most famous of which was a three-year investigation into Ferguson's record as minister of lands and forests during the previous Conservative administration—had come to nothing. In 1923 Ferguson, who had defended himself against government attacks with great determination and skill, was still very much in control of his party. His opportunity to turn the tables on his opponents came after the 1923 election, which resulted in a Conservative victory and the decimation of the Farmer-Labour forces.

Shortly after the Conservatives took office, the new attorney-general, W.F. Nickle, and his officials began investigating the account juggling and general financial mess left behind by the Farmer-Labour government. They soon focused their attention on the former treasurer, Peter Smith, feeding the evidence they uncovered to the legislature's public accounts committee, which was conducting an investigation of its own.

A bald, genial, cherubic farmer, Smith had not been well regarded by the grizzled prophet of the UFO, W.C. Good, but Premier Drury had succumbed to pressure from other UFO members and appointed him to the cabinet as treasurer. Under his easygoing ways, and those of his less than competent deputy, Charles Matthews, the budget of the province mushroomed from $19 million to $40 million, with nary an audit of receipts. The press was filled with tales of financial mismanagement, one of which maintained that money could often be seen sticking out of government filing cabinets. But there was more to this story than simple carelessness and incompetence. Nickle's investigators and the public accounts committee discovered that Smith had regularly received large sums of money from an anonymous source and that these sums, as well as numbered coupons from a large quantity of bonds, had been placed in his Stratford bank account. Digging even deeper, they found strong circumstantial evidence to suggest that Smith was not using the money for party purposes, but for personal gain alone. In the party game of the day, and before the advent of the Election Expenses Act, the political system was paid for almost entirely by kickbacks or simple donations from those who did business with the government. This was expected and accepted, even by the moralistic Drury government. The UFO minister of highways, Frank Biggs, was so closely allied to various contractors that he was described by Howard Ferguson as "the greatest highwayman in Ontario."[10] Nevertheless, it was considered illegal to receive kickbacks for private gain unless such moneys had been channelled by the party into a testimonial fund.

Smith was not the only culprit. The public accounts committee informed Attorney-General Nickle and Provincial Treasurer Billy Price (McRuer's old mentor from Algonquin Park, now Peter Smith's successor), that the highly respected stockbroker Aemilius Jarvis was implicated in Smith's wrongdoing. Reporting that Jarvis had made a suspiciously high profit of $500,000 on the purchase and resale to the Ontario government of some $6-million worth of bonds, the committee strongly suspected that this profit had been split with Peter Smith. The latter's share was $300,000 worth of bonds, the receipts of which were in his bank account.

A handsome old silver-headed sportsman, his bland mouth draped with a bushy "soupstrainer" moustache, his head crowned with a silky black topper in winter and a floppy cream-coloured Panama in summer, Aemilius Jarvis was the sixty-four-year-old grandson of William Dummer Powell, chief justice of Upper Canada from 1816 to 1825. An avid horseman, he was a prominent figure at horse shows and in the Toronto Hunt Club. He was also an accomplished sailor. After his graduation from Upper Canada College he had spent two years sailing, and afterwards he served for two decades as the skipper of the yacht representing Canada in the America's Cup. A leading member of the Royal Canadian Yacht Club, the "Commodore," as Jarvis was known, published in 1922 *5000 Miles in a 27 Tonner*, an illustrated log of his yacht voyage to the Caribbean and back. In the business world, the firm of Aemilius Jarvis and Company, Bankers and Brokers, had anchored 103 Bay Street since 1892, and Jarvis himself was also chairman of the board of the Canadian Locomotives Company and vice-president of B.C. Packers. An unabashed imperialist, he had lobbied indefatigably for the establishment of the Royal Canadian Navy in the years prior to the First World War. Later, he set up a recruiting station at his own expense to man the cruisers *Niobe* and *Rainbow*, established a school of nautical instruction, and helped Sir Robert Borden's Union Government purchase two American warships, one of which became the *Hochelaga* and the other the flagship *Stadacona*. Jarvis was the chief animating spirit of the Navy League, which, with 169 branches across Canada involving more than 50,000 boys, was a powerful lobby group committed to stimulating interest in naval defence.

Unintimidated by such a social Goliath, Attorney-General Nickle ordered evidence to be gathered for a prosecution. To undertake the task, Nickle confidently called on assistant crown attorney Jim McRuer, whose hard work and great aptitude had already been recognized by his seniors. The first instruction McRuer received underlined the delicacy of this messy affair; he was directed never to discuss the case with his own superior, Eric Armour, who moved in the same social circles as Jarvis.

In February 1924, armed with a search warrant and accompanied by several officers and the brilliant A.E. Nash of the accounting firm Clarkson, Gordon and Dilworth, McRuer quietly entered the Bay Street offices of the Jarvis company and asked to examine the files. Jarvis himself was abroad in England at the time, and his firm did not wish to protest against the intrusion for fear of adverse publicity. McRuer was given the material he wanted. For two days, Nash and his assistants searched for evidence of large bond transactions of the type whose coupons had been found in Peter Smith's possession. They got nowhere, and McRuer was growing "more than a little nervous."

On the third day, McRuer was in police court conducting a prosecution when Colonel Gordon, one of the senior partners of Clarkson, Gordon and Dilworth, entered the room, came directly up to him, and whispered in his ear, "I think we have it." Meeting McRuer at noon adjournment, Gordon showed him a very thin file containing a copy of a letter from Aemilius Jarvis Jr. to Brown Brothers, prominent investment dealers in New York City. The letter referred to $368,000 worth of bonds, identified by name but not serial number, with instructions to send them back to one Andrew H. Pepall of High Park Avenue in Toronto, an old friend, McRuer and his investigators already knew, of Peter Smith. Indeed, in earlier days, Pepall had given Smith the distribution franchise for Delco farm-lighting equipment in the Stratford area. More compelling still, Pepall's brother Harry was a salesman in Jarvis's Toronto office. In addition, the bonds matched the type of the coupons deposited in Peter Smith's Stratford bank account, and the amount seemed to be just about right. Why, if the bond transaction had been legitimate, did such an usual, trail-covering procedure need to be followed?

The trail was very hot indeed, but without bond serial numbers and receipts the evidence was still highly circumstantial. McRuer promptly conferred with Attorney-General Nickle and Premier Howard Ferguson, and together they planned a bold course of action. The first idea of the attorney-general was to dispatch the Ontario Provincial Police to Brown Brothers to get the serial numbers. McRuer objected to this course of action, pointing out that Ontario police had no jurisdiction in a foreign country; he also feared that any blunder might result in the evidence being destroyed. Instead he suggested that he and Nash should go to Albany and persuade the attorney-general of New York State to support the investigation. Nickle agreed to this proposal, gave McRuer a letter of introduction, and set up an appointment.

That same night McRuer and Nash left by train for Albany, arriving the following morning. They then met with the attorney-general of New York, who in turn opened a door by introducing them to a Mr. Chambers, the securities commissioner of New York City. Chambers proved to be most helpful, and McRuer and Nash met again with him the following day in his New York City office to discuss strategy. He made an appointment for them with Brown Brothers and told them that, if necessary, he was prepared to issue a subpoena to obtain the documents that McRuer and Nash needed.

The following day McRuer and Nash found themselves sinking into plush leather chairs in the oak-panelled office of the managing director of one of the oldest, most prestigious blue-ribbon merchant banks in the United States. Not to their surprise, the managing director told them that the company's files were confidential. When McRuer mentioned the possibility of a subpoena, however, and then placed a telephone call to Chambers to underline the threat, the director grew more cooperative, explaining that he did not want any trouble. Yet Brown Brothers was not yet ready to capitulate: the firm's lawyer questioned the constitutionality of McRuer's demand. Prepared for this objection, McRuer indicated that he had instructions from the attorney-general of Ontario to engage New York lawyers "to go to the limit" in overturning any constitutional objections that might arise. Adding further power to his argument was the arrival of Securities Commissioner Chambers himself, subpoena in hand. Brown Brothers' managing director gave in, saying curtly "We don't want any litigation here," and handed McRuer the coveted file.

Returning with Chambers to his office, McRuer and Nash opened the file and found a letter delivering $368,000 worth of bonds back to Andrew Pepall of Toronto. To make the case even tighter, the damning letter gave the serial numbers of each bond, and each tallied with the coupon numbers in Peter Smith's bank account. That night Nash and McRuer were on the Toronto-bound train jubilantly clutching photographs, supplied to them as a final favour by Chambers, of the whole file of letters and the serial numbers of the bonds. The fate of Aemilius Jarvis and Peter Smith was all but sealed.

In May 1924 a charge of conspiracy to defraud was laid against Aemilius Jarvis, his son Aemilius Jarvis Jr., Harry Pepall (Jarvis's stock salesman), and Peter Smith. By this time Andrew Pepall had fled to California, and Nickle instructed McRuer to go after him. Though conspiracy was not an extraditable offence, McRuer became inventive and, after three weeks in California, obtained a deportation hearing against Pepall in Los Angeles based on illegal entry into the United States. The court ruled in favour of deportation, but Pepall's lawyer appealed the case to the secretary of labour in Washington and in November the deportation was overturned. A couple of months later, the Government of Ontario took another tack, again dispatching McRuer to California, this time to request Pepall's extradition on charges of theft and bribery. Jim was accompanied by Mary on this second trip; the combination of a holiday and work was helpful to their marriage because Jim was increasingly consumed by his career. He proved successful in his mission, obtaining Pepall's extradition, but it was now July 1925—too late for the trial of Jarvis and the others back in Canada. Pepall himself was later acquitted.

Even without Pepall's testimony, however, the crown prevailed in its prosecution of the Jarvises and Peter Smith. Their case was tried in late

October 1924 by Chief Justice Richard Meredith and a jury. The formidable W.N. Tilley was chief crown prosecutor, with McRuer acting as junior counsel. The Jarvises were defended by the imposing trio of Arthur Slaght, Richard Greer, and I.F. Hellmuth, three of the outstanding trial lawyers of the day; Smith was defended by T.H. Lennox, a well-known Conservative politician. The trial lasted four days, during which even former premier E.C. Drury took the stand, and was marked by high drama, incisive questioning by Tilley, and much stirring eloquence on the part of Lennox and Slaght. In the end, Jarvis Sr. and Peter Smith were found guilty of conspiracy as charged, while Jarvis Jr. and, at his later trial, Harry Pepall were acquitted. Mr. Justice Meredith sentenced Smith to five years in penitentiary; Jarvis, on account of his age, was handed only a brief six-month term in the county jail, but was forced to pay a whopping $600,000 fine. The following March, the Court of Appeal sustained Jarvis's jail term but reduced his fine to $250,000—a decision that, in the eyes a furious Chief Justice Meredith and an equally angry Premier Ferguson—turned Jarvis's punishment into a simple matter of restitution of the amount gained in the fraud.

In March 1926 Jarvis's high-placed friends presented a petition to the federal government demanding not a retrial but a complete pardon and remission of the fine levied by the Court of Appeal. It was signed by a broad cross-section of the Ontario elite, including such leading figures in the worlds of politics, business, and the professions as Sir John Willison, Sir Joseph Flavelle, Hume Blake, Sir Henry Pellatt, and Sir Clifford Sifton. Even Crown Attorney Eric Armour signed the petition, in the belief that his friend Jarvis had been punished enough. In support of their claim that Jarvis was an *"absolutely innocent man,"* the signatories presented many arguments, one of which was that the crown had deliberately tied up Pepall in an extradition case in California to keep him from taking part in the Toronto trial, where his presence would have altered the outcome of the case. They did not name names, but Jim McRuer was obviously one of the villains in their interpretation of events.

The tremendous publicity surrounding the case placed McRuer in a difficult position. Fortunately for him, and for the position of the Ontario government in the affair, the claims set out in the Jarvis petition were demolished in a "private and confidential memorandum" prepared for the attorney-general's office. Written by the distinguished Toronto lawyer McGregor Young, this memorandum argued that the Jarvis petition was inaccurate, superficial, and even unscrupulous, and that, in asking not for a new trial but for a reversal of the conviction, it was without precedent in Canadian law. Young went on to note that Jarvis had been defended by an "army of counsel that in respect of ability and experience in criminal trials and defences could not be duplicated from the entire Bar of the Province."[11] The federal minister of justice, Ernest Lapointe, no doubt received a copy of Young's memorandum, and he apparently informed Jarvis's supporters that the opposition of the Ontario government to any reconsideration of the Jarvis case prevented federal action. But the controversy continued. In 1927 the new Ontario attorney-general, Billy Price, informed Lapointe that any use of the royal prerogative to overturn the Jarvis conviction "would be unheard of, and the suggestion that it be used could only be explained by the large number of very influential men who have signed the memorandum believing it to be accurate, when in fact in the result it is a tissue of inaccuracy."[12] Premier Howard Ferguson, for his part, also held firm on not granting a pardon to Jarvis, even after an appeal from his close friend Sir Joseph Flavelle in October 1928.

Efforts to clear Jarvis's name persisted into the 1930s, and indeed in 1933 the controversy became more intense than ever with the publication in Maclean's magazine of a series of articles by former premier E.C. Drury entitled "Have We a Canadian Dreyfus?" The essence of Drury's case was that the Jarvis-Smith affair was nothing short of a political conspiracy, undertaken by Premier Ferguson in revenge for earlier attacks on his own reputation by the Farmer-Labour administration. Such arguments cut little ice in Ottawa with the Conservative government of R.B. Bennett, but in 1936, with the Liberals once again in power, Minister of Justice Ernest Lapointe bowed to pressure from Ontario (now governed by Mitch Hepburn's Liberals) and asked the Ontario Court of Appeal whether a new trial should be granted. Its decision—that a retrial was not warranted—put a close to the affair, though Jarvis himself continued to protest his innocence until his death in 1940.

McRuer never had any sympathy for Jarvis, and on more than one occasion he felt compelled to defend the fairness of the trial and the propriety of his own role in it. He had even less sympathy for Peter Smith. As a minister of the crown, Smith had behaved shamelessly, exploiting the public trust for his own private benefit. McRuer always regarded his conduct as, quite simply, unforgivable.

Following the conviction of Smith and Jarvis, Attorney-General Nickle, who was increasingly impressed by McRuer's tenacity and fearlessness, gave him the task of assisting in the prosecutions resulting from the fall of the Home Bank. The bank's failure had ruined many small depositors, and its directors were charged with "negligence in the performance of their duties." The prosecution in this series of trials was handled by D. Leighton ("Lally") McCarthy, a terrifying dragon of the legal profession, McRuer again serving as junior counsel. Acting for the defence was a tremendously talented team of lawyers—W.N. Tilley (as was common in those days, he acted in his career as both crown and defence counsel), Newton Wesley Rowell, R.S. Robertson, I.H. Hellmuth, Gordon Shaver, and two junior contemporaries of McRuer, Salter Hayden and John W. Pickup. Together, they were a galaxy of future chief justices and officers of the Law Society.

In answer to the defence's request for "particulars," McRuer adopted a strategy that he later described in these terms: "If you're asked to give particulars, give so many particulars that you swamp the other side." Endless sessions with George Clarkson, the liquidator, and investigating accountants A.E. Nash and H.D.L. Gordon produced an impressive volume of detailed evidence, and then, in July 1924, the trials began. They lasted for eight months, until February 1925. During that time McRuer was in legal heaven, studying with profound delight the style and techniques of the stars of the legal profession and always enthralled by the razor-sharp mind of Lally McCarthy. Initially, the prosecution was successful, winning convictions in each of the trials. On appeal, however, the convictions were overturned on the grounds that the directors were not responsible for the bank's management. The federal government eventually came to the aid of the depositors, giving them 35 cents on the dollar.[13]

The only person who did not appeal his conviction, simply because he could not afford to, was the bank's diminutive accountant, Ocean Smith. He had been the least "negligent" of the bunch, McRuer felt. Smith's sentence had been suspended and he was placed on probation. On the day before Christmas, a few months after the trial, McRuer saw Smith boarding a downtown streetcar and hailed him. Finding the man in a bad way—he was trying to start without much success a new career as an insurance salesman—McRuer bought from him a five-year, $10,000 life policy. By this time Jim had accumulated a little money and wanted to give his family some security. So the attorney who prosecuted Smith now provided him with a commission that saved his Christmas, earning the man's lasting gratitude.

Someone else was grateful to McRuer. After the first trial, D.L. McCarthy told Attorney-General Nickle that McRuer had "been of great assistance to me in all these cases." An "indefatigable worker," McRuer, he said, had "relieved me to a great extent and enabled me to save my strength during this somewhat tedious and protracted trial. He was at all times a complete master of the details of the intricate accounts which he had to deal with, and was always ready and willing at all times, no matter how great the personal inconvenience, to come to my aid when I was being hard pressed for time to keep matters going, and in the preparation at night of material for the coming day."[14]

These flattering words were an impressive tribute to McRuer's role in the Home Bank trials and an accurate measure of the disciplined work habits that always marked his career.

BEFORE THE JARVIS-SMITH and Home Bank cases had burst upon the public scene, McRuer's activities in prosecuting stock-market criminals led to widespread demands for more efficient ways of dealing with the problem. He himself argued for reform, proposing that the crown attorney be given authority to send accountants into companies if complaints had been received and if there was reasonable and probable cause to believe that a fraud had been committed. McRuer thought that the existing law "was much too anaemic" to deal with stock frauds.[15]

His recommendations fell on the receptive ears of Attorney-General Nickle. A fastidious, principled lawyer with an independent cast of mind, Nickle fully agreed with McRuer's contention that the ordinary citizen buying securities should have governmental assurance of fair dealing. He quickly caused a bill to be drafted containing McRuer's suggestions for the search and seizure of corporate books. Then, in a rather extraordinary initiative, Nickle invited McRuer to attend a meeting of the Conservative caucus to recount some of his experiences with stock fraud and to explain the purpose of the bill. At that meeting, McRuer outlined the practical problems faced by the office of the crown attorney in dealing with stock-fraud allegations, and emphasized the need to send accountants into companies to see whether there was any justification for the seizure of books—a much milder and less drastic course of action than dispatching the police right away. Some members of caucus were quite antagonistic. One older member, a wizened Bay Street veteran, growled, "I'm not going to have any Crown Attorneys snooping around in the companies I'm concerned with."[16]

The securities bill was passed in 1923 but not proclaimed; instead, it was put on hold until the need for it became more apparent. Five years later, after the Jarvis-Smith and Home Bank cases had again under-lined the need for stock-market regulation, another act came into force. Stronger than the 1923 measure, the Securities Fraud Prevention Act, as it was known, established the Ontario Securities Commission, which, by demanding a statement of financial structure and operation from every public company, went a long way towards eliminating stock-market cor-ruption.

In addition to their significance in the development of public policy in Ontario, the Jarvis-Smith and Home Bank cases threw light on McRuer's personality and values. Just as his battles with bootleggers revealed his determination to uphold the law, regardless of his doubts about its wis-dom, so did his record in fraud cases illuminate his commitment to fair-ness and justice. The Jarvis-Smith and Home Bank cases, in particular, made clear his adherence to two principles—that everyone, rich or poor, was equal before the law, and that no one should be able to escape jus-tice merely by virtue of the legal talent arrayed on his or her side. These were basic principles to McRuer, and they would always remain so. His belief in them likely predated his experiences with Jarvis, Smith, and the Home Bank, but these cases greatly tested his resolve in putting his convictions into practice. He passed that test easily, as he would again many times in the future. Throughout his career as a lawyer and later as a judge, there was never any doubt about McRuer's commitment to legal equality and justice.

The Jarvis-Smith and Home Bank cases, along with the other fraud cases he handled in the early 1920s, are significant for other reasons as well. As a result of these cases, McRuer gained a greater respect for strong political leaders who would not succumb to pressure when public confi-dence in the rule of law was at issue. And that respect was reciprocated. After the Jarvis-Smith trial, McRuer was held in high esteem, not per-haps by those whom he had prosecuted and their powerful friends, but by most other people in politics, business, and the law. Decades later, on 27 May 1957, he received a letter from Toronto lawyer William A. Price, who, remembering the Jarvis case, said simply: "That took courage."[17]

5

LAWYER AT LARGE

JIM AND MARY MCRUER found that his comfortable income, improved health, and good prospects as a hard-working lawyer gave them a new confidence in their life together. A particular delight for them was their daughter, Mary Louise, who would be dressed up in a white dress and bonnet and proudly taken on Sunday afternoon visits to the in-laws. A further source of happiness came with the birth of a second daughter, christened Katherine, on 20 May 1923. Soon the new child, like her sister before her, provided a good excuse for the McRuers to move once more. The couple felt that they needed more space for their enlarged family, and Jim still remembered from his early years of searching titles and closing real estate deals the financial benefits of turning over properties at regular intervals. So that year the duplex was sold in exchange for a house at 244 Armadale Avenue in Toronto, and again the Tom Thomsons were rehung.

In others areas of McRuer's life, the period from the mid-1920s to the mid-1930s saw him build upon his earlier accomplishments as a lawyer and even take a new direction, shifting from government work to the potentially more lucrative realm of private practice. At the same time, these years witnessed a definite broadening of McRuer's interests. Not content any longer with a single-minded devotion to the law, McRuer began a part-time teaching career and also spent considerable time attempting to improve the training and advance the interests of Ontario's police. Through all of this, he kept an eye trained on the world of politics—a world that fascinated him as much as ever—and even involved himself directly for the first time in Liberal Party policy-making and electoral campaigns. The law was interesting and challenging, to be sure, but politics still had an appeal that no McRuer could resist.

McRUER's WORK FOR THE FERGUSON GOVERNMENT had not gone unnoticed by the federal Liberal Party, and by Prime Minister William Lyon Mackenzie King in particular. McRuer had a name and a reputation for personal integrity, and he was also known by the Masseys, Rowell, and others as a good Liberal. An unusual personal connection was that Jim's brother, John, had befriended King's brother, Macdougall, when the two men were patients residing at the tuberculosis sanitorium in Denver, Colorado. King, like McRuer, had journeyed to Denver to bring home to Canada his brother's remains.

Doubtless feeling that McRuer's presence in the Toronto crown attorney's office was simply maintaining Conservative Premier Ferguson's prestige, King wanted the star attorney in his fold. In 1925 feelers were sent out and McRuer was quietly approached by Fred McGregor, for years King's personal secretary and now commissioner of the Combines Act. Minister of Labour James Murdock, who, in his earlier career as a colourful, rough-and-ready railwayman, had sometimes run his union meetings with a gun on the table, also was sounding out McRuer.

McGregor had been at King's side during the latter's stint as deputy minister of labour in the Laurier government and later during his consulting work with the Rockefellers of New York. His passion was combine busting, and he thought that McRuer's experience in fraud cases made him an ideal candidate to assist the federal government's work in this area. The first case McGregor had in mind for McRuer proved how highly Jim was thought of—it involved a complex and powerful combine in the fruit industry of western Canada. The federal departments of justice and labour, both grappling with the administration of the Combines Act, were experiencing a great deal of difficulty in prosecuting a Vancouver combines case against the Nash-Simington fruit syndicate—a branch organization of the great Nash-Finch Fruit Corporation of the United States.

The Nash-Finch organization had originated in 1908 in Grand Forks, North Dakota, as a produce business in a small provision shop. With a novel conception of produce marketing, W.K. Nash rapidly extended his operations and by the mid-1920s the company's annual turnover was estimated at $360 million. In Canada, the Nash-Simington combine stretched, like the arms of an octopus, from Winnipeg to Victoria. Consisting of no fewer than forty-two companies, the combine effectively removed competition in the fruit business by owning or controlling the middlemen firms that dealt on a consignment basis with the fruit farmers. Market control was exercised at the broker level since the brokers were able to claim to the fruit farmers that their margins were low, whereas in truth they were returning rents or dividends to the wholesalers that were kickbacks pure and simple.

The practice of the Canadian organization was to conduct, through its branch companies, all the transactions that took place between the first purchase from the grower and the final sale to the public. Its own broker companies did the buying from the producer on the fruit farms of British Columbia. They "sold" to their own jobbing and warehousing companies, which, in turn, on occasion, even "sold" again to vendors in the combine. Thus the unsuspecting grower was duped. When he protested against the low price paid him for his produce, he was told by the broker company that the jobbers would not pay more and that warehousing charges had increased. In every conceivable way he was induced to part with his fruit; if he required money, he was given cash in advance and sometimes even tied to long-term contracts with the combine. And so the swindle went on. In time the relative prices paid to the grower and those demanded from the public became grotesquely unfair.

The first outcry came in the summer of 1923 from the small fruit growers of the Okanagan valley, but it was not until the Victoria Hothouse Association on Vancouver Island joined in that official action was taken. A prosecution was launched by British Columbia Attorney-General A.M. Manson against the fruit-broker company Mutual (Vancouver) Ltd. Unfortunately, for lack of substantial evidence, the case was dismissed at its preliminary hearing by the local police magistrate. The fruit growers of the province, however, were not to be deterred by the incompetent prosecution. They turned to the Government of Canada for help, and in the spring of 1924 a young Toronto lawyer was appointed head of a royal commission to investigate the fruit-marketing conditions in western Canada. His name was Lewis Duncan—an Osgoode classmate of Jim McRuer and nephew of Jim's former partner in Proudfoot, Duncan, Giant and Skeans.

Lewis Duncan proceeded on a tour of the western cities, interviewed officials of the Nash-Simington organization, examined their books, and heard the grievances, first hand, of the growers. A few months later he

made his report to the King government—a report containing sensational charges against Nash-Simington.[1] Federal action was hindered,
however, by the weaknesses of the Combines Act. What was needed was
an imaginative, concerted campaign using all the legal weapons in the
federal government's arsenal—the kind of case that was McRuer's spe-
cialty. In Toronto, Duncan arranged to meet McRuer for lunch at the
National Club. Acting as McGregor's emissary, "Lew" Duncan, as Jim
knew him, concluded the meal by offering his friend and classmate
the job of chief prosecutor for the Government of Canada in the Nash-
Simington case.

As it happened, Duncan's offer was well timed. McRuer had begun
to feel confined in the crown attorney's office, and increasingly he was
drawn to the more diversified and lucrative world of private practice.
The fruit combines case offered him a perfect opportunity to launch out
on his own. It also had the potential of opening doors in the Liberal
Party—still one of McRuer's passions, despite his work for the Conservative government of Ontario. He agreed to take on the Vancouver assignment when his one condition, that he be permitted to retain his own
accountants, was granted. A further indication of how much the federal
government wanted McRuer came when Labour Minister Murdock told
Jim directly: "Don't take instructions from anyone but me—and I'll give
you none!"[2]

McRuer then announced his resignation as assistant crown attorney
to Attorney-General W.H. Price, the man who had been instrumental in
getting him the job in the first place. Price accepted the resignation with
regret. A friend of Jim's from law school, Norman Macdonell, gave him
a temporary base in his office in the Sun Life Building, and McRuer was
off and running. The Nash-Simington case would fully occupy him for
the next nine months.

The first thing McRuer had to do was move his pregnant wife and
the two little girls—Mary Louise was now four and Katherine two—to
Vancouver, his home base for the next several months. He then had to
pore over Lewis Duncan's report on the case, and, once he had done so,
prepare his plan of attack. True to form, McRuer ignored the Combines
Act altogether and went after the market manipulators with a favourite
charge, section 498 of the Criminal Code, an old provision from the
common law dealing with conspiracy to defraud. This was perhaps an
easier charge to prove than combination in restraint of trade, and in the
fruit combines case the fraud in question was the action of Nash-Simington brokers in taking goods on consignment to sell to themselves.

Compiling incriminating evidence on such prestigious figures as Aemilius Jarvis, Peter Smith, and Andrew Pepall had been difficult enough, but now McRuer was faced with the even greater challenge of seizing the books of forty-two separate companies in four different provinces. To start with one or two would tip off the rest. Lightning raids on company offices—by now a McRuer trademark—were necessary, and the campaign had to be planned with military precision. All the necessary search warrants were prepared in secrecy and with great meticulousness. Fortunately, the commissioner of the RCMP was a justice of the peace for all jurisdictions in western Canada, a fact that simplified matters considerably. Accounting firms were alerted to expect special business, and the RCMP commanding officers in Winnipeg, Regina, Saskatoon, Calgary, Edmonton, Vancouver, and Victoria as well as in a number of smaller towns were given sealed operational orders with instructions to open them only at a synchronized time—coordinated for the different time zones—in all locations. McRuer had done everything humanly possible to ensure the secrecy of the operation, including preparing and sealing the envelopes himself. Now all he could do was nervously wait for zero hour.

Before dawn on 17 July 1925, Mounties in each of the detachments intended for the massive operation read their orders, and then, together with accountants, moved in to seize the books of the suspect companies. Within an hour the crown was in possession of an overwhelming mass of evidence—some 200 tons. Only one firm offered token resistance and attempted, without success, to quash the search warrant. Although the companies were informed that they could have access to their books at RCMP headquarters, it was also made clear that life could be made distinctly uncomfortable for any firm that showed a lack of cooperation with the investigators.

Under the direction of McRuer's old friend Jay Howson, the accountants soon developed a clear pattern of how produce sales were conducted by the combine, and they quickly found damning evidence in the seized correspondence. Several letters told branch operators how to run the combine and show false returns to the fruit farmers. While the accountants did their painstaking work, detailing the whole operation of the network, McRuer scurried about western Canada—a cocky thirty-five-year-old crime-buster in a wing collar, yellow bow-tie, and creamy white boater with black band—spending a few days here, a few days there, overseeing the accountants' work, assessing their evidence, and plugging holes in their information.

All this work was taking place quietly behind the scenes; news of the seizure of company records had not been made public, and the syndicate was not exactly publicizing the matter either. It had been a year since the release of the royal commission's report, and the government was being accused of procrastination. Meanwhile, the books required for courtroom presentation were moved to the Vancouver courthouse where McRuer's defence team continued working on the indictments for a common-law charge of conspiracy to defraud. During these preparations for trial, McRuer had to restrain the brilliant Lewis Duncan from being overly meticulous and getting lost in a maze of esoteric legal threads or irrelevant financial detail. When Duncan, who felt a proprietary interest in the case because of his earlier role as royal commissioner, began to give McRuer instructions about how he should proceed, McRuer "laid down the law very firmly to him," emphasizing that he intended to handle the case in his own way—an edict that Duncan "graciously accepted."[3]

Court proceedings opened in early October 1925. McRuer showed a real flair for the dramatic when, on stepping forward to be introduced to the presiding judge, he produced from the folds of his gown a sixteen-page indictment containing 256 charges against the Nash-Simington syndicate. Forty-two branch companies and eleven individuals were named in it, fifty-three defendants in all. Before an astonished court the judge read out the indictment to the grand jury, which in twenty-four hours returned a true bill. The prosecution was not dismissed this time, the way it had been when attempted by British Columbia's attorney-general. News of the event quickly travelled throughout the country.

By this time Mary, almost due to give birth again, had returned with the girls to Toronto. Jim joined her at Christmas and on 3 January 1926 their third child and first son was born. They christened him John, the name the McRuers had, for seemingly endless generations, given the first-born male; Jim McRuer, like a good lawyer, delighted in following the precedent. Ten days later he was back in Vancouver as the long-awaited trial got under way before Mr. Justice McDonald of the Supreme Court of British Columbia.

As lead counsel for the crown, McRuer was assisted by two other seasoned courtroom lawyers, Stuart Lane of British Columbia and Jim Frawley of Alberta. E.P. Davis of British Columbia led the battery of defence counsel on hand. With fifty-three defendants, McRuer knew that he would be in for plenty of delaying tactics as Davis and his colleagues tried to find technical reasons for not getting to the substance of the trial. Anticipating their objections, McRuer had paved the way

as smoothly as he could prior to the trial. No arguments about jurisdiction of the court could be made: the federal minister of justice had
already given Mr. Justice McDonald jurisdiction over all four western
provinces. By a further special order of the attorney-general of British
Columbia, the usual preliminary hearing was waived; the trial could
proceed immediately.

Still, every manoeuver by McRuer to speed up the trial was blocked by
the defence. No sooner had the court convened than the defence threw
up obstacles, focusing on the jury selection; each defendant had the
right to exercise twelve peremptory challenges, and exercise it they did.
After a day and a half, only two jurors had been sworn, out of 160 on the
panel. McRuer, understanding that the prosecution could play the jury
game as easily as the defence, asked for a week's adjournment and went
to work. The RCMP were requested to go through the phone books and
gather the names of 1,000 "prospective jurors" to summon. Eight hundred people were recruited, and on the date of sitting the courtroom was
choked with potential jurors, while other stragglers packed the halls and
a meandering line stretched out into the street. McRuer watched with
delight as journalists joined the throng and gleefully reported the sticky
mob scene in their newspapers. Eventually, the defence saw that McRuer
was not going to be smothered, and so they speeded up the selection and
ten more jurors were chosen. In the process, a record in Canadian legal
history had been set: the court had summoned 1,200 jurors before the
panel of twelve was finally selected.

The next procedural victory went to the defence. Despite the stubborn
efforts of McRuer and his crown colleagues to prevent it, Davis secured
a court order which forced the prosecution to produce in court all 200
tons of evidence. Then, every single sheet of this evidence brought forward by the crown had to be filed as an exhibit before it was accepted
by the defence. Finally, the crown presented its carefully prepared case.
For thirty-six days the jury followed McRuer as he proceeded through a
tangle of facts and documents.

At the trial's close, each of the defence counsel summed up his arguments to the jury, and then McRuer offered his own concluding remarks.
In a four-hour address he lost the attention of the jury only once, and
the fault lay not with him but with the opposing side. One of the four
defence counsel, E.P. Davis, a well-known tippler, had been leaving
the courtroom at regular intervals, then wobbling back, his eyes a little glazed, overly careful about where he placed his feet. The jury began
to notice this delectable little spectacle, and several spectators tittered

at the sight. McRuer had just read out one particularly damning piece of correspondence and was summing up his case—"Now gentlemen of the jury, as sober businessmen ..."—when Davis suddenly blurted out, in a loud whisper, "Does he mean *me*?" Pandemonium ensued; the jury was convulsed in fits of laughter, and even the judge shared in the joke. McRuer, standing there with a rueful smile on his thin lips, was totally upstaged.

Judge McDonald, in one of the most exhaustive charges ever delivered from the bench of a British Columbia court, then handed the case to the jury. The jurors retired and began deliberations which lasted for a dramatic twenty-four hours. Tension in the courtroom neared the breaking-point, but McRuer remained confident. On Saturday, 13 March 1926, the jury returned its verdict. The four most senior executives of the syndicate, although not the brokers and jobbers, were found guilty. During its deliberations, one of the defence counsel had asked McRuer his opinion on the nature of the sentence. "Arrange to have a lot of money here Monday morning," he replied. The syndicate executives were collectively given a $250,000 fine, at that time a colossal amount. Soon the combine cracked to pieces.

McRuer was delighted when one of the convicted men, impressed by the thoroughness of the prosecution's case and depressed by Davis's consumption of liquor—"more than was necessary to promote the welfare of their case," he said—personally congratulated him, saying that if the defence had worked as hard "we wouldn't be where we are tonight." However, it was evidence that convicted, not just hard work. In a final neat footnote, the cartel members tried to mount an appeal, but they dropped the idea swiftly when McRuer made noisy preparations to appeal the sentence and ask for a jail term.[4]

In an editorial of 15 March 1926, under the heading "Justice Done," the Vancouver *Morning Star* praised the long trial as exemplifying "the high traditions of Canadian justice, modelled on the old British pattern." The headlines were good, too; even the *Daily Express* of London, England, reported the story, under the banner "Great Fruit Fraud Exposed."[5] McRuer returned victoriously to Toronto; the Nash-Simington case had been an outstanding way of announcing that he was now in private practice. Having scored a singular triumph in the eyes of Prime Minister King, he fully expected further legal work from the federal government and even a riding nomination.

McRuer soon learned, however, that he had not yet paid all his dues to the Liberal Party. In the summer of 1926 the King government suffered defeat in the House and, on being denied a dissolution by the governor-general, was replaced by a Conservative administration under Arthur Meighen. An election followed in September, and McRuer was asked to return for a time to Vancouver to campaign for Liberal candidate Dugald Donaghy. His name and face well known from the recent flashy trial, McRuer campaigned vigorously on behalf of Donaghy. The goal was not only to elect a Liberal candidate but also to force Donaghy's prominent Conservative opponent, Minister of Customs H.H. Stevens, to stay out of the national campaign as much as possible. In a vigorous address on the evening of 7 September, McRuer played to his local renown as a prosecuting attorney, presenting an "indictment" of Stevens on five "counts" relating to liquor smuggling. The *Morning Star* reported that McRuer's "scathing" attack on Stevens employed "all the powers which have brought him into prominence as one of Canada's ablest prosecuting attorneys."

When McRuer, back in Toronto one week later, watched the election results come in, he was jubilant. King's Liberals won 116 seats, and the Conservatives only 91; 33 other newly elected MPs (Farmers, Progressives, and Liberal Progressives) would likely support King. The Liberals had almost been driven out of British Columbia, however, winning only one seat. Donaghy, despite McRuer's efforts, had been roundly defeated by Stevens. Still, with the Liberals in office nationally, McRuer could take both partisan and professional comfort.

On returning to Toronto from Vancouver in the fall of 1926, Jim McRuer opened his own law office in the Sun Life Building. Before long, however, it became clear that two heads were better than one in juggling the competing demands of a law firm, and so McRuer entered into a partnership with J.A.R. Mason, whom he had come to know and respect when Mason was assistant solicitor for the City of Toronto. The two ensconced themselves in the Northern Ontario Building on Bay Street, their spartan offices decorated with wooden benches and tile floors— no sofas and broadloom in those days. At first, work was erratic, but it picked up gradually. Although these were the days before the Law Society required audits from lawyers, McRuer wanted to run a tight ship. He and Mason were therefore assisted by an accountant, none other than McRuer's friend and fellow trust-buster Jay Howson. Their secretary and all-round office manager was an immensely capable woman, Olive Luke, who would stay with McRuer until he became a judge.

McRuer specialized in "briefs at trial"—a reflection of his preference for courtroom work as a barrister over office work as a solicitor. He had truly had his fill of real estate law earlier in his career, and so he now built a litigation practice that included both civil and criminal cases; in some of the latter he acted for the crown, and in others he was defence counsel. A measure of his success—and that of Mason, too—was the firm's gradual expansion over the late 1920s.

The first lawyer to join their ranks was V. Evan Gray, who arrived in 1927. Though a competent lawyer, Gray also enjoyed the good life, and when, in 1933, he took a fancy to the attractive wife of one of the other partners, McRuer kicked him out of the firm. Also in the late 1920s, McRuer and Mason recruited, for contract and real estate work, A.J.P. "Pat" Cameron, an old friend of McRuer from Victoria Presbyterian Church and also an active Liberal campaign worker in west Toronto. Shortly afterwards they hired a brilliant third-year student, Andrew Brewin. Like his father, Canon F.H. Brewin of St. Simon's Anglican Church, between Bloor and Howard streets in Toronto, Andy Brewin was dedicated to improving the lot of the underprivileged. During the Depression he and his family fed great numbers of starving young people who had no work and no place to go, and, in spite of McRuer's never-ending attempts to recruit him to the cause of Liberal Party, he would remain an unabashed democratic socialist, running time after time for the CCF and NDP before finally being elected to the House of Commons in 1962.

A coveted symbol of recognition for any lawyer is to be appointed "one of His Majesty's Counsel learned in the law," and by the late 1920s there was no doubt that McRuer qualified. On 5 June 1929, at Queen's Park, he was raised to the dignity of King's Counsel. By this time he was also comfortable financially, and he remained so after the beginning of the Depression. Although he lost $10,000 in the 1929 crash, he was still prosperous enough in 1931 to build a new home—a Georgian-style house on Glenayr Road in the newly developed suburb of Forest Hill.[6] During the rest of the decade both McRuer and his firm continued to prosper, owing partly to the demand for McRuer's services in the combines area and partly to the never-ending bread and butter litigation of automotive-accident defence work. Away from the office, McRuer curled, fished, and golfed. His exploits on the golf course won him the title one year of "Toronto's Best Golfer" and were frequently reported in the sporting pages of the city's newspapers.

McRuer's professional success was mostly the result of his unquestioned ability and hard work, but a bit of luck was also involved—especially at the start. In the federal election of 1930 the Conservatives under

R.B. Bennett achieved a landslide victory, ousting McRuer's beloved Liberals and, more particularly, his patron, Prime Minister King. Although
McRuer was the acknowledged expert in combines prosecution, the
election of the Conservatives would have cut him off from federal government work were it not for a fortunate turn of events. The Department
of Justice had already engaged McRuer and Arthur Slaght to prosecute
a plumbers' combine in the Windsor area, and this case was well under
way before the election. Also in hand was an appeal to the Privy Council
about the constitutionality of the Combines Act itself.

In 1929 McRuer had agreed to a request from a genial and colourful
Welsh lawyer, Sir William Gwyn-Jones, that he act for a private organization Jones had pulled together in an imitation of a similar outfit in Britain, called the Proprietary Articles Trade Association. Known as PATA, it
was intended to control the sale of patent medicines and heavily adver-
tised brand products such as Bayer Aspirin and Eno's Fruit Salts. The
association used these goods as loss leaders, selling them below the
agreed retail price, and retailers who signed on with PATA agreed not to
market with wholesalers who allowed price cutting. McRuer, who knew
the Combines Act thoroughly, was afraid of the results and advised
Gwyn-Jones and PATA to find a way out of probable criminal prosecution. Delay was best—he suggested petitioning the minister of justice
to refer the act to the Supreme Court for a ruling on its constitutionality. Gwyn-Jones followed this advice, and the minister in turn did ask
the Supreme Court for a decision. When the court upheld the act, PATA
decided to take the case all the way to the Privy Council in London for
a final ruling.

McRuer's decision to represent PATA irked the deputy minister of justice, Frank Edwards, prompting him to ask whether McRuer thought it
proper to act for a private client, since he had previously been retained
by the government in a separate but similar prosecution. McRuer was
disturbed by this suggestion of conflict of interest, but both the treasurer of the Law Society and Newton Wesley Rowell gave him their support. While this was going on, Justice Minister Ernest Lapointe and
Fred McGregor, seeing that McRuer was tied up, had asked the eloquent
Arthur Slaght to prosecute the Windsor plumbers, but Slaght replied that
he would take the case only if he could get McRuer as his associate. With
the Department of Justice holding firm to its view that McRuer could not
defend one combine and prosecute another, he resigned his brief with
PATA, prompting Frank Edwards's snide comment that Jim had "returned
from the land of the Philistines."[7] Subsequently, PATA asked W.N. Tilley

to take charge of the appeal to the Privy Council. There the case languished, and PATA had dissolved before the Privy Council confirmed the act's constitutionality in 1931.[8]

As the first prosecution in Ontario under the Combines Act, the Windsor plumbers case was an important one. The initial investigation of the plumbers by Commissioner Gordon Waldron—complete with corporate documents stating quite clearly how the prices were to be fixed—made preparation easier. The plumbers had tried to create an organization of retailers to control prices paid by plumbers to the wholesalers, much like PATA, and they operated entirely in the open, convinced by their counsel, Louis Singer, that they had nothing to fear.

The trial began just as word came from Tilley about the Privy Council's decision. The presiding judge was Mr. Justice Wright, a solemn and sober man who could keep a straight face better than anyone. (Once, when McRuer had appeared before him on a criminal negligence case, an elderly and distracted court registrar read out the charge that "the accused did on a certain day at a certain time in a certain township drive his motor car negligently and recklessly and caused the death of so and so and did thereby commit adultery." While the courtroom dissolved in chuckles, Justice Wright kept up the dignity of the court and did not crack a smile, but only announced in his booming voice that the charge was "manslaughter, manslaughter.") Slaght led off against the plumbers, but he was always happier on the defence and McRuer carried the weight of the prosecution. After R.B. Bennett's victory in the federal election, Slaght, a high-profile Liberal, was pulled off the case and replaced by McRuer's Tory friend, Lally McCarthy. Though McRuer, too, was a known Liberal, he was sensibly kept on by McCarthy as his junior. Louis Singer, the lawyer who advised the plumbers and organized the combine, was eventually convicted at trial and fined $8,000, although the president of the association was found not guilty.[9]

Two other significant combine cases prosecuted by McRuer in the early 1930s further delineated the rules of doing business in Canada. One, the case of *Regina* v. *Container Materials*, developed the jurisprudence of the Combines Act to a great degree and entrenched its provisions firmly in Canadian criminal law. This case concerned a company that had organized a combine to control the manufacture of kraft cardboard boxes. McRuer proceeded first as an adviser to Fred McGregor's Paperboard Shipping Containers Commission, assisted by Andrew Brewin and J.L. McLennan, an articling student of his, as well as by Robert M. Fowler, later a corporation lawyer specializing in combines. The manufacturing companies all freely belonged to Container Materials and worked out cooperative pricing agreements through it. There was no fraud involved, no conspiratorial criminality or secret codes as in another combine, the Canada Wire and Cable Company, but the companies had made a trade agreement that stepped over the boundary line and violated the act. McRuer won a conviction and then took the companies all the way to the Supreme Court of Canada to have this conviction confirmed.[10]

The other case, in which McRuer failed to secure a conviction, involved a conspiracy to fix prices in the tobacco industry in western Canada. Since the case was being heard in Edmonton, McRuer had to take an examination to join the Alberta bar. When he had joined the British Columbia bar in 1925 to prosecute the Simington fruit combine case, McRuer had simply applied and paid a $400 fee. "They were very kind to me," he later recalled. Yet Alberta was going to be much tougher. The Law Society had directed that one of its benchers should examine McRuer as to his qualifications. Two hours before the exam for which McRuer had been thoroughly studying, the busy examiner Gordon Steer (later chief justice of Alberta), merely called him up and said, "Well, I have another appointment, the examination is over. You passed."[11] McRuer then happily paid his fee and was in business. Unfortunately for McRuer and the crown, the case—R. v. Macdonald Tobacco Company— was dismissed without leave to appeal due to a double jeopardy from an abortive earlier prosecution.[12] Still, McRuer's stay in Edmonton was far from wasted; a friendly fellow barrister, Stanley McCuaig, lent him his car that summer, and he, Mary, and the children happily toured Alberta.

FUNDAMENTALLY, McRuer's decision to launch himself into private practice reflected a desire for new challenges. The same desire lay at the root of two other departures in these years, his decision to undertake part-time teaching and his efforts on behalf of Ontario's police.

In 1932 McRuer was appointed lecturer in criminal procedure at Osgoode Hall. He taught there for an hour per day, focusing not on the rights and wrongs of a case but on the all-important business of correct procedure. Among his students were Bora Laskin and Wilfred Judson, both of whom would rise to the pinnacle of the legal profession as justices of the Supreme Court of Canada, and John Arnup, later a judge on the Ontario Court of Appeal. McRuer continued to teach criminal procedure at Osgoode Hall until 1936, impressing his students with his thoroughness as well as his seriousness. When he was elected to sit as a bencher of the Law Society, he relinquished his teaching because of the long hours of committee work that the Society now required of him, and because, as a bencher, he could receive no remuneration for teaching. He had enjoyed teaching and, in his reserved way, meeting the law students, although there was one aspect of the job that he definitely did not like—marking papers. His daughter Mary Louise remembers how much he resented having to spend June afternoons in the garden poring over exams. He was once delighted when a student responded to a long question with a one-word answer—No. The student got full marks.

Another significant initiative on McRuer's part, dating from 1930, combined his interest in teaching with his awareness of the need for better training of policemen. At that time, Toronto's police were led by their lionhearted chief constable, Brigadier-General Dennis Draper, a bustling, mustachioed little man, just short of the police department's own five-foot, eight-inch height limit. Draper was a tough-minded administrator who carefully reorganized the city police—which was quickly replacing militia as the prime aid to civil power—and implemented fair but strict internal disciplinary procedures. He also greatly improved the force's *esprit de corps*, making promotion dependent not on membership in the Orange Lodge, as had previously been the case, but on merit. Under the new regime that Draper instituted, a policeman's ability and so his suitability for higher rank was to be demonstrated by course work and examinations.

Draper had been greatly impressed with McRuer's impartiality and attention to procedure when he was crown attorney, and in 1930 he retained Jim as counsel for the Toronto Police Commission. In the months that followed, Draper, appreciating the time that McRuer gave to police chiefs and officers in instructing them in the correct and clear performance of their duties, gradually drew him into greater involvement with the police. It was a cause always close to McRuer's heart. He was fascinated by forensic science, and he also appreciated what he had learned first hand about the important and difficult work police officers are called on to do. In a 1934 letter to a Windsor police officer, McRuer wrote that one of his chief "hobbies in life" was advancing the interests of policemen, whose "earnest and conscientious manner" made him sympathize with "their eternal struggle against political interference."[13] That same year McRuer gave a tangible demonstration of his support of the police by becoming counsel to the Police Association.

Draper and McRuer worked well together, and one of their most important collaborative projects was the creation of police-training programs. The first result of their efforts was the opening in 1932 of a Toronto police school, located atop the Stewart Building at Queen's Park. Holding the title of "Advisory Dean" at the school, McRuer taught the police recruits criminal law and, by popular demand, wrote a pocket-sized bestseller called *The Police Constable's Manual* (published by McClelland and Stewart) so that officers could have a ready reference book and not have to carry around a bulky copy of the criminal code as they performed their duties. When the financial constraints of the Depression forced the school to shut down late in 1934, it was back in operation again within four months, owing to McRuer's relentless lobbying of the attorney-general, Arthur Roebuck.

In 1935 McRuer, in cooperation with the Ontario Provincial Police and the Toronto Police Commissioners, started laying out plans for an Ontario police college open to officers from all across the province. RCMP training was taken as a model, and McRuer and Draper communicated with police schools in the United Kingdom for information about courses and methodology. The reorganized Ontario Police School was officially opened on 11 March 1935 in the old Toronto Teachers' College on College Street, west of University Avenue.

The approach to criminology at the Toronto police school and its provincial successor was original and full of vitality. Policemen were instructed in the criminal code, demeanour and appearance, equipment, discipline, arrests, execution of warrants, use of force, evidence, and identification of criminals. English literature also became part of the curriculum, with the object of improving officers' written reports and presentation of evidence in court. The resources of the nearby University of Toronto were tapped for experts in forensic science. Professor Rogers of the chemistry department would cross the road to talk about chemical analysis and identification, and others would lecture on fingerprinting and ballistics. McRuer himself gave practical, unacademic lectures on the procedures to be followed during the course of duty, particularly in an arrest. Other lecturers included William J. Dunlop, head of the extension department of the university (and Ontario minister of education during the 1950s), judge Hawley Mott of the Juvenile Court, Ontario Fire Marshall E.P. Heaton, Chief Inspector George Guthrie, Crown Attorney J.W. McFadden; crown counsel (and later deputy attorney-general) William B. Common; Joseph Sedgwick from the office of the attorney-general; and Chief Constable Dennis Draper, who lectured on "Crime Prevention, Sobriety and Character."

To sceptics who doubted the need for a police college, McRuer frequently quoted an authority that invariably stopped them short—the Magna Carta: "We will not make any Constables but of such as Know the Law of the Realm and mean duly to observe it." Over time, the college succeeded far beyond McRuer's expectations, turning out forty graduates for each three-month session. Many graduates told him how much they appreciated the chance to get some professional training, some of them never before having had the chance to study even the criminal code. One Toronto constable, J.H. Lougheed, wrote McRuer after graduation, praising his talent of explaining legal technicalities in a way the average policeman could grasp and understand: "Listening to men like you and Judge Mott is an inspiration to me to be true to the higher ideals in life." McRuer's personal dignity and manners left an impression on his students. To quote from Lougheed again: "I'm presuming, from your demeanour, that you are a Christian gentleman. I don't believe I heard a vulgar word from you, which is unusual among professional men, as well as policemen. I feel I must make mention of this because I feel that none of us can afford to neglect our spiritual well-being, we being immortal creatures."[14] McRuer treasured Lougheed's letter, keeping it in a family scrapbook.

McRuer's support of police was especially evident in his relationship with the Dorland inquiry, which had been set up in 1933 after a political storm had erupted about the Toronto police's use of "go-betweeners" or informers. Often dismayed by the contrast between the strict conduct of court proceedings and the lax conduct of government commissions of inquiry, McRuer felt that this royal commission on alleged police irregularities and the activities of convicted criminal Albert Dorland was a perfect case in point. The events leading to the creation of this commission were strange and shadowy, and at their centre was McRuer's friend Chief Constable Draper.

Draper had more than his share of enemies. Gambling operators and hoodlums resented his efforts to crack down on organized crime, and the Orange Order, which had long controlled the police force, opposed his administrative reforms. Together they formed a formidable opposition, and in 1933 they tried to use an aborted bank robbery as a pretext to do away with their nemesis once and for all. It happened like this. Information had come to the police from a shady character named Toohey that the Dorland gang was going to attempt a bank robbery at the corner of Wellesley and Church streets. Inspector of Detectives Alex Murray and Chief Constable Draper discussed the matter and then told Toohey to "keep in touch with these fellows and let us know the details of when they are going to commit the robbery." When he learned the exact time and place, Murray sent five detectives to stake out the bank. Evidently they failed to conceal themselves well enough, for the robbers grew suspicious, got back in their car, and took off. The police followed in hot pursuit and, after a furious chase, their cars collided with that of the robbers on Wellesley Street; then, in an assault that became known as "The Battle of the Plains of Wellesley," the police fired away at the get-away vehicle until Dorland and his gang surrendered. Nobody had been hurt, and the robbers were tried and convicted, but the case triggered a concerted campaign to discredit the Toronto police and force Draper's resignation.

Draper was criticized in the legislature and in public on his use of informers and for allowing his men to shoot at the robbers. The newspapers, always hungry for headlines, gave the story great play. Eventually, the government caved in and authorized a royal commission of investigation under Mr. Justice Kingstone. Peter White was counsel for Draper; McRuer represented Alex Murray. Though he was not a wealthy man, Murray did not have to worry about being unable to afford McRuer. Toronto fuel merchant Alfred Rogers, no stranger to the race courses of Ontario, invited McRuer to his office, told him that he was indignant about the charges against Draper and Murray, and retained him to appear before the commission on Murray's behalf. "Go the whole course," he growled at McRuer, "and send me the bill."

The inquiry was tilted against Draper and Murray from the start, and the commission's report, presented to the government in July 1933, was harshly critical of what it viewed as a Keystone Cops melodrama. Kingstone felt that the police had gone too far in encouraging Toohey to participate in an entrapment plot, and that, following the aborted robbery, the officers had acted in an unwarranted and dangerous fashion—first by conducting a high-speed car chase through the streets of the city and then by launching a "murderous fusillade." He also documented inadequate control of the "sting" operation and raised other issues that suggested a lack of professionalism on the part of the Toronto police. While the report fell short of condemning Draper outright, it did single out Murray as being "a party to the commission of a crime" since he had advised Toohey to accompany the robbers. The end result of the commission's investigation was that Murray was permitted to resign, a heavy but perhaps necessary sacrifice to pay to keep Chief Draper himself in power.[15] McRuer was happy that at least Murray had not been fired—in that event, as he pointed out, the police officer would have lost his pension—but the entire investigation left a bad taste in his mouth. To his mind, Kingstone's ignorance of law enforcement was compounded by his obvious partiality, a combination that turned the investigation into something of a kangaroo court.

DESPITE HIS HECTIC SCHEDULE in the late 1920s and early 1930s, McRuer also found time for politics—of the Liberal variety, of course. In 1927 he was instrumental in the creation of a Liberal discussion group in the Toronto area, an initiative for which he was warmly thanked by Prime Minister King.[16] This group appears to have been short-lived, but McRuer's interest in Liberal Party organization continued and indeed became stronger than ever when the King government went down to defeat in 1930. The day after the election, he wrote to King to say that "as a Liberal I am very much disappointed in yesterday's results, and I am more disappointed as a true Britisher. I feel that you gave the country a leadership that it has seldom had in our Canadian history. I also feel that the expression of the polls was not a rejection of the policy of British Empire Trade, but was one of those results brought about by conditions over which no Government had any control." McRuer went on to express the hope that "yesterday's vote will result in the consolidation of the Liberal interests throughout Canada. These have been divided under different groups and this has impaired the strength of Liberalism. It may be that the realization of Tory ascendancy will be effective to bring together all these interests for the national benefit."[17]

Other Liberals were thinking along the same lines. One of them was Vincent Massey, the godfather of Ontario Liberals, who took a leading part in the campaign to return Mackenzie King to power. Appointed by King to the post of first president of the National Liberal Federation, Massey soon fastened on McRuer as one of the rising members of the Liberal Party and asked him to form another study group to assist in policy formation. With Massey's support, a number of such round-table groups were formed and called Twentieth Century Liberal Clubs, or Century Clubs for short.

McRuer assisted the Liberal cause in other ways. In the early winter of 1933 Massey asked McRuer to help him in setting up a Liberal policy conference at Port Hope, in imitation of the British Liberal Party's Oxford Summer School. The conference was to be strictly unofficial, but King was nonetheless worried about Massey's motives, regarding him as a possible pretender to the throne. McRuer, however, had no such suspicions. Agreeing with Massey that the party was adrift and needed new, carefully thought-out policies, particularly in the economic sphere, McRuer volunteered to give a speech at the conference and lead a round-table discussion on the securities marketplace.

The timing of the conference could not have been better. In 1933 the depression that had begun with the stock market crash of 1929 still showed no sign of lifting. Unemployment stood at nearly 20 per cent, the wheat economy of the Prairies lay devastated by drought, and, in the absence of the social "safety net" of a later age, those without work were dependent on charity. Amidst these grim conditions, there was a crying need for new economic policies to replace those that had failed so abysmally. In the United States, this need was answered with the election in 1932 of Democrat Franklin Roosevelt as president, under whom a "New Deal" was gradually put in place to rebuild a shattered economy and restore a sense of hope. Canada, however, was still drifting in 1933; R.B. Bennett's main solution to the Depression had been to "blast" Canada's way into world markets, and this approach seemed to be futile in the face of mounting protectionism around the globe. The Liberal Party obviously had an opportunity to portray itself as the party of new ideas, the party of hope, and the Port Hope conference was intended to be the first step in its revival.

Opening on 4 September and continuing for six days, the "First Liberal Summer Conference" attracted over 300 delegates and a good smattering of newspaper reporters to Massey's Batterwood House in Port Hope and then to seminar rooms in Trinity College School, located in the same town, to discuss "present day problems." Discussion ranged over the various ways in which governments might intervene practically to manage the capitalist economy, without either abolishing the market system or granting it unfettered freedom to do what it liked. After addresses of welcome by Mackenzie King and Vincent Massey, McRuer led off on the afternoon of 4 September with a round-table discussion on "The Protection of the Investor." In two other groups, King's former secretary, Norman Rogers, then a political science professor at Queen's University, spoke on federal-provincial relations, and Carl Goldenberg, McGill lawyer and economist, conducted a seminar on "Trade, Tariffs and Preferences."

In the days that followed, group discussions dealt with such issues as budgets, unemployment relief, agriculture, banking, and foreign policy. The leaders of these discussions included T.A. Crerar, former leader of the Progressive Party ("Transportation Problems"); O.M. Biggar, former chief electoral officer ("Electoral Reform"); and the former minister of national defence, Colonel J.L. Ralston ("Trade as a Factor in Recovery"). Addresses were given each evening, two of the most influential being delivered by members of President Roosevelt's "brain trust," Averell Harriman and Raymond Moley. Harriman was a member of Brown Brothers, the merchant-banking firm that McRuer had visited during the investigation of the Jarvis-Smith affair. (McRuer discreetly chose not to mention this incident in his chats with Harriman.) Two other speakers who made trenchant remarks on the economic crisis were J.W. Dafoe of the *Winnipeg Free Press* and Floyd Chalmers of the *Financial Post*. But the real star of the Liberals' Port Hope conference, since Massey was unable to lure John Maynard Keynes, was Sir Herbert Samuel, the grand old man of the British Liberal Party. For Mackenzie King's part, he only spoke twice at the conference, first to raise the curtain on the proceedings and then to lower it at the conclusion.

McRuer's own seminar was a relaxed session of give and take. The Companies Act and the 1928 Security Frauds Prevention Act were discussed; the latter measure involved a field in which McRuer had special knowledge because of his stock fraud prosecutions and his role in helping draft Ontario securities legislation. The consensus emerged that there should be greater restrictions placed on limited companies so that subscribing shareholders would have some assurance of the scope of the company's operations. Directors should be required to have some real and tangible financial interest in the company, shareholders should be given more information, and minority shareholders should have greater protection. There were some "silly suggestions," duly reported by McRuer in his address, that preference shareholders be given voting rights, or that dividends should be eliminated altogether, but overall the recommendations were sensible. McRuer's only complaint to Massey was that there were too many journalists present, and he expressed the view that they should be kept out of future sessions. All things considered, however, McRuer regarded the conference as a success.

Now fully involved in the formation of Liberal policy, McRuer followed up his role at the Port Hope conference with a series of speeches to local Liberal clubs in 1933 and 1934. He corresponded extensively with Norman Lambert, national secretary of the Liberal Party in Ontario, and Vincent Massey about the success of these endeavours.[18] He also began to pay closer attention to politics at the provincial level, where a Liberal revival was taking place.

At the beginning of the Great Depression, Ontario Liberals were

wracked by discord over liquor and religion, and both the federal and
provincial Liberal parties were pathetically organized. But the greatest
problem, at least at the provincial level, was leadership. The Ontario Liberal Party was led by the pipe-smoking prohibitionist Bill Sinclair, an
old-fashioned Presbyterian Grit lawyer from Oshawa so out of date, so
pedestrian and lacklustre, so bereft of political guile that the wily Tory
Premier Howard Ferguson was able to play with him like a cat with a
mouse. McRuer once took the timid Sinclair a draft of a bill he had prepared to provide for the relief of widows and their dependants. Sinclair's
only response was an ineffectual shrug and the remark that "oh, if I take
that up, Ferguson will tear it to pieces."[19] Despairing of action, McRuer
eventually leaked his draft to Billy Price, and Ferguson happily appropri-
ated it and put forward a similar bill in the legislature two sessions later.

At the opposite extreme from the "dry" Sinclair were the increasingly
influential Liberal "wets," a group that included such men as the lawyer
Arthur Slaght and the business barons Percy Parker and Harry Sifton.
In between were the "reform" Liberals, who included McRuer, lawyer
Arthur Roebuck, Paul Martin of Windsor, and, at the centre of their net-
work, Joe Atkinson of the *Toronto Star*. All could see that Sinclair was
getting nowhere, and their frustration grew when Ferguson resigned in
1930 and the Liberal Opposition seemed unable to capitalize on the obvi-
ous weaknesses of his successor, the decent, solid, but fumbling George
Henry. It was therefore in some desperation that the Ontario Liberal
Party, in its 1930 convention, gambled, and going against the wishes of
Mackenzie King, chose as its leader the thirty-four-year-old Mitchell F.
Hepburn.[20]

Hepburn, a dairy farmer from Elgin County, had sat in the House
of Commons since 1926. Cherubic-faced and dimple-chinned, he was a
natural clown and showman, but there was more to him than that—he
was also an immensely shrewd politician. After his election as leader of
Ontario's Liberals, he gave the party a new lease on life by broadening its
base to include farmers and labour and by attempting to heal party divisions, especially those caused by the issues of prohibition and Roman
Catholic separate schools. To party pros such as Senator Frank O'Connor
and Arthur Hardy, and to experienced backroom boys such as Arthur
Slaght, all engaged in rebuilding the Ontario Liberals from the grassroots
up, Hepburn was a ferocious campaigner in the mould of Huey Long
who could get people excited, even mesmerized. In their eyes, Mitch's
vast repertoire of quips and colourful stories were a welcome relief from
the antique oratory of R.B. Bennett and the pious homilies of Mackenzie

King. The people needed excitement, and someone to make them laugh in that season of hardship and economic discontent. They needed an excuse to vote Liberal, and Mitch gave it to them.

The more severe eye of Jim McRuer looked somewhat askance at Hepburn's antics—he later described him as a man who "lacked loyalty to the people"—but for the time being he kept his reservations to himself. Like other Liberals he thought that Hepburn could win, and he watched with satisfaction as the Conservative government of George Henry squirmed under Hepburn's attacks. When the provincial election was called for June 1934, McRuer even considered running as a candidate in Premier Henry's riding, York East; eventually, resisting pressure from such veteran Liberals as William Mulock, he decided against the idea.[21] Yet he did not remain on the sidelines during the campaign. On the contrary, he became one of a stable of four Liberal speakers—the others were Slaght, Roebuck, and ex-Alberta agriculture minister Duncan Marshall—who stumped the smaller centres of the province spreading the Liberal message while Hepburn himself handled the larger crowds. A measure of how much attention these efforts attracted was a statement made by Premier Henry. Speaking in Gravenhurst on 31 May, Henry criticized Hepburn's "henchmen lawyers" who were "going around the country speaking from a Liberal platform."[22]

By now Hepburn, capitalizing on the misery of the Depression and the ineffectiveness of the Henry government, was the dominant figure in Ontario politics. His compelling brand of political evangelism had awakened Ontario voters to the potential of politics as an instrument of change, and large crowds congregated at country schoolhouses across the province to hear the Liberal Party's message. Expecting an Ontario version of the Roosevelt New Deal, they were eager to hear the colourful oratory of Hepburn and other Liberal showmen, but their new interest in politics also conditioned them to listen to the more sober message purveyed by solid, earnest, safe speakers such as McRuer. Besides doggedly cataloguing government waste—the chauffeur-driven Cadillacs and Packards, the high salaries, the marble-panelled offices, the reckless expenditure on public buildings—McRuer eloquently argued the desperate need for greater public assistance to the unemployed, and set out in detail the evidence of pervasive corruption in government.

Mary McRuer helped her husband practise his speeches at home, and advised him on what not to say. She was not a particular admirer of his abilities as a stump-speaker, but in fact Jim himself was his own harshest critic. As he said himself, he was inclined to crack open a subject as though it were an egg, carefully and methodically. His earnest style was in striking contrast to the dynamic performances of fellow lawyer Arthur Slaght, whose approach to speechifying was summed up in his remark to McRuer that "regardless of what is here we'll dress it up to look good."[23] When McRuer and Slaght appeared on the platform together, as they did all around the province, they were a strange team, but somehow an appropriate one in the campaign to make Mitch Hepburn premier of Ontario. McRuer supplied the facts and analysis, Slaght the emotional power.

On one occasion McRuer himself combined facts and emotion. In a speech delivered at McGregor's School, in Premier Henry's riding of York East, on 9 April, McRuer began by presenting a matter-of-fact analysis of the increase in the public debt under the Conservative administration. His research was impeccable but the subject rather dry; the one lively moment came when he denounced the government for wasting "public funds by reckless expenditure in times of prosperity" and then, as a consequence, having little choice but "to throw thousands of men out of work in times of adversity." But it was not until he turned to other subjects—government corruption and insensitivity to the plight of working people and the unemployed—that McRuer's speech caught fire. Reviewing evidence of government misconduct in the management of the province's natural resources, he thundered that the defence of ignorance was no defence at all: "If they were such children they have no right to hold office. If they were not such children, the wrath and condemnation of the Province should be upon them. In any case they should be driven from office as utterly inefficient."

On the subject of poverty, McRuer became even more impassioned. "We have been now four years in one of the most devastating depressions that Canada has ever seen," he said. "Throughout these four years there has been unprecedented production and abundance of wealth, but in great centres like Toronto and the Yorks almost one-quarter of our people have been destitute and starving." The cause of this misery was not a "lack of wealth" but inadequate "distribution of wealth." Aggravating the problem was the failure of the provincial government, and particularly the Department of Labour, to take any action at all to alleviate "the suffering of the people." As an example, McRuer cited a recent strike by workers in the city of Stratford's furniture factories and packing houses. This strike had been triggered by the workers' inability to survive on the starvation wages they were being paid, but the government's only response to their grievances was brute force: "Two detachments of trained soldiers, armed with rifles and bayonets, four machine guns, and four baby tanks armour-plated and capable of shooting 500 rounds a minute. Thus were the strikers of Stratford met with force and intimidation." McRuer's speech ended with a rousing piece of political rhetoric that revealed the depth of his commitment to the "common man":

"The time has come for a drastic change in the Province of Ontario. If we are to have any prosperity in the future there must be a drastic reduction in the public debt. Burdened with debt and taxation, the people cannot be prosperous. There must be provision for unemployment insurance.

"The dissipation of the wealth of the forests by the barons of finance must cease. The people of the Province are entitled to their birthright. The wealth of the mine is for the prospector and the legitimate investors, and it is time for the Government to see that they get it, instead of the ruthless promoter and speculator who spend their lime mining the public.

"The wealth of the farm is for the farmer and the toilers, not for the milling company, the dairy company, the bread company, and all the financial interests that have been exploiting it.

"The time has come for us to approach the problems of Government, not in the interests of the financier, as has been the record of the past, but in the interests of humanity as a whole. The welfare of the individual, his comfort, happiness and health, are entitled to consideration, and exploitation must cease if we are to be a happy Province."[24]

All the speeches and barnstorming came to an end on 19 June 1934, when the voters of Ontario toppled the largest Conservative majority ever and gave Hepburn the biggest Liberal majority in provincial history to that date: sixty-six Liberals were elected to seventeen Conservatives, and not a single Tory MPP was left in the old Grit heartland from Toronto to Windsor. Jim McRuer had found the campaign exhilarating, and he felt proud about the part he had played. Owing in a small measure to his efforts, Queen's Park was again controlled by the Liberal Party—a party that, in his eyes, still represented the forces of progress. In a telegram he sent to Hepburn congratulating him on the victory, McRuer noted that "you and Arthur Slaght conducted a faultless campaign. All Ontario is thrilled."[25]

By the end of 1934, then, McRuer had made a successful move into private practice—no mean accomplishment in the midst of the Great Depression—had branched out into the areas of teaching and policing, and had made a significant contribution to the federal and provincial Liberal parties through his new-found roles as policy adviser and election campaigner. He had every reason to look forward to the years ahead with optimism and anticipation.

He was not disappointed. In the immediate aftermath of Hepburn's victory, former premier George Henry had predicted ruefully that the people of Ontario were "in for interesting times."[26] No one would find these times more interesting than Jim McRuer.

6

REFORM BY REFORMERS

For Jim McRuer, the year following Hepburn's victory in Ontario was exceptionally busy. First, he served as the defence counsel representing Ontario Hydro in a high-profile provincial commission of inquiry. Then, in the space of about six months, he wore two other hats—as counsel to the controversial MP Agnes Macphail in a federal government inquiry, and as a Liberal candidate in the federal election. The first of these appearances on the public stage, the one involving Ontario Hydro, placed him in the middle of a complicated and messy affair that implicated a former premier of Ontario and a former prime minister of Canada. One of its chief protagonists was none other than McRuer's new patron at Queen's Park, Mitch Hepburn.

After becoming Liberal leader, Hepburn had been eager to ferret out evidence of government waste and corruption, and one of his favourite targets was Ontario Hydro. His crusade against the utility began in late 1931 and revolved around two claims: that Ontario Hydro had made excessive purchases of power in contracts with private Quebec companies; and that—Hepburn was here drawing on evidence presented at a parliamentary inquiry in Ottawa—the Beauharnois Light, Heat and Power Company had made a kickback payment to the Ontario Conservative Party in exchange for a power contract. The federal inquiry, whose main concern was the ties between Beauharnois and the former Liberal government of Mackenzie King, eventually dismissed this allegation of wrongdoing on the part of Ontario Conservatives, but Hepburn still smelled blood and used the Beauharnois revelations with telling effect in a by-election held in South Wellington in November 1931.

Calls for a full investigation of Hydro affairs increased, and in February 1932 the Henry government capitulated to public pressure and launched an inquiry. Much to Hepburn's astonishment, this inquiry exonerated Hydro and the government in a report presented that November, but the Liberals were still not prepared to let the matter drop. Hepburn, assisted by the ever-active Arthur Slaght, continued looking into Hydro's affairs, and in early 1933 their efforts were crowned with success. In the late 1920s Ontario Hydro had contracted to make annual purchases of power from the Ontario Power Service Corporation (OPSC)—a subsidiary of the Abitibi Pulp and Paper Company, set up to produce power in the Abitibi Canyon north of Sudbury. With the onset of the Depression, however, financially strapped Abitibi defaulted on its bond payments, and the Henry government entered into negotiations to take over OPSC. The negotiations were almost concluded in March 1933 when Hepburn and Slaght discovered that both Henry and former prime minister Arthur Meighen had a financial interest in OPSC. On 5 April, Henry, in answer to repeated questions about the matter in the legislature, admitted that he had $25,000 invested in OPSC bonds and that Meighen was the director of companies which held OPSC bonds worth several hundred thousand dollars. Humiliated, Henry privately told Howard Ferguson, "I will never forgive myself."[1]

The premier was able to survive the Opposition's attacks by claiming that he was guilty only of carelessness, not of any impropriety. Still, his reputation was badly damaged, and the OPSC scandal was a hot issue in the 1934 election. Following the Liberals' victory in that contest, Hepburn, acting on the advice of Mackenzie King, established an investigation (known as the Smith-Latchford Commission) into the operations of Ontario Hydro in general and the dealings of Henry and Meighen in particular. This inquiry was not to be neutral and dispassionate. Jim McRuer was given the job of counsel for the Ontario Hydro Commission—a rather curious role for a Hepburn ally—while Arthur Slaght was appointed counsel to the inquiry. Another Hepburn appointee, Stewart Lyon, was not directly involved in the commission but he played a key part in its proceedings nonetheless. As the new chairman of Ontario Hydro, Lyon acted in a somewhat compromising fashion, feeding evidence of waste, incompetence, and corruption in the organization he now headed to the commission. W.N. Tilley defended the Henry government; Arthur Meighen, judging from the people Hepburn had put in place that the inquiry was to be more political than legal, decided to defend himself.

Hearings took place in July and August 1934. McRuer's task was mainly to protect the corporate interests of Ontario Hydro and to present its documents as evidence; Tilley, however, charged that McRuer in fact assisted efforts to sully Hydro's reputation. In one exchange, McRuer referred to the "somewhat violent personal attacks" that Tilley had levelled against him and said that he was willing to dismiss them as "spoken in the heat of these arguments." To this Tilley replied that "there was nothing inadvertent" about what he said; his remarks were "quite intentional."[2] Slaght, for his part, happily used colourful, headline-provoking language in dealing with the former prime minister, and Meighen responded emotionally to Slaght's ruthless attacks by calling the commission "the most diabolical political inquisition ever held outside Turkey. The conduct of it would put to shame Pontius Pilate."[3] McRuer felt sorry for Henry and especially for Meighen, who personally had held only $3,000 worth of OPSC bonds. On one occasion, late in the proceedings, while McRuer was walking out of the hearing room, Meighen said to him, with a heavy sigh, "Mr. McRuer, I have been a fool in this case. I made a grave mistake in not having a lawyer with me."[4]

The commission's report, issued in October 1934, found both Henry and Meighen guilty, not of wrongdoing, but of impropriety resulting from an apparent conflict of interest.[5] No penalty was attached to the finding, but the blot on their reputations as pre-eminent public men was punishment enough. A short lime later, in April 1935, the Hepburn government attracted still more publicity when it introduced a bill that repudiated Ontario Hydro's contracts with Quebec companies, contracts that both Hepburn and Attorney-General Arthur Roebuck described as inequitable and illegal. The bill passed eleven days later to shrieks of pain from bondholders and the financial community but to acclaim from the public at large. McRuer was one of the staunchest defenders of this action; he argued that breaking the contracts was not nearly as iniquitous as entering into them in the first place.

Around this time, McRuer waded into a furious public controversy concerning Hepburn's minister of welfare, David Croll. In 1934 Croll decided to scrap the system whereby government-issued vouchers could be redeemed for food at authorized stores. Believing that the system was both rife with abuse and an insult to the people it was supposed to help, Croll instituted in its place direct cash payments to the poor. This move struck many as diabolical, and an official of the United Church, George

Little, even went so far as to denounce Croll as a "border city Russian Jew." McRuer was outraged. He acted immediately, writing directly to the moderator of the United Church, the Reverend Richard Roberts, to protest the "abusive manner" in which Croll had been attacked. "We all feel that the United Church stands for good will to all men, no matter what their race or creed may be," McRuer said. Little's remarks indicated that "he was not fit" to occupy an important position in the church, and McRuer was certain that "it will take some years to repair the damage that Mr. Little has done to the United Church of Canada by attempting to stir up a wholly unchristian and vicious racial strife."[6]

Croll later recalled that "there wasn't anything for me to say once McRuer had spoken. He won the day completely." McRuer's letter, Croll noted, was "so well written, and so well said, and it came from authority. It's a great statement of his passion for justice." Croll believed that Little's attack achieved the paradoxical result of legitimizing "the Jew in politics." "The very fact that he went after me because I was a Jew—people didn't like that." Helped by McRuer's courageous repudiation of anti-semitism in all its forms, David Croll said that his Jewishness would "never again be a barrier" for him over his next fifty years in Canadian politics. All his life, he remembered McRuer's "noble questure."[7]

While Mitch Hepburn and David Croll were busy shaking up Ontario, Jim McRuer's gaze was shifting from Queen's Park to Ottawa. For some years he had contemplated becoming a member of parliament, and in 1935 the goal seemed within reach. By January of that year, the federal Liberal machine, busy planning for an election, had asked McRuer to put his hat in the ring in the riding of High Park, his old neighbourhood in Toronto's west end. Liberal organizers considered him brittle in his relations with others, but they also appreciated his rising reputation and his diligent efforts on the party's behalf. In the previous election, the Liberal candidate, A.A. Bond, had failed to capture the riding, losing by a margin of more than 6,000 votes. McRuer was not dissuaded by Bond's defeat, however. The horrible state of the economy would work in the Liberals' favour, and, in High Park in particular, McRuer told Mackenzie King that the riding could probably "be won, as the Conservative candidate won in the Provincial election by a narrow margin of less than one thousand votes, and the Liberal, although a good organizer, was a Roman Catholic and to this fact his defeat was attributed notwithstanding a very fine campaign put up by him."[8] He agreed to let his name stand in nomination.

The nomination meeting, held at Mavety Hall on 15 February before an audience of several hundred cheering Liberals, had about it all the political fireworks of the time. By way of returning an old favour—McRuer's campaigning on behalf of the Vancouver Liberal candidate Dugald Donaghy in 1930—British Columbia Liberal chief Ian Mackenzie spoke in support of McRuer. Taking second spot to no one in his delivery of the Liberal Party line, not only in theme but in rhetoric, Mackenzie gave a speech that conveyed fully the temper of the times. In a display of unrestrained Grit partisanship, Mackenzie volubly criticized the Bennett government as a "bureaucratic, dictatorial despotism that reared its ugly head above a puppet Canada, a usurping assumption of the reins of power over the minions of a servile state, and an accentuated, aggravated, intensive, selfish materialism." Then, his voice rising in pitch, the lines coming slower now, he asked the good Liberals of High Park to continue pursuing "the broad free path of Liberalism, avoiding on the one hand the wild-eyed visionaries; the miracle workers, the peddlers of paradise on the left, and on the Tory right the secret and sinister policy of fascistic sabotage."[9]

McRuer took a more cerebral approach in his address, although his intense partisanship was fully on display, too: the Conservatives were the "enemy" and Prime Minister Bennett a "dictator." He spoke of his membership on a 1930 committee which drafted an unemployment insurance policy for the Liberal Party; he criticized the Bennett New Deal—a package of reform legislation assembled in the last months of the government's mandate—for not going far enough; he supported a national health insurance plan, a lower tariff on "all of the necessities of life" (such as sugar, food, gasoline, and textiles), a publicly owned Bank of Canada, and mortgage relief in the form of fixed 5 per cent interest rates. All of this came straight from the platform of the Liberal Party, but McRuer did add two or three "reforms" of his own. Drawing on his personal experiences, he proposed tightening up the Combines Act and enforcing it more vigorously, protecting Canadians from stock fraud, and reforming the penal system. His speech demonstrated both his commitment to the cause of Liberalism and his generally thoughtful approach to issues of public policy. The audience was impressed, and McRuer was nominated without opposition as the Liberal candidate in High Park.[10]

FOR JIM McRUER, the pace now picked up considerably, and the next turn of events brought an opening that any lawyer would savour, particularly if he was a candidate for parliament. In the early spring of 1935,

McRuer received a prominent visitor in his Toronto office. Gerard Beaudoin, a well-known, reform-minded Ottawa lawyer, had come on behalf of Agnes Macphail, the first woman elected to the House of Commons. Macphail, the MP for the Ontario riding of South East Gray, had entered parliament in 1921 as a representative of the Progressive Party. A plain-spoken feminist, known for her keen intelligence and razor-sharp wit, she crusaded tirelessly for the rights of women and of other disadvantaged groups. By 1935 one of her causes—prison reform—had landed her in political hot water.

Prison reform was an issue tailor-made for Macphail. She instinctively disliked confinement, and in her own life she had broken out of the sense of imprisonment experienced by many women, fighting hard against the restraints imposed by her rural environment, her sex, and a political culture inhospitable to her reformist proposals. Macphail's "intense concern over prison problems," it is said, "followed directly from this emotional bias" against restraint.[11] When first made aware of the appalling conditions in Canadian jails, she had been reluctant to get involved. Her parliamentary role as champion of Canada's farmers was satisfying and fully consumed her time. She relished it, and the farmers were her constituents—the prisoners were not. Yet the need for penal reform touched her conscience. She could not pass it by.

In the early 1930s "Aggie" Macphail repeatedly spoke in the House of Commons about the need for an objective inquiry into prison conditions. Without a doubt the most prominent advocate of prison reform in the political arena—Macphail eventually would found the Elizabeth Fry Society of Canada—she was assisted by like-minded crusaders in other walks of life. Both the Toronto *Globe* and *Maclean's* published a number of hard-hitting exposés of prison conditions, and the appearance in 1933 of O.C.J. Withrow's *Shackling the Transgressor: An Indictment of the Canadian Penal System* kept the issue in the public eye. From Kingston, former attorney-general W.F. Nickle, who had acted as defence counsel for the leader of a prison riot, Murray Kirkland, added his own allegations in a letter to the Reverend Canon Scott of Quebec City, who in turn delivered a widely publicized sermon on the scandalous conditions in the prisons.

In becoming a leading agitator for reform of the penal system, Macphail had, time and time again, embarrassed successive ministers of justice by presenting allegations of corruption within the penitentiaries to the House of Commons—allegations that often led to sensational headlines in the country's newspapers. Generally, her information was sound and she was able to detail conditions clearly, relying on information gathered through a network of informants inside and outside the justice system which she had enthusiastically—and sometimes recklessly—developed over the years. But her determination and resourcefulness had few admirers in government. As her charges became more and more shocking, the reaction of ministers grew increasingly strident. Politically, Macphail was a marked woman.

An opportunity to undermine her credibility came the government's way in February 1934. Kingston inmate Charles Bayne had told Macphail that he would die of tuberculosis unless he was moved to a jail farm, where working in the fields provided the fresh air and sunlight helpful to TB victims. Macphail went to bat for the man, even though the Department of Justice would not give her the details of his crimes which she regularly requested. When she spoke highly of Bayne in the House, calling him "a man with a fine social outlook ... I know him well," Minister of Justice Hugh Guthrie happily lowered the boom. Taking Bayne's record, he read it out to the MPs, omitting the gorier "bestial" details of a long career of indecent assault, forgery, theft, and gross indecency."[12]

To a strait-laced woman such as Macphail, Guthrie's revelations about Bayne's offences, sexual and otherwise, were embarrassing and cruel. After this episode, Macphail was personally devastated and publicly discredited. Still, she had recovered her nerve by the late winter of 1934–5 and her resolve was strengthened when she received information that Guthrie had made a surreptitious attempt to manufacture further evidence against her. In April 1934 Guthrie had sent the senior inspector of penitentiaries, J.D. Dawson, to Kingston Penitentiary to cajole Macphail's principal informant into testifying against the MP. They wanted it to be made clear that Bayne, a liar and cheat, was the source of her information on conditions in the prison. During the course of his visit, Dawson also met with another inmate, who later informed Macphail that Dawson had told him, "Aggie made a goddamned fool of herself in the House of Commons, but when we are finished with her she will never be able to lift up her head in the House again."

On 18 March 1935 Macphail rose in the Commons to request that Guthrie produce all papers relating to Inspector Dawson's visit to the Kingston Penitentiary in April 1934. On the 19th Guthrie replied that there was "no foundation" to the reports of Dawson's attempt to discredit her, but on the 20th Macphail virtually accused Dawson of lying. In the end, Guthrie was forced to bow to Macphail's demand for a parliamentary inquiry into the matter. Macphail then attempted to capitalize on her victory by insisting on a full-scale investigation by a royal commission into conditions in all of Canada's penal institutions. The government flatly refused. If Macphail thought her parliamentary privileges had been breached, the government would examine her special case. However, there were no grounds, said the government, for a general inquiry into prison conditions.

Guthrie appointed the former arch-Tory partisan, judge E.J. Daly, as commissioner of the inquiry, and R.H. Greer, also a stalwart Toronto Tory, as commission counsel. When Macphail asked to be provided with counsel, however, Guthrie refused. The injustice of the situation was obvious. Greer, whose task was to exonerate the government, was to have his fees paid by the government; Macphail, as the victim of the alleged improprieties, would have to mount her case with personal resources that could not possibly match those of the government.

On his visit to McRuer's office, Beaudoin asked McRuer to take up Macphail's case. As their meeting concluded, McRuer not only agreed to this request but indicated that he would not charge Macphail a fee. The case was an irresistible one. It promised to place McRuer right in the middle of a scintillating drama while at the same time broadening his experience with public inquiries. It also involved an issue—prison reform—that had become increasingly dear to his own heart. The sensibilities he had on this score—based especially on his observations of jails and prisons and experiences with convicts during his time in the crown attorney's office—soon became acutely developed as a result of his exposure to Agnes Macphail.

McRuer knew that a whitewash of the government was in the works, but he also believed that the inquiry could offer a great opportunity to preach the message of prison reform to a national audience. Yet not all of his motives in taking up Macphail's cause were idealistic. The case also held out the prospect of political gain, both for McRuer and for the Liberal Party. Defending Macphail offered McRuer an opportunity to strike a blow against the federal Tories and, at the same time, would assist Mackenzie King's efforts to maintain the alliance between the Progressives and the Liberals. As if this was not incentive enough, the case would generate a wealth of publicity that would be beneficial to McRuer's own election campaign in High Park—a fact that was not lost on his opponents. In the days ahead, Greer would accuse McRuer of taking the case only for selfish "political ambitions," and Commissioner Daly echoed this assertion in a number of sarcastic remarks from his dais. The theme was soon taken up by several editorial writers across the country and particularly by the *Toronto Telegram*, a booster of the Conservative cause. McRuer took this all in stride—after all, the accusation was not far off the mark. Years later, with a twinkle in his eye, he made the following admission: "I wouldn't say that I didn't feel at the time that it wouldn't do me any harm politically to be involved in an attack on the government." Macphail was delighted to have McRuer representing her; in a letter written to him in late May, she said that "it lifts a great load off my mind to know that you will be here."[13] For his part, McRuer found working with Agnes Macphail an inspiring experience. The two had a lot in common. Both had been born in 1890, both had inherited the political instincts and values of rural Canadian Scots, and both had supported the passage of the 1918 act granting women the right to vote in federal elections and of the 1919 act that permitted women to sit in parliament. Intellectually, too, Macphail and McRuer were kindred spirits. As was true of McRuer, Macphail's incessant efforts on behalf of society's underdogs—the poor, women, farmers, prisoners, and others—sprang from a deep sense of justice.

The Daly inquiry bore out all of McRuer's suspicions that the odds were stacked against him and his client. During its hearings, which were held in Ottawa and Kingston, Daly frequently interrupted witnesses with sarcastic comments, and efforts to admit evidence bearing on Macphail's charges and allegations were often turned down by the judge after protests by Greer. Still, McRuer did manage to get two authoritative witnesses to speak out for the record, and the problems at the penitentiary which they described could be ignored only by the most cynical observer. Father W.T. Kingsley, the Roman Catholic chaplain at Kingston, called Inspector Dawson "full of conceit, self-opinionated, and holding the belief that experience was not necessary in the conduct of the penitentiary."[14] Kingsley accused Dawson of duplicity and incompetence, and launched a scathing attack on Canada's penal system. Even Daly did not dare to cut off the testimony of this reputable witness, and the press reported the priest's statements with enthusiasm. The second witness called by McRuer was a fine old soldier, Colonel W.B. Megloughlin, emergency warden during a riot in 1932 and in charge of the prison at the time of Dawson's visit. Megloughlin described some sadistic beatings at the penitentiary, outlined Dawson's attempts to suppress Bayne's evidence, and repeated Dawson's now famous comment that Macphail had "made a goddamned fool of herself."

The inquiry also featured many fiery exchanges between McRuer and Greer. When Greer contrasted his experience with McRuer's lack thereof, McRuer shot back: "I have a duty to perform here, and I shall

not be directed by my learned friend as a schoolmaster directs his pupils.
I am determined to have a full inquiry, and I am content to let the public
judge as to my experience and standing at the Bar and my conduct."[15] On
another occasion, McRuer denounced as "dastardly and unfair" Greer's
argument that Communists were behind Macphail's call for an investigation of Canada's prisons.[16] According to one newspaper reporter, "judge
Daly attempted to spread oil on the troubled waters and preserve the
dignity of the inquiry but his voice was almost lost in the din as the
three men stood up and shouted at each other, gesticulating, at the same
time."[17]

Gerard Beaudoin, who acted as McRuer's junior in the proceedings,
was present in the courtroom every day. He, Macphail, and McRuer had
come to a shared belief that they were exposing the prison problem to
the light of day. This sense of mission helped them overcome their feelings of frustration. So did Macphail's buoyant sense of humour. When
McRuer—tall, dark, and dignified—and Beaudoin—short and bald—
arrived to accompany her to the courtroom one morning, she looked
them up and down, grinned, and said, "Well, what's the long and the
short of it today?"[18]

One day in late spring, while in the midst of the hearings, McRuer
received word that his father had died. Judge Daly immediately
adjourned the inquiry, and McRuer returned to Toronto by the next
train. He had been preparing himself for this news, because his father,
in his eighty-fifth year, had been ill for some time, but it still came as a
shock. Much of what he had done in his own life had been motivated by
a desire to prove himself to his father. Just a couple of months earlier, his
father had been immensely proud when Jim won the Liberal nomination in High Park; sadly, however, he would never witness what his son
was convinced would be an even greater triumph—election to parliament. John McRuer's funeral was simply and solemnly conducted at the
family home on Gothic Avenue. His body was then taken back to Ayr
for burial in the cemetery overlooking the village. In the same southwest
Ontario soil he had worked for years as a farmer and had long yearned
to leave behind, John McRuer now rested beside his eldest son.

When judge Daly brought down his report several weeks later,
Macphail and McRuer were disappointed—though not surprised. Ignoring the testimony of Megloughlin and Kingsley, Daly exonerated Dawson completely. He refused to consider whether Justice Minister Guthrie
had been involved in the affair, and he also avoided any discussion of
the general state of Canada's penitentiaries.[19] As for Macphail, she wrote

a defiant letter to McRuer: "The judge did do a fine whitewashing job, putting it on thicker than I expected. But in spite of his decision we have won the first round ... The good old *Globe* has been hammering away with one editorial after another."[20]

Both Macphail and McRuer realized that they might have lost a battle, but not the war. The Daly inquiry had proceeded, as best as judge Daly and commission counsel Greer could ensure, within the extremely narrow terms of reference drafted by a government determined to keep the prison problem out of sight and therefore out of mind. Yet the publicity surrounding the case, and particularly the controversy aroused by the government's attempt to bury the issue of prison reform, resulted in a widespread view that something was fundamentally wrong in the penitentiaries system and that only a full-scale public inquiry could set things right. Among the proponents of this view were many of the country's newspapers.

Much of the press had been antagonistic to Macphail at the outset of the inquiry. Some newspapers saw the whole exercise as a colossal waste of time and money, trivializing the affair by suggesting that it was all a matter of whether or not an official had called Agnes Macphail "a goddamned fool." The St. Thomas *Times Journal* was one of these, its editorial position summed up in the claim that Macphail was "making a mountain out of a mole hill. She should forget about it."[21] In the end, however, Daly's clinging to his narrow terms of reference, along with McRuer's skilful advocacy, had changed many minds. At the same time, those already converted to the cause of prison reform used the Daly inquiry to promote their views. Harry Anderson, managing editor of the Toronto *Globe*, was especially active on this front, as was *Maclean's* magazine.[22]

In the wake of the Daly inquiry, Macphail and McRuer were determined to make prison reform an important issue in the approaching federal election. Macphail, however, with her life-long suspicion of Liberals and Tories alike, was modest in her expectations. In the same letter to McRuer in which she damned Daly's report, Macphail conceded that the coming election looked "like a walk-away for the Liberals, which, so far as you are concerned makes me happy. But my confidence in the Liberal Policy is not great. Nor do I see courageous leadership at the head of it. This is the Liberals' great chance, but if they fail to distribute goods and services they will be in as unhappy a position as Mr. Bennett when the term is out. I am banking on you."[23]

McRuer, as a good Liberal, had no such doubts. Like Macphail, he was delighted that the Daly inquiry had generated valuable publicity for

the cause of prison reform, and, as an added bonus, had further blackened the reputation of the Bennett government. Unlike her, however, he
was optimistic that a Liberal victory in the approaching election would
result in significant change, not only in terms of prison reform but for
Canadian society generally. His friendship with Agnes Macphail and the
experience of the Daly Inquiry had infused him with a new sense of mission, and he was eager to put his views before the public. For him, the
election could not come soon enough.

THE FEDERAL ELECTION CAMPAIGN of 1935 began in mid-summer and
lasted until early fall. It occurred in the midst of the Great Depression,
and voters throughout Canada were looking to the political system for
solutions to their problems. Some continued to place their faith in the
established parties, but others looked elsewhere. The Conservatives and
Liberals faced a challenge on the hustings not only from the Communists but from three new parties. The Reconstruction Party, the Social
Credit Party, and the Co-operative Commonwealth Federation (CCF),
each for the first time contesting a national election, had pushed the
number of candidates for the House of Commons to a record high of
894. In the riding of High Park, the Social Credit Party, though fresh
from an electoral victory in Alberta and hopeful of repeating its success
at the national level, did not field a candidate. Still, McRuer faced a four-
way race.

   Carrying the Tory colours in High Park was the incumbent MP, Alexander James Anderson, also a lawyer. Although McRuer considered him
hard to attack because he was "a very nice man, well known in the community," there were chinks in Anderson's armour. Nationally, the Conservatives entered the campaign at a severe disadvantage, handicapped both
by their past failure to end the Depression and by their unpopular leader,
R.B. Bennett, who, with his bombast, pomposity, and seeming insensitivity to the plight of the unemployed, had become widely disliked across
Canada. Added to these difficulties were discontent and division within
the party. Bennett's autocratic rule had made him personally unpopular
with many Tories, and the problem had been compounded by disagree-
ments over policy. In the early years of his government, Bennett had
fought the Depression with traditional remedies, and in so doing had
lost the support of progressive elements in the party. Then, in a series of
radio broadcasts in January 1935, he had unveiled a sweeping New Deal,
which alienated party moderates and traditional Conservatives.

The CCF, predecessor of the New Democratic Party, had been launched in 1932 in Calgary. An alliance of farmers, trade unionists, and intellectuals led by the widely respected J.S. Woodsworth, the CCF described itself as "a Dominion-wide movement for better food, better clothing, better homes, more education and culture—in short, a more abundant life."[24] In its Regina Manifesto of 1933, the CCF called for public ownership of key industries and utilities as a necessary step in the reorganization of society, and for the establishment of a welfare state through the introduction of such measures as universal pensions, health insurance, unemployment insurance, family allowances, and workers' compensation. In the riding of High Park, the CCF candidate, Donat Marc Le Bourdais, stood little chance of winning the riding but nonetheless threatened—along with another protest candidate—to siphon votes away from the Liberals.

The other protest candidate was Dr. Minerva Ellen Reid, who represented the Reconstruction Party. This party was led by Harry H. Stevens, the former federal Conservative cabinet minister whom McRuer had publicly attacked in the previous election. Since then, Stevens had been forced to resign from the Conservative Party because of policy differences with the prime minister. He and his fellow Reconstructionists argued that the most pressing issue of the day was the control exercised by the selfish and greedy rich over the main economic institutions of Canadian society. The party's platform promised a comprehensive public works program, a national housing scheme, special assistance to farmers, workers, veterans, and the young, and the elimination of unfair trade practices and excessive profits. Though lacking a national organization, the Reconstructionists fielded candidates in every province. In all, there were 174 candidates campaigning under the Reconstruction banner.

On the national stage, the Liberals campaigned on the slogan of "King or Chaos." In a contest that focused on unemployment as "Canada's most urgent national problem," the sixty-year-old Mackenzie King, confident of victory, took a casual and cautious approach. Rather than setting out a detailed program of his own, King concentrated on attacking the flaws of his opponents. He and his colleagues denounced Bennett as a dictator, criticized the Conservative administration's inability to lead the country out of the morass of the Depression, and promised voters a conciliatory, cooperative brand of government that would usher in a more harmonious era of federal-provincial relations and set the stage for economic renewal. Across the country, circumstances favoured the Liberals and the Conservatives bore the full brunt of popular discontent.[25] In Toronto, however, it was a closer race.

Buoyed initially by the publicity of the Daly inquiry, and running on the adrenalin that an election contest generates in candidates, McRuer entered the political fray in earnest. At the start of the campaign, he wrote an ingratiating letter to Mackenzie King commending him "on a magnificent opening address which should have a great settling effect on the public mind. The political gymnastics of our three political opponents are designed only to exploit human suffering. Your address comes as a refreshing and solid foundation on which to build our reform programme."[26]

The riding of High Park ran back from Lake Ontario through many factories and tree-lined streets densely built with solid red-brick houses. McRuer's campaign team included many local stalwarts of the riding association, not the least of whom were his parents-in-law, Dr. James and Katherine Dow (both life-long ardent Liberals). For the opening event of the campaign, Mavety Hall was filled to capacity. The candidate's slogan—"Reform by Reformers"—was emblazoned across the south wall in large red letters on a white background. On the stage with his mother-in-law and a half-dozen others, McRuer waited as one speaker arraigned the Bennett government during a forty-minute oration, and then he himself took the podium to declare: "The flag is up. Come, fight with me, and drive out the enemy." He warned his supporters that it would be a long and hard fight, and that "every trick and every artifice of election engineers" would be used by the Conservatives. "But I tell you and I tell the enemy in High Park that all the Tory campaign chest cannot buy the people in High Park."

McRuer launched his campaign by issuing a little fold-out card-brochure containing his sixteen-point program, with a picture of him on the cover, shyly smiling at the electorate under his brown-rimmed pince-nez glasses and his black toothbrush moustache. He learned from his official agent, H.H. Gibson, why the brochure was printed by the Kendal Printing Company: that company was a union shop, and the union logo printed on the card would send a signal of support and solidarity to the workers of High Park. McRuer was certainly grateful that party "pros" were tending to these finer details of constituency campaigning, because he was making his appeal on a very different level indeed.

One detail that was not so finely handled was the matter of his home address. When McRuer listed it as City of Toronto rather than Forest Hill Village, his opponents concluded that "he has decided his beautiful home on the hill is a disadvantage in this present campaign." In marked contrast to the Liberal candidate, the Conservatives noted, the incumbent MP "has both lived and worked in this riding for the past forty-four years. It is not necessary to journey by motorcar to the secluded isolation of Forest Hill Village to obtain the assistance of Mr. Anderson."[27]

There were no all-candidate debates—other than a comical attempt at one when the candidates gathered at the returning office for the formality of filing their nomination papers. Promptly at the 2 o'clock deadline, returning officer W.A. Carter received the candidates' papers and declared the meeting adjourned. "There will be no speeches," he said. Both McRuer and CCF candidate Le Bourdais challenged this decision, and various people fought to make themselves heard in the ensuing uproar until the manager of the building threatened to evict everyone. The Conservative MP left during the turmoil and in so doing prompted McRuer to ridicule, when back at Liberal committee rooms, "Mr. Anderson's fear of facing the other candidates." In fact, Anderson had left to attend the funeral of a friend. "Mr. Anderson, as a gentleman, had no option but to do as he did," explained a local paper.[28] After that, candidate McRuer confined himself to addressing his own meetings and debating the other candidates through the newspapers and in campaign literature.

McRuer set out at length his party's positions on the issues of the day—old age pensions for veterans, lower interest rates on mortgages, negotiation of a trade treaty with the United States, unemployment and health insurance, and so on. Juggling his law practice as he campaigned, and supported by stalwarts such as Bob Fowler (later head of the Pulp and Paper Association) and Jim McLennan (later an appeal court judge), he depended much more on public meetings than on door-to-door canvassing. Every Wednesday night for three or four months candidate McRuer held a public meeting in one of his committee rooms to discuss each of his policy planks in turn. Sometimes other Liberal candidates—such as Sam Factor from the riding of Spadina—joined him for these meetings. It was an educational approach, a reach-the-voters-through-their-minds method that reflected an idealistic view of how elections ought to be conducted. Soon, however, the same faces kept appearing at his meetings—a sure sign that his instructive lectures were not reaching the masses. By no means an extrovert, and fond of his dignity, McRuer demurred when asked to sell himself like soap by standing outside the industrial plants at lunchtime and soliciting the votes of the workers. He had a distinct distaste for the glad-handing side of political campaigning, not because he did not recognize its value but because he personally felt so uncomfortable with it.

McRuer was much more at ease delivering a series of radio addresses on CFRB. From 18 September to 10 October, in well-prepared and closely argued talks, McRuer set out his views before a listening audience still drawn by radio's dramatic impact. The broadcasts covered a wide range of subjects—trade and tariffs, railways, the key election issue of unemployment, control of credit, and even Mackenzie King's record as a statesman—and none was more eloquent or passionate than the talk addressing the issue of prison reform. On 2 October, his voice fairly crackling over the CFRB airwaves, McRuer declared: "We pride our-selves on British institutions and British law…but [Canadians] can-not look back with pride on that branch of the administration of the criminal law that is involved in the punishment of those who have offended against it." McRuer, still angered by the Daly inquiry, decried the fact that some 4,000 men and women were incarcerated in Canada's seven penitentiaries, at an annual cost of approximately $500 each. He charged that the Conservative Minister of Justice, Hugh Guthrie, was carelessly mismanaging the penal system and allowing the superinten-dent of penitentiaries, General D.M. Ormond, to impose a militaristic rule that showed no regard for human dignity. "Militarism may crush," he asserted. "It may punish. But it has no place in a policy of reform." Pointing out that Liberal leader Mackenzie King had previously called for a thoroughgoing royal commission into conditions in the penitentia-ries, listing a number of abuses for which Guthrie and Ormond should be held accountable, and recommending the creation of a non-partisan board to oversee Canada's correctional institutions, McRuer insisted that justice be done: "I call on the people of Canada to *demand* a com-plete reconstruction of the penitentiary system of the Dominion. Justice to the moral delinquents demands it, and not only that, but justice to society itself demands it."

As much as McRuer enjoyed his radio campaigning, and as effective as it may have been in helping the Liberal cause, the major publicity drive for his High Park campaign came at a series of public rallies. One of the most memorable was a picnic on 13 July at High Park which was billed as "the biggest political meeting ever held in West Toronto." It was a beautiful summer day and there were races for all, from tots to seniors, as well as special events—tossing the shoe (women only), a mixed three-legged race, a race for elderly women, and a fat man's race. Milk and ice cream were distributed for the children, and a lucky draw was held—with a washing machine as the grand prize.

As the events drew to a close and the picnic baskets were gathered up, the crowd of 2,000 to 5,000 people (the size depended on whether one accepted the Conservative or Liberal estimate) happily sat back and listened to oratory from J.C. Elliott, a former Liberal minister of public works, William Mulock, MP for North York, the next provincial Liberal candidate in High Park, J.G. Culnan, and finally, with the crowd well primed, McRuer himself. After the candidate's "forceful" speech, the master of ceremonies for the picnic introduced a surprise guest, Agnes Macphail, who, by remarkable coincidence, had been driving into Toronto when she heard about the picnic and decided to attend. "Just delighted" to be there, she explained how, in need of the best legal counsel available, she had turned to J.C. McRuer. It was a fine endorsement, and she would repeat it on 9 October at a public meeting in her own constituency, where she stated that "Canada needs now, more than she ever needed, representatives of the calibre of Mr. McRuer, men who put the interests of the public first and, even at personal sacrifice, are ready to give public service to causes which they realize are for the country's welfare."[29]

The biggest rally of all—billed as a "Monster Liberal Party" and an organizational triumph of the highest order—took place in the Ravina Gardens on 4 October and was attended by 7,000 cheering McRuer supporters. Premier Mitch Hepburn himself came to add a little lustre and his famous common touch to McRuer's campaign, and Vincent Massey and Professor Norman Rogers of Queen's University, another prominent Liberal candidate, were also there to boost the party's effort in High Park. Hepburn, whom the *Globe* described as the "stellar attraction in the galaxy of talent" at the rally, walked alongside McRuer as they entered the arena. As they did so, the premier turned to Jim and said, "Jim, it's all in the bag."[30]

The rally was an outstanding success, but a week later, at the eleventh hour of the campaign, Conservative candidate A.J. Anderson dropped the Tories' bombshell. Anderson asserted that McRuer had received $44,000 in legal fees from the former King administration—a hefty sum to voters in the Depression—and this charge was repeated on radio by none other than McRuer's own mentor, Colonel Billy Price. McRuer was furious and fought back. He insisted that Anderson had grossly exaggerated the amount; he noted that he had been retained by the Conservative governments of premiers Ferguson and Henry and for this work had been paid fees just as high or higher; and he reminded voters that he had gotten results in busting trusts—the work for which he had been paid—and that, if elected as an MP, he would be ineligible for any more government work in the future. This counter-attack was followed, five days before voting, by another blast from McRuer's opponents. An article in the *Telegram* claimed that McRuer was drawing the "quite considerable salary of $3,500 per year for his very nominal duties as solicitor to the Police Commission." He should, said the paper, "be content with one foot in the trough." The final campaign brochure from the McRuer camp pointed out that he had been appointed to the police commission by the previous Conservative administration, that he was paid on exactly the same basis as other appointees, and that his work for the commission was strictly non-political.

Yet the damage was done. Not even an editorial page endorsement in the *Globe*[31] and the support of Agnes Macphail helped. On election day, 14 October, a drained and tired McRuer was encouraged by some early results. Soon he saw how the tide was running, however, and telephoned Anderson to concede defeat. He had lost by a decisive 2,600 votes, although he could save some face by claiming that Anderson's margin of victory from the last election had been cut substantially. A significant factor in his defeat, besides the charges of Anderson and the *Telegram*, was the vote-splitting among the candidates; the CCF and Reconstruction candidates combined took almost as many votes as McRuer. Had the election been a two-way Liberal-Conservative fight, McRuer would surely have been elected.

The Liberal Party nationally had scored a smashing victory—171 seats to 39 for the Conservatives, 17 for the Social Credit, 7 for the CCF, 1 for the Reconstructionists, and 10 others. While this was some consolation for McRuer, his own defeat weighed heavily on him. Demoralized by the sour ending of the High Park campaign, and still saddened by the death of his father, he dropped everything and, accompanied by his wife, went north to the Big Chief Lodge near Orillia for some much needed rest.

Upon reflection, McRuer realized that he had enjoyed the 1935 campaign. It had brought him much public attention, and it had yielded valuable insights into human nature and the ways of the political world. Still, his defeat was a bitter blow, and it would take him some time to get over it. A few weeks after the election, the new minister of finance, Charles Dunning, consoled McRuer by telling him that he was lucky not to have won—a sentiment with which McRuer's wife agreed. Mackenzie King's sweep, Dunning noted, had brought so many junior MPs into the House of Commons that McRuer would have been a very frustrated backbencher for a long period. McRuer saw the aptness of Dunning's remarks, and, as the years passed, the scars of the 1935 campaign healed.

With time, he even began to realize that he had never been suited to politics anyway. Accepting his limitations—his inability to mix easily with
other people, his dislike of political glad-handing, his mediocre talents
as a public speaker (a high and reedy voice was not the least of his weaknesses in this area)—he concluded that he had been blessed in his near
escape from a life in politics. He also became convinced that he should
never seek election again. In a letter several years later, on 27 March 1940,
to another unsuccessful Liberal candidate, Joseph Bench of St. Catharines, McRuer said that he often recalled Dunning's words. The "exigen-
cies of political life," he remarked consolingly, "are often cruel to their
victims."

MCRUER'S ADJUSTMENT to electoral defeat was only beginning when he
had to make another accommodation with his world in 1935. Two weeks
after the election, a sombre McRuer attended St. Andrew's Church
in Toronto for the funeral service of his old bible class teacher, Frank
Yeigh. McRuer had done more than just keep in touch with Yeigh over
the years; he had been become president of the "Frank Yeigh Old Boys'
Association," which included among its activities the raising of money
for various charitable projects. One of the causes supported by the association was the Grenfell Mission hospital in Labrador, and, after Yeigh's
death, McRuer set himself to providing the hospital with a new, fully
equipped ward. The ward opened in 1936 and was known as the "Frank
Yeigh Memorial Room." In it hung the same picture of Yeigh that had
decorated the bible classroom for so many years.[32]

By the end of the year 1935, then, Jim McRuer had his share of wounds
to nurse. Yet he was not the kind of person who reacts to reverses by
lapsing into inactivity. On the contrary, he had more reason than ever
to throw himself into his work—of which there was no shortage. In
addition to his private practice, McRuer soon received a new assignment from government. Mackenzie King, ensconced once more in the
prime minister's office, was aware of McRuer's sacrifice in the election.
He cabled him a telegram of regret and shortly afterwards, in early 1936,
rewarded him with the position of chief counsel to a royal commission.
This commission, headed by Mr. Justice W.F.A. Turgeon of the Saskatchewan Court of Appeal, had been set up by the Liberal government to
investigate the Canadian textile industry. The pretext for the creation of
this commission was the decision of the Dominion Textile company to
close its plant in Sherbrooke, Quebec; the commission's mandate called

for the gathering of "full and complete information" about Dominion Textile's operations, and the textile industry in general, so as to enable the government to reach "sound conclusions" regarding this industry's position "in relation to British and foreign competition, and in particular, the extent to which the employer can reasonably and properly be expected to maintain employment over periods of temporary difficulty."[33] Factory closings do not normally spawn royal commissions, but in this case Mackenzie King—an expert on labour relations—appears to have been angered that an industry long protected by tariffs could shut down factories and so cause significant social distress without divulging the reasons for its decision. This was not the whole story, however; the government also had a political agenda. King, long an avowed foe of the tariff-coddled textile manufacturers, had learned during the 1935 election that employees at several textile companies found a note in their pay packets advising them to vote Conservative. The Liberal prime minister was determined to get higher wages for textile workers, and a lower textile price for Canadians, by freer trade. He also wanted revenge.

By the time the commission began operation, Dominion Textile had actually reopened its doors. If this action was intended to undercut the commission's work at the outset, however, it failed. The commission paid special attention to the operations of the Dominion Textile conglomerate and its organizing genius, Montreal millionaire Sir Charles Blair Gordon, who was also president of the Bank of Montreal and Royal Trust and a director of the CPR, Sherbrooke Cotton, and Drummondville Cotton; coincidentally, Gordon even happened to be chairman of Penman's Mills of Paris, Ontario, the firm that had awarded Jim McRuer a $12 high school entrance prize thirty-one years earlier. Moving beyond the specific case of Dominion Textile to consider the industry as a whole, the commission investigated complaints that retailers and importers were being squeezed and textile workers paid starvation wages while the companies, protected behind tariff walls, returned vast profits to their investors—some of which ended up in the coffers of the Conservative Party.

For McRuer, it was comforting to get back into this kind of groove, where his talents could be channelled more productively than on the dangerously unchartered tracks of political campaigning. He was also delighted to be closely associated with Justice Turgeon. Highly educated, beautifully fluent in both English and French, with a powerful and analytic mind, Turgeon had a great capacity for remembering facts, stories, and names, from the bellhop at the Fort Garry Hotel to leaders in all walks of life. Further adding to the interest of the commission's work was the presence of Aimé Geoffrion as Sir Charles Gordon's chief counsel. Geoffrion, who had frequently argued cases before the Supreme Court and Privy Council, charmed McRuer with his concise brilliance and conducted the defence of Gordon without a word of acrimony or ill nature, all of which led, as McRuer said, to "a very pleasant investigation."

"Pleasant" described the relationship among those doing the investigation, not the subject nor their approach to it. As commission counsel, McRuer prepared and submitted his own lengthy legal brief to the commission, arguing that "it is a common law right of every citizen of Canada to purchase the goods he wants in the cheapest markets of the world. Unless legislation imposed by government restrained him from doing so, no court in the land can deprive him of that right. When, however, a protective tariff was lawfully applied against the importation of any article, the effect of such was to give the manufacturer of that article in Canada the private right of taxation." McRuer felt that the government was quite correct in asking companies what they did with their high profits, and if they were applied to capital, "was it fair that the customer should again be required to pay for profits earned upon it?" At another point in the brief, McRuer offered an even more revealing statement of his political philosophy:

"The evidence shows that in its relations with the public and its employees the leaders of this industry have maintained little regard for human relations. The laws of power appear to have dominated and directed the policy of the industry, rather than regard for justice.

"The strife between capital and labour will continue with unremitting bitterness as long as employers seek legal advantages and special privileges from various governments of the dominion and arrogantly deny to their employees, on whose behalf these advantages are obtained, any share in or control over the direction of the policies under which the fruits of those advantages and privileges are distributed."[34]

This message was subsequently quoted with approval by the leader of the CCF, J.S. Woodsworth.[35] The business community was less impressed. Describing McRuer as a "decent, competent, quiet Toronto lawyer who made an excellent Sunday school teacher," the *Financial Post* wondered "what it is that turns men of such reserved temperament into headline-seeking corporation baiters." McRuer had castigated specific textile companies for making excessive profits, but the *Financial Post* asked whether he himself was not guilty of the same sin—his $150-per-day fee as commission counsel amounted to a substantial profit on the money he had "in his pockets when he started in the law business." Chastising him for "building up the idea that to earn a profit is sinful," the *Financial Post* concluded that "Mr. McRuer at the moment is not a lawyer but a manu-facturer—a manufacturer of headlines."[36]

The work of the Turgeon commission occupied McRuer for six months. Its report, which was not tabled in the House of Commons until March 1938, exonerated Gordon, placing the blame for the closing of Domin-ion Textile's Sherbrooke plant on the local manager. On the larger issue of the relationship between government and the tariff-supported textile industry, the commission concluded that "there is an undertaking on the part of the manufacturer, so long as he continues to enjoy the advan-tage of the tariff, to refrain from throwing workmen out of employment especially in times of distress, without reasonable justification or excuse." Operating from this perspective, the commission recommended that the Customs Tariff of 1931 be amended to allow the government to withdraw tariff protection from any companies who ignored their responsibilities to the community.[37] It was a daring recommendation—perhaps too dar-ing. In the end, no direct action was taken on the commission's report. From 1939 on, the government was too preoccupied with fighting the Second World War to give much thought to reforming the Canadian tex-tile industry. A few months after his work with the Turgeon commission came to an end, McRuer received yet another offer of employment from the federal government. Although he was initially reluctant to accept it— he still burned over allegations that he was always getting large fees from Liberal governments—he could not ultimately refuse: the offer appealed to his most basic convictions about justice, drew on his recent experi-ence with Agnes Macphail and the Daly inquiry, and promised not only to broaden his own horizons considerably but also to result in tangible and far-reaching social reform. The King government wanted to appoint McRuer to a royal commission investigating conditions in Canada's pris-ons—the very thing he had advocated so vigorously in the recent elec-tion. As it turned out, his involvement in the commission would plunge him into a world whose injustices and horrors were worse than anything he had encountered before.

7

INSIDE CANADA'S PRISONS

THE CREATION OF A ROYAL COMMISSION on Canada's prison system was mainly the result of the efforts of McRuer's friend Agnes Macphail. After her re-election in 1935, Macphail continually pestered the King government for her long-cherished investigation of the country's prisons, and at length Prime Minister King and Minister of Justice Ernest Lapointe gave in. On 27 February 1936 the government passed an order-in-council creating a royal commission "to inquire into and report upon the penal system of Canada."[1] For the post of chairman of the commission, known officially as the Royal Commission to Investigate the Penal System of Canada, the government selected Mr. Justice Joseph Archambault, a judge of the Superior Court of Quebec. Assisting Archambault were two other commissioners: R.W. Craig, a prominent Winnipeg lawyer and former attorney-general of Manitoba, and Harry W. Anderson, the editor of the Toronto *Globe* who had made prison reform a personal mission.

The Archambault commission encountered remarkable difficulties at the outset. Indeed, there were enough ghoulish signs surrounding the commission to make the superstitious prime minister leery about having anything more to do with it. Shortly after the order-in-council of February 1936, Archambault was involved in serious accidents that left him with two broken legs; he was totally immobilized for several months and walked only with the greatest difficulty thereafter. (Agnes Macphail, reflecting on the commission's misfortunes in its early days, remarked that, if Archambault had had more than two legs, "they would have gone also."[2]) Then, on 28 April 1936, Harry Anderson suddenly died. This came as a great blow to those interested in the commission, for Anderson, a keen student of criminology and penal reform, had been counted upon to push forcefully for the cause. Yet more bad news was to come. Anderson's replacement, the editor of the *London Free Press*, Mel W. Rossie, died before he could receive his official appointment.

The Liberal government then revisited its files. King and Lapointe needed a man with three essential qualifications to fill the open position on the Archambault commission. First, and most important, the individual must have a proven record as a reliable Liberal and Mackenzie King loyalist. Secondly, the candidate should, at least in the eyes of the public, be a person of independent judgment and possess some credentials in the field of penal reform. Thirdly, King wanted both a man to whom he owed something and one whom he could use in the future. Hating to waste any opportunity of capitalizing on his power of granting patronage, he intended to use this appointment to pay off old political debts. At the same time he hoped to invest in the future by contracting new debts in his own favour through this appointment—a goal that could be accomplished only if the candidate in question had a promising career ahead of him. Weighing these considerations, King decided on James McRuer.

Lapointe telephoned McRuer on 14 September to offer him the job, and McRuer, without an ounce of superstition in his body, accepted. The only condition he stipulated concerned the matter of his fee. Still feeling stung by attacks on his integrity during the election, and worried that he would be criticized as a lawyer looking only for government briefs, he insisted on receiving no fee whatsoever. In the end, he agreed to accept a $35-a-day expense allowance.[3] His appointment as commissioner was made official by order-in-council on 17 September 1936.[4]

McRuer's appointment raised a few eyebrows in informed circles, for everyone who knew him realized that he meant business. This legal terrier was not the kind of person Mackenzie King should have appointed, they thought, unless he had the idea of seeing the project through—all the way. Macphail, although not one of the doubters, was jokingly apprehensive. Before McRuer's appointment had been announced, she wrote to a friend: "I believe now McRuer, the lawyer who gratuitously acted as counsel for me in the minor investigation a year ago, is to be offered the third place. Much as I want him to accept it, one fears for him if he does."[5] McRuer himself, however, had no fears. Fresh from an unhappy experience in the recent election, he was slowly coming to understand that he was most likely to achieve his goals, not by seeking elective office, but by working through the judiciary and other appointed branches of the government. He was certainly aware of the many ways in which politicians abused royal commissions by treating them as excuses for inaction, but he steadfastly believed that such independent bodies of inquiry formed an integral component of the British constitutional tradition. The custom of seeking the advice of experts on especially troublesome problems, McRuer believed, protected society from the machinations of unscrupulous politicians.

These beliefs were to be sorely tested in the years ahead. In the fall of 1936, however, McRuer was full of optimism. The Archambault commission was finally getting under way, and McRuer was hopeful that its investigation of Canada's prisons would herald the dawning of a new age for those confined within their walls.

THE ARCHAMBAULT COMMISSION, after its ill-fated launching, began work in early October 1936. With breaks for travel, special planning sessions, and the rare day off, the commission took evidence for the next fourteen months, until 15 December 1937. In the course of a long stretch of hearings, the commissioners visited all seven federal penitentiaries in Canada—Dorchester Penitentiary, in New Brunswick; St. Vincent de Paul Penitentiary, just outside Montreal; Kingston and Collins Bay penitentiaries, both in Ontario; and the Manitoba, Saskatchewan, and British Columbia penitentiaries. McRuer missed only Dorchester, and for the hearing at that penitentiary he later read every word of the evidence in transcript form. When visiting each of these penitentiaries, the commissioners also went to the affiliated facilities for women. In addition, they visited about fifty provincial institutions, including prisons, hospitals for the insane, detention homes for girls and boys, training schools, and police stations. Numerous interviews were conducted, as well, outside these institutions. Finally, after visiting nineteen similar prisons in the United States and nineteen more in England, the commissioners realized that, given the number of institutions they still hoped to examine, the time had come to divide up their efforts. So, either singly or in pairs, they next visited three institutions in Scotland, three in Holland, eight in Belgium, six in France, five in Germany, and one in Switzerland. In all, the commission visited 113 institutions in nine different countries.[6]

The commission was determined to let everyone in the penitentiary system have a fair opportunity to express themselves. In advance of a visit to a federal penitentiary, they had notices placed around the institution informing all prisoners, guards, and support staff that the commission wished to interview anyone who had anything at all to say. Interviews— whether with a night cleaner or a convicted mass murderer—were held strictly *in camera*, with not so much as a guard present to protect the commissioners. Only after all these interviews were conducted did the commission meet in Ottawa to hear the evidence of the superintendent of penitentiaries, the three inspectors, the chief engineer, the head of the Remission Branch, the deputy minister of justice, and the undersecretary of state. By adopting this method, the commissioners were convinced that they gained the confidence of both officers and inmates and that, as a result, information was obtained which otherwise might have been withheld. This method also deterred witnesses from seeking publicity, the commissioners believed, and prevented the publication of distorted reports that would have conveyed erroneous impressions.

Others—a number of newspaper editors, Conservative MPs, federal bureaucrats responsible for the penal system, and private citizens—took a more jaundiced view of the commission's approach. These critics charged that, by granting the top officials in Ottawa an opportunity to address the commission only at the last stages of the inquiry, the commissioners gave the impression that the officials were being put on trial by countless and nameless witnesses in Canada's penal institutions. Moreover, since the identities of the earlier witnesses were protected, the authorities were effectively denied the right to face their accusers. Under the cover of anonymity, it was suggested, the witnesses were also bound to seek revenge on the authorities through exaggerated stories and false allegations. Even before the commission brought down its report, then, there were many people who were predisposed against it.

During the course of their inquiry the commissioners were repeatedly shocked by the things they witnessed. Between 1932 and 1937 there had been sixteen full-scale riots in Canada's seven penitentiaries, and the commissioners soon began to see why.[7] The superintendent of penitentiaries, General D.M. Ormond, was a good military man but seriously miscast in his role as head of the prison system. A stickler for rules and discipline, he had issued a set of no less than 724 regulations which were designed to govern virtually every aspect of life in the penitentiaries with draconian rigour. Nowhere was there evidence of any genuine attempt to effect the prisoners' rehabilitation; on the contrary, the entire emphasis was on punishment, and severe beatings were regularly meted out for the most trivial reasons. There were no parole boards at this time, only a ticket-of-leave system that operated on political influence. The treatment of prisoners in the penitentiaries depended on the whims of different wardens, some of whom were fine men, some of whom were not. In any case, the military discipline of the system meant that the guards had to adhere strictly to almost military orders, which made humanitarian intervention in particular cases almost impossible. On top of all of this, the penitentiaries lacked any system of classification of prisoners. There was no segregation of different types of prisoners; young offenders, convicted of their first crime, found themselves side by side with hardened criminals. The mentally ill were frequently locked away without treatment. Even those with infectious diseases were often left to rot away, lost in the general prison population.

Long after the commission's hearings were over, McRuer was haunted by the nightmarish scenes he had witnessed. The sight of a man ranting to himself, alone, strait-jacketed in a padded cell, kept coming back to him. No help was available to this suffering soul because of a situation that was almost Kafkaesque: incarcerated in a federal prison, he could not be transferred to a hospital for the mentally ill because such institutions fell under provincial jurisdiction and his province refused to admit him to one. Nor could McRuer ever forget the so-called "conversation hour" in St. Vincent de Paul Penitentiary in Quebec. In this institution, the prisoners were enjoined to keep silent for all but one hour each day. One of the prisoners, in for a white-collar crime, pleaded with the commissioners, "Whatever you do, do away with the conversation hour." McRuer decided to witness this spectacle himself, and one afternoon he went into the dome of the prison, a huge round building with several circular tiers of cells around an open courtyard with a skylight. At the sound of a bell, the prisoners were allowed to talk. During the hour that followed, the noise was horrendous: inmates locked in their cells would shout to their friends down the corridor, scream at the guards, and rant and rave at themselves or the universe, venting the hopelessness pent up inside them. As McRuer stood there and heard the din, he thought he was in hell, consigned to the most awful bedlam imaginable. It reminded him of the ape house at the Riverdale Zoo in Toronto. The only difference was that the animals at the zoo were treated better.

Also at St. Vincent de Paul, a guard escorted McRuer to the "solitary" section to see two dangerous prisoners who were not allowed to mingle with the other men. McRuer found a raving insane man in a completely bare cell, the Black Hole, urgently clutching the bars and howling, "They're taking the gold out of my teeth!" At another institution, the penitentiary at Prince Albert in Saskatchewan, McRuer was outraged by the stupidity of the "keepers." Here the usual prisoners' reports of ill-treatment had an unusual twist. Each and every one of them complained that their food, especially the porridge, was constantly contaminated with mouse droppings. At first the commissioners did not take these complaints too seriously, since stories about bad food usually masked concerns about brutality. McRuer's temper was unusually long for a Scot, but after hearing the charge about contaminated food repeated again and again, he finally had had enough. He demanded a tour of the prison's kitchen and storehouse, and there, to his amazement, he saw mice running everywhere. He even found one large bag of oatmeal with the bottom chewed out by mice and a hole as big as his hand. The cook explained that it was impossible to keep the mice out, but this excuse did not rest well with McRuer. Casting his eyes knowingly about the room— once a farm boy, always a farm boy—he quickly spotted the source of the problem: a chewed hole gaped in the corner of the kitchen's wooden door, through which mice were running with all the efficiency of the London tube system. He then exploded, instructing the staff to put a piece of tin over the hole "or answer to me."[8]

If stupidity and incompetence sometimes angered McRuer, cruelty always made his blood boil. He could scarcely believe the ways in which corporal punishment was administered in Canada's prisons. Prisoners were routinely given ten lashes when they entered the prison, and, no matter how well they behaved during incarceration, another ten lashes when leaving, by way of good riddance. This final whipping was designed to keep a man on the straight and narrow by reminding him of the awfulness of life in prison. The sight of the fresh whip wounds, the theory went, would also have a salutary effect on the ex-convict's friends and acquaintances who greeted him upon his return to society.

The procedure was brutal, and the weapons barbaric. Typically, the man was called into an office and made to strip naked. A table was produced, and his ankles were bound to its legs. He was then forced to bend forward over the tabletop. Official explanations pointed out that this arrangement ensured that the guard assigned to administer the whip would have a clear shot at the prisoner's back. In practice, it guaranteed that his testicles would be struck—inflicting excruciating pain. No warden of a Canadian prison had been known to object when the torturer's scourge slipped below the back of the prisoner.

In fact, Canadian penal authorities had shown unaccustomed efficiency in developing their instruments of torture. The commissioners found that the instruments used—whether to execute the sentences of the courts or for purposes of prison discipline—were not uniform. A number of different whips were officially authorized by federal regulations. The basic instrument was a leather strap, perhaps one-quarter of an inch thick and three inches wide. The application of this strap would ensure stinging pain without necessarily doing much damage to the skin surface. The second officially sanctioned scourge, a variation on the first, had holes about the size of a fingertip drilled through the strap. When applied with customary force, this strap would bite into the skin. If used "efficiently"—and there is no record of mercy being shown in these cases—the drilled strap could easily produce great welts in the prisoner's skin after only a few applications; one or two more lashes generally pulled the prisoner's skin off in patches. The commissioners would recommend its abolition. The third method of torture sounds more innocent. After all, it was only made of rope. But this unmatted rope whip was a version of the cat-o'-nine-tails, and, when its hard cords of twine were applied, a guard could hit a prisoner on the back of the neck and on the testicles with a single stroke.

Several other officially sanctioned modes of torture were variations on this whip. One was a rope whip, the strands of which had been knotted—the real cat-o'-nine-tails. Needless to say, the knots bit like daggers into the skin, always drawing blood. Another was a cat-gut version of the cat-o'-nine-tails. As the officials so very well knew, whereas rope applied with force cuts through the body like barbed wire, cat-gut acts like a razor. The last whip was made of knotted cat-gut: the ideal means of breaking a body.

Everywhere McRuer went he asked the professionals and inmates the same question: "In your opinion, what is the greatest cause of crime?" And everywhere the answer was the same—"broken homes," whether by failed marriages or the death of one of the parents. Sometimes the question boomeranged. On their visit to the penitentiary in Winnipeg, McRuer, Archambault, and Craig were trapped for half an hour in a 6' × 4' elevator with a talkative convict-witness, Harry Carlson, who regaled them with his "cure-all for crime"—a good job for everyone. The incident was reported to the papers and one headline gleefully noted, "Penal Commissioners Get a Taste of Cell Life in Stalled Elevator."[9]

Some of the sessions were exhausting. The commissioners spent six weeks in Kingston alone, determined to gather as much evidence as possible. They grilled General Ormond for eight days and found that he had "no concept whatever of the human side of the operation of penal systems" and had created a bureaucratic, nightmarish regime.[10] Nor did

Ormond have any sense of the right of prisoners, on being accused of misconduct, to a fair hearing. The superintendent saw "nothing wrong in a man being flogged for an offence he had never been tried for."[11] His 724 regulations, issued without consultation with the wardens, had contributed to low morale and to the sixteen riots between 1932 and 1937. He showed little concern over the fact that, during one riot, guards had shot at a prisoner in his cell—a prisoner who happened to be Tim Buck, convicted as a Communist subversive but in truth the leader of the legally recognized Communist Party of Canada. Ormond had even banned the baseball games instituted at the Kingston penitentiary by warden W.B. Megloughlin.

On their visits abroad, the commissioners adopted a more low-key, less intrusive approach. Mindful of the sensitivities of their hosts, they contented themselves with interviewing local officials and observing conditions in the prisons during guided tours. Yet the trips were immensely useful. McRuer, for one, believed that he was able to identify clearly some solutions—and some examples to avoid—as a result of his time in the United States, Britain, Belgium, Holland, Austria, and France talking to the experts and comparing the various systems of penal servitude and reform. In Holland, he was shaken by the spectacle of prisoners forced to wear paper bags over their heads to prevent visitors from seeing them; and in France he felt that the authorities put too much of a premium on harsh work. In Britain, however, he was impressed. The Borstal system, he concluded, was doing a superior job in educating low-risk young prisoners by placing them in unguarded institutions that were operated like carefully run schools, each with about fifty offenders under a house-master. McRuer was taken with the sincerity of one instructor at a Borstal institution who was personally distressed when a boy escaped because he felt it was a poor reflection on his abilities in rehabilitation. McRuer was also struck by the amount of volunteer help available in British jails. At Wichfield prison in Devon, McRuer met a young school teacher who taught mathematics to an inmate for two hours a week. The director of prisons in England assured McRuer that he had no trouble in getting reliable volunteers, and that they were carefully screened.[12]

Over the course of 1937, much of the commission's work devolved upon Archambault and McRuer, since Craig had fallen in love with a woman from New Jersey, whom he met while the Archambault commission was visiting the state. Indeed most of the leg work was always McRuer's, since the still-crippled Archambault had to walk with two canes. Working so closely together for such a long period of time proved to be a strain for both men, and it was therefore no accident when they decided to go their own ways on their trip to Europe in 1937. Archambault disappeared with his devoted wife, who had hovered about him with both the discretion and the care of a guardian angel throughout the proceedings. McRuer, for his part, juggled arrangements so that he was able, at his own expense, to take his wife Mary and his daughter Katherine to Europe. After he had finished touring prisons, the trio paid a visit to Vienna.[13]

After concluding their hearings the Archambault commissioners began the work of compiling their report. By this time Archambault and McRuer had entirely given up on Craig—partly because he had not been pulling his weight, and partly because he did not share the views of his fellow commissioners. Throughout late 1937 and early 1938 Archambault and McRuer maintained an intense dialogue between themselves about the commission's findings, and the two men agreed on how they would collaborate in the production of the commission's report. Archambault drafted certain chapters while McRuer looked after the rest. They exchanged each other's draft chapters, criticized them, and then sat down together to work out the details. When the commissioners completed their report on 4 April 1938, they felt satisfied that they had formulated a detailed, far-reaching blueprint for penal reform. No one, not even their critics, would have disputed that assessment.

THE ROYAL COMMISSION ON THE PENAL SYSTEM of Canada formally presented its report, dated 4 April 1938, to cabinet in June. This report presented eighty-eight recommendations in nearly two dozen different categories. The categories included centralized control, reorganization of administration, classification of prisoners, prison discipline, use of firearms, recreation, education, medical service, religious services, prison employment, prison pay, women prisoners, internationally standard minimum rules, amendments to the Criminal Code, prevention of crime, statistical information, juvenile and family courts, adult probation, reports to sentencing judges, ticket-of-leave and parole, rehabilitation, and penitentiary conditions.

The report's central conclusion was that "there are very few, if any, prisoners" who did not leave penitentiaries "worse members of society than when they entered." Its underlying goal, which the commissioners urged on all Canadians, was the evolution of a penal system with the primary purpose of protecting society. "It is of the greatest importance

that this system should be characterized by that firm dignity that is traditional in the British administration of justice. There is no place in it for
weak sentimentality or for cruel severity."[14]

One unequivocal recommendation was the immediate removal of
General Ormond as superintendent of Canada's penitentiary system.
The commissioners' report was sprinkled throughout with criticisms of
Ormond, and his role in the "unsatisfactory aspects of the administration of the penitentiaries" was described in detail. "He has displayed,"
the report concluded, "an irritating manner of exercising authority," and
this failing on his part was "one of the major contributing causes of the
sixteen riots or disturbances which have taken place since the Superintendent assumed office." Ormond, the commissioners asserted, had
"completely lost the confidence of the staffs of all the penitentiaries and,
without this, no administration can succeed."[15]

This sharply worded condemnation of Ormond, which contrasted
with the balanced tone of the rest of the report, bore more of Jim McRuer's style than of Archambault's; one writer to the Ottawa Journal, a paper
that denounced the Archambault report's "vindictive tone," described
McRuer as a "very aggressive, dominating lawyer...whose temperament is the opposite of judicial."[16] Ultimately, the commission's attack on
Ormond was counter-productive, for it sparked a political row that distracted attention from the report's more substantive recommendations.

Apart from the immediate removal of General Ormond as superintendent, the commissioners believed that an essential first step in the reform
of Canada's penal system was the comprehensive reorganization of the
system's administration. They maintained that all prisons in Canada
should be placed under the control of the federal authorities, except for
a small number designed specifically "to provide for offenders against
provincial statutes, prisoners on remand, and those serving short sentences."[17] The national penal system should be directed by a powerful and
independent three-member prison commission, but individual prison
wardens should, in concert with this body, be granted more authority to make executive decisions at the local level. Penitentiary officers,
probation officers, and parole officers should become a well-paid professional group trained through innovative university programs and a new
school specializing in penal matters. Merit, not political considerations,
should govern all decisions about appointments and promotions, and
"all hopelessly incapable officers should be retired."[18] Prison regulations
should be completely revised and permanent boards of visitors should
be established at the local level to ensure that these regulations would

be enforced on a continuous basis. At all times, rules and procedures in the prisons should be based on four essential principles: the protection of society; the safe custody of inmates; strict but humane discipline; and the reformation and rehabilitation of prisoners.

For this new administrative system to meet its objectives efficiently, the Archambault commissioners believed that a comprehensive means of classifying and segregating prisoners had to be introduced. All prisoners should be assessed medically and psychiatrically. The seriousness of their crimes, their age, and the likelihood of their reformation and rehabilitation should be evaluated. Separate institutions ought to be established for incorrigible offenders, young offenders, mentally handicapped offenders, insane prisoners, drug addicts, and so on, and within each institution further distinctions should be drawn between those who were reformable and those who seemed destined to a life of recidivism. Proper classification and segregation of prisoners, the commissioners believed, would bring a number of benefits woefully absent under the system they had seen, Such measures would promote the rehabilitation of convicts, ensure that hardened criminals would be prevented from "contaminating" their fellow inmates, and allow the authorities an opportunity to administer justice within the system on an equitable basis.[19]

Next, the commissioners insisted that a scientific and fair system of reward and punishment be enforced in all the penal institutions. All prison offences ought to be tried before a properly constituted prison court, and prisoners should have the right of appeal to the local board of visitors. In a radical departure from Canadian tradition, the commissioners also recommended that "corporal punishment should be abolished except for the offences of assaulting an officer, mutiny, and incitement to mutiny."[20] Moreover, prison officers should be allowed to use firearms only in the most extreme situations, and misuse of those weapons should be treated as a criminal offence.

Pursuing this theme, the commissioners reasoned that, just as the use of punishment should be better regulated, so the use of rewards for appropriate behaviour should be extended. More recreation time, better access to reading and writing materials, and increased visiting privileges should all be introduced for convicts who showed respect for the rules of the system. Above all, educational opportunities should be enhanced, and young offenders in particular should be given the chance to acquire the skills they needed to succeed in society after release. Finally, medical services should be reorganized to meet the genuine needs of the individual prisoner, and better access to religious services should be provided.[21]

The last recommendation was dear to McRuer. Many of the other recommendations, aimed at curbing cruelty and injustices within prisons, had been motivated by anger and disgust. Yet the recommendation regarding religious services came from a different part of McRuer. It was based on his understanding that, while many of the broken people ending up inside Canada's penitentiaries could be trained for re-entry to society, they would not be truly rehabilitated and set on a new course unless and until something new—the light of religious conscience—was sparked inside them.

The commission maintained that all services provided or made available to inmates, whether religious, medical, or educational, should encourage their social readjustment and should always provide tangible evidence of society's good will. As a reward for good behaviour, the commissioners recommended that prisoners be allowed to earn a small monetary compensation through compulsory work in a new system of prison farms and industries. While these economic projects should not be allowed to compete with private enterprise, they should be able to provide essential goods and services to the penal system and other government departments. Properly managed prison farms and workshops, it was felt, could make Canada's prisons self-sufficient in many areas, and in the process prisoners could acquire valuable skills and work experience. The commissioners recommended that all able-bodied prisoners be compelled to work at least ten hours per day. That the human resources of the prison population could be left unexploited while prisoners languished in their cells hour after hour seemed nothing short of a national disgrace to Archambault and McRuer.[22]

The commissioners then turned to the custody of female prisoners, and their treatment of this problem was marked by some subtle insights into the role of women in Canadian society. It began with an observation about the "comparatively unimportant part played by women in crime in this country." Crime was overwhelmingly a male enterprise, and women accounted for only a very small portion of the criminal population. "However," the commissioners went on to point out, "the fundamental principles of reformation apply equally to both sexes, and, therefore, the principles of classification, training, and education for men prisoners recommended in other chapters should be applied as far as possible to women."[23] Yet the commissioners qualified this recommendation by noting that "when the sick have been deducted, the number of trainable women is very small, and the women prisoners, apart from young prisoners, who are capable of deriving benefit from continued education would constitute a small class."[24] In short, while the commissioners' analysis proceeded on the idea that women and men prisoners should be treated equally, the thrust of their recommendations pointed in other directions, based in good part upon the differences in the size of male and female prison populations. At the time of the Archambault inquiry, women accounted for just 6 per cent of total convictions and 1 per cent of the total population of Canada's federal prisons.

In 1936 there were thirty-two female inmates in the women's penitentiary at Kingston and 2,053 in provincial reformatories and jails.[25] The commissioners were particularly struck by the types of crimes for which women were being incarcerated. For example, they found that, if federal and provincial prisoners were added together, eight women across Canada were imprisoned for abortion-related offences, twelve for prostitution, and 173 for keeping or being inmates in houses of "ill-fame." Another thirty-five had been convicted for breaches of the peace; 206 for being drunk and disorderly; forty-six for "selling or giving liquor to Indians"; two for using "abusive and obscene language"; four for incest; five for bigamy; and three for indecent exposure. No less than forty-five women were locked away as "lunatics and persons unsafe to be at large." A startling 412 women were imprisoned for vagrancy, and 446 were incarcerated for truly minor social offences against public order. The commissioners found that a distressingly large proportion of Canada's female prisoners was drawn from the ranks of the poor.

Equally distressing to the commissioners was the fact that fully 47 per cent of all female convicts (fifteen of the thirty-two) serving penitentiary terms were imprisoned for charges of murder, attempted murder, or manslaughter. Only a small percentage of female prisoners were convicted for premeditated thefts, frauds, and similar crimes, and—rightly or wrongly—the commissioners concluded that most female inmates were really victims of their own feminine nature. "These women are not a crime problem," the commission asserted, "but are of the occasional or accidental offender class, who have been carried away by the overmastering impulse of the moment, often the outbreak of long pent up emotion. They are not a custodial problem, and could be cared for as well in a reformatory as in a penitentiary."

The commissioners concluded that Canada's prison for women at Kingston, and the many provincial reformatories to which women offenders were sent, were generally well kept and under-utilized. They recommended that these institutions should be converted for use as prisons for men, and that most female prisoners could be sent to more humane

facilities designed to meet the special needs of the female prison population. Whether this conclusion was an early blow struck in the cause of
women's rights or simply an example of a sexist set of assumptions about
"woman's nature" is problematic. It is certainly clear that McRuer was
troubled by seeing women locked away, especially in thick-walled cells
and behind walls that were much higher than necessary. Generally, the
commissioners' approach to women's issues in the penal system reflected
a special concern for the problems of females—especially young ones.
They believed that, whenever possible, young women should be placed
on probation rather than institutionalized.[26]

The commissioners were not yet finished. They also demanded that "a
complete revision of the Criminal Code should be undertaken at once"
and that all revisions should meet an acceptable international standard.
This reform should encompass everything from providing legal services
for the poor to restricting the sale of firearms. Moreover, a new effort
should be made to prevent crimes of all sorts, based on three radical
principles, each of which bear McRuer's distinct imprint. First, Canada's
police forces must be thoroughly reformed. Political influence should
have no place in police administration, and all police officers should be
trained according to exacting standards through new educational programs. Secondly, community involvement should be "enlisted in an organized manner" through church and school groups, social service agencies,
and other such vehicles to drive home the message that crime prevention
begins at home. Finally—and most startling to many of the Archambault
report's readers—the state should become actively involved in promoting
social welfare. In the words of the report: "The responsibility of the state
for the financial support of community clubs, boys' and girls' clubs, and
leisure time programs should be recognized. They are a means of preventing or, at least reducing, juvenile and adolescent delinquency."[27]

The commissioners also recommended numerous administrative
reforms to the judicial system. Better methods of keeping statistics
about crime should be developed. Juvenile and family courts should
be reconstructed to prevent the system from inadvertently turning
confused children into hardened criminals. A viable probation system,
staffed by professionals, should be introduced nation-wide. A strict but
compassionate system of parole should be developed. Judges should be
supplied with carefully prepared reports on each prisoner before sentencing, and they should be required to visit prisons on a regular basis in
order to maintain a proper perspective on the kind of sentence that was
appropriate in a given case.[28]

Such were the central recommendations of the Archambault commission. After the report was presented to cabinet, the commissioners waited anxiously for the government's response. In their view, the social fabric of the country faced a serious threat unless the federal government, working in cooperation with provincial authorities, acted quickly to implement their recommendations. As events unfolded, however, it became quite apparent that the commissioners' hopes for immediate reform were destined to be disappointed.

POPULAR REACTION to the Archambault commission's report was decidedly mixed. The *Ottawa Journal* was critical, the *Ottawa Citizen* supportive. That set a pattern, for across the country virtually every newspaper commented editorially over the next few years on the report's recommendations. On balance, a slight majority of the papers supported Archambault and McRuer's findings, particularly that Ormond be removed and replaced by a prison commission. A smaller number supported their suggestion that psychiatric services be provided and that a proper system of parole be set up at the national level. Some got beyond generalized support or opposition and focused on the specific reforms proposed for women prisoners and the calls for centralized administration and better classification of prisoners. Support for the commission's report also came from church groups and organizations such as the Elizabeth Fry Society and the John Howard Society, the Canadian branch of which had been founded recently by McRuer's friend Dennis Draper, chief of police in Toronto. A general view was that prisoners should be punished, not rehabilitated.[29]

In the political arena, the reaction was much the same. Justice Minister Ernest Lapointe introduced a bill in late June 1938 to overhaul the old Penitentiary Act, but its only important change was that respecting the creation of a new penitentiary commission—as recommended in the Archambault report—consisting of three members and vested with the responsibility for the management of the prison system. Lapointe explained that the report's other recommendations would be "carefully studied ... and could be dealt with later by legislation if necessary."[30] The government, always half-hearted in the matter of prison reform, had been driven to create the Archambault commission by the agitation of Agnes Macphail, CCF leader J.S. Woodsworth, and several crusading newspapers. Now, with the release of the commission's report, the government seemed even less enthusiastic about its findings.

A heated debate followed in the House, and the views expressed indicated the wide gulf separating those who "blushed with shame as they
read of the barbaric state of affairs" in Canada's prisons and those who
were "still in favour of running our penitentiaries as places of punishment rather than clinics for the assuagement of jaded nerves."[31] Primarily, however, the issue centred on Superintendent D.M. Ormond—the
Liberals and CCF agreed with the recommendation of the Archambault
commission that he had to go; the Conservatives, led by R.B. Bennett in
the House of Commons and Arthur Meighen in the Senate, vigorously
defended this "Canadian Dreyfus" who was being treated as a scapegoat
and whipping boy.

The debate ended when Lapointe said that, if the penitentiary commission was not created, he would not accept responsibility for the prisons.
In reply, the suddenly reasonable Bennett said, "Had the Minister said
this before we would not be opposing this bill." The Conservatives abandoned their blockade tactics, and the bill passed the Commons without
a dissenting vote on 29 June 1938. Only the formality of Senate approval
remained. Yet it soon became apparent that the wily Tories had supported the bill in the Commons merely to lull the government to sleep.
On 30 June, with many Liberals away on vacation, the bill was resoundingly defeated in the Senate.

The Conservatives' position was that the way to get better penitentiaries was to appoint better wardens. This view, however, cut no ice with
McRuer. When he read the *Globe and Mail*'s headline on 1 July—"Senate
Kills Prison Board Measure"—he flushed with anger. Almost as galling
as the bill's defeat was Meighen's statement in the Senate that he admired
Mr. Justice Archambault and R.W. Craig, but, as for the third commissioner, "the less I say about him the better."

The irony for McRuer was that, though he disagreed vehemently with
Meighen and was devastated by the bill's defeat, he realized that the penitentiary commission had been proposed in part as a way of getting rid
of Ormond. The idea may have been too cute by half; it certainly had not
worked. As it turned out, there had been all along a much more direct
way to oust Ormond, and it was the route now followed by the government. On 13 July the cabinet approved an order-in-council abolishing
the position of prison superintendent and removing Ormond from public service.

An even larger irony for McRuer was that he saw the aborted bill as a
most inadequate response to all that the Archambault had recommended;
if he had been sitting in parliament, he would have voted against it, too,

on the grounds that it should be redrafted to have more substance added. The government was promising to take up the matter again, but parliament was now prorogued and, by the time it would resume sitting, war clouds over Europe diverted attention from the issue of prison reform.

For a while, McRuer and Archambault acquiesced in the King government's reluctance to act. After all, they were familiar with how the political system worked, and they knew that "things take time." With the outbreak of the Second World War, however, McRuer in particular lost his patience. Whereas the government, not unreasonably, focused all its attention on the war effort and placed other issues on the back burner, McRuer took the position that the war underlined the need for fundamental reform of the prison system. At a time of national crisis, when all the country's resources must be mobilized in what veterans such as McRuer knew would be an all-consuming struggle, there could be no justification—in McRuer's eyes—for having thousands of able-bodied men wasting away in prisons. Overhauling the prison system, in short, would increase the supply of manpower available both for military service and for civilian employment. It was inextricably linked to a successful prosecution of the country's war effort.

McRuer pursued three strategies in mobilizing support for the recommendations of the Archambault commission. In close collaboration with Archambault, he began by mounting a discreet but firm letter-writing campaign directed at King and his ministers. On 4 December 1940, for example, McRuer wrote to King, pressing him to place the Archambault commission's recommendations concerning penal administration on the agenda of a forthcoming federal-provincial conference. Citing statistics on the rapid rise of crime in Canada, McRuer concluded that "in time of war the conviction and confinement of such large numbers of able bodied men is a serious handicap," and he assured King that he would willingly commit all the necessary time and effort to finding a solution to this problem if only the federal authorities would cooperate.[32] King's "confidential" reply on 11 December made it clear that penal reform was one of the last things on his mind. "The scope of the conference is already very extensive and the inclusion of other matters might increase the difficulty of reaching agreement and jeopardize the success of the conference without anything having been accomplished in the way of furthering the ends you have in view. At the same time, any addition to the agenda would create a precedent which would make it difficult for the government to resist the pressure to have other matters ... included within the scope of the discussions."[33]

Also typical of the King government's attitude was the reaction of Justice Minister Louis St. Laurent to constant entreaties from Archambault and McRuer for a meeting on the issue of prison reform. On 16 January 1942 Archambault wrote to McRuer: "I have just received a letter from Mr. St. Laurent which is disappointing. He tells me in his letter that he has noted very carefully the remarks made in mine and that he is giving this matter all the importance which it deserves. He adds, however, that it will be impossible for him to see us before he makes a complete study of the whole matter and he terminates his letter by stating that he would be very anxious later on to have your views and mine on the matter. In my view this means that the matter will drag, especially when the Session will open and Mr. St. Laurent will be taken up with war matters. I do not know what to do."

By the time that McRuer received this despondent letter, he had already launched out on his other two tacks. One of these involved the media. Angered by the government's disregard for a commission that it had created, McRuer encouraged the press to seek interviews with him, and the result was a steady stream of exposure of, and editorial comment upon, the report of the Archambault commission.[34] He even arranged to have the magazine *Saturday Night* print a lengthy article setting out his views on prison reform. In explaining his resort to *Saturday Night* as a means of furthering his goals, McRuer noted that government would not act on the issue of prison reform unless "public indignation" was aroused.[35]

McRuer's third tack was related to the second: he launched a public-speaking campaign. In every available public forum, McRuer hammered away at the King government for failing to implement the recommendations of the Archambault commission. During a speech delivered in Montreal on 7 May 1942 to the Canadian Conference on Social Work, he opened with a blast against the very nature of Canada's economic order. "It is not unfair to say that no government in Canada can show a convincing record of accomplishment in any achievement designed to save men and women, and especially young men and women, from the demoralizing effects of the thirties," he charged, in the rasping tenor voice which always betrayed the fact that his emotions were in high gear. He then went on to assert that the failure of successive Canadian governments to reform the economic order lay at the root of most crimes. Nothing short of a radically new approach to the improvement of the lot of the common Canadian, he said, could put an end to the current rise in crime. Canada's penal system, according to McRuer, should be "put out of business" by a comprehensive renovation of social conditions within the country.

Some eight months later, during an address to the Women's Canadian Club of Montreal, McRuer again underlined the social injustice at the core of the existing prison system: "A man may be an unmitigated scoundrel who has built up a fortune extracting the last ounce of strength from the humblest workman at the lowest pay, yet he will be admitted freely to the finest drawing rooms, while an unfortunate individual who has served a term for a paltry offence committed under the most extenuating circumstances, must in normal times walk the streets in search of any lowly employment because both employers and employees have toward him a particular attitude of mind that cannot be denied." Asserting that "the days of branding have not passed," McRuer reached an unequivocal conclusion: "There is so little official consideration given to the moral, spiritual and physical betterment of the individual that I fear there are few who enter prison for the first time that are not scarred in their very souls by the burning iron of sordid association."[36]

McRuer's wartime lobbying on behalf of prisoners took other forms, too. In 1940–1 he served on the United Church Commission on Crime and Penal Reform, and three years later he chaired a Canadian Bar Association committee on the punishment of juvenile offenders. He also took an interest in individual cases. He personally helped an ex-convict find good work in British Columbia, and he successfully protested to the minister of national war services for reinstatement of a man who was discharged without a hearing from war work because of his criminal record. Then there were the people he was unable to help. In 1942 he received a handwritten note from a woman who had read about McRuer's views on penal reform in the *Montreal Standard* and who was struck by his recommendation that deserving convicts should be released from prison to serve in the army. This one example speaks for the dozens of other similar cases he encountered. The woman sadly noted that her husband, by whom she had three small children, was serving three and a half years in Kingston Penitentiary. Convinced that her husband had been hoodwinked into participating in a crime devised by someone else, she described her own situation in these terms: "Mr. McRuer, my three children are all small, the oldest just turned 6. And I am in very poor health … I have to be on relief until my husband comes home … I can not live on what I get on relief … Mr. McRuer, if there is anything or any place you can advise me to do or any one I can write to who will be able to help me out & help my husband to get the chance to join the army

I would be very glad to receive any information on it. My husband is perfectly innocent of the crime on which he was sent to Kingston for." McRuer wrote back to the woman on 12 June, suggesting that she redirect her request for remission to the Department of Justice and that she contact the lawyer who had acted for her husband at the time of conviction. He was deeply moved by her situation and kept her letter in his permanent files, privately resolving to do all he could to ensure that the number of letters he received from such women would be reduced in the future.[37]

It was an uphill battle, but McRuer and other advocates of reform gradually began to make headway. In the early 1940s the King government was finally able to proceed with the creation of a national prison commission, which had some of the authority that the Archambault report had recommended. A variety of improvements to prison conditions—better food and medical care, more liberal visiting privileges, greater emphasis on education and vocational training—were also made in these years, all of which culminated in 1947 with the passage of a comprehensive penitentiary act.[38] During the next decade, further progress was made. Of the Archambault report's eighty-eight recommendations, sixty-eight required action on the part of the federal government, while the other twenty involved joint action by Ottawa, the provinces, and local municipalities. With regard to the first category, at least fifty recommendations had been acted upon by 1958, when the Diefenbaker government created a national system of parole."[39] In subsequent decades, still other reforms were introduced, including an increasing emphasis on rehabilitation, the abolition of corporal punishment, and the introduction of minimum security institutions, training programs for both prisoners and guards, and paid work for prisoners. All of these reforms were in keeping with the spirit of the Archambault report; indeed, in many respects, the prison reform movement of the post-war decades took its inspiration from the recommendations of the Archambault commission. The result was the evolution of a new kind of penal system, one that was far more humane than the system investigated by McRuer, Archambault, and (sometimes) Craig in the late 1930s.

McRuer never lost his deep commitment to prison reform. Following the war, he made several speeches calling for a variety of fundamental changes to make prisons more humane,[40] he became involved with the Canadian Penal Association, and he served as first chairman of the Canadian Corrections Association. Always passionately proud of the Archambault report, he had been frustrated for many years by the indifference of some and the hostility of others to the report's recommendations. Yet, as time passed, he had the satisfaction of seeing the cause prevail. The slow remaking of the country's prisons that occurred from the late 1940s on was, in his mind, in the best interests both of the prisoners and of society as a whole. More than anything, however, these reforms were a matter of common decency and fairness. Prisoners, for McRuer, were human beings, and they had the right to be treated as such regardless of the crimes they had committed. They, too, were entitled to justice.

8

LAW, POLITICS, AND WAR

PENAL REFORM was by no means Jim McRuer's only interest in the period from the mid-1930s to the early 1940s. Despite the Depression, his legal practice remained reasonably busy in these years—with both corporate and criminal clients—and he was still deeply involved in Liberal Party politics. While no longer tempted to run again as a candidate, McRuer continued to be active in the backrooms and became an important figure in attempts to deal with the growing rift between Ontario Premier Mitch Hepburn and Prime Minister Mackenzie King. Finally, though his legal practice, political activities, and work with the Archambault commission combined to create an extraordinarily hectic schedule, McRuer found time to "do his bit" during the Second World War in ways both public and private.

A personally satisfying landmark in McRuer's legal career during these years was his election in 1936—after the blow of an unsuccessful attempt five years earlier—as a bencher of the Law Society of Upper Canada. Typically, he took on his new responsibilities with gusto. He buried himself in special projects on legal education, income tax, and foreign exchange control, and began organizing classes on these subjects at Osgoode Hall. He showed his concern for the integrity and rights of the legal profession through his work chairing the Law Society's unauthorized practices committee, which sought to curb unauthorized conveyancers of property (the unaccountable upstarts who were cutting in on the legal profession's turf). He also lobbied hard for the princi-

ple that magistrates should owe their appointment to their legal training and experience rather than to political influence. McRuer, seeking
to end political patronage in these appointments, stressed in one speech
that "if a man is not qualified to determine the sentence an accused person ought to serve, he is not qualified to try the accused man and decide
whether or not he is guilty."[1]

Besides his work with the Law Society, McRuer was at the centre
of some dramatic murder trials in these years. The most spectacular—
and his only prosecution—occurred in 1936. At 11 p.m. on a black and
rainy night, a young woman by the name of Ruth Taylor, wearing a blue
angora sweater, left her job at the Toronto General Trusts Company and
boarded the Gerrard East streetcar. She got off at Coxwell Avenue, and
then, in a driving rain, began walking home along a slippery sidewalk
illuminated by a few street lamps flickering under the waving trees. She
never arrived. Toronto police searched the area the following day and
found her body in a ravine. She had been sexually assaulted and afterwards killed with blows to the head. The weapon had been a heavy piece
of broken concrete.

Chief Constable Dennis Draper, who had developed the most meticulous investigative practices for crimes such as this, directed that the
ravine be thoroughly searched by an army of constables. The police
discovered a mechanic's wrench. Draper also engaged a senior and
well-known forensic expert, Professor Joslyn Rogers of the analytical
chemistry department of the University of Toronto, to do the analysis
of the wrench and other evidence. In short order, the police's suspicions
fastened on a mechanic named Harry O'Donnell, who had spent three
years in Kingston Penitentiary for an attempted rape committed several
years before in the same ravine, but a block south of where Ruth Taylor
was killed. On searching O'Donnell's flat, detectives Jim McIlrath and
Bert Waterhouse found his clothes hanging in a closet soaking wet. His
shirt contained 294 blue angora rabbit hairs closely resembling those
in the murder victim's sweater, and Professor Rogers and his assistant
found that they reacted the same way under chemical analysis of the dye.
The burrs on his trouser legs matched those at the scene of the crime.

McRuer was brought in as crown prosecutor. The day before the case
was to go to the grand jury, detective Waterhouse told McRuer that he
had discovered some red stains and the initials "O.D." stamped on the
wrench. McRuer quickly suggested that he send out a squad to examine O'Donnell's tools and to look for the dies used to stamp the wrench.
When this investigation was conducted, twenty-two other tools were

found with the same initials, and the die for the "O.D." was also discovered.

The only defence argument—a hoax developed by counsel Frank
Regan and an "expert" by the name of Zeidler—was that O'Donnell had
been visiting his wife in hospital, where she had just given birth, and
had hugged her. She was, it was claimed, wearing a blue sweater at the
time. This theory was completely demolished by the meticulous fore-
sight of McRuer, Rogers, and the police, who had already taken a clipping off Mrs. O'Donnell's blue sweater and found it completely different
from the one worn by the victim. McRuer also called as a witness the
matron of the hospital, who swore that Mrs. O'Donnell had never worn
the blue sweater during her stay there; it had been locked away in her
suitcase. McRuer subjected Zeidler to a fierce cross-examination and
finally obtained an admission that Dr. Rogers's scientific conclusions
were correct. After the trial Mr. Justice Jeffrey summoned McRuer into
his chambers and congratulated him on being "one of the few men who
know how to cross examine an expert."

O'Donnell was convicted and sentenced to be executed. An appeal
was dismissed.[2] On death-row, he confessed his great sin to a priest, who
persuaded him to write it down. O'Donnell admitted that he had done
the deed as McRuer had described it, but said that he had acted out of
a loss of control—he had been overcome with sexual desire. At any rate,
an appeal for clemency (and commutation to life imprisonment) on
the grounds of motivation was turned down by the federal cabinet and
O'Donnell was executed.

On another occasion, McRuer served—for the first time in his
career—as defence counsel in a murder case. Charles Cline was a prominent seventy-one-year-old doctor in London, Ontario, who performed
abortions. In early 1938 Dr. Cline ended up in court because one of his
abortions had resulted in the death of a Detroit schoolteacher, Mary
Wilkinson. On the witness stand, Cline's nurse stated that he had accidentally penetrated the woman's uterus and then, to relieve her pain, had
given her a heavy dose of chloroform, which killed her. Stupidly, Cline
put the corpse into his car and, after a short drive, dumped it into the
Thames River. On a technicality, McRuer was able to get the charge
reduced to manslaughter. Crown counsel Cecil Snyder had overlooked
the fact that he could not bring in more than the allowed five experts
without leave. Since he had failed to seek leave, he was not able to prove
the cause of death and therefore was forced to agree to the lesser charge,
to which McRuer's client pleaded guilty. The trial was publicized fero-

ciously in the newspapers and became so popular that spectators were banned after a crowd trying to get in the courtroom wrenched a heavy oak door right off its hinges.[3]

In the days before legal aid, lawyers quite often took on a case without charging a fee, as part of their professional responsibility. McRuer was no exception. One of the cases he handled on this basis occurred in 1938 and involved a man named William Manchuk. A Polish immigrant, Manchuk had done well in Canada and owned his own home in St. Catharines. The origins of his eventual downfall lay in a series of violent arguments that Manchuk had with his next-door neighbour John Seabright over the location of the fence that divided their properties. This dispute about the boundary line escalated on 6 June 1936 when Manchuk tore down the fence. Two days later Seabright began to rebuild the fence, and Manchuk, who could not speak much English, became furious. Using violent and threatening language, he and his wife insisted that the fence-building stop, but Seabright refused. In a horrible rage, Manchuk got an axe from the house and inflicted three blows to Seabright's head, killing him. He then went to Seabright's house and did the same to his wife, Amy, killing her with two blows.

Manchuk was tried for the murder of John Seabright, but the defence of "provocation" was accepted by the jury and so he was convicted on the reduced charge of manslaughter and sentenced to twenty years imprisonment. At the next assize in 1937 he was tried for Amy Seabright's murder, convicted, and sentenced to be hanged on 31 May 1937. The verdict was appealed on the grounds that the trial judge's charge to the jury had improperly served to nullify the defence of "provocation" and therefore only a conviction for murder—as opposed to provoked manslaughter—was possible. The appeal was allowed and a new trial ordered.[4] The crown then appealed this decision to the Supreme Court of Canada, hoping to keep the murder conviction in place, but that appeal was dismissed.[5] For a second time, accordingly, Manchuk stood trial for the killing of Amy Seabright, and for a second time he was convicted. Once again he was sentenced to be hanged; once more he appealed.[6]

It was at this appeal stage that McRuer became involved in the case, drawn primarily by his sympathy for the defendant. It was his contention that, in the first two trials, the judge had not given a correct explanation to the jury of the defence of provocation (which reduces murder to manslaughter), and that in the second trial Mr. Justice F.D. Hogg had insinuated that the Court of Appeal already considered Manchuk guilty of murder. The presiding judge, Mr. Justice W.E. Middleton, who had called McRuer to the bar over twenty years earlier, took the rare and unusual step of summoning McRuer and his opposite number, the deputy attorney-general, to his chambers and telling them that he would dissent on the issue of provocation, which would allow McRuer to proceed to the Supreme Court of Canada and argue the issue there. McRuer, however, suggested to Middleton that the defects in the judge's charge to the jury provided a stronger case, and so Middleton eventually dissented on the whole judgment. This decision gave McRuer more leeway in planning his defence.

On appeal to the Supreme Court, McRuer presented his argument concerning the defective jury charge in the first two trials. Chief Justice Sir Lyman Duff, whom McRuer considered "the greatest jurist Canada has ever produced," inquired with a tone of mild exasperation: "Mr. McRuer, Do you know if there is any case in Canadian history where a man has been sent to be tried four times for the same murder?" McRuer replied briskly: "No, I don't think so, My Lord, but I am not asking you to send this case back for a new trial. I ask you to convict him for manslaughter because I think that is the proven case and it is the proper verdict to sentence him as you think he ought to be sentenced." Duff, in turn, agreed with McRuer, substituted a verdict of manslaughter for that of murder, and sentenced Manchuk to life imprisonment.[7] In prison, Manchuk, twice sentenced to hang, eventually died of natural causes. His story subsequently inspired a National Film Board "short" called "Neighbours."

Other McRuer cases in these years did not involve life and death but were important nonetheless. One of them saw him acting as defence counsel for the Mining Association of Canada. In this case, gold nuggets had been smuggled by miners out of northern mines, particularly Noranda, passed south, and then melted on the sly in Toronto where the stolen gold was sold as bars. A number of criminal charges had been laid in connection with this operation, and since it involved a network of relationships, the Mining Association itself had been included in the proceedings on the grounds that its officers knew of the miners' actions and so were part of an organized conspiracy. When the case came to trial, everything went smoothly for McRuer until, to his astonishment, the trial judge, James Parker, stood up and—without any warning or allowing any questions—announced, "I have come to the conclusion that I have no jurisdiction to try this case, since the offence, if there was one, was committed in Quebec." He then walked off the bench, leaving the lawyers open-mouthed. McRuer applied for an Ontario Supreme Court *mandamus* to direct the judge to continue, and an amused Mr. Justice Hogg granted it. When court convened a second time and the trial continued to its conclusion, McRuer succeeded in having the charge against his client dismissed.[8]

Another case stretched back to the 1920s. In 1926 McRuer had taken up the cause of Toronto investor J.P. McLaughlin in a major lawsuit against Solloway, Mills, a roaring twenties "bucket shop" in the city's financial district. This company operated by not putting sales through the stock exchange at all; phoney transactions would be reported to the client. The scheme worked only as long as the company could stay ahead of its clients, and, after the stock market crash of 1929, the chickens came home to roost. McLaughlin, represented by McRuer, claimed that he had been defrauded by the company and sued for damages of $150,000. The company responded by declaring bankruptcy; McRuer responded by continuing the suit against the two owners of the company, I.W.C. Solloway and Harvey Mills.

Andrew Brewin, McRuer's junior in the law firm, prepared most of the case, with all its painstaking financial detail, and the matter dragged through the courts for seven years. In the first trial, Mr. Justice Patrick Kerwin gave judgment for McLaughlin. The company, represented by Arthur Slaght, then resorted to the Court of Appeal, which—with Justice Macdonnell dissenting—dismissed the case. In February 1936 the Supreme Court of Canada allowed McRuer's appeal in part, awarding McLaughlin half the amount claimed. Both sides appealed and counterappealed, and finally, by July 1937, McRuer was in England to thrash out the case before the Judicial Committee of the Privy Council.

Thoroughly prepared and confident, McRuer carefully outlined his client's case, and on 29 October the law lords dismissed the appeal of Solloway, Mills and reinstated Kerwin's original judgment at trial. On returning from England, McRuer went to see his old friend Justice Macdonnell, who was mortally ill. He informed Macdonnell that the Privy Council had agreed with his dissent, a piece of news that cheered him greatly in his last days.[9]

In addition to trial work, McRuer also became involved in yet another of his major judicial inquiries, this one involving the John Inglis Company, operator of the Bren Gun plant near Toronto. As early as 1936, Canadian military planners had determined that the army would need 7,000 Bren machine guns—superb light weapons that had to be manufactured with great precision. Britain had acquired the licence to manufacture the weapon from the Czech engineering company that had invented it, and the plan was to have both the British and Canadian governments set up factories for this purpose. In Canada, General Andrew McNaughton presented a massive $30-million scheme to refit the Dominion Arsenal plant at Valcartier, Quebec, to produce the Bren, but in fact nothing ever came of this experiment in public enterprise. Struck by the speed of German rearmament and the slowness of the British response—a publicly owned Australian Bren plant was still not operating either, after two years of planning—the Canadian cabinet, influenced particularly by the arguments of Minister of Transport C.D. Howe, resolved that private enterprise should build the weapon.

With the urgency of the international situation becoming increasingly clear, the Department of National Defence approached Major James Hahn, a Toronto lawyer and manufacturer of radio sets, and gave him $20,000 in preliminary planning funds to obtain the licence and plans from the British government. Hahn had emerged as a tireless lobbyist in this matter, because, according to McRuer, "he understood what was going on in Germany much better than the politicians or the people of Canada. He was sure there was going to be another war and he knew we were not doing very much toward getting ready for it." One of the reasons for the prevailing lethargy in rearmament, McRuer noted, was that "there were not many people who were enthusiastic about making arms. They were infected with the Beverley Nicholls concept that it was the manufacture of arms that was the basic cause of all wars." Hahn himself, in describing the desperate situation, pointed out that "in England they were only beginning to draw chalk marks on the floors as to where to put the machines that would produce the tools to make the guns."[10]

On 31 March 1938, without tender or competitive bids, the King government signed a contract with Hahn for 583 guns by 1941 and the balance of the 7,000 by 31 July 1943. In return, Hahn was to be paid on a cost-plus basis. The Canadian and British governments were to pay for and own all the tools; Hahn was lent all the old Ross Rifle manufacturing equipment taken over in the First World War and stored at Valcartier, and the government agreed to pay executive salaries, travelling expenses, legal fees, and many office expenses. However, the profit margin of Hahn's company, British Canadian Engineering, was to be limited to 10 per cent. The guns were to be manufactured at the mothballed John Inglis appliance factory outside Toronto, bought by Hahn for $250,000, and British Canadian Engineering, chartered on 23 November 1936, was allowed to use the John Inglis name. With the promise of Canadian government support, Hahn also got a concurrent contract for another 5,000 Bren guns in the United Kingdom and the War Office agreed to pay one-third of the cost of the operation.

A brouhaha over this Bren Gun contract erupted on 1 September 1938 with an article in *Maclean's* magazine entitled "The Canadian Armament Mystery." Written by George Drew, who three months later was to become leader of the Ontario Conservative Party, the article objected to the government's action in letting the contract out to private industry, awarding the contract without tender, and giving the contract to a firm that was apparently owned and controlled by a stable of Liberal lawyers. Drew's article pointed out that, of British Canadian Engineering's 250,000 shares, 107,964 were held by Hahn, 25,000 by the stockbroker firm of Cameron, Pointon and Merritt, and a total of 117,031 by two fictitious companies—Investment Resources Ltd. and Anglo Engineering Company Ltd. The nominal directors of Investment Resources and Anglo Engineering were employed—as secretaries and a law student—at Plaxton and Company, a good Liberal law firm.

The scandal was the last thing Mackenzie King needed as the war clouds gathered. After an attack on the contract in parliament, he appointed a royal commission into the affair under the chairmanship of Mr. Justice Henry Hague Davis of the Supreme Court of Canada. Aimé Geoffrion was retained to act for Major Hahn; Colonel J.L. Ralston (still in private practice in Montreal, but soon to enter the federal cabinet) acted as counsel for the commission; and J.C. McRuer was retained as counsel for the John Inglis Company, which had interests to defend in the matter since its name was being used by Hahn as a public relations cover. Determined to extract the maximum personal publicity, George Drew appeared for himself, and, like Arthur Meighen in the Hydro scandal five years earlier, he may have made a very serious mistake in doing so.

During the hearings, McRuer and Drew slung facts at each other and scrapped over details, Geoffrion pored over statements and statutes and manuals of procedures to try to ensnare Drew on some technicality, and Ralston maintained a scrupulous position of dignity and neutrality. Working hard, McRuer produced a massive statement that set out all the essential points about the contract. Each day about five o'clock Geoffrion would call him in for a consultation, discuss the events of the day, and then, after a half hour say, "Well, that's all. Goodnight." He then left, leaving McRuer to work alone through the evening hours.

Yet McRuer did not mind. It was a privilege to work with the man—

his mind was so quick and sharp, so adept at discarding the irrelevant or inconsequential, and his decisions were invariably right. Just at the time McRuer was about to present his summarizing arguments, Geoffrion came into his office and said that he had been looking at the Inquiries Act and that it stipulated that no report could be made against a person unless a charge had been made against him as well. Drew had spoken out about many things, but he had never formally charged Hahn with impropriety. Consequently, said Geoffrion, he would tell Justice Davis that by statute he could not make any report against Hahn.

McRuer watched, highly amused, as Geoffrion made this argument before Davis in a neat twenty-minute speech. Davis's face dropped. He knew that Geoffrion had closed the door on him, and that all he could do was report the facts but without giving any findings bearing on Hahn. Drew had been scuppered.

Davis did express great concern about the absence of competitive bids, which he found objectionable, and he suggested the establishment of a defence purchasing board to handle contracts with private indus-try.[11] That much was quickly done, and the new board proved vital in the intense military procurement of the war years. As the rest of the com-mission's report got lost in a Commons-Senate joint committee, Bren guns began to pour out of the John Inglis plant and were shipped to Brit-ain in ever-increasing numbers (250,000 by war's end). In wartime, the Bren Gun inquiry, which normally would have led to the worst sort of scandal mongering in the House of Commons, was allowed to fizzle out. For McRuer and everyone else concerned in the Davis inquiry, as well as for the general public, there were more momentous matters to confront.

IN THE YEARS immediately after the federal election of 1935, McRuer faced a political problem that was thorny, time-consuming, and a cause for some despair. This problem involved Premier Mitch Hepburn and Prime Minister Mackenzie King.

In the latter half of the 1930s, Mitch Hepburn did little to address the economic problems of the day, but he was certainly successful in changing the face of provincial politics. Apart from cancelling Ontario Hydro's contracts with private power companies in Quebec, Hepburn was no sooner in office than he auctioned off government limousines in a giant fire-sale at Varsity Stadium, Toronto, and, as further proof of his determination to usher in a new era in Ontario politics, dismissed large numbers of civil servants appointed during the previous administration.

Such moves spoke volumes about Hepburn's penchant for political theatrics, and the same flamboyance would always remain a trademark of his style of governing. It would also characterize his personal life. Unlike his predecessor, the staid "Farmer George" Henry, Hepburn was something of a wild man. Ensconced in his private suite at the King Edward Hotel in Toronto, Hepburn spent much of his time drinking with his cronies and consorting with women of questionable virtue. A visitor to his hotel suite in 1937 met "two attractive girls who sprawled on a sofa and called the Prime Minister 'Chief'" and a "bodyguard-cum-gentleman's servant" named "Bruiser" who mixed drinks for the premier and his guests.[12]

At the King Edward and elsewhere, Hepburn conspired against his real and imagined enemies. One of those was a fellow Liberal, Prime Minister King. The rift between the two men was largely based on personality, the gregarious, earthy Hepburn having nothing in common with the introverted, dignified Mackenzie King, and over time its fires were stoked by Hepburn's stubbornness, sensitivity, and pride. The feud began shortly after the federal election of 1935, when King declined to make two cabinet appointments requested by Hepburn. In the years that followed, a number of substantive issues divided the combatants, including the sharing of tax revenue between Ottawa and Queen's Park, the federal government's refusal to allow the export of Ontario waterpower to the United States, and the amount of federal relief payments to the provincial government. For Hepburn, however, these issues were not the cause of the dispute, but just further insults heaped on his early injuries at King's hands. Spoiling for a fight, he was quite ready to reduce his differences with King to the level of personal attack. Beginning in 1936, he denounced King furiously, ridiculed him, and worked behind the scenes to undermine his leadership. King himself, a master of self-control, took the high road, ignoring the insults and suggesting possible compromises.

McRuer closely followed the goings-on at Queen's Park throughout Hepburn's premiership, and, as time passed, he was increasingly angered by the premier's antics. Indeed, within a couple of years of Hepburn's victory in 1934, McRuer had reached the conclusion that Hepburn was not what Ontario, or the Liberal Party, needed at this point in history. For the serious-minded and progressive McRuer, Hepburn's substitution of cheap carnival for real policies was a serious failing. So were his irresponsible demagoguery and authoritarianism. The premier's instincts, McRuer more and more believed, were those of an unscrupulous charlatan eager to trample on the rights of others, the due process of law, and parliamentary democracy whenever he saw a chance to enhance his own power or destroy an opponent. On a personal level, McRuer found Hepburn's womanizing and boozing as distasteful as his politics. His most grievous sin in McRuer's eyes, however, was his disloyalty to the Liberal Party. King was not perfect, to be sure, and in the late 1930s his inaction on the report of the Archambault commission left McRuer deeply disappointed. Yet King was well intentioned, McRuer believed, and in any case he was a Liberal—a fact that excused a multitude of wrongs. He deserved better than to have his name dragged through the mud by the erratic, irresponsible Hepburn.

In short, McRuer was disgusted by the whole spectacle of the Hepburn-King feud and he knew whom to blame—the premier of Ontario. As a good Liberal, however, he was distressed by the internecine feuding, and in the mid-1930s he tried to act as peacemaker. On 5 October 1936 he indicated to Tim McQuesten, Hepburn's minister of highways, and to Harry Johnson of the Ontario Liberal Association that a meeting of the Ontario Reform Association should be convened as soon as possible. The ORA—McQuesten was its president, and McRuer sat on its management committee and was chairman of its resolutions committee—was a policy-discussion group whose concern was unity between the national and provincial Liberal parties. McRuer got nowhere, however; the meeting he suggested was never held. Matters then deteriorated rapidly. Hepburn ordered a cessation of campaign contributions from the Ontario Liberal Party to its federal counterpart, instructed McQuesten not to award any highway contracts to companies friendly with King and his supporters, and, exactly a month after McRuer's attempt to convene an emergency meeting of the Ontario Reform Association, directed Harry Johnson to separate the Ontario Liberal Association from the National Liberal Federation. Then, in April 1937, Hepburn detected further evidence of Ottawa's perfidy in its response to the Oshawa strike. The principal issue in this strike was the attempt of workers at the General Motors plant to establish a union affiliate of the United States-based Congress of Industrial Organizations. Hepburn saw in the strikers' demand the influence of "foreign labour agitators" and the threat of Communist subversion, and he was astonished and enraged when the federal minister of labour, Norman Rogers, expressed reluctance to send the RCMP to Oshawa to assist the provincial police in preventing picket line violence. Two other prominent Liberals viewed the Oshawa strike differently. Arthur Roebuck and David Croll opposed Hepburn's uncompromising anti-union stance, and, as a result, Hepburn dismissed them from his cabinet.[13]

Hepburn, however, saw no reason to change any of his policies or attitudes, including his contemptuous view of the prime minister. In June 1937 he openly announced that he was still a reformer but no longer a "Mackenzie King Liberal ... I will tell the world that, and I hope he hears me."[14] A few months later Hepburn declared that "Mr. King was never friendly to Ontario, I happen to know because I was with him and watched him in Ottawa."[15] Such declarations, along with Hepburn's image as an heroic crusader against the Red menace, were popular with most of the electorate and helped give Hepburn another decisive victory in the election held in October 1937.

McRuer remained essentially on the sidelines in the 1937 provincial election campaign, preferring the tranquil isolation of his in-laws' cottage at Stoney Lake. Developments after the election confirmed him in the belief that Hepburn was out of control, and convinced him that the premier needed to be removed is soon as possible if the Liberal Party and Ontario as a whole were not to suffer irreparable damage.

Armed with his new mandate, Hepburn continued to do battle with King in a variety of ways. After George Drew became provincial Conservative leader in 1938, the Hepburn government and the Official Opposition cooperated more and more, especially on issues related to the developing crisis in Europe. Many Liberals were disgusted by this spectacle, particularly since the purpose of the Hepburn-Drew alliance was to discredit the foreign policy of the King government in Ottawa. They were equally disgusted by Hepburn's refusal to participate in a joint United States-Canada seaway development on the St. Lawrence River unless he could get permission to export more hydro power, and by his harsh attacks on the Rowell-Sirois commission—a body established by King in February 1937 to "investigate the economic and financial basis of Confederation, and of the distribution of legislative powers." In these maneuvers, Hepburn found a willing ally in Quebec premier Maurice Duplessis who, like Hepburn, was highly hostile towards—and suspicious of—Ottawa.

McRuer was appalled by the Hepburn-Duplessis alliance, for in his mind the Quebec premier was a "scoundrel ... a wicked man politically in every way ... and no kind of man to have the Premier of Ontario scheming with." He was especially appalled by rumours that Hepburn and Duplessis were in the process of creating an interprovincial political organization that would control central Canada regardless of which party held power in Ottawa. Though there was little substance to these rumours, many people—McRuer included—saw no reason to doubt them. McRuer himself first heard the story of the Hepburn-Duplessis plot at a dinner party in Ottawa. The couple hosting the party—the woman was a close friend of Mary McRuer—were often guests at Hepburn's farm in St. Thomas, and they told McRuer what a good thing it would be, and how much in the national interest, if a Hepburn-Duplessis coalition could force King from office. Knowing that he was being sounded out, McRuer said nothing, but he reported the conversation— along with other evidence of scheming by Hepburn and Duplessis—to Mackenzie King and Minister of Labour Norman Rogers. On 7 December 1938 he told Rogers that "liberalism in our province in its best sense is being somewhat trampled on, and it is imperative that some action ought to be taken in the near future."

King himself had heard that Hepburn and Duplessis had some conspiracy in the works, and he moved quickly to nip it in the bud. With his blessing, C.D. Howe made the alleged conspiracy public in his renomination speech in Port Arthur on 10 December 1938, with Norman Rogers on the platform. At that point, opposition to Howe collapsed, and he was renominated by acclamation. Afterwards, Hepburn called a press conference where he threatened "a fight to the limit" and talked of supporting the newly elected federal Conservative leader, Robert Manion, in the next federal election—"at least he's human," he snorted. Then he called Norman Rogers a "pink socialite" for his reformist views.[16]

McRuer saw in the ever-accelerating confrontation between Hepburn and King, not just a power struggle, but the emergence at Queen's Park of profoundly anti-democratic, unconstitutional, and near-fascist forces which threatened the foundations of Ontario society—liberalism and parliamentary democracy. Many of his fellow Liberals felt the same way; indeed, in reformist Liberal circles in Toronto, near-hysteria prevailed. Atkinson's *Toronto Star* frantically described the Hepburn-Drew alliance as an axis in the manner of Hitler and Mussolini, writing ominously of Mussolini's march on Rome to overthrow democracy and establish a fascist dictatorship. Hepburn was no longer leading the Liberal Party but "some sort of third or fourth party ... that substitutes uncouth rudeness for courtesy in public life, promotes Canadian disunity instead of unity, and is allied with a non-Liberal party in Quebec." All through December 1938 the *Star* ran two-column, front-page editorials calling on Liberals to remain true to Mackenzie King and democracy.[17]

Deeply troubled by the political climate, and knowing full well the kind of power Hepburn could muster if he wanted to, McRuer wrote Mackenzie King on 13 December 1938 to thank him for the stand he had taken "in respect to the difficulties that we are having in Liberal politics in the Province of Ontario." Emphasizing that he had long been "quietly urging that this issue should be faced squarely, and whatever the result it must be fought out as the principles involved are all too important to be sacrificed for any immediate political expediency," McRuer painted a grim picture of what the prime minister and all good Liberals were up against: "I am convinced that we are experiencing a revolution in the Liberal Party that is inspired by sinister influences that have not the public good at heart." To deal with this crisis, McRuer stressed the need for new "ways and means" of organization among loyal Liberals—the existing Ontario Reform Association was nothing but a puppet of the Hepburn government—and he gave his support to King's suggestion that a special caucus of Liberal MPs and Senators be held. On the second point, however, he modified King's proposal slightly, suggesting that the meeting also include those Liberal candidates, or at least those in Ontario, who had been defeated in the last federal election. The purpose of this meeting would be to develop plans for improved organization and for putting before "the people of the Province the case for Liberalism in the Dominion at large." In answer to Hepburn's charge that the King government was the prisoner of a "laissez faire do-nothing" mentality, the meeting could also consider ways of publicizing "in a comprehensive and thorough manner the accomplishments and achievements of the Government." All of this, McRuer said, "should be done at once aggressively, and not as a defensive measure. It is difficult to defend insidious attacks of this character, but it is easy to present the case in the offensive." His letter concluded with a declaration of his "intense personal loyalty to yourself and your leadership."[18]

King welcomed McRuer's "helpful constructive suggestions."[19] On the evening of 15 December 1938, a Thursday, a telegram went out from Liberal party whip Bill Fraser, and co-signed by Norman Rogers, C.D. Howe, Postmaster-General J.C. Elliot, and Trade and Commerce Minister W.D. Euler, inviting MPs, Senators, and defeated candidates to meet the following Monday at 11:00 o'clock in the railway committee room of the Parliament Buildings in Ottawa. The meeting was being called "to discuss recent developments touching particularly the Liberal Party in Ontario."

On Saturday, 17 December, his birthday, Mackenzie King received a call shortly after lunch from Hepburn loyalist Arthur Slaght. Instead of offering him birthday greetings, Slaght told King that Mitch Hepburn had collapsed after making a speech at the Empire Club and was now seriously ill in St. Thomas, Ontario. Indicating that Hepburn would probably resign in a few days, Slaght expressed the hope that King would not make Hepburn's condition any worse than it was by threatening to expel him from the Liberal Party. King, however, was not impressed. "My size up of the situation," he wrote in his diary, "is that once Hepburn found he was squarely faced with a fight, he has taken to drink and probably in a bad way."[20] In this he was supported by a former Hepburn ally, *Globe* publisher George McCullagh, who quipped privately to friends that Mitch Hepburn was "not fit to be premier of a pub."[21]

At the same time that Slaght was phoning King, McRuer received an urgent phone call from Norman Rogers asking him to go to Ottawa on Sunday, the day before the caucus meeting, for a meeting at Rogers's house. McRuer dropped everything and took the overnight train. When he arrived at Rogers's home after church, he found his host with C.D. Howe, Norman McLarty, an MP from Windsor, and Bill Taylor from Simcoe, the chairman of caucus. As they talked matters over, they reached a consensus about the need to keep the caucus meeting under control and particularly to prevent party loyalists from attacking Hepburn supporters, one of whom was Bill Fraser, the whip and secretary of caucus. With his fine sense of procedure, McRuer suggested the preparation of a draft resolution that would force discussion along certain lines; the chairman would be formally requested to appoint a committee to consider the resolution and bring it forward for a vote, and, after the voting, all the members of caucus would be asked to come up to the front and sign the resolution. This idea went over well, and McRuer agreed to work on a draft. Then the five of them chose a slate for the committee that Taylor could appear to pull out of his hat at random.

The following day, the Liberal MPs, Senators, and defeated candidates convened in the cavernous railway committee room. The whole affair went most smoothly. Following a comment by McRuer that they ought to have something specific to consider, there was some mild discussion on the motion to nominate a committee to prepare resolutions. It was seconded and passed. Then Taylor, a master actor, gazed out over the audience, and, as if spontaneously picking out names at random—"Ah, Mr. McRuer, would you be willing to serve on this committee?"—he got the committee he wanted, composed of the exact slate prepared the day before. At this point McRuer had the resolution endorsing King's leadership in his pocket. In committee, it was worked over nicely by McLarty, and improved, and then half an hour later was brought back to caucus. There was no mention of Hepburn in the resolution, merely a pledge of "loyalty, devotion and support for the future" to Mackenzie King and his leadership at a time when "democratic institutions which have been won at great sacrifice are so gravely imperilled." After a minimum of discussion, no one dared to vote against the resolution in front of their colleagues, and besides, most of them had had no lunch and wanted to wrap things up. The resolution was passed unanimously. Taylor quickly wrote the resolution on some foolscap, signed it with a great flourish of his pen, and passed it across to his caucus secretary, Hepburn crony Bill Fraser, who swallowed hard and signed as well. Then all other members were invited to affix their signatures, which they did .[22]

The passing of the resolution was a great victory for McRuer, and for Mackenzie King, but many Ontario Liberals were still squeamish. The Hepburn machine had helped them tremendously in the 1935 election, and, since the federal and provincial Liberal riding associations overlapped so much, they took seriously his threat to help Manion and the Conservatives in the coming federal campaign. Yet the caucus meeting of December 1938 did turn the tide against Hepburn. Realizing this, Mackenzie King wrote McRuer on 29 December to thank him for his work at the caucus, having "learned from others how much you contributed to its proceedings." King expressed the hope that McRuer would "continue to take an increasing interest and important part in the affairs of the Party."[23] McRuer, for his part, was satisfied with the results of the meeting, but he still worried about the Liberal Party's future. In July of the following year he expressed to J.L. Ralston his continuing hope that "the undesirable influences of the Liberal Party will not succeed in gaining control."

Within a year of the Ontario caucus meeting, Hepburn made a fatal mistake. After Canada entered the war against Germany in September 1939, Hepburn began to rail against the federal government's military effort, telling reporters that "the situation in Ottawa would break your heart... Mr. King apparently hasn't yet realized there is a war on... Mr. King has not done his duty to Canada—never has and never will."[24] On 18 January 1940, in reply to a comment by George Drew about federal inactivity, Hepburn introduced in the Ontario legislature a motion criticizing Mackenzie King for his weakness in prosecuting the war and regretting that "the government at Ottawa has made so little effort to prosecute the war in the vigorous manner the people of Canada desire to see."[25] With Hepburn threatening to resign if the vote went against him, the motion, supported by George Drew and all the Tories, passed forty-four to ten. Ten Liberals voted against the motion, and a majority of Liberal members were not present, many having tiptoed out to avoid voting.

In Ottawa, Mackenzie King, protesting that he could not fight a war and Mitch Hepburn at the same time, knew that providence had handed him the excuse he had been looking for. Using the Ontario motion of censure as a pretext, King called a snap general election for 26 March 1940 in spite of his earlier promise to Conservative leader Robert Manion that parliament would sit for another term before going to the country. Having helped to defeat the Duplessis machine in the Quebec election the previous October, King's Quebec cabinet ministers, Chubby Power, P.J. Cardin, and Ernest Lapointe, were eager for another fight, especially since the Tories were unprepared, lacking both funding and a plan of attack.

Inevitably, McRuer was asked to run. He had decided after 1935 to make his career outside parliament, but his success with the caucus meeting in Ottawa—to say nothing of the sudden rush of excitement as the election got under way—caused him to reconsider. Much soul-searching ensued, but in the end he decided to decline the offer. After ten years of the likes of Mitch Hepburn, he felt more than ever that he was not cut out for the brutality of a career in politics. "When it became clear that McRuer would not run, one of his law partners, Pat Cameron, took up the challenge and was nominated for the Liberals in McRuer's riding of High Park. McRuer now played a different role, happily toiling away as chairman of the Liberal Party's election campaign speakers committee.

McRuer spent the election in-doors, nestled in a big office in the *Toronto Star* building. Secure from the blizzards that raged across Canada that winter, and assisted by Bob Fowler and a talented younger lawyer, J.J. Robinette, McRuer churned out one mimeographed policy statement after another. Never a good campaigner, but always keen on organization, procedure, and the orderly articulation of ideas and policies, McRuer had found his political niche in "the greatest multigraphing election ever," showing the government's program of action in a crisp daily bulletin packed with tid-bits of information. Facing him and the rest of the Liberal campaign team were the listless Tories led by Manion. To his great disadvantage, Manion was persuaded by the likes of Mitch Hepburn and George Drew to make "union government" the only plank in his election platform, and in following this strategy the Tories even changed their name from the Liberal-Conservative Party to the nondescript "National Government Party." As for Mackenzie King, who was counselled by Norman Lambert to campaign with "dignity and calmness," his only comment on union government was a milky complaint about changing horses in mid-stream.

On 11 March 1940, two weeks before the election, a disgusted and dejected Harry Nixon, the Ontario provincial secretary and Hepburn's seat-mate, resigned from cabinet, declaring that the Hepburn-Drew alliance was "particularly repugnant" since it seemed to exist "for the sole purpose of concentrating every possible attack and embarrassment upon the federal government."[26] A delighted McRuer immediately wrote Nixon: "Heartiest congratulations on the stand you have taken. You are giving Liberalism in this Province real leadership when it is sorely needed. You probably know, as all the rest of us do, that the discontent and dissatisfaction with the attitude of the Premier has been such that if someone did not take a stand for the course that was right, the party was prepared to assert itself in no uncertain manner. From what I can learn throughout the country, Dr. Manion, George Drew and Mr. Hepburn are going to be in for one of the greatest drubbings that any group ever got, and I should have been very sorry to see you and some of my other close personal friends suffer at the hands of the people.

"Undoubtedly your action has been courageous, as it is not easy to definitely break with one who has given the party such excellent leadership at other times. The most charitable view we can take of the present situation is that Mitch's health is such as to completely warp his judgment on important public matters. As one of the old guard that fought the battles against overpowering Toryism along with you in 1927 and again in 1929, I must say that it is with great sorrow that I find the leader we chose in 1930 has drifted so far from the ideals that we held for him at that time. You can rest assured that your multitude of friends will back you stoutly, and that your days in public life in this province are far from being at an end."

Unfortunately for McRuer, Hepburn persuaded Nixon to change his mind, and the following day, Nixon announced his return to the cabinet. A smiling Mitch Hepburn called in newsmen to Nixon's Royal York suite and happily tore up Harry's resignation. Yet Nixon, in the exchange, had also got something from Hepburn. With the assistance of McRuer, who spent some time with Nixon on his farm, a deal was struck and a truce of sorts made between the Hepburn government and the federal Liberals. Three days later, Nixon appeared on the same platform as Mackenzie King in a monster rally in Massey Hall and forged the Liberals together again with these simple words: "My good wife and I just drove down from the farm to be here and to say to you that come what may, we are behind Mr. King."[27]

On 26 March King romped to the largest majority in Canadian political history to that day, gaining thirteen more seats, mainly in Quebec and Alberta, for a total of 181 to the Conservatives' 40. If McRuer himself had run, he realized, he likely would have been elected. Well known, a veteran, he could have easily surmounted Anderson's plurality in High Park. As it was, Pat Cameron lost by only some 200 votes. Yet McRuer was quite content serving his party and his country in other ways; a career in politics was no longer one of his ambitions. Happy working behind the scenes, he took great delight in a Liberal victory that he him-self had worked hard to achieve. As soon as the votes were counted, he fired off a telegram to King offering his "most sincere and hearty congratulations on the victory in Canada. It is a fine tribute to your leadership. We particularly feel that the endorsation in Ontario rightfully expresses the feelings of the Ontario Liberals toward you personally."[28] This telegram was followed the next day by a letter in which McRuer again congratulated King on the Liberal Party's "magnificent victory," a victory that all his friends regarded "as a great personal tribute to the leadership you have given over a long period of years, and more than that … [as] an indication that statesmanship can prevail over political adventurers." He added: "The whole campaign conducted throughout Canada by yourself and your associates was on such a high plane, and that conducted by your opponents on such a low one, that the verdict of the people is reassuring to those who are interested in public life. I feel that men who would make very able public servants are often kept out of public life for the simple reason that they do not wish to expose themselves to a tirade of vilification and abuse at the hands of those who believe that that is the road to power. I believe the result of this election will do more to create in Canada a tradition [of civility] than anything that has happened in many years. Never did we have a campaign that was conducted from such diametrically opposite schools of thought, and never have we had such a pronouncement from the people."

McRuer then expressed the hope that the political situation in Ontario would improve in the wake of the federal election. "It is of manifest importance to the people of Ontario and to the growing generation that the affairs of government should be carried on with a consciousness for the public welfare, and not merely as a sort of slapstick political comedy involving the personal abuse and ridicule of all those who might disagree with the erratic course being followed."[29]

McRuer's hopes were disappointed in the short term, for, despite King's strengthened position, Hepburn could still cause trouble. In the spring of 1940 Hepburn and like-minded champions of provincial rights had been infuriated by the report of the Rowell-Sirois commission, which recommended that the federal government should be granted sweeping and exclusive taxation powers in exchange for assuming existing provincial debts, taking over such expensive social programs as unemployment insurance, and paying the provinces a national adjustment grant. In January 1941 a federal-provincial conference was called to discuss the report's recommendations. Before it convened, Hepburn wrote to his friend, federal cabinet minister Chubby Power, another politician with a well-known fondness for the bottle, that he was "going to the conference in Ottawa with blood in my eye and dandruff in my moustache—but of course that's the way you expect me."[30]

At the conference itself, Hepburn, supported by premiers William Aberhart of Alberta and Duff Pattullo of British Columbia, dismissed the recommendations of the recently released Rowell-Sirois report. Claiming that the report was the "product of the minds of three professors and a Winnipeg newspaperman," he vowed to "stand solidly behind Quebec if at any time her minority rights are threatened." The whole affair was a callous waste of time, said Hepburn. It was "unthinkable that we should be fiddling while London is burning." After two days of acrimonious discussion, Hepburn announced that the Ontario delegation had no choice but to return to Toronto and "leave these wreckers of Confederation ... to carry on their nefarious work."[31] The conference adjourned without a single achievement to its credit.

Yet, in the end, Hepburn lost and King won. During the years 1939–45 the federal government, faced with the national emergency occasioned by the war, assumed all of the functions and taxing authority envisaged by the Rowell-Sirois report. This shift in the balance of federal-provincial power, which the King government justified by citing its responsibility under the BNA Act for peace, order, and good government, was never made formal and permanent through constitutional amendments, but it was still very real. The result was that the Ontario government, like all provincial governments, was little more than a "glorified county council" during the war.[32] It was forced to give over its power to tax in return for direct federal grants. Its major work during its extended life (beyond the normal five-year limit between elections) seems to have been its unanimous passage of a bill to change the name "undertaker" to "funeral director and embalmer." Ontario's citizens understood the irrelevance of its provincial government, and, despite his bravado, so did Hepburn.

The 1941 federal-provincial conference was Hepburn's last hurrah. Early the following year he was personally humiliated by the result of a federal by-election in the riding of York South: the Conservative candidate, former prime minister Arthur Meighen, whom Hepburn supported, lost to the CCF candidate, Joseph Noseworthy, by almost 4,500 votes. McRuer was delighted with the by-election result and sent Mackenzie King a telegram congratulating him and expressing confidence in his leadership. At about the same time, he stressed to the prime minister the need for "some wide-spread organization of Liberals in Ontario for the purpose of getting behind your leadership" and getting rid of Hepburn. Indicating that "Mr. Hepburn will soon remove any small measure of confidence that any Liberals may have in him," McRuer underlined the gravity of the situation in the starkest terms: "This goes far beyond any question of political expediency. There are forces at work that, for their own political and monetary advantage, are quite willing to sacrifice the unity of Canada and the ultimate welfare of Canada. These forces can only be properly countered by united effort." In short, McRuer concluded, it was time to revive efforts—suspended because of the outbreak of the war—to provide the Liberal party in Ontario with a firmer organizational base. As a beginning, he suggested that a "strong body" be established to put the government's case to the people in the proposed referendum on conscription.[33]

By now Hepburn's mind was beginning to wander—the effect of medication and years of burning the candle at both ends—and he intrigued with Aberhart of Alberta, the federal and provincial Tories, the autoworkers, and even Communist Party leader Tim Buck in the hope of lighting the old fire against King. None of it worked, and he grew tired of the whole business of politics. On 23 October 1942 he handed in his resignation as premier (though not as party leader or member of the cabinet) and asked the lieutenant-governor to swear in Attorney-General Gordon Conant as his successor. Although such a manoeuver was constitutionally acceptable in a technical sense, Hepburn's action shocked the province and astonished most Ontario Liberals, including McRuer. Their candidate for premier and party leader was not Conant, a colourless Oshawa lawyer without any evident leadership qualities, but Brant County MPP Harry Nixon. They were convinced that a leadership convention should be held, and, if it were, that Nixon could win.

Two days after Conant assumed the premiership, a concerned McRuer wrote him a letter offering congratulations and support but also warning him of the necessity of holding a convention to confirm his leadership as soon as possible. McRuer noted that leadership "is only the gift of the party itself, properly called in convention. I feel sure that anyone who would attempt to hold the leadership of the Liberal Party without consulting the Party as a whole is bound to fail." Strong medicine, this, but McRuer felt that Conant needed frankness, and he told him that the same words were on everybody's lips.[34] He sent a copy of his letter to Sir William Mulock, a former minister in the Laurier government and a former chief justice of Ontario, noting that he had "couched it in as moderate terms as I can, and I hope it will impress him."[35]

In November the Liberal caucus, while agreeing to support Conant for the coming session, resolved that a leadership convention would be held within two months of the session's close. Conant then held on while the party tore itself apart. Hepburn remained on the scene as provincial treasurer and continued to attack Mackenzie King's "Nazi tactics"; Nixon resigned from the cabinet in disgust and began preparing furiously for a leadership convention. Conant finally lost patience with Hepburn and in March 1943 informed him that his resignation from the cabinet (originally handed in when he had resigned as premier) would now be accepted—a move that an almost apoplectic Hepburn denounced in a letter to the press as evidence that King's political machine had set up a "Quisling Government in Ontario."

The Liberal convention was held on 28 April 1943 at the King Edward Hotel and was attended by a big posse of federal cabinet ministers led by C.D. Howe and Ian Mackenzie. The result was a foregone conclusion: Harry Nixon easily defeated three other candidates and became the new premier of Ontario. Yet, for Ontario Liberals, the passing of the torch came too late. On 4 August 1943 Harry Nixon led his party to its most crushing defeat since the rise of the United Farmers of Ontario. The Liberals came in third with only fifteen seats, while the Conservatives under George Drew's leadership won thirty-eight and the CCF thirty-four. Within two years Drew's minority government suffered defeat in the legislature and went to the people again. Astonishingly, the Liberals, demoralized and confused, turned again to Hepburn, making him party leader at another convention. McRuer was dismayed by this turn of events. It was clear in his mind, if in no one else's, that memories of past Hepburn victories were no substitute for clear thinking in the present. He refused to take any part in the 1945 campaign; instead, he channelled all his political energies into the federal Liberal cause.

As the campaign wore on, most voters began to realize that Hepburn's old magic was gone. On election day, McRuer, a dyed-in-the-wool Grit,

voted Liberal; he rationalized his action by saying that he was just supporting the good Liberal candidate in his constituency. Provincially, the
Liberals were trampled in a Tory landslide, winning only eleven seats
compared to sixty-six for the Conservatives and eight for the CCF; even
Hepburn lost his seat. The Ontario Liberal Party would not win another
election until 1985.

McRuer's worst fears about Hepburn's political legacy for Ontario
Liberals had come true.

IN THE LATTER STAGES of Hepburn's turbulent premiership, McRuer,
like all other Canadians, had one eye trained on Canada and the other
on a Europe once more in the throes of war. For an old soldier such
as McRuer, the Second World War was reminiscent of the first—but
with one important difference. This time, civilization and freedom were
threatened, not just by an authoritarian, expansionist Germany, but by
a Germany that was controlled by one of the most morally abhorrent
regimes in history.

McRuer strongly supported the King government's management of
the nation's military effort, as we have already seen. He also did what he
could to counter the charges of the government's critics. On 28 November 1939, for example, he wrote to inform his close friend in Ottawa,
Minister of Defence Norman Rogers, about a "whispering campaign of
"a most malicious nature that is being carried on in the City of Toronto."
Army recruits in Canada, it was said, had not been given socks, they
were freezing in unheated huts at the base in Valcartier, Quebec, and the
government was not issuing any medical equipment to the military hospitals. McRuer characterized all these stories as "complete prevarication"
and speculated whether they emanated from "enemy sources," namely
Nazis or Communists.

The one criticism of the government McRuer did accept was that it
was failing "in respect to publicity." "We must realize," he reminded Rogers, that "we have been brought up in a country where people have been
taught that they have a right to know what is being done by the Government, and that national effort may be greatly impaired by lack of public
support if the public is not kept well informed." Spurious charges such as
the ones now making the rounds in Toronto, McRuer concluded, "should
be met with facts so that those of us who have the greatest confidence in
the extraordinary, able and conscientious effort that is being put forward
by everyone in a position of trust in Government at the present time,

may have the opportunity to meet such criticism before a prairie fire has been started that may result in a great conflagration."

On one occasion, McRuer attempted to win over critics of the war effort by bringing them together with the minister of defence. In December 1939 a group of concerned Toronto businessmen and professionals led by James M. Macdonnell, soon to be elected as a Conservative MP, approached McRuer and asked him to join them on a trip to Ottawa, where they intended to meet with federal politicians and express their anger over Canada's lack of military preparedness. Macdonnell had known McRuer for a very long time, and he and his group were anxious to obtain his help not only because of his reputation as a prominent Liberal but also because of his close friendship with Minister of Defence Norman Rogers. While McRuer was not sympathetic to their cause, he agreed to accompany them to Ottawa on the condition that they act not as a self-constituted body but as delegates of organizations such as the Board of Trade and the Canadian Manufacturers' Association. This condition was an astute one—the group would have made no headway with government if they were merely a collection of aggrieved citizens—and Macdonnell and his colleagues readily agreed to it.

With McRuer's help, the group soon obtained an interview with Rogers in Ottawa. Arriving in his office in a fighting mood, they harangued the defence minister for over an hour and a half for the government's apparent lack of will and ability—a state of affairs best manifested, they thought, in stories that guns were being taken away from the militia and that recruits were being trained with sticks. When Rogers had heard them out, he leaned back in his chair and thanked them for their concern. Then, after warning them that they were prevented by the Official Secrets Act from disclosing any information he gave them, Rogers somewhat sadly proceeded to set out what he called "the facts of life." When the war began, he said, Britain was very short of weaponry of all kinds and the Canadian government had agreed to ship overseas all the rifles in its armories. As they spoke, Churchill was still asking for any kind of firearm, even shotguns and sport rifles, and Canada was continuing to collect and deliver arms to Britain, with the result that there were no rifles for either the recruits or the militia. This revelation of how bleak and desperate the real situation was had an instant and humbling effect on the delegation, and they thanked the minister for his frankness and his trust.[36]

When the group filed out, Rogers asked McRuer, Macdonnell, and a Quebec representative of the Canadian Legion to stay behind. Once they were alone, Rogers requested their help in devising a scheme whereby the training and valuable military experience of First World War veterans could be usefully employed. This was a request that McRuer and his colleagues could not refuse, Given access to the Department of National Defence's records for the 1914–18 war, they developed the outlines of a plan over two or three days, and McRuer was left with the job of filling in the details. By June 1940, with the "phoney war" in Europe ended and the Wehrmacht sweeping across France, McRuer's draft plan for the Veterans' Guard of Canada was ready, and he eagerly planned to present it to Rogers when the latter came to Toronto on 10 June to give an address to the Canadian Club. But Rogers never arrived. Half-way between Ottawa and Toronto his plane crashed and he was killed. McRuer was devastated. He had lost a friend whom he greatly admired, and the country had lost an able defence minister in the midst of a war.

Chubby Power, the minister with responsibility for the Royal Canadian Air Force and for the British Commonwealth Air Training Plan, stepped temporarily into Rogers's shoes as acting defence minister. On 5 July he was replaced by J.L Ralston, and together they brought the Veteran's Guard plan before cabinet. It was approved substantially as McRuer had written it, and a subsequent order-in-council established the Veterans' Guard of Canada under the control of the minister of national defence. It provided for the establishment of twenty-nine infantry companies composed entirely of First World War veterans. These companies were responsible for guarding locations vulnerable to enemy sabotage, such as war plants, railways, and power stations. In addition, they were posted as a military guard at the fifteen isolated internment camps holding enemy aliens resident in Canada and captured German soldiers (as well as, in time, Canadian citizens of Japanese, Italian, and German origin). Some well-trained reserve companies were eventually attached to various units of the Reserve Army.

McRuer was active in other ways during the war. At the request of his law partner Andrew Brewin, he spent much of his spare time—what little of it he had—in the early days of the war helping to found the Civil Liberties Association of Toronto. This organization came into being on 11 March 1940, and, besides McRuer and Brewin, its members included Agnes Macphail, B.K. Sandwell, the editor of Saturday Night, and two Conservative MPs, James M. Macdonnell and Leopold Macaulay (a former Ontario minister in the George Henry government). McRuer had a complex view of the association, seeing it as a vehicle both to educate the public about the importance of democratic rights and also to justify government restrictions on those rights in wartime. Specifically, McRuer saw the imposition of the War Measures Act as a necessary measure to safeguard freedom by limiting democratic liberties temporarily, though he also urged the need for government restraint in its use of the act.

This point of view made McRuer's position in the Civil Liberties Association somewhat uncomfortable, At the first public meeting of the association on 13 March, some members of the audience—apparently Russian sympathizers (Hitler and Stalin were then allies)—rudely shouted during Macdonnell's middle-of-the-road speech. They reserved their worst treatment for McRuer, however, booing him loudly when he declared that the war was not a Sunday School picnic and that Canadians were going to have to make temporary sacrifices, including the surrender of some civil liberties. It was the only time in his life that he was booed—and it happened at a civil liberties meeting where he was expressing his opinions![37]

Nine months later McRuer, "more in sorrow than in anger," resigned from the Civil Liberties Association because he felt that his belief in the need for the War Measures Act was proving too much of a burden for the organization. After his resignation, he repeatedly called upon the government to restrain itself in applying the War Measures Act, and, while he did not oppose the government's decision in 1942 to intern the Japanese Canadians of British Columbia, he did urge that the policy be made more lenient. That same year, when it was proposed that Japanese domestics be barred from Toronto, McRuer wrote to the mayor opposing such a move. In a letter of 9 June 1942 he noted that "at the present time the domestic situation in the city is extremely difficult, and many women who are giving valuable time and service in war work are going to find it very difficult to carry on with the war services they are giving and do their own housework at the same time." He then added, still keeping sentiment safely at a distance but hinting at his preference for firmness tempered with mercy: "These Japanese girls must live somewhere in Canada, and it would appear that, under proper supervision, they can be as safely kept in Toronto as any other place. Of course, I quite agree that they should be with responsible parties, and under all the supervision that the necessities demand."

The McRuer family, like many other Canadian families, went through changes during the war. In 1939 Mary Louise left home to begin studies at the University of Toronto. She could have continued living with her parents, but, since the McRuers were prosperous enough now to pay university residence fees, she took a room on campus in Whitney Hall.

Her busy father had not even realized when she left on a Saturday night in September that she would not be returning, and so he missed saying goodbye and wishing her well. In a way, that was fortunate, because he sat down on 25 September to write a fatherly letter in which he expressed himself far more openly than he could have done in person. "You will find university life something new. There is a spirit and atmosphere about it that you do not find in any other place. You will make there many new friends and I think the loyalty of friends made at the university stage of your life surpasses that of all other friends. They are your friends because they like you for what you are, not for the place you hold in society and the direct or indirect influence you may have and I am sure those are the only friends worth while." He wrote about how she would be missed at home but also about how glad he was that she would be "living in." This would give her an opportunity, he noted, to meet students from out of the city. "Never forget," he then added, "that they will look with some jealousy on the Toronto girls and the greener a freshman is the greater he or she appreciates a kindly smile." After cautioning her to avoid "all cliques"—something he had always done in his own life—he raised a practical matter. Inquiring if there was a bank at the university where she could cash a cheque, he explained that he wanted to "arrange to have money for you when you need it." He closed his letter with "Lots of love, Daddy" and tucked in the envelope a ten-dollar bill for "pin money."

Everyone was in for more learning in this period. Daughter Katherine left Toronto altogether, headed for Queen's University in Kingston. Her father offered her the same kind of advice he had given Mary Louise, and he recounted as well some of his own experiences in Kingston during the First World War (he had found the town so dull as a soldier that he told Mary, "If they held a funeral here it would cause a commotion"). Katherine had talent as a writer and, as she described it, a "quirky mind" that allowed her to observe details from a fresh perspective, but to her frustration her father frowned on journalism and directed her instead toward university and a professional career. After graduation, Katherine would "do her bit" by enlisting in the Royal Canadian Air Force. She experienced no break with her father over joining up, however, as Jim had with his own father in 1916. He was, in contrast, proud of her.

Son John, moving with no particular happiness through the disciplined routine imposed by the University of Toronto Schools, finished grade 12 and then decided, at age seventeen, to enrol at the Royal Roads Military Academy on the Pacific Coast, a busy and exciting spot to be in the midst of the war when Canadian naval patrols scanned the horizon and secluded landing areas for Japanese invaders. When he graduated, John realized a boyhood dream by joining the Royal Canadian Navy—a step that also set him free from his domineering father.

Mary, too, became part of this educational exodus from Glenayr Avenue. In the early 1940s Mary decided to take Jim up on his prenuptial promise that, one day, she would be able to resume her university education. She enrolled at the University of Toronto and graduated with a first-class honours degree in fine arts in 1943, the same year that her two daughters graduated. The simultaneous arrival on the scene of three McRuer women with university degrees was newsworthy enough for the *Toronto Telegram* to send a photographer to the family home the next day, but—apart from the satisfaction of seeing their picture in the newspaper—what particularly stood out for the two daughters was the fact that Mother's marks were higher than theirs.

During the war, the McRuers opened their home to an evacuee from bomb-torn London, a young girl named Jennifer Barton who was the daughter of Jim's friend Wilfred Barton. John, still living at home, could hardly talk with Jennifer—she cried endlessly during her first year at their home, distraught over the war, missing her parents, anxious about living in a strange country, and basically miserable. Mary McRuer, at her wits' end "more or less despaired." At least she had one escape: after preparing supper, she would head off to the university for her classes, leaving behind tearful Jennifer, and, when he was home, Jim, who would wash the dishes and clean up. Over time, Jennifer pulled herself together and enrolled at the Bishop Strachan School for Girls (Jim's solid income was helpful in a number of ways). Still unhappy, however, she risked an Atlantic crossing in 1944 to return home to England. Arriving safely, she went on to become an expert in modern languages, especially German, and to work for MI-5 in counter-espionage.

In 1940 McRuer experienced a personal tragedy. His mother had been ill with cancer for some time, and in the last months of her life she was cared for by Jim's sister and her husband, Solomon Hannant, who moved into the Gothic Avenue house. Jim visited frequently but felt sad each time he left. As Mary's illness worsened the Hannants found themselves increasingly unable to cope, and eventually she was moved into a nursing home. In July 1940 she died, and, after a quiet family funeral, she too was taken back to Ayr for burial. Jim was grief-stricken. Others in the family had found her austere, but he had always loved her deeply.

On a happier note, the war brought an unusual opportunity McRuer's

way. In 1940 he received a request from a friend to act as honorary consul in Toronto for The Netherlands government, now in exile in London.
Crown Princess Juliana of The Netherlands and her two daughters had
taken refuge in Ottawa and made their wartime home in the capital city
while Prince Bernhard stayed in England to serve with the Royal Air
Force. While extremely busy with other work, McRuer agreed to act on a
voluntary basis as the consul for The Netherlands and soon received his
royal patent signed by Queen Wilhelmina. Giving the consulate secretary a room in his own law office, McRuer helped sort out many conun-
drums for Dutch nationals in the Toronto and southern Ontario region,
issued a steady stream of passports to Dutch citizens, mainly refugees
who wished to travel, and provided a general clearing-house and introduction bureau for the many Dutch who had fled from their German-
occupied homeland. The work had its satisfactions, but John McRuer
remembers that his father found "Dutchmen stubborn and difficult to
deal with." On one occasion McRuer assisted Prince Bernhard in his visit
to the Free Dutch army training centre near Stratford, Ontario, and in
1943 he and his wife attended the christening service for Princess Margriet, born as a Dutch national in a ward of the Ottawa General Hospital
temporarily declared by parliament to be Netherlands territory. McRuer
wrote letters to newspapers regarding Holland and the war, and he made
public appeals to Canadians to support the "wear a daisy" campaign; the
daisy—called a "Margriet" in Dutch—was being worn in Holland as a
commemoration of those who fell during the Nazi occupation. McRuer
even sold the flowers at his office on Bay Street.

As the war neared its end, McRuer was just as busy as he had ever been,
with his law practice, politics, and various wartime activities all making
demands on his time. In taking stock, he had good reason to be pleased
with his accomplishments. Since his call to the bar in 1914, McRuer had
risen slowly but steadily to the senior ranks of the Canadian legal profession, acquiring a reputation as a smart, hard-working lawyer capable of
tackling all manner of cases. His flourishing legal practice had made him
financially comfortable and also had given him an entrée into the world
of politics. Though unsuccessful in his one attempt to win a seat in parliament, he nonetheless had emerged as an important player in the Liberal
Party's backrooms, and his political contacts combined with his legal reputation had given him a chance to undertake one of the most challenging assignments of his life as a member of the Archambault commission
on prison reform. There were disappointments and frustrations along
the way—the federal government's inaction on the Archambault com-

mission's report, the nasty business of dealing with the impetuous Mitch Hepburn, and the Ontario Liberal Party's devastating defeat in 1943. In all, however, McRuer could pride himself on how far he had come and on how much he had achieved.

Of course, McRuer was never one to rest on his laurels. By 1944 he was starting to cast around for a new challenge—one that would offer him opportunities different from those he had had before. With so many accomplishments to his credit, and with so many friends in high places, he did not have to wait long. Before 1944 had run its course, McRuer had accepted an offer from the Government of Canada that would set the course of his life for the next two decades.

9

ON THE BENCH

DURING THE EARLY AUTUMN OF 1944, the Ontario legal world was abuzz with rumour. Chief Justice Hugh Edward Rose of the Ontario High Court of Justice was widely expected to request retirement on the grounds of failing health. Members of the legal profession—whether aspirants to the bench or not—speculated about his successor and other imminent personnel changes in Ontario's judiciary. Jim McRuer was far from oblivious to this situation, but his involvement in the matter ran much deeper than many people suspected.

McRuer had been offered a judgeship a few years earlier but, with two children in university at the time, he declined the promotion because he still needed the higher income that his legal practice was generating. By 1944, however, the financial pressures on him had lessened; Katherine and Mary Louise had graduated from university, and Katherine and John were in the military. The time now seemed ripe for a "move up." McRuer believed that every good lawyer should aspire to service as a judge, and he now realized, as someone in his mid-fifties, that the impending shakeup of Ontario's judicial corps was an opportunity he should not overlook if he was serious about acquiring a place on the bench. Given his three decades of experience in practising and enforcing the law, he was confident that he would make a good judge.

McRuer was certainly well placed for promotion to the bench. Apart from his impressive qualifications as a lawyer and federal government commissioner, he had a record of service in the Liberal Party and was well known to both Prime Minister King and Minister of Justice Louis St. Laurent. McRuer and St. Laurent had come into contact through the Turgeon commission, the Canadian Bar Association (of which St. Laurent was honorary president from 1941 to 1946), and the Law Society of Upper Canada. In addition, McRuer had a valuable ally in the person of Dalton L. McCarthy, the current treasurer of the Law Society. McCarthy, who had been a colleague and friend of McRuer since the days of the Home Bank case twenty years earlier, was quite close to St. Laurent and was putting in a good word on McRuer's behalf.

In the fall of 1944 McCarthy paid a visit to McRuer's law firm and asked if he had time for a short walk. In a few minutes they found themselves under a gloomy Toronto sky, surveying the neighbourhoods around McRuer's offices. McCarthy recounted that, at a recent meeting he had had in Ottawa with the minister of justice, he had recommended McRuer as successor to the ailing Chief Justice Rose. St. Laurent was warm to the suggestion, and McCarthy now wanted to know how McRuer felt. After a brief silence, a smiling McRuer assured McCarthy that he was prepared to serve his country in any suitable capacity.

Several days later McRuer received a telephone call from Fred Varcoe, deputy minister of justice in Ottawa, who asked him if he would accept an appointment to the Exchequer Court of Canada. This was not what McRuer was expecting. Perplexed, he replied that he knew very little about the working of the Exchequer Court, except that it concerned itself with patents, trademarks, and copyright, and that he was not interested in the job. Varcoe said that he was not surprised, and shortly afterwards he phoned back with another offer—an appointment to the Ontario Court of Appeal. Of course, Varcoe said, McRuer was still a leading candidate for the post of chief justice of the Ontario High Court, and his acceptance of a position with the Court of Appeal would not stand in the way of further promotion in the near future.

On 13 October 1944 Prime Minister Mackenzie King signed the order-in-council appointing James Chalmers McRuer to the Court of Appeal for Ontario. A new chapter in his legal career had begun.

DURING MCRUER'S TIME ON THE BENCH, the Supreme Court of Ontario was the highest court in the province. It was comprised of two branches, the "Court of Appeal for Ontario" and the "High Court of Justice for Ontario." The Court of Appeal was headed by a chief justice called the "chief justice of Ontario" (the highest-ranking Ontario judge), and the

High Court was headed by a chief justice called the "chief justice of the High Court" (the second-highest-ranking Ontario judge). Judges were appointed to one or the other of the two divisions; all such judges were judges of the Supreme Court as well as judges of the particular division to which they were appointed.

Trials were held before judges of the High Court, and appeals from their decisions were heard by judges of the Court of Appeal. The latter court also heard cases being appealed from the county or district courts and the lower magistrates' courts. Any cases from Ontario's courts that eventually found their way to the Supreme Court of Canada would first have been heard by the Ontario Court of Appeal. The High Court was located at Osgoode Hall in Toronto, but it also moved in circuit to all counties and districts of the province; the Court of Appeal sat only at Osgoode Hall.

McRuer remained on the Court of Appeal for fourteen months, from 14 October 1944 to 27 December 1945, and during that time he was called upon to adopt a legal perspective entirely different from the one he had held as a lawyer. In the Court of Appeal, neither plaintiff nor defendant appeared in person, there were no jurors, and only a few spectators were present. Counsel for both sides argued the most intricate subtleties of the law with calm deliberation, while the judges, with only the written record of the original trial before them, weighed the legal arguments in the light of extensive research which they themselves conducted during long hours in the library. As is still true today, the work of the appellate judge was arduous, not only because of the hours of solitary study the job entails but also because of the heavy responsibility involved in reversing or upholding the decision of another court.

As McRuer arrived at the Court of Appeal in 1944, the eight other justices he was joining were, in order of seniority, William Renwick Riddell, Robert Grant Fisher, William Thomas Henderson, Charles Patrick McTague, John Gordon Gillanders, Roy Lindsay Kellock, Robert Everett Laidlaw, and Wilfrid Daniel Roach. All nine were led by Robert Spelman Robertson, chief justice of Ontario—a situation that made McRuer uncomfortable. Although he and Robertson had a high regard for each other's talents, they did not get along well. Their poor relations dated to the 1920s when they were on opposite sides in several cases.[1]

For all lawyers who become judges, promotion to the bench is followed by a transitional period during which they adjust—often with mixed emotions—to their new role. In McRuer's case, the adjustment was especially difficult because, when all was said and done, he did not find his work on the appellate court especially satisfying. McRuer toiled away at the written record, poring over abstract scholarship, lost sometimes for days in mazes of evidence, argument and counter-argument, before emerging with pearls of judicial wisdom. His intellect was engaged by the research side of his work, and he was also stimulated, in a narrow way at least, by the legal reasoning to which he was exposed. Still, he longed to have closer contact with the people whose lives his decisions affected. Missing the "real life drama" of the trial court, he began to wonder whether the conclusions he drew from the dreary documents that now circumscribed his professional life were as valid as those reached by judges and jurors who had seen the parties to the dispute in the flesh. Years later, in a lecture on "The Role of the Judge" given to the Advocates" Society on 1 November 1974, McRuer was speaking from personal experience when he expressed the view that appointees to the appellate court would be much better judges if they first had some experience in trial court.

Although McRuer's tenure on the Appeal Court was characterized by long stretches of monotony, it certainly did not begin that way. The first case that he heard—*Yachuk* v. *Oliver Blais Co.*—fascinated him and resulted in his writing a precedent-setting judgment. His decision was reversed by the Supreme Court of Canada in 1946 but then upheld by the Judicial Committee of the Privy Council in London.

The case began in Kirkland Lake on a hot summer's day in 1944, when a nine-year-old boy and his younger brother were pretending to be Indians on the warpath. Remembering a movie in which a war dance was accompanied by burning torches, they marched to the edge of a nearby marsh and collected a bunch of bulrushes. Somehow they found matches, but, since the bulrushes had not been dried, they were unable to light them. Frustrated yet not willing to give up, the older brother obtained an empty lard pail from home and, with the five cents his mother had given them for chocolate milk, the two young boys went to a local gas station. The attendant, who did not warn the boys about the explosive nature of gasoline, filled half the can with the volatile fuel. The boys then returned to their secret hiding-place in the woods, and minutes later the community was thrown into turmoil. In attempting to light the bulrushes, the older boy spilled quantities of gasoline on his clothing, and when he struck a match to light the torches he exploded into a ball of flames. Although he survived, he would be disfigured for life.

An action for financial compensation was brought by the boy's parents against the operator of the service station. Mr. Justice George Urquhart, the experienced trial judge who heard the case, awarded large damages of about $10,000. However, since both sides had contributed to the accident taking place, he apportioned the degree of fault and negligence between them—25 per cent to the service station employee and 75 per cent to the small boy.[2] This meant that the boy would receive just one-quarter of the damages, or $2,500. The boy's parents were not satisfied and their lawyer, J.L.G. Keogh, appealed the judgment to the Ontario Court of Appeal. Chief Justice Robertson asked McRuer and Mr. Justice Wilfrid D. Roach, who had also been recently appointed to the Court of Appeal, to sit with him in hearing the case. It came before the court during McRuer's first week on the bench, and he followed it with fascination.

The case raised some delicate points of law, particularly the issue of whether a nine-year-old boy could be guilty of negligence in his handling of a highly flammable substance. Robertson, McRuer, and Roach decided to reserve judgment. At the end of the week, when the time came to allocate work on reserved judgments, Chief Justice Robertson asked his associates if they had any preferences. McRuer volunteered with enthusiasm to take the gasoline case. After studying it for some time, he concluded that no nine-year-old boy could be expected to grasp the full dangers involved in handling gasoline, and that the service station attendant who sold the fuel to him was fully negligent and bore exclusive responsibility. The entire liability, he recommended, should rest with the service station attendant, which meant that the service station, or most likely its insurance company, would pay the full amount of the $10,000 damages to the boy. Once his written reasons were prepared, McRuer, with some mixed feelings, took the text to Robertson, whom he knew to be a most careful man. The chief justice read it closely and then said only, "Well, you worked that out pretty well." Like a schoolboy receiving a high mark on one of his assignments, McRuer felt a surge of satisfaction. His judgment won Roach's concurrence, too, and so it became a unanimous decision of the court.[3]

The defendant's lawyers reacted more negatively and appealed the judgment to the Supreme Court of Canada. There McRuer's ruling split the court. Two judges held that the boy was entirely to blame and that there was no liability whatsoever on the attendant at the service station; two others held that Mr. Justice Urquhart at the trial had arrived at the proper decision and that his original apportionment of fault was correct. Only Mr. Justice Ivan Rand upheld McRuer's decision that the boy was entitled to full damages.[4]

This division of opinion in the country's highest court settled nothing. A further appeal was accordingly made to the Judicial Committee of the Privy Council, and this body restored the judgment of the Ontario Court of Appeal.[5] Not only was McRuer satisfied with this vindication of his decision, but he saw the Yachuk case as a landmark along the path towards the recognition of the special rights of children under the law in Canada—a cause that he believed in deeply and that would benefit from his further interest in the years ahead.

During his time on the appellate court, McRuer became preoccupied with the problems involved in appeals of sentences. While he recognized that the right of appeal against a sentence was essential, he had growing doubts about whether such appeals achieved the best results. Even before his elevation to the bench, McRuer had believed that trial judges usually proceeded carefully and wisely in the imposition of sentences, basing their decisions on the nature of the offence, the circumstances under which it was committed, the character of the accused, and the needs of the community where the crime had taken place. Another of his longstanding beliefs, based upon his years of courtroom experience as both crown prosecutor and defence attorney, was that trial judges were in a good position to reach sound decisions: they were most familiar with local circumstances, came to know first-hand the witnesses and the accused, and, by listening to testimony day after day, absorbed not only the details but the whole atmosphere of the case. Although these judges imposed varying sentences for what, to an outside observer, appeared to be similar or identical crimes, McRuer was convinced that such discrepancies in sentencing were appropriate as long as each case had been weighed according to the principles of law and local conditions.

McRuer's views on all these matters did not change after he became a judge; on the contrary, his doubts about the role of appeal judges in sentencing even increased. McRuer would observe in 1983 that "some of the Appeal Court judges have never tried a criminal case. In fact, some have never tried any case, having been named directly from the bar." He then added: "We trust a jury of men and women to try the innocence or guilt of a person accused of a crime, and I have sometimes thought that a review board of solid citizens such as we get on juries would do an appropriate job of reviewing sentences imposed by judges. I know, of course, that all my legal friends would claim that idea complete heresy. Yet the question of law hardly enters into the matter of sentence, if there is to be punishment for the offence committed."[6]

McRuer's reflections on sentencing were set out in an article in the *Canadian Bar Review* in November 1949. Entitled "Sentences," this arti-

cle largely grew out of his experiences on the Court of Appeal. McRuer
began his analysis by stressing the importance of sentencing, the complexities it involved, and the need to retain flexibility. "There is probably no more difficult task that any judicial officer has to perform than
the imposition of the appropriate sentence on a person convicted of
crime, and there is no place in the administration of justice where there
is greater danger of injustice being done," he reasoned. "The limits of the
discretion of the court, although bounded by law, must necessarily be so
wide that the discretion is exercised with little definite legal guidance."[7]

McRuer then outlined his view of the philosophy of sentencing underlying Canadian law, namely that punishment should act as a deterrent
to others and "in some measure serve to rehabilitate the offender."[8] Noting that the American Bill of Rights limited the severity of punishment
by stipulating that "excessive fines ought not to be imposed or cruel or
unusual punishment inflicted," McRuer set out a similar axiom: "Swift
and sure punishment always does much more to regulate society effec-
tually than the severity of punishment."[9] Studious moderation, he concluded, should always be exercised when sentences are imposed.

McRuer next surveyed the five ways in which offenders could be punished in Canada at that time: "(1) sentence may be suspended, with or
without conditions; (2) the offender may be fined; (3) the offender may
be imprisoned (a) in the common gaol, (b) in a provincial reformatory,
(c) in the penitentiary; (4) the offender may be whipped; (5) the offender
may be executed."[10] After evaluating the effectiveness of these means of
punishment and finding them wanting in various ways, McRuer advocated a number of reforms that were largely based on the findings of
the Archambault commission's report. A probation system should be
established for the supervision of all persons released on suspended sentences. Probation officers should be available to make reports on convicted persons for the information of the court before sentence is passed.
Minimum or fixed sentences should be abolished except in the case of
murder. Whipping should be regulated as to the character of the instrument to be used, the maximum number of strokes, and the time when
the punishment is inflicted (at the start of incarceration, not mid-way
or near release). The administration of the Ticket of Leave Act should
be under the commissioner of penitentiaries and those recommending
tickets of leave should act in close cooperation with the prison instruc-
tors. Those released on a ticket of leave should be supervised by probation officers. Finally, the administration of the federal penitentiaries and
provincial reformatories should be unified.[11]

As for the review of sentences within the Canadian judicial system, McRuer stated unequivocally that the usefulness of the Court of Appeal's role in this area was decidedly limited: "The right of appeal to the court of appeal against sentence, although an important right, is quite insufficient to give assurance that there will not be many grave injustices."[12] This fact, combined with the other deficiencies in the system that he had isolated, underlined the need for fundamental change. McRuer himself strongly believed that an integrated approach to sentencing was essential. Judges, magistrates, police officers on all levels, prison officials, members of parole boards, and remission officers and parole officers should not face "strict regimentation of the parts they play in this branch of government." Instead, McRuer urged, there should be "close co-operation toward attaining the end to which they are all working."[13]

At the end of 1945, McRuer was still buried in his work as an appellate judge, and, with the exception of the odd case or two, not enjoying it any more than usual. Then, however, came salvation. On 28 December Jim and Mary McRuer were enjoying themselves at a Christmas-week party at the Toronto Skating Club when a message came through that he was wanted on the telephone to receive a long-distance call. Somewhat annoyed by the interruption of one of the few moments of pleasure that he had allowed himself lately, McRuer went to the phone thinking to himself, "This had better be important!" On picking up the receiver, he had difficulty in keeping his composure when he recognized the voice of Prime Minister Mackenzie King. As McRuer listened, King launched into one of his hyperbolic addresses, always an indication that he was in a fine mood. Eventually he got to the point: cabinet had that day passed an order-in-council appointing McRuer to Ontario's High Court as successor to Chief Justice Rose, who had just died after months of suffering. This was the offer that McRuer had been anticipating since his appointment the previous year to the Court of Appeal. He quietly returned to the party and, when an appropriate break in the conversation came, discreetly told Mary that he had accepted King's offer.

Thus began yet another chapter in the career of Jim McRuer, one that would last more than eighteen years until his resignation as chief justice on 1 July 1964. This new role on the bench was not to be the final stage in his career—even though he began it at age fifty-five and left it when he was seventy-three—but it was an active and challenging one, taking him to every corner of Ontario and to many places throughout the world. To the surprise of those who did not know him well, and the delight of those who did, McRuer approached his new position with an enthusiasm that had been noticeably missing during his fourteen months on the Court of Appeal.

As CHIEF JUSTICE OF THE HIGH COURT, McRuer had responsibilities far greater than those he had exercised on the Court of Appeal. Besides heading Ontario's superior court of criminal jurisdiction, he was also in charge of the organization and operation of the province's far-flung system of circuit courts.

McRuer began his term as head of the High Court by vowing that he would personally preside at one time or another in every single county or northern district where assize courts were held, even though there were forty-eight such places in the province and this had not been the custom of Ontario's past chief justices. He wanted to acquaint himself with the local officials of the judicial system, evaluate their effectiveness, and become familiar with the vast diversity of the local communities comprising Canada's most populous province. Above all, McRuer wanted to guarantee that all the people of Ontario had equal access to the courts and that they themselves believed in their equality under the law. Like a missionary, McRuer set out to communicate his sense of justice to all Ontarians, and to put the judicial system at the service of the people whenever and wherever they needed it.

There was one trip that McRuer never forgot—or wished to repeat. On a tour of northern Ontario during the winter of 1956, McRuer found himself billeted in a modest hotel only a few minutes' walk from the courthouse. The case he was hearing dragged on into late afternoon, and after adjournment he spent several extra hours in the courthouse weighing the evidence, failing to notice that a severe blizzard had descended upon the town. When he finally closed his books and stepped out on the street, the driving snow had formed a blinding wall of ice that surrounded him. He literally inched his way through the storm towards his hotel, and when he finally found his way to his quarters he quietly gave thanks for his safe arrival. Only then did he realize that his nose had frozen. After the storm passed, he sought medical attention, and the doctor assured him that his nose would heal in time. This experience taught McRuer that sentencing was not the only area of the law where the dispensation of justice must be guided by a certain respect for local conditions.

McRuer applied this lesson in another case that he heard in the north country. He had been presiding over a process of jury selection in which the contending barristers had shown unusual petulance. At the end of a long day, the judge felt relieved when the jury was finally filled. Then, to his great astonishment, McRuer was approached by a somewhat scruffy man who had been selected for jury duty. "I have to go home to milk my cows," he said. "My wife's been sitting out in the car all day waiting for me, and she don't drive. Ain't no way for her to get back to our farm." Fully aware that a judge must not have private conversation with a sworn juror, McRuer was tempted to charge the man with contempt. Then he remembered his frozen nose. After warning the farmer never to address him "in this manner" again, and sternly announcing that "I will not tolerate this sort of thing in my court," McRuer the former farm boy continued: "I will make sure that someone looks after your cows... and your wife." He then instructed a local policeman to drive the woman home and find someone who would be willing to milk the juror's cows during his term of jury service. The officer was somewhat surprised, but he was not prepared to question the instruction of the chief justice of the High Court. After dealing with the matter, he reported to McRuer. "I delivered the lady to her home," the officer noted. "Only problem was that she's not the juror's wife. Seems she was the wife of the next-door neighbour. Anyway, the neighbour agreed to look after his wife's boyfriend's cows for the time, if you see what I mean, Your Lordship."

Mostly, McRuer liked to keep to himself while on the assize circuit. "After all," he would say to local authorities who were trying to arrange some form of entertainment for their distinguished visitor, "I have my responsibilities, and the court must convene on time in the morning." However, just how sociable, or circumspect, McRuer chose to be when visiting the counties and districts of Ontario to conduct trials varied with the time and the place—depending on how much time he had on his hands, and whether there was the prospect of good fishing. Occasionally he relaxed by playing bridge. Several of the lawyers in the county towns were his friends, and they included a number of bridge players. One of them was Fred G. MacKay, who played host to McRuer in Owen Sound until he was appointed to the Court of Appeal in 1950. Campbell Grant, who practised in Walkerton until his appointment as a judge in 1962, was another. Grant later remembered that, at evening bridge parties with McRuer, "the business of the Court was never discussed."[14] The lawyers, particularly junior counsel, enjoyed these opportunities to meet with McRuer, even though the chief justice played each game to win. Chattering was not allowed.

Once, when McRuer finished the Walkerton Court sittings early, MacKay arranged for him to spend the afternoon fishing for speckled trout in the stream of the Hepworth Anglers Club, a club formed in 1870 by bankers, lawyers, and other well-to-do fishermen. Even though McRuer did not catch much on that particular outing, he enjoyed the afternoon on this beautiful stream. He had, in fact, become an ardent fisherman, and, now that he could afford the hobby, he often visited with a group of his friends the salmon rivers of New Brunswick, where he whipped the waters with his fly rod with considerable success.

Even while he was taking the High Court to the people, McRuer retained a strong love of tradition. One example of his traditionalism was his reaction to the abolition of appeals to the Privy Council in 1949. In a letter that year to Britain's lord chancellor, Lord Jowitt, McRuer observed that the end of appeals to the Privy Council was "a natural development of the growth of Canadian nationality," a sign that Canada was "moving forward into new eras." Still, he could not suppress "a twinge of regret" for, in his view, "our association with the British jurisprudence through the appeals to the Judicial Committee has had a wholesome effect on the development of law in Canada."[15]

In a similar vein, McRuer's strict personal discipline had significant repercussions for the way the courts operated. As chief justice, he insisted on a more rigorous observance of formal procedure in all the courts under his supervision. For instance, McRuer's first visit to Windsor as chief justice proved to be a sobering experience for just about everyone. "The first visit of Chief Justice J.C. McRuer to Windsor has been followed with interest by police officers, members of the legal profession and even the local magistrates and judges," wrote local journalist R.M. Harrison. "They're all learning things." Some of the lessons that McRuer taught the court officials in Windsor were the same ones he took to all corners of Ontario. McRuer admonished counsel not to get "chummy" with their clients when they were in the witness box; he directed lawyers to keep their place by the table (rather than parading around in front of the judge's bench or the jury box); and he instructed witnesses to maintain an erect posture in the stand so that everyone could hear their testimony clearly. Further, he took a "prominent Windsor barrister to task for appearing to 'scold' an independent witness for the Crown." Those citizens who offer evidence to the court out of a sense of responsibility to the community, McRuer admonished, should not be subject to "abusive examination by defence counsel." McRuer also criticized a policeman for failing to take accurate measurements at the scene of an accident.

At another point in the trial, he turned to the crown attorney, who had objected that bringing to Windsor a witness incarcerated near Kingston would be a waste of public money, and silenced the courtroom by declaring that "giving the accused full justice is to be placed first, above monetary considerations."[16]

His no-nonsense manner was revealed in other ways, too. Throughout his years in the courtroom McRuer was dismayed by how the legal process could be stalled simply through the lassitude of the court officials in charge. As chief justice he resolved to curtail such inefficiency, and he made his intentions clear from the outset. In the words of one reporter, "Chief Justice McRuer has set a shining example of punctuality. His courts start on the dot, which means a lot when scores of jurors, witnesses, lawyers, police officers and so forth are waiting around. His Lordship told one court official about recesses: 'When I declare a to-minute recess, it means 10 minutes, not 11.'"[17] In Hamilton in 1962, when all forty-six cases on the docket for civil jury hearings were settled out of court at the last minute, McRuer objected that the courts were being used as an "adjustment bureau."

This commitment to procedural correctness and efficiency went hand in hand with a steadfast determination to maintain judicial formalities. When sitting for the first time in one rural courtroom which displayed only the Ontario coat of arms, McRuer refused to proceed until that emblem was replaced by Canada's royal insignia. Though knowing that some would criticize this action as an example of pomposity and formalistic nonsense, he believed that a simple, fundamental principle was at stake. The powers that he exercised in court did not derive from the Province of Ontario, but from the crown; the decisions of Canada's courts, in McRuer's estimation, achieved their validity on the basis of this authority. His decision in this instance to delay proceedings until the right coat of arms was mounted on the courtroom wall was a serious inconvenience to those involved in the trial, but McRuer, the formalist, a stickler for proper procedure, saw forms as indispensable in a civilized society. He wanted to make an example that would teach a clear lesson about the nature of the courts which he was now responsible for administering.

In 1946, soon after becoming chief justice, McRuer realized an idea that he had nurtured for many years—and that again related to his sense of judicial dignity and propriety. Until this time, the judges of the High Court wore either no gowns or the same black silk gowns as those worn by king's counsel and judges of the Court of Appeal. This distinguished them from the average barrister but did not set them apart from the host of KCs appearing before them. McRuer's period of military service had convinced him of the importance of distinctions in dress in hierarchical organizations, and his experience in foreign courts (which he always loved to visit on trips abroad) had shown him how effective distinctive robes could be in impressing on the litigants the solemnity of the judge's role. Enlisting the support of Mr. Justice John Keiller Mackay, whom he regarded as "a real traditionalist,"[18] McRuer launched a campaign to have robes designed for the justices of Ontario's High Court.

The idea of distinctive gowns was welcomed by most of the members of the judiciary, and, despite a few outcries from the political left, the judges were soon outfitted with the scarlet sashes, purple robes, and deep pink cuffs that they wear to this day. The new garments were patterned on the robes worn for fifty years by judges of the King's Bench in Upper Canada and later Ontario and for centuries by the judges of England's King's Bench at the trial of civil actions during the Easter and Hilary terms. When McRuer first appeared in his new gown (at the January 1947 opening of the winter assizes in Toronto), he believed that he had made a bold statement about the nature of Canadian justice—a statement that would be repeated thereafter every day that Ontario's High Court justices appeared in their courts. In the same letter to Lord Jowitt in which he reflected on the abolition of appeals to the Privy Council, McRuer wrote regarding the new gowns for High Court judges: "I feel greatly satisfied that we have forged this link of tradition with the heritage of jurisprudence that we have from England."[19]

McRuer's strict sense of courtroom decorum could also manifest itself in a way that appears prudish today. On one occasion, in 1952, a young female reporter for a Toronto newspaper was asked to leave a trial on the instruction of the chief justice. Her crime? She was wearing a sleeveless dress. A court official asked her if she had any garment with which to conceal her arms, and when she said she did not, he informed her that the chief justice did not want her reporting the case in a sleeveless dress. A woman's bare arms, McRuer felt, might be enough distraction to cause a fine point of law to be missed. Ever attentive to the smallest details involving respect for the court, McRuer was not about to allow that to happen.

McRuer's years on the bench would be filled with remarkable cases and several landmark decisions in law, but he also had an impact through the power of his personality, his dedication to justice, and his strict and severe judicial manner. For many people across Ontario, in fact, it was McRuer's character rather than his legal mind that made a lasting imprint on their memories.

Lawyers who appeared before McRuer learned early on that he expected them to be fully prepared for their cases and intimately familiar with the law involved. He disliked "florid, theatrical appeals to a jury's emotions" and took a certain credit for helping eradicate such practices during his years on the bench. "Judges," he proclaimed, "do not tolerate forensic gymnastics any longer."[20] According to Campbell Grant, who appeared before McRuer in court at various times in Walkerton, Owen Sound, and Goderich, the chief justice "followed the evidence carefully and was always familiar with the law involved and usually delivered judgment immediately following argument of counsel." In court, Grant observed, McRuer "never interfered with counsel so long as they were complying with the rules of practice."[21] But he did not hesitate to correct them when they departed from the rules.

Grant believed McRuer to be an ideal judge, able to grasp the heart of the matter through his knowledge of human nature and his own standard of fairness and integrity. "He possessed," Grant said, "the proper personality to dispense justice."[22] His experience as a lawyer was undoubtedly an asset, and so too was his involvement in politics. In 1985 Attorney-General Ian Scott, who had been a lawyer at McRuer's firm, recalled an experience that suggests some of the significance of McRuer's political experience to his work as a judge. During his days at law school, Scott and fellow student Pierre Genest sometimes skipped boring lectures on mortgages to attend court sessions where trials that interested them were under way. There Scott first saw Chief Justice McRuer preside in a commission of inquiry into electoral irregularities in the Toronto riding of St. Paul's. "I was impressed, indeed stunned, by the particular knowledge that the Commissioner had of the workings of the system—not the irregularities—the workings of the system. And it was only many years later that I learned that all that had been obtained when he was the unsuccessful Liberal candidate in High Park riding."[23] McRuer himself felt that another of his experiences—growing up on a farm—had been invaluable to him in his work on the bench. In a speech delivered in 1960, he told his audience—as he would tell many others over the years—that a person born and raised on a farm has a "rich heritage of human affairs, things which a city dweller cannot know."[24]

Yet McRuer was not without his faults as a judge. At least in his early days on the bench, he seemed incapable of ridding his mind of the attitudes and practices of the advocate. This failing was sometimes revealed in his practice of questioning witnesses himself after counsel had completed their cross-examinations. More seriously, his lawyerly instincts occasionally led him to ignore judicial impartiality and jump into the courtroom fray. For instance, in the Evelyn Dick case, recounted in more detail in the next chapter, McRuer repeatedly took sides and stepped outside his allotted function to offer advice that only a lawyer consulted by the party in question could properly give. Apparently the chief justice did not always appreciate or entirely accept the well-known axiom that "the Crown never wins and never loses."

It is unclear whether McRuer ever realized that his handling of the Dick case alienated the jury. What is certain, however, is that he was not inclined to much self-doubt. In an interview with the *Toronto Star* on the eve of his retirement as chief justice in 1964, McRuer revealed that "I don't let past decisions worry me and keep me awake. I forget them very quickly, and very soon afterward I have to go to the record to recall. It's no use worrying about things you can't do anything about, I do the best I can, and then my mind is at rest. It was the same way when I was practising law. If I won I didn't gloat; if I lost I didn't worry. You cannot let your emotions enter into your judgments. If you did you'd be distraught."[25] What he meant by "emotions" was not deeply felt feelings—he had plenty of those—but sentimentality.

Assessments of McRuer's abilities as a judge varied considerably. A *Globe Magazine* article, also published just before his retirement, claimed that McRuer's decisions during his eighteen years as chief justice "were sometimes considered harsh but were more often applauded." The article pointed out that "though some may debate the extent of his compassion, his perception and his grasp of human motivation are acknowledged." Yet it noted as well that McRuer's "objective intensity" apparently caused "considerable squirming—even fear—in his court."[26] Others agreed. Rendall Dick, who became deputy attorney-general of Ontario, recalled his early days in McRuer's court: "He could be a fearsome personage for a young counsel."[27] Another lawyer, now on the bench, described McRuer as "a son of a bitch. He was rough, and very Crown minded." The lawyers whom McRuer blasted were usually those whom he considered incompetent or who had come to his courtroom ill-prepared. He was not critical of all lawyers. McRuer remarked once that he was "always anxious to see young men of real capability develop to the best of their talents." An illustration of this interest was a letter he wrote in November 1954 to a Belleville lawyer, Ronald Cass, who had just won a case before him. He congratulated Cass and offered "in all kindness" one or two suggestions for his conduct in future cases. Cass responded gratefully, alluding to his limited court experience, the "care, consideration and fairness" with which McRuer had presided over the trial, and the assistance that had always been forthcoming from the bench.

It was not only counsel who benefited from McRuer's thoughtfulness. In a special representation to McRuer, dated 7 March 1946, a Whitby jury expressed their "grateful thanks for your Lordship's consideration for our health and comfort." The jurors' experience with McRuer's manner and that of other officials in his court had "given to twelve citizens of Ontario County increased admiration for the administration of Justice, a greater regard for the police protection afforded by the Crown, and a higher valuation of the privileges and duties of our Canadian Citizenship."

McRuer's relationship with his fellow judges was somewhat mixed. In his early years on the High Court the sailing was not smooth. He was somewhat younger than most judges at that time, and not all of his brethren agreed with the way he was running the court. In the Toronto trial sittings of the court, for example, the preparation of the weekly list of cases to be tried was an important procedure; cases of unusual importance or those that presented exceptional legal problems were usually assigned to a senior judge or one particularly qualified to try the case. On one occasion, Mr. Justice Walter Schroeder studied the list and saw that, according to it, he was to preside over an important murder trial in Toronto. On the morning the trial was to begin, Schroeder discovered to his amazement that the chief justice—a great lover of murder trials—had supplanted him. Schroeder was so chagrined that he went straight home and refused to report for duty for some time. The feud between these two strong-willed men elicited front-page coverage from the press, but eventually they were reconciled. By the time of McRuer's retirement from the bench, he and Schroeder had come to like and admire each other.[28]

Essentially, McRuer's problem with people—as illustrated by this episode—was twofold: he could go after something with great determination and be oblivious to the side-effects on others, and he never apologized. In some respects, these qualities helped him to move ahead in his career and also enabled him to undertake tasks that would have intimidated others. Yet the same qualities made it difficult for him to establish close relationships. He was a man whom most people respected, but whom many feared or disliked.

McRuer's early years on the High Court were marked, not only by clashes with his fellow justices, but also by frequent reversals of his judgments in the Court of Appeal. He found these reversals upsetting but did not complain about them. Nor did he point out that the cases he presided over personally were often ones of the greatest difficulty, a fact that helps to explain the fate of his judgments on appeal. If his sense of duty as chief justice had not governed his actions, he might have allowed some of these thorny cases to be dealt with by other High Court judges. In any event, as the years passed and McRuer became more accustomed to life on the bench, his decisions fared better. Indeed, in the latter part of his career on the High Court, from about the mid-1950s on, there were far fewer appeals from his decisions and most of them proved unsuccessful.

Over these same years, McRuer also came to be highly regarded by most members of the legal profession, judges and lawyers alike. William R. Poole, who appeared before McRuer in five murder trials and later served with him on the Ontario Law Reform Commission, offers this assessment: "He was one-hundred per cent on the side of justice."[29] Another colleague, judge Wishart Spence, in a letter to McRuer dated 10 June 1963, wrote: "For thirteen years and a few months I have worked in your court ... and everyday I have found pleasant. It is most conservative to say this is due in no small measure to your wise counsel and firm loyal friendship ... There could be no one who was a member of that Court who would fail to have for you a profound respect and a real deep affection. Believe me I am grateful ... for the priceless opportunity I have had to serve with you." Similarly, Mr. Justice William Gale (later chief justice of Ontario) wrote to McRuer on n November 1963 praising his "vast graciousness and deep understanding of other people."

The respect that McRuer earned, in spite of his difficult personality, was based mainly on his work as a jurist. Yet it also derived in part from his talents as an administrator. There was nothing going on that affected the operation of the High Court or the work of judges anywhere in the province that McRuer did not know about, and, especially after his much publicized confrontation with Schroeder, he also worked hard to foster a collegial relationship between himself and his colleagues. Another reason for McRuer's fine reputation in the eyes of his peers was his formidable appetite for work. From the beginning of his term on the High Court, McRuer worked every bit as hard if not harder than the rest of the judges, taking on the difficult cases and making himself available at all times to discuss legal or administrative problems with any of them. Moreover, he adopted the same approach with judges all across Ontario. John Brooke, later a judge on the Court of Appeal, telephoned the chief justice one night from out of town with a difficult question about the admissibility of evidence in a criminal case and the consequent jury charge. He and McRuer discussed the pros and cons of the issue and McRuer gave his opinion. The next morning McRuer awoke early and, sometime after 7:00 a.m., closeted himself in the judges' library at Osgoode Hall. He studied the relevant books, confirmed the opinion that he had formed, and telephoned Brooke to give him the additional details.

Such incidents were not unusual. On any given day McRuer might receive a long-distance telephone call from a judge in Kenora or Cochrane or Windsor. They had no judicial colleagues with whom to discuss a case, nor did they have much time available to do research on an intricate point of law that they needed to decide promptly. These summonses for help came at unpredictable times, and fatherly guidance from McRuer usually put a crisis in perspective. For example, at home late one evening, McRuer received an appeal from a new judge who had been asked by a crown attorney to cite someone for contempt of court. McRuer replied firmly that he should simply tell the crown attorney to "go away and do his own business. If he thinks that somebody has committed a contempt of court he can lay a charge. He should not ask the judge to do his work!"

Many years after he stepped down from the court, McRuer assessed the heavy administrative load of the chief justice:

"The judges were independent men and at the same time they had to be managed because you had to shift them around. And at times a judge would be on his free week and yet some judge had taken sick so you would have to ask him to give up his free week and go sit in Windsor or Chatham or some place like that. He has had all his plans made for that week and his home life and so on ...

"I had no administrative officer at all and I delegated to Mr. Smythe duties to keep in touch with all the courts that were sitting throughout Ontario ... every Thursday they would report to him what the position of their list was, if their list broke down before Thursday the registrars would report at once. Well I kept that line of communication through the registrars and then Mr. Smythe would keep constantly in touch with me. And I might be sitting in Cochrane. But he would phone me long distance and every Thursday he would phone me as to what the position of the lists were all through Ontario where the courts were sitting ... it was, without any question, the most difficult judicial office in Ontario."

On 1 November 1974, a decade after his retirement from the High Court, McRuer lectured on "The Role of the Judge" to the Advocates' Society. The product of many years experience on the bench, this lecture provided a summing up of his judicial philosophy and demonstrated how far he had come from the days when, as a neophyte chief justice, he could not restrain himself from questioning witnesses, instructing counsel, and even taking sides. Declaring that the "first duty of the judge sitting at trial is to control the trial and ... the court" to prevent the proceedings from degenerating into "a sort of legal cock-fight," McRuer expressed some misgivings as to whether trial judges, in criminal trials at least, had been given sufficient authority to "safeguard the administration of justice as an institution ... through control [of] conduct in the courtroom." Yet he also pointed out that judges should command respect through their own behaviour rather than by intimidation. As to the question of how far a judge should interfere in the course of a trial, McRuer recognized that it was a delicate point, dependent on the circumstances, On the whole, he believed that judicial interference "should occur sparingly and always with the objective of fairness in mind."

Another matter raised in McRuer's 1974 lecture was the use of plea bargaining as a means of expediting the administration of justice. It did not surprise his listeners that he found plea bargaining appalling. Terming this practice "moral bankruptcy" and "a philosophy of disaster," he maintained that the solution to the problem of clogged courts was not plea bargaining but the allocation of a greater budget for court facilities. At the very least, McRuer insisted that a judge should have no participation in any discussion about pleas or probable sentence except in open court.

LIKE MANY OTHERS, McRuer had made a financial sacrifice in relinquishing his law practice for a career on the bench. In 1944, when Canada's "abler lawyers" were observed by the *Toronto Star* to be earning "from $20,000 to $50,000 or more per annum,"[30] the chief justice of Ontario's High Court made less than $6,000. For at least his first two years as a judge, McRuer was able to supplement his salary by continuing to collect a healthy share of the revenue from his old law firm—a not uncommon practice in those days. Nevertheless, the fact remains that his income as a judge never approached what he could have earned as a lawyer. In a 1953 letter to John Robinette, McRuer wrote that "notwithstanding the fact that my family had all received their education when I went on the Bench, nevertheless I many times doubted whether I was being fair to their future and to my wife."[31]

In any case, for McRuer, monetary considerations were secondary.

His decision to accept promotion first to the Court of Appeal and then to the position of chief justice of the High Court had been motivated by natural ambition, a desire for new challenges, and, most important of all, a commitment to bring about real change both in the legal system and in Ontario society as a whole. His passion for justice went hand in hand with a deep-seated attachment to tradition, but there was no contradiction in that. In McRuer's eyes, tradition was central to the life of any society, and his own vision of the law as well as his commitment to justice drew inspiration from history in general and more particularly from the British legal heritage that Canada shared as a member of the commonwealth. Forged over the course of his long career in the law, McRuer's legal philosophy would be evident throughout his years on the bench, whether he was traversing the judicial districts of northern Ontario or presiding over a trial in the sedate surroundings of downtown Toronto. Underlying his decisions as a judge was his unyielding determination to make the noble traditions of the law serve the interests of all people.

The substance of McRuer's judicial philosophy was revealed in cases dealing with such varied subjects as spies and murderers, the environment, native people, women and children, and workers. It was in these cases that McRuer the judge was put to the test.

10

SPIES AND MURDERERS

MCRUER HAD BARELY TAKEN HIS SEAT as chief justice of the Ontario High Court when he found himself presiding over the trials of several persons charged with espionage following the shattering revelations of Igor Gouzenko. Heralding the beginning of the Cold War, these trials not only involved the fundamental security of the country but also raised far-reaching questions about civil liberties in a democratic society—questions that McRuer fully recognized and sought to address.

The Gouzenko affair began on the early evening of 5 September 1945, when a cipher clerk at the Soviet embassy in Ottawa left his office for the last time. Concealing under his clothes hundreds of secret documents that showed the existence of a Soviet spy ring in Canada, Igor Gouzenko spent almost three days making the rounds of the *Ottawa Journal*, the RCMP, and the Department of Justice before he was finally taken seriously and given protective custody. In October the King government passed an order-in-council under the authority of the War Measures Act (which was still in effect) authorizing the arrest and interrogation of persons suspected of espionage. Matters then remained at a standstill until February of the following year, when the federal government established a royal commission, composed of Supreme Court judges Robert Taschereau and R.L. Kellock, to investigate Gouzenko's claims. An even longer delay would no doubt have occurred had not Drew Pearson, an American radio commentator, forced the Canadian government to act by reporting rumours about the existence of the spy ring. Several people were arrested, held incommunicado, and interrogated by the commission. Eighteen of them were formally charged with breaching the Official Secrets Act by conspiring to communicate secret information to a foreign power. Among the accused were three National Research Council scientists, Raymond Boyer, a high explosives expert, and two engineers, Edward Mazerall and Dunford Smith; Gordon Lunan, an army officer serving with the Wartime Information Board; Scott Benning, an official in the Department of Munitions and Supply; Emma Woikin, a cypher clerk in External Affairs; Kathleen Willsher, deputy registrar in the British High Commission; Eric Adams of the Industrial Development Bank; and Fred Rose, the Labour-Progressive (Communist) MP from Montreal.

The circumstances surrounding their arrests aroused intense debate in the country. The Toronto *Globe and Mail* attacked the government for holding "secret trials without counsel and violating the fundamental human rights,"[1] and the *Winnipeg Free Press* lectured the King government that "there are very strict limits beyond which the democratic government cannot and must not go."[2] In the House of Commons, the leader of the Conservative opposition, John Bracken, expressed support for the government's efforts to stamp out espionage but noted his concern that many Canadians were expressing feelings of "unrest and criticism ... through lack of understanding of the ... extraordinary procedure followed by the Government in holding certain Canadians incommunicado in connection with this matter." Describing "the refusal of *habeas corpus* proceedings, the holding of men without a legal charge against them, without the right of bail and without the right to have counsel" as a violation of "the principles of British justice," Bracken asserted that "the Canadian people are not in sympathy with any departure from the regular procedures of our courts, established over long years, for dealing with matters of this kind, unless the circumstances are most unusual, such as, for instance, the safety of the state being endangered."[3] In support of Bracken, MP John G. Diefenbaker railed at the "star chamber method" of a government hiding behind the authority of the War Measures Act.[4]

It was against this background that the Gouzenko trials began on Tuesday, 14 May, in the Ottawa courthouse before Chief Justice McRuer. All through the proceedings, McRuer later recounted, there was an eerie feeling that foreign powers were watching, absorbed by the revelations and keenly interested in how everything would turn out. Spectators thronged the courtroom each day, hanging on every word and gazing with fascination on the curious figure of Igor Gouzenko, who wore a hood and was protected by a RCMP bodyguard.

Four of the accused conspirators were tried by McRuer personally: Edward Mazerall, Scott Benning, Kathleen Willsher, and Eric Adams.[5] Though the trials involved espionage—something almost unprecedented in Canada to that time—the issue of conspiracy around which they revolved was not unusual in Canadian law; indeed, in his own career as a lawyer, McRuer himself had prosecuted a number of conspiracy cases. Each of the Gouzenko trials had its own peculiar wrinkles, but all essentially followed the same pattern. In trial after trial, Igor Gouzenko testified and produced certain of the documents that he had smuggled out of the Russian embassy. The prosecution (one of whose members was the distinguished John Cartwright, later a chief justice of the Supreme Court of Canada) did not have to prove the existence of a conspiracy—that was an undisputed fact—but it was required to prove that each of the defendants was involved. On the other side, the defence lawyers, who included the formidable Joseph Sedgwick, attempted to cast doubt on the participation of their clients in the conspiracy, and this effort was supplemented by appeals to the jury's sympathy and by claims that the publication of the royal commission report had prejudiced and coloured any conclusion a jury might reach. McRuer turned down Sedgwick's request, made in the trial of Kathleen Willsher, for a change of venue, stating that there would be no place in Ontario where there would not have been publicity about the royal commission.

As for the evidence submitted, McRuer allowed the admission of the defendants' statements before the Taschereau-Kellock commission, but not anything they said to police officers while in detention. In charging the jury in each of the trials, McRuer defined a conspiracy, explained the kind of evidence required to convict the accused of this crime, and outlined the relevant provisions of the War Measures Act. He also instructed them that they could not find the accused a party to the conspiracy on the basis of Gouzenko's testimony or of evidence he had produced. They could, however, make this finding on the basis of statements the accused had made before the royal commission inquiry.

The Gouzenko trials continued until the end of 1946. Of the defendants, several—including Boyer, Benning, Lunan, Mazerall, Smith, Willsher, Woikin, Rose, and Alan Nunn May (who was tried in Britain)—were found guilty and sentenced to penitentiary terms. Some won their cases, and others were convicted but later acquitted on appeal. As historians Robert Bothwell and J.L. Granatstein have noted, the acquittal verdicts did not really throw much doubt on the evidence brought forward by Gouzenko. Rather, they suggest, the acquittals had more to do with some legal problems in accepting as evidence stolen embassy materials, and also with the government not always being able or willing to introduce in court the evidence presented in secret to the royal commission.[6]

In later commenting on the Gouzenko trials, McRuer expressed agreement with the view that the people arrested had been treated improperly in not being allowed to see counsel or friends. "There were two very highly skilled counsel employed by the Commission and the commissioners were judges of the Supreme Court," McRuer said, "and yet the accused were never told that they could object to answering questions on the grounds that it would tend to incriminate them ... They went in and answered the questions put to them by counsel or the Commissioners. Then, when it came to the trial, that evidence was used, which was very substantially the evidence that convicted them. There was, however, no rule under which I could have excluded it." On the last point, McRuer was undoubtedly correct. Nevertheless, the troubling events of the Gouzenko affair made such an impact on him that years later, as a one-man Ontario royal commission on civil rights, he recommended changes in the provincial Public Inquiries Act to ensure the right of witnesses to refuse to answer any questions that may incriminate them or subject them to civil action. A similar provision was implemented, at McRuer's recommendation, for the protection of witnesses at a coroner's inquest.[7]

The Gouzenko trials did not mark the end of McRuer's involvement with the spy affair. The next stage involved the Americans. Gouzenko's revelations had predictably caused a great deal of consternation in Washington, particularly after the Alger Hiss trial, which convinced many Americans that fifth columnists and subversive "fellow travellers" were occupying positions of responsibility in the United States government. The House of Representatives soon established its own committee on un-American activities, while the Senate's Internal and Security Subcommittee of the Judiciary Committee (known popularly as the Jenner-McCarran Committee), not to be outdone, wished to bring Gouzenko down to Washington and have him testify. Gouzenko nervously refused to leave Canada and the Canadian government, not wanting American politicians interviewing Gouzenko in public about Canadians, and possibly destroying in the process the reputations of some prominent Canadians, supported him. When Lester B. Pearson, the minister of external affairs, passed word to American authorities that anyone was at liberty to interview Gouzenko if he wished to be interviewed, but that the RCMP could not protect him in the United States, there was a furious exchange of highly charged opinions on both sides of the border, the Chicago *Tribune* in particular writing scathing and abusive editorials aimed at the Canadian government and Pearson in particular.

By December 1953 the Canadian government had relented somewhat, and Pearson made a secret deal with Secretary of State John Foster Dulles: the Americans could question Gouzenko, providing that Canada had the final say on what information would be made public and that the interrogation would be presided over by a Canadian. The minister of justice, Stuart Garson, contacted Chief Justice McRuer to see if he would agree to preside at an interrogation of Gouzenko by senators William Jenner and Pat McCarran of the Senate subcommittee. McRuer agreed. He told his wife that he was going to Ottawa for two or three days, but that she should say, to anyone who asked about him, that she did not know where he was. On Saturday night, 2 January 1954, he was about to leave for Toronto Union Station in a taxi when news came over the radio that two United States senators from the Jenner-McCarran committee had just left Washington for Montreal. "Now I know where you are going!" said Mary, excited but apprehensive.

The press soon guessed as well. McRuer narrowly avoided a television crew staked out at Toronto's Union Station as he boarded the Ottawa train with his court reporter, Noel Dickson. At 2:00 p.m. the following day he met with External Affairs Minister Pearson, Minister of Justice Garson, his deputy minister, Frederick P. Varcoe, A.C. Smith and G.G. Crean from the Department of External Affairs, David W. Mundell, representing the attorney-general of Canada, and A.J. McLeod, legal adviser to the RCMP. Garson stressed the extreme delicacy of the affair. All that afternoon the seven men planned the interrogation while McRuer drew up air-tight rules and procedures. He noted in a private personal memorandum: "Having regard to the history of the inquiries in Washington and the actions of Senator McCarthy, it was apprehended that the meeting in Canada might develop so as to create ill-will and international tension, not only abroad but in Canada as well. For this reason the procedure to be adopted was most carefully considered so as to bring it within the understanding between the two governments and to fully protect any innocent persons from being smeared by accusations that could not be substantiated." Pearson had no desire to import a McCarthy-style witchhunt into Canada. McRuer understood the dangers equally well and knew that his role would be vital.

Late that afternoon, ready to proceed to the next stage, McRuer was driven by Mundell and McLeod along the north shore of the Ottawa

River. They travelled east toward the Seignory Club in Montebello, Quebec, a massive log structure specially opened up in the depths of winter for the interrogation. The gates were heavily guarded and the grounds patrolled by the RCMP. McRuer was quartered in the lodge next to United States Ambassador Douglas Stuart, recalled from a California vacation. Stuart, a genial and kind man, appreciated the delicacy of the situation. McRuer chatted with him for a short time, and both studiously avoided any substantial mention of the matter at hand. That evening, while Stuart travelled to Montreal to brief the American senators, McRuer went over the proceedings with Dickson, Mundell, and McLeod. They agreed that Canadian authority should be maintained at all times and that the American visitors were to be treated with courtesy and respect.

That same day, under television lights and with all the glare of media publicity, hard-bitten, horn-rimmed demagogic Republican Senator William Jenner, chairman of the Senate subcommittee, arrived in Montreal by train with his vice-chairman, Nevada Democrat Senator Pat McCarran, J.G. Sourwine, the subcommittee's counsel, and a reporter. The American senators wanted maximum publicity—on leaving Washington, they had announced that they would give a major press conference on their return. Canada wanted none. Ambassador Stuart met them at Windsor Station in Montreal with RCMP and External Affairs officials, and they gave a press conference at the Windsor Hotel. Then they were whisked out the back door under escort to an unknown destination, successfully avoiding (from the Canadian perspective, at least) further press questioning.

On Monday morning, 4 January 1954, the interrogation began in the ballroom of the Seignory Club. The place had been redesigned as a courtroom, with a raised dais and two sets of tables. In his firmest voice, McRuer read the regulations for the proceedings to all assembled, his austere manner suggesting that he would not entertain any objections. The rules were primarily reminders to the Americans not to question Gouzenko about any Canadians, since Canada had its own way of enforcing criminal law and must be permitted its own procedures. As McRuer recalled the proceedings, Gouzenko, hooded as always, "was brought in and the regulations were then read again. He was then interrogated most of the forenoon and afternoon by Mr. Sourwine. The Senators present took very little part in the proceedings. Everything passed off very agreeably after the introductory questions submitted to Mr. Gouzenko." Those preliminary questions, however, did alert McRuer to possible danger. To quote again from his account: "I thought the interrogation was

proceeding on such broad lines that it might develop into an interrogation with regard to Canadian affairs. I drew their attention to the fact
that Mr. Gouzenko had been interrogated many times during the Royal
Commission and that he had conveyed all the information he had up
until that time and that any information pertinent to the United States
had already been conveyed to the proper authorities of the United States
and that I hoped it would not so develop as to cover the same ground as
had been covered by the Royal Commission. Whether it appears in the
record or not, Mr. Gouzenko said, 'I hope it will not too.' Thereupon Mr.
Sourwine confined himself to very well prepared questions that were
put forward in a manner that was entirely unobjectionable and in fact
very commendable. At the conclusion of the interview Senator McCarran asked the one question too many that is so often asked. He asked Mr.
Gouzenko whether the regulations that had been laid down prevented
him from giving them any information that he otherwise could give and
his answer was 'No.' He said that the regulations were quite agreeable
to him. Senator Jenner said that there were some things in the regulations they didn't like but they had to accept them as 'the ground rules.' I
rather deduced that as between Senator Jenner and Senator McCarran
they were sparring for political position over the matter."

For two hours, Sourwine had read out a long series of names from
several filing boxes of cards, "Do you know the name of so and so?"
Gouzenko's answer each time was "No." The ebullient McCarran's only
question was, "Is there anything you would have said to us alone, that
you don't feel free to say at this hearing?" Gouzenko said that there was
not. The general impression McRuer had was that the senators left the
interrogation empty-handed and with their tails slightly between their
legs.

Their quest fruitless, the senators raced off to Montreal to catch the
Washington train. On facing reporters back in the United States, Jenner
and McCarran announced that they had no comments other than to say
that they had met with Gouzenko and interrogated him. As for McRuer,
he had a leisurely drive back to Ottawa, a debriefing at the Department
of Justice, and a quiet dinner with Lester Pearson before going to the
airport for a comfortable flight to Toronto. Pearson's parting words said
it all: "There will never again be an inquiry like this for you to preside
over."[8]

As he flew back to Toronto, McRuer could reflect that no innocent
person had been hurt, no one hunted down, no liberty threatened by the
Gouzenko interrogation. He was satisfied with the outcome, and also

with his own role in ensuring that American-style witchhunts had been kept south of the border.

FOR McRUER, the Gouzenko trials were a fascinating way to begin his term as chief justice. The trials he presided over in later years did not have the same international significance, but many of them were just as intellectually compelling and some came close to matching the spy trials' emotional drama. Of these, the ones he found most gripping involved the crime of murder.

McRuer's attraction to murder trials partly derived from his understanding of their social role in satisfying society's deep-seated need to see justice done; most people, McRuer believed, wanted those guilty of the ultimate crime to pay with their own lives, and the murder trial was therefore a public ritual with profound sociological and psychological importance. McRuer relished murder trials for other reasons as well. He loved the courtroom drama that invariably attended murder trials, he was fascinated by forensic experts whose knowledge and skills could turn up vital clues or decipher otherwise obscure pieces of evidence, and he keenly enjoyed using procedural and evidentiary rules in the high-stakes game of life and death. Knowledge of law counted, too, and McRuer felt enormous satisfaction plunging into the relevant statutory provisions and case law, and applying them to the facts of the human tragedy unfolding before him in the courtroom.[9]

When McRuer mounted the bench in 1944, the sentence of death was provided for murder, rape, treason, and acts of war by the subject of a foreign state then at peace with Canada. The last two offences were rarely the concern of a Canadian judge. As for the second offence—rape—judges almost never imposed the death penalty for this crime.[10] Murder was a different matter. The sentence of death for murder was mandatory, and only the exercise of the royal prerogative of mercy could commute this punishment to life imprisonment or something less. In a murder trial that resulted in a guilty verdict, the procedure followed was always the same. After the jury made known its finding, the judge was required to ask whether they wished to make a recommendation of clemency. The number of jurors for and against such a recommendation were set out in a report, also obligatory, from the judge to the solicitor-general. If a sentence of death was imposed, the judge had to appoint for the execution of the sentence a day far enough in the future to allow sufficient time for consideration of the case by the federal government. The practice in Canada, since Confederation, was to have every capital case reviewed, from the point of view of clemency, by the governor-general in council. This was done after all legal remedies had been exhausted or abandoned. Practically speaking, if the solicitor-general believed that there should be no interference in the death sentence, he could merely refrain from taking any action and the accused would be executed at the appointed time. On the other hand, if he felt that the sentence should be commuted, he would have to seek the concurrence of his cabinet colleagues; if they agreed, an order-in-council commuting the death sentence would be issued.[11]

McRuer firmly supported the role of executive clemency in the judicial system, but he always adhered to the view that "the prerogative is one of *mercy and grace*, not one of *right*."[12] When extenuating circumstances such as the mental health of the convict warranted commutation of a death sentence, McRuer was happy to recommend leniency to the crown. In the absence of these circumstances, he was equally satisfied to see murderers hang—as they often did. McRuer passed so many death sentences during his years on the bench that, among trial lawyers, he gained the nickname of "Hanging Jim." Some even quipped that he took his own rope with him to a murder trial.

The following are just six of the dramatic murder trials which Jim McRuer presided over during his tenure as chief justice of Ontario's High Court.

Evelyn Dick and the "Torso Murder"

In 1946 Mrs. Evelyn Dick of Hamilton was accused of brutally murdering her husband, John Dick, and horribly mutilating his body before dismembering it. She was also charged simultaneously with manslaughter in connection with the death of her infant son. Convicted and sentenced to death on the murder charge, she was later acquitted at a retrial ordered by the Ontario Court of Appeal. In terms of McRuer's own career, the Dick case perfectly illustrated his difficulty during his early days on the bench in distinguishing the judge's role and the role he had played so often as a prosecuting attorney.

During Dick's two murder trials, the newspapers, delighted to have the kind of story that formed the bread and butter of so many American and British tabloid publications, fed a continuous stream of revelations to a public eager for sensational gossip. A host of freelance writers also rushed to publish lurid descriptions of the case in books and articles (and eventually even a stage play). Much of the material the newspapers and writers drew on for their accounts came from the extraordinary confession—or rather confessions, plural—of Evelyn Dick herself. While in jail awaiting trial, Dick time and time again made statements to the police, at all hours of the day or night, either to retract previous statements or to add new gruesome details; in all, she made at least eleven statements. Dick seemed to delight in the attention she received from the police and to revel in the horror of the murder. Yet, while the confessions were the principal evidence linking Mrs. Dick to the crime, it was not clear whether she was mentally competent to make accurate statements about the murder. Nor was it clear which of her many so-called confessions should be believed and which were admissible in court.

Apart from the public's fascination with her confessions, the rules governing confessions were a hot issue in the Canadian courts of the day, the Supreme Court of Canada having just ruled in 1943 in *R. v. Gach* that a confession could not be admitted unless the accused had been formally warned at the time of the confession that statements he or she made could be used as evidence against him, or her, in court.[13] This ruling caused an outcry among the public and in the ranks of the legal profession, and it was later overturned by a second Supreme Court of Canada ruling, *R. v. Boudreau* (1949). The Boudreau judgment said that, although warnings should normally be given, the necessity of a caution depended upon the particular circumstances of the case; the crucial issue was whether the statement was voluntary.[14] At the time of Dick's trials, however, the first ruling of the Supreme Court of Canada was still in force.

In the 1940s, another issue—the mental state of an accused person when making statements to police—was becoming the subject of a growing debate in the legal profession. McRuer himself was soon to head a one-man royal commission on the subject, but in 1946, when Evelyn Dick went to trial, guidelines for judges dealing in this area of law were vague and judgments varied considerably.

To a large segment of Canadian society, the murder of John Dick seemed an open-and-shut case. Mrs. Dick had repeatedly admitted hacking her husband to death, and she had even gone so far as to claim that she enjoyed the experience. No balanced person could have committed such a crime, but, in the eyes of many Canadians, the showing of leniency towards a brazen murderer on the grounds of insanity would serve only to lower the barriers of legal protection from deranged people.

Ontario's courts had more difficulty in judging the case. At the first trial, before Justice Barlow and a jury at the assizes at Hamilton, the judge admitted virtually all of Dick's statements to the police as valid evidence. In addition, Barlow did not give detailed instructions to the jury either about the use of confessions in court or about the use of insanity as a defence under the law. The jury returned the expected verdict of guilty on 16 October 1946.[15] At this point, a rising lawyer from Toronto, John Robinette, was retained to act for Mrs. Dick on her appeal. On 21 January 1947 the Ontario Court of Appeal overturned the guilty verdict in the first trial, on the grounds that the judge had erred in admitting statements made by Dick to the police and in failing to instruct the jury properly. A new trial was ordered.[16]

In view of the importance of the case, Chief Justice McRuer decided to preside himself. At this second trial, the crown wished to introduce the seven statements made by Mrs. Dick that it had introduced at the first trial, as well as four additional statements made by her. McRuer ruled them all inadmissible. In his mind, the Court of Appeal's express findings as to the admissibility of the first seven statements applied to all the statements tendered by the crown, and he believed himself to be bound by that court's ruling. To his disappointment, neither the lawyers for the crown nor those for the defence presented the kinds of rigorous arguments that he would have liked to hear. Privately, he thought that the crown should have pressed for the admission of some of the statements made by Dick to the police which the Court of Appeal had earlier rejected, and he also believed that the defence should have explored Dick's mental state and treatment at the hands of the police in finer detail. McRuer did not hesitate to state at trial that, had he not felt bound by the Court of Appeal, he would have admitted some of the statements. What more could a defence lawyer hope for?

In McRuer's own personal judgment, Mrs. Dick had very likely butchered her husband while in a state of insanity. Yet, in the absence of the one statement that counsel for the crown had admitted was the only confession of real importance, the case against Dick was weak. Increasingly frustrated with how the trial was proceeding, McRuer intervened repeatedly, offering advice to the crown attorney and lecturing the accused and her counsel. Among those shocked by his behaviour were the members of the jury. According to one of its members, the jury took an intense dislike both to McRuer and to the senior crown counsel, Timothy Rigney. They felt that McRuer and Rigney were most unfair to the defendant and her counsel, John Robinette, for whom they developed a great admiration during the lengthy trial.

In the end, the jury ignored the arguments of McRuer and the crown counsel, acquitting Mrs. Dick on 6 March 1947, exactly one year after the date of the murder the crown had so persistently alleged she had committed.[17] With "perhaps a slight edge in his voice," noted a reporter, McRuer discharged the jury and retired to his chambers. Deeply unhappy with the conduct of counsel and the findings of the jury, he longed to lecture all the parties involved on the principles of the law and to announce to the world what his own verdict would have been. One of those lawyers he wanted to lecture was, of course, John Robinette, who became famous as a result of Dick's acquittal. The view of Robinette, and of the criminal bar generally, was that Mrs. Dick was acquitted despite McRuer's best efforts to see her convicted.

Following the trial, McRuer carefully reviewed his own role in the proceedings. After going over the case again and again in his mind, he concluded that Mrs. Dick had been given a fair trial under the law. The principles of British law had been strictly observed, he reasoned, and as chief justice he could have done no more or less in this case. The verdict was unsatisfactory to McRuer, but justice had been done.

Yet matters did not rest there. The crown appealed Dick's acquittal to the Court of Appeal on the sole ground that McRuer wrongly rejected as evidence statements made by the accused to police officers, but the acquittal was unanimously upheld by a five-member panel.[18] McRuer then took the highly unusual step of privately advising the crown attorney about how he might improve his case if he appealed to the Supreme Court of Canada—an astonishing action that again showed how his strong personal feelings about the justice of a case could obliterate his often-espoused respect for judicial proprieties. Yet no further appeal was made, and Evelyn Dick went free—for the time being. She was subsequently convicted of manslaughter in the death of her son and spent the next eleven years in jail.

The Case of the Incriminating "Love" Letters

In June 1950 McRuer, sitting with a jury in Napanee, heard a sensational murder trial involving family violence and the defences of insanity and provocation. The defendant, James Fosbraey, was accused of murdering his wife, June.

Fosbraey, who was twenty-nine years old at the time of his wife's murder, was born in England and had served both in the British army and in the Royal Air Force. While in the air force he was sent to Canada for training and here he met June Curran, an attractive girl from Napanee. The two were soon married and a child, Carol, was born in 1946. Upon his discharge from the RAF, Fosbraey moved to live with his wife in Napanee, but he soon found that neither life in Canada nor life with a wife and child would be as easy as he had hoped. The Fosbraeys were chronically short of money and so had to live in June's parents' home. Tensions mounted in the crowded house and exploded in the autumn of 1949 when June confessed to being romantically involved with another man. On 6 October a quarrel broke out, and Fosbraey struck his wife, giving her a black eye and bruised cheek. That day June borrowed $200 from her uncle so that Fosbraey could return to England. When Fosbraey stormed out of Napanee he vowed to get a divorce in England and shouted that June would never hear from him again. Once in England, however, he had a change of heart. Emotionally upset and unable to find employment, Fosbraey became obsessed with his adulterous wife.

In the forty-two days between 11 October and 22 November 1949, Fosbraey wrote no less than seventy letters to his wife in Napanee; in fact, on one day alone, he sent her eight letters. The letters showed wild swings in emotion which struck terror in June. He was thinking of committing suicide, he said; he was going to kill her; he would divorce June and carry off their child; he wanted nothing more than to be reunited with her. Most letters contained endearing terms and pleas for money and understanding. He constantly upbraided June for betraying him and, whenever the subject of her unfaithfulness arose, more threats followed. Finally June received Fosbraey's letter of 11 November, in which he said that he was returning to Napanee and would be staying with Hugh Jaynes, a friend. Fosbraey arrived in Napanee on the 22nd and made some contact with June, who was so frightened by the encounter that on the following day she grabbed three of Fosbraey's letters, threw on her scarlet coat, and hurried to the local police station.

There, Corporal Smith of the Ontario Provincial Police examined the letters carefully. They all contained extremely abusive language and threats of violence. In one, Fosbraey wrote: "I'll be back. Your black eye was [just the beginning]. I should have killed you both right there had I known what I know now. You say you want a divorce and Carol. Well you can't have either." Another letter included the following lines: "You will pay very dearly for your mistakes, both of you. Especially you. I have only one aim in life and that is to meet face to face with you … I'm really mad now. Gosh if I was only in Napanee now I would really use the thing I'm reloading in my hand right now." Smith was naturally

John and Mary McRuer (sitting), with sons Jim and John and daughter Margaret, pose for a formal photograph in front of their farmhouse near Ayr, 1896.

Four-year-old Jim McRuer poses with his brother and sister in Bauslaugh's Photo Studio in Paris, Ontario. He would later say that he hated the kilt because "it made me look like a girl."

The graduates of Paris High School, class of 1907, with Jim McRuer sitting in the front row, left.

A nineteen-year-old Jim McRuer articles at Huntsville in Muskoka. The artist Tom Thomson took this picture in the spring of 1910. COURTESY NATIONAL GALLERY

Jim's brother, John, a medical doctor, seen at the Scotia Junction train station. Another Tom Thomson photograph, it was taken during the same spring outing in 1910.

A trick photograph in 1910 captured five sides of the young McRuer. Later, many people would claim to know Jim McRuer, but few truly understood all dimensions of this complex man.

On a winter day at the Highland Inn, Algonquin Park, McRuer (left), ill, broke, and depressed about his career, met W.H. Price (right). Price helped Jim obtain the post of assistant crown attorney in Toronto, a development that McRuer would later call "the turning point in my life."

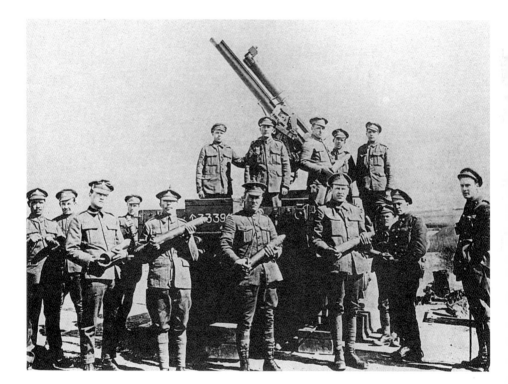

Lieutenant McRuer (right) commanding Canada's first anti-aircraft unit, No. 4, Section E Battery, shortly before the Canadian victory at Vimy Ridge, April 1917.

While serving in the First World War, Jim carried this photograph of Mary Rowena Dow in his wallet. They were married in September 1919.

Mary McRuer with her new baby, Katherine, and two-year-old Mary Louise, 1923. Son John would be born in 1926.

In 1935 McRuer ran for parliament in the riding of High Park but was defeated. Jim (back row, centre) is seen here with his twelve fellow Liberal candidates in the Toronto and York County ridings, including Vincent Massey (front row, hand in pocket).

Wigged and robed, McRuer prepares to plead a case before the Judicial Committee of the Privy Council, London, 1937. He won the case for his client, who had been swindled by the firm Solloway, Mills in a Roaring Twenties financial scam.

The McRuers loved travelling. Here Jim and Mary, her father, Dr. Dow, and their daughter Mary Louise prepare to fly across the English Channel to France in 1936.

The three members of the royal commission on Canada's prisons—R.W. Craig, A.J. Archambault, and McRuer—visit Lincoln, England, to study the "Borstal system." Their 1939 report called for sweeping prison reform.

Mother and two daughters graduate from university simultaneously, May 1943. Katherine (left) and Mary Louise (right) flank Mary McRuer. The Evening Telegram, TORONTO

Unveiling ceremony, 1947, of a bust of Sir Lyman Duff (centre, profile), retired chief justice of the Supreme Court of Canada. Others, left to right: Justice Minister J.L. Ilsley; J.C. McRuer; MP *and incoming* CBA *president John T. Hackett; Prime Minister W.L.M. King; and the new chief justice, Thibodeau Rinfret.* LITTLE, NATIONAL ARCHIVES OF CANADA, PA 134980

As chief justice, McRuer swears in Nathan Phillips as mayor of Toronto, January 1956. The two had studied law together at Osgoode Hall. TUROF-SKY, TORONTO

In 1967 McRuer reviews recommendations with John W. Morden, a counsel to the royal commission inquiry into civil rights. This commission would help transform Ontario law and the relationship between the individual and the state. GERALD CAMPBELL

In 1968 McRuer holds a press conference at Queen's Park to unveil the first three volumes of his inquiry into civil rights. Two more volumes followed in 1969 and 1971. MAIER, Globe and Mail

Jim and his second wife, Robena Dow (a cousin of his first wife, Mary, who died in 1967), emerge from their wedding service at Deer Park United Church, March 1968. MAIER, Globe and Mail

The founding commissioners of the Ontario Law Reform Commission, 1965: W. Gibson Gray, William R. Poole, Richard Bell, McRuer (chairman), and H. Allan Leal (vice-chairman). ONTARIO DEPARTMENT OF TOURISM AND INFORMATION, 4K670

McRuer receives an honorary doctor of laws degree from the University of Toronto, 1962. With him are J.A. Corry, Lord Devlin, Cecil "Caesar" Wright, and Dean Erwin Griswold. JACK MARSHALL, #621314-5

Governor-General Roland Michener invested McRuer into the Order of Canada at a ceremony in Rideau Hall, Ottawa. BREGG, CANADIAN PRESS

In both his public and his private life, McRuer always attached much importance to the interests of children. Here, a happy ninety-two-year-old McRuer embrances his grandson Geordie, son of John McRuer.

James Chalmers McRuer—an observant man and an attentive listener, reflective and tireless in his various endeavours—was driven throughout his long life by a passion for justice.

concerned about these letters, but he also knew that idle threats were frequently made when one of the partners to a marriage felt betrayed. He arranged to meet with both June and her husband that evening, 23 November. In his testimony at the trial, he said that June did not appear to be unduly afraid of Fosbraey at that encounter, but he took the precaution of ordering Fosbraey to remain in north Napanee, where he was staying, and not to cross the river into south Napanee, where June lived with her parents.

In the next five days Fosbraey's activities were noted with alarm by many local citizens. On Friday, 25 November, he visited his acquaintance Jack Mascal, who had just come in from hunting. Mascal became concerned when Fosbraey showed an unusual interest in Mascal's hunting gear. Fosbraey pressed Mascal for detailed instructions on how to use a hunting knife and then asked about the killing power of his shotgun. "Could I kill someone with this at 75 yards?" Fosbraey asked. Before Mascal could answer, Fosbraey pointed the gun at Mascal's head and asked with a grin, "How about at this range?" Mascal was relieved when Fosbraey left.

On Saturday Fosbraey purchased his own hunting knife and then returned to Hugh Jaynes's house, where he was staying. He did little but talk about his wife all day. On Sunday he upset his host by his incessant chatter about his wife and by his compulsive behaviour. Three or four times in an hour he would go through the motions of putting on his tie, jacket, and coat and then taking them off again. That night, neighbours saw him lurking about in the vicinity of June's parents' home.

Meanwhile, June had not been sitting quietly at home. On Saturday she and her lover drove to Kingston and checked in at the British American Hotel. On Sunday they returned to Napanee and afterwards went to a dance outside town. Missing the last bus home, they returned to Napanee by taxi in the early hours of Monday morning. That same morning, Fosbraey visited Lieutenant Gardner of the Salvation Army, seeking his assistance in effecting a reconciliation between himself and June. When Gardner visited June, she refused to have anything more to do with her husband. For much of the day Fosbraey was seen loitering around the bridge leading to south Napanee. He also visited the Benn family, where he again did little except talk of his wife.

At 7:00 p.m. on that Monday Fosbraey entered Lieutenant Gardner's office and was told of June's resolve to leave him. Twenty minutes later he was seen on the Napanee bridge talking with a woman in a scarlet coat. At 8:00 p.m. a neighbour heard a hideous scream and ran out to find June, dressed in her coat, lying in a snowbank, covered in blood. Her heart had been torn open by three deep gashes from a sizeable knife, and her thumb had been almost completely severed by a fourth thrust of the blade. She died before she could be taken inside.

In June 1950 James Fosbraey was brought before Chief Justice McRuer, charged with the murder of his wife. The court sat for six days, hearing the testimony of numerous witnesses, reviewing forensic evidence, and examining, among other things, a large collection of letters written by the accused to his wife in the weeks before her death. Although the case was straightforward on the surface, counsel for the defence skilfully presented an intricate case supporting a plea of not guilty by reason of insanity, and both McRuer and the jury were called upon to grapple with this problem in considerable detail. For McRuer, the case crystallized some of the key difficulties involved with the defence of insanity. How can the court distinguish between a disturbed individual and an insane one? What marks the line between a moment of irrational passion and a temporary condition of mental illness? Is there a difference between culpability and responsibility for a crime? These and other considerations preoccupied McRuer as he pondered the case.

During the trial, counsel for the defence quoted extensively from the various letters the accused had sent to his wife in an attempt to show that he was definitely deranged. The sheer volume of letters and the shifting moods that they reflected, the defence maintained, proved that the accused was at the very least schizophrenic. The defence also called expert witnesses to substantiate its claim that Fosbraey was insane, but McRuer was not convinced that proper diagnostic tests had been performed. Defence counsel argued as well that the admission of adultery made to Fosbraey by his wife immediately prior to her death constituted legal provocation. McRuer ruled that such admission was not provocation in law, however, and he specifically directed the jury that a verdict of manslaughter could not be considered or returned.

The issue of insanity presented more of a challenge. In his chambers, McRuer systematically studied the huge collection of Fosbraey's letters. He spread them all out, arranged them in strict chronological order, and then painstakingly reread every single word. At length he reached the conclusion that Fosbraey had been enraged by his wife's infidelity and then had grown desperately lonely and depressed. Yet could these symptoms be considered evidence of insanity? What man could fail to have such emotions when confronted with the fact that his wife was unfaithful? McRuer noted as well that most of the letters were filled with professions of love and regret for past difficulties, and he considered that these sentiments also were normal for a husband going through marital breakdown.

What seemed unusual to McRuer was that Fosbraey's threats of violence became more frequent as time passed. Far from coming to grips with his sorrow, it was obvious that Fosbraey was seeking consolation in planning revenge against his wife and her lover. Notwithstanding Fosbraey's final visit to the Salvation Army on the day of his wife's murder, all of his words and deeds pointed to the fact that he planned to murder his wife. After all, why did he take such pains to learn how to use a hunting knife, and why did he buy one when he had never been a hunter? Above all, why was he carrying that knife when he crossed the bridge to south Napanee during the snowstorm on the night of Monday, 28 November?

McRuer worked through the night preparing a lengthy charge to the jury which set out his views on the rules of evidence and the defence of insanity. He was proud of his charge; indeed he felt that he had produced something of a masterpiece. On 7 June 1950, it took the jury only fifty-two minutes to bring down a verdict of guilty, whereupon McRuer pronounced a sentence of death with the words that had been used again and again down through the years. "On 21 September," he solemnly told Fosbraey, "you shall be taken to the place of execution and there hanged by the neck until you are dead. And may the Lord have mercy on your soul."[19]

After passing the mandatory sentence of death on Fosbraey, and in the quiet of his chambers, McRuer began to puzzle about a fact that he wished had come out in the trial: had Lieutenant Gardner said a word of prayer with the condemned man when the two met only minutes before June Fosbraey was found dead in the snows of Napanee? To most, this question would seem odd or irrelevant; nothing in the trial had turned on it. The fact that such a thought occurred to McRuer underlines the importance of religious faith in his life, as well as the feelings of a judge when condemning a person to death.

James Fosbraey sat on death row, measuring out the days to his hanging. Then, just five days before he was to walk to the gallows, his lawyers, Walter B. Williston and R.E. Nourse, obtained an order from the Ontario Court of Appeal. The court, in deciding to allow their application on behalf of Fosbraey, ruled that under the criminal law any question about whether an accused had been provoked to commit a murder must be left to the jury to decide. This issue of "provocation" was vital, since under

the Criminal Code culpable homicide (which would otherwise be murder) could be reduced to manslaughter if the person who committed the
act did so in the heat of passion caused by provocation; in this case, the
penalty would be less severe than it would be for murder. Previous cases
had determined that, when there was uncertainty in the evidence about
provocation, it was the jury—properly charged—and not the judge who
must decide the matter. Because Fosbraey's letter, written at the time of
the murder, contained some expressions which could be considered evidence of provocation and others which suggested a premeditated murder, the Court of Appeal concluded that "the learned trial Judge erred in
withdrawing the matter of provocation from the jury and the result is
that there must be a new trial."[20]

On 6 November 1950 Fosbraey's second trial for the murder of his wife
began, this time in Picton, Ontario. In the interval since the first trial,
his lawyer had succeeded in persuading the court to order a change of
venue on the grounds that it was impossible to find an impartial jury in
Napanee. Before Mr. Justice R.W. Treleavan and jury, R.E. Nourse again
presented the case for the defence and William Common prosecuted for
the crown. The trial was a replay of the same tragic story, except that the
jury now considered the matter of provocation. After deliberating for
four and a half hours (compared to less than an hour for the jury in the
first trial), the new jurors found Fosbraey guilty of manslaughter—the
reduced charge—but recommended no mercy. James Fosbraey was sentenced to life imprisonment at Kingston Penitentiary.[21]

Death in the Chateau and Contempt in the Courtroom

In 1951 the case of R. v. Sullivan gave McRuer the opportunity to grapple
with yet two more controversial legal problems: acceleration of death
and contempt of court.

On 15 November 1950 Toronto lawyer Francis J. Sullivan, age fifty-two,
and his wife, Marion Gough Sullivan, age forty-eight, checked into the
Chateau Laurier Hotel in Ottawa. Sullivan was the chief solicitor for the
Ontario Lands and Forests Department, and he was in Ottawa to attend
provincial tax-appeal hearings.

At around 3:30 in the morning of 18 November, Mrs. Sullivan phoned
the hotel management to say that she had found her husband lying on
the floor of their room. The hotel detective and the hotel doctor, Dr.
Lorne Gardner, arrived, found Sullivan dead, and notified the coroner.
The hotel room contained some smashed glass as well as the bruised,

cold, and nude body of "Frank" Sullivan. He had been dead for some hours before his wife had notified anyone.

Mrs. Sullivan was charged with murder, which was later reduced to manslaughter, and the case came before McRuer on 31 January 1951 in Ottawa. The trial continued until 13 February 1951. Although numerous witnesses were examined, in McRuer's mind everything came to depend on the testimony of the pathologist, Dr. Max Klotz of the Ottawa Civic Hospital, who had performed the autopsy on Sullivan. In examining Sullivan's corpse, Klotz had counted no less than sixty severe bruises around the victim's head and upper body. He had also discovered, however, an old aneurism which had burst in the back of Sullivan's brain. When pressed to state his final opinion as to whether Sullivan had died from the blows he had sustained or from the eruption of this aneurism, Klotz replied, "In that area I have some doubt."

To McRuer, this simple statement closed the books on the Sullivan case. The crown maintained that Mrs. Sullivan was guilty of manslaughter because her blows had at the very least accelerated her husband's death. McRuer was satisfied that Sullivan had not self-inflicted the sixty-odd serious bruises that Klotz had found, and he felt fairly certain that the Sullivans had become embroiled in a brawl in their room at the Chateau. Yet, since the pathologist was in doubt about the precise cause of death, and since the crown could not prove that the blows had actually accelerated the eruption of the aneurism, Mrs. Sullivan could not be found guilty of causing her husband's demise. At the very least, McRuer believed, Mrs. Sullivan was, in fact, guilty of committing a brutal assault, but the crown had not elected to charge her with that crime. McRuer concluded that Sullivan should be found not guilty of manslaughter, and the jury eventually reached the same conclusion.[22]

During the course of the Sullivan trial, there was another game in play. McRuer became increasingly concerned about the behaviour of the press and the attitudes of the public. The *Ottawa Journal*, under the editorial direction of the renowned Grattan O'Leary, had taken a particular interest in the case, and McRuer's courtroom became packed with spectators, many of whom appeared only to be seeking cheap entertainment. Because the *Journal* portrayed Mrs. Sullivan as a pathetic character who had suffered years of abuse at the hands of her husband, she was gathering considerable public sympathy. As the Sullivan jury was not sequestered, McRuer began to worry that its verdict might be unduly influenced by such media coverage.

McRuer always encouraged the public to observe the legal process in the courtroom, and he was known as one of Canada's staunchest defenders of the right—even duty—of the press to cover trials fully and fairly. Still, he was equally vehement in maintaining that the freedom of the press must never take priority over the right of the accused to a fair trial, and two incidents convinced him that the press and the public had gone too far in the Sullivan case.

On 13 February 1951, when the jury returned its verdict of not guilty, the Ottawa courtroom, which contained more than 300 spectators, erupted into brief but loud applause and cheering. McRuer, who earlier had ordered the sheriff to warn all spectators not to indulge in such displays, was scandalized. "There will be order in this courtroom!" he cried, with unusual force. "This is not a theatre! Order!" In the next instant, McRuer directed the sheriff to take into custody two men in the rear row of the spectators' gallery. After freeing Mrs. Sullivan and discharging the jury, McRuer dealt with these two men. Both admitted that they had applauded the verdict. As they stood before him, McRuer lectured the courtroom about the principles of law, the rights of the press, and the rights of the accused. He then turned his gaze back to the two nervous men standing before him. "It is impossible for me to comprehend why people come into a court of justice, where other people's liberty is at stake, and treat that court like a vaudeville show," he chided the men. He found them guilty of contempt, but, since it would be unfair to punish only two out of the many who had behaved improperly, he let them go without fine or imprisonment.[23]

This occurrence attracted national attention for a short time. A second incident at the same trial, however, had more long-lasting effects, thrusting McRuer into a lengthy debate which continued over the next several years and which would even be referred to in 1994 in connection with a publication ban on a trial conducted in St. Catharines, Ontario. On the Saturday of the first week of the Sullivan trial, 3 February 1951, the Ottawa Journal published an article under the headline "Mrs. Sullivan To Tell Own Story." On Monday the defence counsel, Royden Hughes, approached the chief justice and said that he had never intended to put his client on the stand and that neither he nor his associate had made any statement to the press on the matter. Hughes feared that the Journal story would damage the defence's case by creating the impression that, if she now failed to testify, it must be because Mrs. Sullivan had something to hide. McRuer completely agreed, but he decided not to take any action against the Journal until after the jury retired to consider its verdict. Nevertheless, he did caution members of the jury that they must not be guided by anything that might appear in the press while the trial was in progress.

Once the jury retired, McRuer moved boldly. He directed the sheriff to cite for contempt the editor of the *Journal* and the two reporters, Ainslie Kerr and Ross Smith, who had written the offending article. These three individuals appeared before McRuer after the Sullivan jury delivered its verdict. McRuer addressed them, pointing out the seriousness of the article which they had published. Some might consider this a trivial matter, he admitted, especially since the *Journal* story did not seem to have had a direct bearing on the outcome of the trial; in fact, Mrs. Sullivan had "told her story" to the coroner and to the police, and the jury had acquitted her. Under other circumstances, however, such an article might well result in the condemnation and even execution of an innocent person. McRuer expressed his astonishment that a publication as distinguished as the *Journal* could have interfered with the judicial process in this manner. Such irresponsibility might eventually cause a backlash which would subvert the freedom of the press. In finding that the *Journal*'s article represented contempt of court, then, McRuer saw himself as defending rather than restricting the rights of the press.

Before pronouncing sentence, McRuer asked whether the *Journal* staff had anything to say. Grattan O'Leary then rose and delivered a short speech which McRuer would always remember as one of the most eloquent statements he ever heard in a courtroom. O'Leary began by formally apologizing for the offending article. He accepted full responsibility for making an error in editorial judgment when he approved its publication. Though he assured the chief justice that he had acted in good faith, he now realized the seriousness of his mistake. O'Leary then closed by stating his own conception of the rights and responsibilities of the press when dealing with the workings of the courts.

McRuer was satisfied that he had made his point, and he thought the matter would die after he levied what he considered to be "very moderate" fines of $3,000 against the paper and $300 against each of the journalists.[24] Not for the first time in his career, however, McRuer was to discover that controversy is easier to stir than to settle. Newspapers and magazines across Canada turned their editorial scrutiny on the chief justice's finding of contempt, and McRuer was once again subjected to the bitter-sweet experience of being both pilloried and lauded for applying his standards of justice to the world around him.[25]

He was also soon deluged with invitations to speak about contempt of court at a variety of public meetings. Although always pressed for time, he accepted many of these opportunities to address a wider audience, for he believed more strongly than ever that the public needed educa- tion about the nature of justice—the foundation of all freedom. In the months after the Sullivan trial, McRuer earnestly expounded his views in addresses to the Canadian Managing Editors' conference, the Toronto Press Club, the Toronto Lawyers Club (of which he was a past president), and similar organizations.

As a result of all this interest in the issue of contempt, McRuer was invited to publish an article on the subject in the *Canadian Bar Review*. Appearing in March 1952, this article was tellingly subtitled "A Protec- tion to the Rights of the Individual." In it, McRuer reviewed the his- tory and nature of criminal contempt of court, emphasizing "that the law of contempt of court does not exist for the protection of judges but for the protection of the individual right of every citizen to an inde- pendent administration of justice free from influence or intimidation by improper conduct of any sort." While admitting that the rights of the individual can be abused in many ways through criminal contempt, McRuer dwelt at length upon what he considered to be the growing prob- lem of press interference with the legal process. Throughout his article McRuer stressed that the press should become even more involved in reporting the facts of cases to the public. Yet he also expressed the hope that the press would behave responsibly. He warned that judges must show greater vigilance in ensuring that the press not interfere with the proper administration of justice, and that they must be prepared to act decisively when the rights of the individual were at stake. In his view, all parties concerned with the legal system needed to accept the full weight of their responsibilities in order to preserve the full measure of their freedoms.[26] This was becoming a recurring theme in McRuer's reflec- tions on the legal system.

By the end of the debate about contempt of court that arose from the Sullivan trial, McRuer had emerged as one of Canada's experts on the issue.

The Boyd Gang Grows Smaller

In September 1952, while Chief Justice McRuer was still involved in the controversy over the Sullivan case, yet another sensational murder trial came before him. The case of *R* v. *Suchan and Jackson* was always recalled by McRuer as a fine example of why it is important to involve the press in court proceedings. Indeed, the public interest aroused by the press in this case, McRuer believed, became instrumental in facilitating the speedy resolution of the trial.

In the Toronto of the early 1950s, the notorious Boyd gang loomed large in the public imagination. To many, Edwin Alonzo Boyd was nothing more than an Irish-Canadian gangster who ruthlessly exploited the poor of the city while living a life of luxury financed by an empire of crime and corruption. To others, Boyd was a modern-day Robin Hood who enjoyed being free with his favours to common people almost as much as flaunting his disdain for the established order. In any case, Boyd was a classic example of the kind of underworld entrepreneur who in the mid-twentieth century seemed to be defying the law.

Because Leonard Jackson and Steven Suchan were alleged to be active members of the Boyd gang, their case grabbed big headlines in Toronto's dailies—the *Telegram*, the *Star*, and the *Globe and Mail*—and in newspapers across the province. On 4 November 1951 Leonard Jackson, William Jackson, and Boyd were being held on charges of robbery in the Don Jail in Toronto when they escaped by using a smuggled hacksaw to cut through a barred window, lowering themselves to freedom with numerous sheets tied into a rope. The press jumped on the story, and soon virtually every household in southern Ontario had detailed descriptions of Jackson and his two fellow escapees.

By February 1952 Jackson was living in a rented apartment in Montreal and spending a good deal of time with Steven Suchan. The two returned to Toronto at the beginning of March 1952, staying in the rented house of Suchan's girlfriend, Anne Camero, at 190 Wright Avenue in Toronto. On 6 March 1952 the landlady heard neighbours' complaints about unusual noises in the house on the previous evening. Upon investigation, the landlady discovered that Suchan and a second man (later identified as Jackson), equipped with air pistols, were passing their time pumping bullets into a dummy torso and head in the basement of the house. She called the police, who reacted quickly but cautiously. After all, complaints about tenants from landlords poured in virtually every day. As a preliminary measure, Detective-Sergeant Edmund Tong and Detective-Sergeant Roy Perry of the Metropolitan Toronto Police were sent to the scene. It would be Tong's last assignment. Suchan and Jackson, armed with loaded revolvers, having left Wright Avenue, drove along College Street and stopped for a light at Lansdowne Avenue. The two officers who had followed them pulled the men over, but when Tong approached the fugitives' vehicle on foot he was shot four times; he was to die from these wounds later that month. Perry, who had started to get out of the police vehicle, was shot twice, but survived. Suchan and Jackson fled the scene and drove back to Montreal, where they were both apprehended in less than a week.

On 22 September 1952 Suchan and Jackson were brought to trial before McRuer, charged with the murder of Detective-Sergeant Tong. J.J. Robinette, by now one of Canada's most prominent criminal lawyers, was defending Suchan, but Jackson had no counsel. In the days before free legal aid in Ontario, Jackson simply could not afford to hire a lawyer. Typically, McRuer loathed the idea of proceeding with a case in which one of the defendants had no proper legal representation. Giving up his lunch hour, he walked the corridors Osgoode Hall until eventually he came across a likely candidate. Finding the young barrister Arthur Maloney in an elevator, McRuer asked for a private word. By the end of their chat, McRuer had persuaded Maloney to take Jackson's case without fee. Arthur Maloney would later gain prominence as an ardent advocate of the abolition of capital punishment, and McRuer always maintained that the case of Suchan and Jackson played a great part in shaping Maloney's views on this question. It was an observation made by others who knew Maloney well.

In custody, Suchan admitted firing the fatal shot; Jackson denied firing at all, although Perry testified that he had. When the trial began, defence counsel rested their case on two basic questions: Who fired the gun that killed Detective-Sergeant Tong? And had they both intended to shoot their way out of any difficulty? Maloney maintained that, unless all doubts on the second question could be resolved, Jackson should go free. Robinette argued for, at most, a verdict of manslaughter against his client, Suchan, the admitted source of the fatal bullet or bullets, on the ground that his client had not intended to kill anyone, only to shoot at the police car. In challenging these arguments, the crown argued that the fatal shot had been fired by one or the other of the two men "in carrying out their common intention formed for the unlawful purpose of resisting, with their revolvers, the apprehension of Jackson, then a fugitive from justice and, therefore, both were parties to the offence of murder."

McRuer thought that Jackson and Suchan had formed a common criminal intention, that Tong had died as a result of their joint action, and that the accused were therefore equally culpable under the provisions of the Criminal Code. In charging and recharging the jury, however, he scrupulously emphasized that it was up to them to decide beyond a rea-

sonable doubt whether Jackson and Suchan had had a common criminal intention to resist Jackson's arrest. His duty done, he was satisfied
when, on 30 September 1952, the jury returned a verdict of guilty against
each man.[27] These convictions were upheld by a unanimous decision of
the Ontario Court of Appeal,[28] and on 12 December 1952 the Supreme
Court of Canada refused leave to appeal.[29] On 15 December the cabinet accepted a report from Department of Justice lawyers that there was
nothing to justify executive clemency, despite the "scores of telegrams"
the government had received asking for a stay of execution.[30]

McRuer was certain that justice had been done when both Suchan and
Jackson dropped through the trap door of the gallows at Don Jail at 12:14
on the morning of 16 December 1952. As the execution took place, Mary
McRuer answered the ringing telephone in the family home on Glenayr
Road. She then began to tremble as the anonymous caller threatened her
husband for his role in the Jackson and Suchan case.

The Case of the Maroon Studebaker

In the early afternoon of Thursday, 15 October 1953, a twenty-four-year-
old Canadian soldier was careening across southwest Ontario in his
maroon Studebaker, seeking a place of refuge. On that same afternoon
a fourteen-year-old farm boy was aimlessly pedalling his bicycle along
the back roads near Iroquois in eastern Ontario. At 3:00 p.m. the lives of
these two individuals became entwined.

The farm boy, Dale Hutt, was gazing wistfully at the countryside when
he saw something curious. Dismounting from his bicycle, he cautiously
edged towards the ditch by the side of the road and, on pushing back
the foliage, he was terrified by his discovery—the nude body of a young
woman, stiff with *rigor mortis*. Streams of blood from her nostrils and
mouth had dried into a harsh shade of rust. Her knees were skinned,
and she was covered in bruises. A necklace of abrasions surrounded her
slender throat. Deep gouges appeared in her abdomen and below each
breast. Her left eye socket was ripped apart; her skin was slit open by a
linear slash which extended from her genitals to the level of her nipples.
Dale Hutt had discovered the corpse of twenty-year-old Marie Anne
Carrier, known to her many friends simply as Annie.

Meanwhile, across the province in the village of Beachville, near
Woodstock, Ontario, the soldier in the maroon Studebaker pulled into a
tourist camp and rented a cabin. Identifying himself as 2nd Lieutenant
Peter Balcombe of the 4th Canadian Guards Regiment, he said that he

had spent the night travelling from Quebec City. He wanted a room for only a few hours, after which time he intended to get on the road again, heading for the Canadian west. Balcombe, however, did not leave his room until the following morning, Friday, 16 October.

On Wednesday, 21 October, five days after Balcombe's departure from the cabin in Beachville, Harley Cousins, who operated Roselawn cabins, the small tourist camp in which Balcombe had stayed, opened the daily newspaper. There he saw a photograph of a maroon Studebaker that the police had just impounded in connection with the murder of Annie Carrier. Cousins showed the paper to Charles Clayton, who assisted in running the out-of-the-way tourist operation. As Clayton had checked Balcombe into the camp only the week before, he immediately recognized the maroon Studebaker. Clayton and Cousins then decided to do some detective work in Balcombe's cabin.

They combed the cabin looking for a murder weapon but found nothing unusual except a discarded label from a brassiere, stating its size and place of manufacture. They then remembered that each of their cabins had a trap door in the ceiling which opened onto a small storage space. Cousins cautiously pried open the hatchway and poked through the darkness with his flashlight. He made an eerie discovery. In the cabin's storage space Cousins found a woman's top coat, hat, gloves, bracelet, and assorted undergarments, all of which were later positively identified as belonging to Annie Carrier. The brassiere label found in the room matched a torn brassiere discovered in the storage space. In addition, a used condom was uncovered wrapped up in the clothes. The condom was scarred with marks which were consistent with the bracelet stowed in the loft.

By this time, Balcombe had been arrested. On leaving the Beachville cabin on Friday the 16th, he had driven to his father-in-law's house near London, Ontario. Balcombe's wife and children were staying there temporarily while he was on leave from the camp in Valcartier, Quebec. Everyone remarked that Balcombe seemed unusually anxious, and his father-in-law was surprised to see the excessive care that Balcombe took in cleaning his car. Genuine apprehension set in when Balcombe's commanding officer telephoned from Valcartier.

Lieutenant-Colonel Leduc had been watching Balcombe with concern for some time. Early on in Balcombe's supposed engagement to Annie, Leduc summoned the 2nd lieutenant to his office. He told Balcombe that Annie was a promising woman of excellent character and he hoped that Balcombe, as a married man and officer, would leave her alone. When news of Annie's murder hit the press, Leduc immediately suspected Balcombe. After talking to him on the telephone, Leduc contacted the police, who arrested and charged him with murdering Marie Anne Carrier on or about 15 October. On his arrest, Balcombe told police that he had spent Wednesday night, 14 October, with Annie but then left her alone to drive to London. He claimed to have stopped at Montreal late Wednesday night and started for Toronto Thursday morning.

Police forces in Quebec and Ontario began a massive investigation into Annie's murder. Their combined efforts failed to produce the murder weapon, and the dress that Annie was wearing on the day of her murder was never found. Still, within days the police had compiled an enormous body of circumstantial evidence implicating Balcombe, evidence that McRuer would later describe as "an intricate and resilient web."

Before her death, Annie Carrier had been a young woman of good character. She was one of fourteen children and lived with her widowed mother in Bienville, Quebec, near Lévis on the south shore of the St. Lawrence River opposite Quebec City. A member of the Canadian Women's Army Corps (Reserve), in which she attained the rank of sergeant, Annie was frequently invited to join in social activities organized by the young men and women whom she met in the military. The "CWACS" of Quebec City freely fraternized with the men posted at the base in nearby Valcartier, and Annie's mother was reassured to know that Annie was associating with young men of such good character.

In February 1953 Annie attended a party in Quebec City organized by a fellow CWAC. There she danced with 2nd Lieutenant Balcombe, a handsome and witty officer whose charm distinguished him from the other young men whom she knew. Balcombe asked her for her telephone number, and they agreed to meet the next day. Balcombe acted like a perfect gentleman and treated Annie with a consideration that she had never known before; the only thing he neglected to tell her was that he was a married man with two children.

Over the next few months Annie fell desperately in love with the young officer who drove the maroon Studebaker, while Balcombe lived a double life. Eventually Balcombe proposed marriage, and Annie enthusiastically accepted. Balcombe gave the happy woman an engagement ring as a token of good times to come. Ironically, that ring was all she was wearing when her body was found in the ditch near Iroquois. In the weeks after the engagement, Annie's family and friends became increasingly alarmed by a subtle change in her mood. Something was going wrong between Annie and Balcombe. One day she put her ring away and announced that she was through with the English-Canadian lieutenant. She had uncovered Peter Balcombe's secret. Still, Balcombe was not to be refused. He courted Annie with a bizarre mixture of charm and intimidation, promising to get a divorce, and before long she was wearing his ring again.

Annie was last seen alive on the evening of Wednesday, 14 October, leaving the ferry from Lévis to Quebec City at about 8:30 p.m, one-half hour before witnesses spotted Balcombe in his maroon Studebaker heading for downtown Quebec City from a nearby suburb. About 2:30 a.m. on Thursday morning Balcombe visited a surprised friend in Montreal. Minutes later his Studebaker pulled up to the Tic-Tac Take-away restaurant, located a few blocks away from his friend's apartment. Nobody saw Balcombe's car again until he reached the cabin in Beachville, Ontario, later that day, but two paper cups with the logo of the Tic-Tac restaurant of Montreal were found in the ditch near Annie's body.

Balcombe was tried before McRuer and a jury at the Cornwall assizes between 22 and 27 February 1954. The court heard a remarkable volume of evidence as to the circumstances surrounding the crime and the movements of both Annie and Balcombe in the months and days preceding the murder. Critically important was the forensic evidence relating to the time of death. The pathologist determined that *rigor mortis* had not set in when Annie was placed in the ditch. He also estimated that Annie had lived for about forty-five minutes after suffering her first knife wound. This meant that the murder likely occurred in Ontario, and so McRuer felt that the Supreme Court of Ontario had jurisdiction to try the case. The forensic evidence also indicated that Annie's murderer remained with her as she slowly died, for she was stabbed again about fifteen minutes before her death, once more about five minutes before her death, and several times at or after the time of death.

Defence counsel Joseph M. Kelly, in his jury address, asked for an acquittal on the grounds that Balcombe "could not have committed the crime." He argued that Balcombe could not possibly have placed the body in the ditch and still arrived at Beachville, where he rented a cabin. There was no evidence, moreover, that Balcombe had placed the clothes in the cabin; all the cabins were kept unlocked.[31]

In his charge, McRuer instructed the jury that the forensic evidence presented at the trial meant that the person responsible for killing Annie could not be found guilty of anything less than murder. If she had died of a single wound, the appropriate charge might well have been manslaughter. Annie's killer, however, had watched her die through three-quarters of an hour, and had several times deliberately inflicted further wounds. Whether or not it was Balcombe who was guilty, it was clear that Annie was the victim of a deliberate act of murder.

McRuer also took pains to explain the nature of circumstantial evidence, and he offered the jury the following advice: "I warn you, in considering circumstances do not consider them detached one from another. Consider them all together in relation to the whole thing because inferences to be drawn from one circumstance may be very wrong, or the inferences to be drawn from two; but inferences to be drawn from a multitude of circumstances may direct you to a very safe conclusion. That is your judgment." The chief justice then proceeded through a step-by-step analysis of the circumstantial evidence, providing the jury with concrete examples of how to weigh that evidence. For example, after discussing the discovery of Annie's clothes in the cabin which Balcombe had rented, McRuer told the jury: "You ask yourselves two questions: Is there any realm of possibility that some other person took these clothes from Annie Carrier and by any coincidence in the world stored them in the attic of that little cabin at Beachville, Ontario, on the route the accused was following, where the accused is said to have stayed on the afternoon and night of the 16th? Is there any realm of possibility it was any other person that could have done it than the accused, any other rational conclusion based on the evidence? It is for your judgement, gentlemen, your honest judgement based on your oath as jurors. It is not for me to decide but for you."

McRuer was satisfied that Balcombe was guilty of the heinous murder of Annie Carrier, and the jury agreed.[32] There were simply too many circumstances pointing to his guilt. McRuer made no recommendation of mercy, and, although the case was ultimately appealed to the Supreme Court of Canada, the verdict of guilty was not overturned.[33] Balcombe was eventually hanged.

The case of the maroon Studebaker did not end with Balcombe's condemnation, however, for contempt of court again came into play. During the trial, a local magazine distributor in Cornwall imported a number of American crime magazines containing sensational and even libellous stories about "Canada's Nude CWAC." When McRuer's attention was drawn to these stories, he was outraged, not only because they were morally repugnant but also because they threatened to prejudice the outcome of Balcombe's trial. When counsel for one of the magazines argued that his client should not be found in contempt because he had been "in the dark about the law," McRuer angrily retorted "they will not be in the dark any longer. A glow of light will shine on them after today." McRuer found the magazines to be in contempt and levied fines totalling $14,000 on the three publishers involved; he sentenced the local distributor, William C. Bryan, to ten days in jail. Believing that the effectiveness of a legal sanction did not depend as much on the severity of the sentence as on the swiftness with which it was levied, McRuer ordered Bryan set free after he had spent a night in jail.[34]

When these convictions were appealed, both the Ontario Court of Appeal and Mr. Justice Fauteux of the Supreme Court of Canada expressly rejected the defence's contention that the accused had been irredeemably prejudiced in obtaining a fair trial by the extensive publication and distribution "through the province of Ontario and in particular in the United Counties of Stormont, Dundas and Glengarry from whence the jurymen were selected, of written reports and articles having reference to the case at bar." Fauteux noted that McRuer, not only in his address to the jury but in a statement before the first witness was.called, "instructed [the jury], in the clearest and strongest possible terms," that they were obliged to disregard such publications.[35]

McRuer then received a shock which put an ironic finish to the Balcombe trial. John Diefenbaker, regarding McRuer's act of leniency to the magazine distributor as a sign of weakness and legal impropriety, rose in the House of Commons to complain about a chief justice who dared to overturn his own rulings. When McRuer heard of this, he was astonished that the populist Diefenbaker, "of all people," could have made such a statement. "With men like Diefenbaker in the Tory party," McRuer predicted, "the Liberals could look forward to many more years in power."[36] Three years later, John Diefenbaker was prime minister.

The Last Men to Hang

The Progressive Conservative government of John Diefenbaker came to power in June 1957, and this change in government signalled a dramatic reversal in the longstanding cabinet approach to the death penalty. Diefenbaker had long disliked capital punishment, and his strong views on the subject were increasingly echoed both in parliament (Arthur Maloney, now MP for Parkdale, was a member of the Progressive Conservative caucus) and in the country as a whole. Contributing significantly to the growth of abolitionist sentiment was the controversial case of Wilbert Coffin, hanged in Montreal on 10 February 1956 for the murder of an American hunter. The circumstances of the Coffin case were so shrouded in mystery that profound doubts about his guilt lingered for years.

A measure of how much times had changed was the increase in the number of commutations: in the years from 1953 to 1957, the Liberal government of Louis St. Laurent commuted the death sentences of 45 per cent of convicted murderers; in contrast, during Diefenbaker's tenure, from 1958 to 1962, over 82 per cent of convicted murderers had their sentences commuted.[37] Another reflection of growing unease with the death penalty was legislation introduced by the minister of justice, H. Davie Fulton, in late May 1961. Known as Bill C-92, this amendment to the Criminal Code has been described by one legal scholar, Neil Boyd, as "the most significant restructuring of the legal definition of murder in the history of our country."[38]

In introducing Bill C-92 the Diefenbaker government was following the lead of Britain, the United States, and a number of countries in western Europe, all of which had divided the crime of murder into different categories. Fulton proposed that "deliberate and premeditated" killings should be classified as a separate category punishable by death. He also argued for two other kinds of capital crime, the killing of a police officer or prison guard, and a killing "committed in the course of a crime of violence, such as arson, rape or armed robbery."[39] Following considerable debate, Bill C-92 passed into law in much the same form as had first been proposed to the House of Commons. As a result the Criminal Code now defined murder as either capital or non-capital. Capital murder was defined as any "planned and deliberate" killing, as a death inflicted during "piracy, escape … resisting lawful arrest, rape, indecent assault, forcible abduction, robbery, burglary or arson," or as any action "causing the death" of a police officer or prison guard. All other murder was to be "non-capital," with a sentence of life imprisonment upon conviction.[40]

The legislation did not, however, end the clamour for abolition of the death penalty. As Neil Boyd has noted, the Diefenbaker government continued to commute most sentences of death, in spite of the new category of capital murder. Those Conservatives in favour of capital punishment—Fulton and, later, Finance Minister Donald Fleming—could not sway cabinet from the path of commutation.[41]

At the same time that these grand lines of Canadian public policy were taking shape in early 1961, developments in the Detroit underworld were leading inexorably to the practical consequences that gave such laws their relevance—a gruesome "gangland" murder that would be tried before McRuer and result in his sentencing the accused to death.

Remembered long after it was over, *R. v. Lucas* was far from being the most complicated case that McRuer ever presided over. Nevertheless, because Arthur Lucas was one of the last two men hanged in Canada, it became a landmark in the country's legal history and forever tied McRuer's name to capital punishment.

Lucas, an American, led a hard and troubled life. Born in Georgia in 1907, he grew up in Florida, dropped out of school in grade six, and as a young man earned his livelihood from gambling, drugs, forgery, and prostitution. In the 1930s he was convicted of armed robbery and served a jail term in Leavenworth penitentiary, where prison records described him as a "feeble-minded, psycho-neurotic, anti-social agitator." While he stayed out of jail after 1942, he continued to lead a life of crime, peddling drugs and pimping for prostitutes. Soon a well-known figure in Detroit's underworld, he married Dolores Chipps, a prostitute, in 1953 but then forced her out of the home after they had had a child so that another prostitute, Lillian Boykin, could take her place. Barely literate, Lucas was a mean, brutal man who apparently beat women regularly, but in 1961 he still seemed more of a petty criminal than one destined for the gallows.

Then his path crossed with that of Therland Crater. No less a criminal than Lucas, Crater, known as "Checkerboard" to his cronies, had become a police informant in 1960, assisting the investigations of the Federal Bureau of Narcotics. With his insider's knowledge of the city's underworld, Crater was able to provide the bureau with leads that led to charges being laid against several notorious criminals, including Gus Saunders. In December 1961 Crater was preparing to testify for the prosecution in Saunders's trial on a charge of narcotics smuggling. Saunders wanted Crater eliminated before he could testify, and the contract-killer he selected was Arthur Lucas.

At this time, Crater was living undercover with Carol Ann Newman, a twenty-year-old prostitute, in Toronto. In the early morning of 16 November 1961, Lucas drove into Canada from Detroit in a pink Buick owned by Saunders. The following morning, at 6:30 a.m., Bell Canada operator Elizabeth Williams answered a call from a frightened woman who began shouting hysterically, "You don't have to hold me like that. Let me go!" This was followed by sounds of a struggle and then a scream, "Not my throat!" Williams traced the call to 116 Kendal Avenue, in Toronto's Bloor-Bathurst area. When the police arrived on the scene, they found the bodies of Therland Crater and Carol Ann Newman. Crater had been shot four times and stabbed viciously; Newman had had her throat cut.

Lying on the blood-soaked bed next to Newman's body was a man's gold ring.

Within twenty-four hours the police investigation had moved from Toronto to Detroit. Nine suspects were questioned, including Gus Saunders, his wife, Morris "Red" Thomas (also known as "Polkadot"), and Lucas's estranged wife, Dolores Chipps. Both Thomas and Chipps implicated Lucas: Thomas said that Lucas had driven into Canada on 16 November to sell heroin; and Chipps said that after Lucas returned to Detroit on 17 November he had admitted killing two people in Toronto, one of whom was Crater, and that he was worried about a ring he had lost in the victims' bed. In the early hours of 18 November, Lucas was arrested at the house of his new girlfriend, Lillian Boykin. Soon afterwards, a 38-calibre revolver was found along the Burlington Skyway, a bridge that Lucas would have had to cross in making his way from Toronto to Detroit via Niagara Falls (the fastest route out of the country). Ballistic experts soon concluded that the gun belonged to Lucas, and that powder-markings on his right hand indicated that he could have recently fired the same gun. Another expert, with the scientific bureau of the Detroit police department, discovered that the car used by Lucas on his trip to and from Toronto contained blood stains which matched the blood types of the two victims. Lucas was charged in one indictment with the two murders but the trial proceeded only on the count charging him with the murder of Therland Crater. On 30 April 1962 he appeared in court before Chief Justice McRuer.[42]

Prosecuting for the crown was the tough-minded Henry Bull; Lucas was defended by Ross MacKay, a smart but inexperienced lawyer who was also a bit too fond of the bottle. Bull brought forward fifty witnesses, while only three testified for the defence—Lucas's girlfriend, Lillian; Lucas's sister, Lizzie; and Lucas himself. Lucas had a story ready—he was an old friend of Crater, he said, and he had visited him in Toronto to discuss placing a girl he knew in Crater's Detroit bawdy house—and his lawyer hypothesized that someone else had killed Crater and Newman after Lucas had left the scene.

In the end, however, Lucas's testimony and that of the two other defence witnesses could not stand up in the face of the overwhelming body of circumstantial evidence presented by the prosecution. Lucas himself claimed, perhaps unfairly, that his defence had been seriously weakened by the behaviour of his lawyer, who, he said, stank of liquor "clear across the courtroom."

On 10 May 1962 McRuer delivered his charge to the jury. Like all his charges, it was lengthy and detailed. Running to sixty-five pages, it instructed the jury on key points of law—the meaning of "reasonable doubt," the value of circumstantial evidence—and reviewed each piece of evidence. The jury then deliberated for about five hours before returning a guilty verdict, with no recommendation of clemency. McRuer ordered Lucas to be hanged on 19 October 1962.[43]

The case was appealed, but Mr. Justice Laidlaw of the Court of Appeal ruled that "the only conclusion that the jury acting reasonably and judicially could reach after due and proper consideration of the evidence was that the circumstances were consistent with [Lucas] having committed the offence of capital murder as charged and also that the facts were inconsistent with any other rational conclusion than that he is the guilty person."[44] A further appeal to the Supreme Court of Canada was also dismissed, Chief Justice Kerwin observing, in the court's majority opinion, that McRuer's jury charge had been "thorough, complete, accurate and fair."[45] The Diefenbaker cabinet met in October to discuss the cases of Lucas and two other condemned men: Ronald Turpin, the murderer of a policeman (and, coincidentally, another client of Ross MacKay); and Gary McCarkell, convicted of sexually assaulting and murdering two small boys. McCarkell had his death sentence commuted. In the cases of Lucas and Turpin, however, cabinet decided not to commute their death sentences but only to stay the executions until 11 December. Opponents of capital punishment, including Osgoode Hall professor Desmond Morton, spoke out repeatedly on behalf of the condemned men, but their efforts were in vain. In December, the cabinet met again and decided to let the executions proceed. Diefenbaker defended the decision by pointing out that the jury had not recommended mercy and that since he had been prime minister "no man has been hanged when there has been a recommendation for mercy."[46]

In the words of the Toronto *Telegram*, Lucas and Turpin spent their last two weeks on earth "praying and singing hymns" in their cells in Toronto's Don Jail, attended until the end by a kindly Salvation Army chaplain, Cyrill Everitt.[47] Shortly after midnight, at 12:02 on the morning of 11 December 1962, Lucas and Turpin met their ends on the gallows. It was an ugly scene. Everitt remembered that "Turpin went cleanly. But Lucas, the heavier of the two, had too much rope for his weight. His legs nearly touched the bottom of the floor under the trap. His head was almost torn off … There was blood everywhere."[48] Turpin was pronounced dead at 12:18; Lucas died five minutes later.

The executions of Lucas and Turpin aroused considerable controversy.

On the night of their hanging, a group of about two hundred people stood outside the Don jail protesting the hangings, and a "death watch service" was conducted at the Don Heights Unitarian Church.[49] Press opinion on the executions differed. A *Toronto Star* editorial condemned the hangings and called for the abolition of capital punishment, a "relic of barbarism." The *Telegram*'s editorial took an opposite tack, stating that "repugnant as capital punishment may be, society must exact it for certain crimes—for … deliberate, callously calculated murder." The *Globe and Mail* reiterated its opposition to capital punishment and, pointing to a recent opinion poll indicating that only 47 per cent of Canadians supported the death penalty, called on parliament to abolish it and end the "indecent perennial cliff hanging episodes, when men wait for death and a nation waits to see if it will do them to death."

Both Everitt and the defence counsel for Lucas and Turpin, Ross MacKay, were personally devastated by the executions; Everitt was haunted by the hangings until his death in 1986, and MacKay, equally tormented, slid into alcoholism and lost everything. In the mid-1970s MacKay put his life back together again, but then died of cancer in 1983.[50]

McRuer, in contrast, showed no signs of anguish over the fate of Lucas; in his mind, Lucas's hanging was no different from the other hangings he had ordered over the course of his judicial career. On the morning of 11 December 1962, he read in the newspaper about the executions of Lucas and Turpin but made no comment to Mary. Instead, he simply went back to work, unaware that he would never again have to send a man to his death. In 1967 parliament voted to abolish the death penalty in most cases for a five-year trial period, retaining it only for the murder of police officers and prison guards. Another five-year trial period was authorized in 1973, and a further vote in parliament on 14 July 1976 removed the final vestiges of capital punishment.

ANY REVIEW OF MCRUER'S RECORD in murder trials must address his willingness to impose the death penalty on convicted murderers. This task is difficult, for McRuer was uncharacteristically reticent in discussing the issue of capital punishment. In his later years, he would invariably say that, in sentencing murderers to death, he had done his duty. As a judge, he claimed, he had had a responsibility to impose justice according to the principles of law. Curiously, McRuer spoke out repeatedly during his career for the reform of numerous laws, but when questioned about the issue of capital punishment, he would quietly say that judges do not write the law and they should keep their distance from politics. A student, writing to ask McRuer about the death penalty, received this reply: "I am sorry I cannot be of much help. This is the sort of issue where people have to make up their minds for themselves." After the abolition of capital punishment in 1976, McRuer was once asked whether he would support its restoration; in reply, he said simply, "I do not know." Members of his own immediate family had no idea where he stood personally on the issue of the death penalty.

In the absence of evidence, only speculation is possible. Perhaps the most likely explanation of McRuer's readiness to sentence murderers to death lies in his sense of justice. For McRuer, laws were the foundation of any society, the indispensable prerequisite to civilized existence. Accordingly, while everyone deserved to be treated fairly under the law, those guilty of crimes could not expect to escape punishment. In the case of murder, the ultimate crime in the eyes of the law, McRuer probably operated on the conviction that anyone guilty of taking another person's life should be punished accordingly. He may or may not have seen it as a deterrent—he left no record of his thoughts on that issue. Given his commitment to justice, however, it seems reasonable to conclude that he viewed hanging as an appropriate punishment for a heinous crime. In short, capital punishment in his mind could be an instrument of justice, a way of ensuring that human life was respected and that no person could kill another with impunity. That was the law in any case, and, if government did not see fit to extend clemency to those condemned by the courts, the law should be allowed to take its course.

Yet there was more to McRuer than his reputation as "Hanging Jim." Though his performance was far from perfect in the murder trials he heard during his early years on the bench—the trial of Evelyn Dick is a case in point—he did improve over time. On the whole, his handling of murder cases showed him to be a fair-minded judge, determined to guard the rights of the accused and to extend even-handed treatment to prosecution and defence. His jury charges were very much like the courtroom presentations he had made as a lawyer and the speeches he had delivered in his short career in politics—sober, carefully thought out, and incisive. He may not have been as learned or as eloquent as some of his colleagues on the bench, but he earned respect for his conscientiousness, his understanding of human nature, and his sense of fair play. The murder trials in which he was involved leave no doubt that he was an especially competent and dedicated judge. The same could certainly be said of his record in the other cases McRuer heard, including those dealing with the environment and with native people.

11

LAW, THE ENVIRONMENT
AND NATIVE PEOPLE

EARLY IN HIS YEARS ON THE BENCH, Jim McRuer became known as a champion of the environment. His reputation as a conservationist—the word "environmentalist" did not come into fashion until later—incorporated three fundamental elements: a balanced view of the interests of contending parties, an awareness of the importance of natural resources, and an imaginative application of the law to environmental issues. Just as important was the character of the man himself; McRuer refused to be cowed by the technical jargon of experts, the political power of the antagonists, or the economic consequences of his decisions. Yet his record in environmental cases was not one of unbroken success. Though his judgments against polluters were never overturned by appellate courts, in a number of instances the pollution did not end. Polluters often seemed able to ignore legal sanctions with impunity, while in at least one sensational episode—the renowned KVP case—they used political and economic clout to persuade the Ontario legislature itself to overrule his decision.

The environmental cases that came before McRuer all involved property rights. Several of them may seem trivial; in a few instances they concerned only common sewage. McRuer, however, saw such cases differently. To his mind, property rights lay at the heart of the common law and their maintenance was vital to the preservation of civil peace. Alongside this position were two beliefs that had become central to McRuer's judicial philosophy. First, McRuer was convinced that a violation of the rights of the individual—even in a matter so mundane as a backed-up sewer—amounted to a challenge to the justice system itself and should not be tolerated without the aggrieved person having had a fair hearing before a competent court. Secondly, McRuer firmly believed that the genius of the common law tradition was its blending of continuity and innovation. This process was not static but ongoing, and it required judges to take responsibility for the adaptation of old laws to new circumstances. McRuer saw it as his task—indeed his mission—to address the challenges of a changing world from the proven perspective of the law while at the same time reinterpreting the law itself in the light of those altered social conditions. His efforts to adapt the law so that it would respond effectively to changes in society were especially tested in those cases where property rights overlapped with the cause of the environment.

McRuer's support of the interests of the environment was never so inflexible that it blinded him to other issues. In one case where the inherent rights of native people—rather than property rights—collided with environmental legislation, *R. v. Calvin William George*, McRuer demonstrated the depth of his commitment to one of the most marginalized groups in Canadian society. In his eyes, there was no justification for laws—even those dealing with the environment—that acted as instruments of oppression.

IN ENVIRONMENTAL CASES, as in others, McRuer sought to understand expert testimony by cutting through the jargon. Sometimes this approach involved direct action, as in the case of *Westinghouse Company v. City of Hamilton* in 1948. Westinghouse, the plaintiff, charged that the city of Hamilton had improperly diverted a stream through its property; the water was channelled at one point through an underground sewer, which the company alleged repeatedly backed up and so caused flooding on its lands. As the trial began, McRuer sat patiently through the testimony of several engineers, who attempted to describe the diversion in terms that were favourable to one party or the other. Seeing that the case was rapidly getting nowhere, he suddenly decided, to the astonishment of the counsel involved, that he should examine the diversion personally. Transportation to the site was arranged, and soon the officers of the court were examining with flashlights the dark inside of the dripping sewer. McRuer quickly assessed the situation, and back in court he had no difficulty in finding for the plaintiff. His only regret was that his visit to the sewers of Hamilton resulted in satirical newspaper headlines.[1] He was always sensitive about the need to maintain judicial dignity.

McRuer tried to be practical in resolving environmental cases. In 1951 a farmer in Ontario County claimed that the stream from which his cattle drank was being polluted by sewage discharged by the city of Oshawa. Before the case came to trial McRuer imposed an injunction requiring the city to stop the discharge, but he also granted the city the right to apply for relief from the injunction if unforeseen problems arose.[2] There was a lot of this sort of thing over the years. In the 1962 case of *Esco and Ginsberg* v. *Fort Henry Hotel Company*,[3] a Kingston hotel owner had an easement under the plaintiff's property for a seventy-five-year-old drain, and when flooding occurred the defendant was charged with nuisance. At trial McRuer ruled in favour of the plaintiff, quoting with approval Mr. Justice Denman's words from 1877 in *Humphries* v. *Cousins*, a case that was as old as the Kingston drain in question: "The prima facie right of every occupier of a piece of land is, to enjoy that land free from all invasion of filth or other matter coming from any artificial structure on land adjoining."[4] Again, in the case of *Delhi* v. *City of Peterborough*, McRuer awarded damages against the city for constructing a faulty drain which, on bursting under the plaintiff's greenhouses, caused damage to his property, and he also granted an injunction against further use of this drainage system until it was repaired.[5] Cases such as these did not break new ground and were not considered important enough to reach the law reports. Nevertheless, they provide a glimpse into the workings of the High Court and also shed light on McRuer's approach to legal disputes involving the environment.

As time went on, a number of more high-profile environmental cases came before McRuer's court. The most celebrated—and contentious— was the 1947-8 case of *McKie* v. *The K.V.P Company Limited*.[6] It certainly was reported, not just in the law reports, but on the front pages of newspapers.

The KVP Company (short for Kalamazoo Vegetable Parchment), based in the United States, operated a large manufacturing complex in the northern Ontario community of Espanola, in the Sudbury district. There KVP produced kraft paper by the so-called "sulphate process," which involved the constant discharge of large volumes of chemicals into the Spanish River. While the damage to the environment was clear, KVP had economic arguments in its favour. The Espanola plant was located on the site of a sulphite mill which had been operated by the Abitibi Pulp and Paper Company until financial difficulties brought on by the

Depression forced its closure in 1930. From then until 1946, when KVP purchased the site, Espanola had been a ghost town. KVP's arrival and its opening of an operation that employed two thousand people gave Espanola a new lease on life and provided a dramatic boost to the regional economy. Following on the heels of KVP was the provincial government, which by the late 1940s had also had made large investments in Espanola and vicinity. According to Premier Leslie Frost, these investments (in highways, hydro services, policing, hospital facilities, schools) totalled approximately $20 million.[7]

Yet not everyone was pleased with KVP. Earl and Ted McKie and their fellow plaintiffs, Jack Cifford, Russell and James Vance, and Dr. G. Downe, owned modest tracts of land along the Spanish River downstream from Espanola. Together, they operated a small tourist camp which specialized in outfitting anglers; some of these men were also farmers. They all depended on the river as a source of fresh fish and of water for themselves and their livestock. Finding the river polluted by the operations of KVP, they each launched actions (five in total) against the company which McRuer, sitting in Sudbury, heard as a single case. The plaintiffs claimed damages and asked for an injunction prohibiting KVP from continuing to pollute the Spanish River. The scale of the company's assault on the environment can be measured by the arguments they advanced: their comfort and the enjoyment of their land was adversely affected by the foul odours given off from the water; the water had been rendered unfit for human consumption either in its untreated state or after it had been boiled; the ice taken from the river in winter for domestic use was unfit for the purposes for which it was being used; the water was now repulsive to farm animals and milking cows would not drink it in sufficient quantities to maintain normal milk supply; the water had become unfit to bathe in; the fish in the river were being either killed or driven elsewhere; and wild rice, which had formerly grown in abundance in the waters of the river, forming a feeding ground for wild ducks, had been destroyed.

The plaintiffs, represented by D.R. Walkinshaw, called various witnesses to testify about conditions in and around the river. These witnesses consisted of government officials responsible for the conservation of wildlife and persons living on the banks of the river. KVP hired three lawyers to defend it, J.J. Robinette, J.A. Boles, and James Worrall, and relied heavily on the testimony of experts paid to conduct experiments either in their laboratories or in the company's plant. McRuer, who sat without a jury, later indicated that he was not altogether impressed with

the opinions of some of the well-paid experts. "I think some of these latter witnesses, called for the defendant," he said, "found it difficult to distinguish between the functions of a witness and those of an advocate."[8]
During the trial, McRuer made it abundantly clear that he would base
his judgment on the legal rights of the plaintiffs and the actual conditions of the river and its shores.

McRuer found that following the closing of the Abitibi plant, and
particularly following a flood about fourteen years before which washed
out and cleansed the bed of the river, the fish started to come back to the
Spanish river; indeed, just prior to 1947 the river had once again become
a good fishing ground, with game fish in abundance. As a result, the area
had developed into a desirable resort for fishermen, and, in McRuer's
words, the owners of property on the river "had every reason to expect
that it would continue to develop if there was no interference with it."[9]
Once KVP opened its Espanola operations, however, conditions deteriorated drastically. The water of the river began giving off a foul odour,
likened by witnesses to the smell of rotten cabbage, and its taste also
deteriorated significantly. KVP even admitted that at least three and a
half tons of fibrous material full of chemicals was discharged daily into
the river from its plant. McRuer did not accept the firm's contention that
these substances were adequately diluted by the volume of water in the
river: large numbers of fish had been found dead in the river during 1947,
he noted, and both anglers and provincial authorities had observed a
substantial decline in the fish population. He also specifically rejected
defence arguments that the economic interests of the town of Espanola,
and the livelihood of the employees in the KVP plant, should be given
more weight than those of the plaintiffs. On this point, McRuer minced
no words: "In my view, if I were to consider and give effect to an argument based on the defendant's economic position in the community, or
its financial interests, I would in effect be giving to it a veritable power of
expropriation of the common law rights of the riparian owners, without
compensation."[10]

Noting that "the origin of the common law applicable to this subject goes back to and beyond the Roman law,"[11] McRuer cited the legal
authorities that guided his decision in this case. He then ruled that the
owners of riverside property below the Espanola plant had every right
to relief from the dangerous pollution which, in his view, was directly
caused by the KVP company's operations. He ordered KVP to pay varying amounts of compensation to the individual plaintiffs, and also to
halt its pollution of the Spanish River. An injunction was granted re-

straining the company from polluting the river, with the operation of the injunction suspended for six months "in order to give the defendant an opportunity to provide other means of disposal of its noxious effluent."[12]

Outraged by McRuer's audacity, KVP immediately turned to the Ontario Court of Appeal. When the company's appeal was dismissed by that body in November 1948[13] it promptly made a further appeal to the Supreme Court of Canada. This appeal concerned not the damages the company had been ordered to pay to the plaintiffs (that was still being haggled over separately) but the far more significant injunction.

In presenting KVP's case to the Supreme Court, counsel J.R. Cartwright and J.J. Robinette argued that the company was covered by recent amendments to Ontario's Lakes and Rivers Improvement Act. It was their contention that the revised act, which brought pulp companies within the terms of environmental pollution legislation that was already on the Ontario statute books, empowered the Supreme Court to do any one of several things—refuse to grant an injunction against the owner of the mill under certain named conditions; grant an injunction to take effect after a specified lapse of time or subject to terms, conditions, or restrictions; or, instead of granting an injunction, direct KVP to take measures to prevent or diminish the pollution damage. Cartwright and Robinette pointed out that, under the amended act, the Supreme Court's power was applicable in a proceeding where an injunction had been granted and an appeal was "pending." The idea did not impress. As Chief Justice Patrick Kerwin said in the court's unanimous decision, the amendments to the Lakes and Rivers Improvement Act came into force 1 April 1949, by which time the Ontario Court of Appeal had already given its judgment upholding McRuer's ruling. Since a provincial legislature could not extend the jurisdiction of the Supreme Court of Canada, a measure such as Ontario's Lakes and Rivers Improvement Act could not enable the Supreme Court to give a judgment that was impossible in law at the time of the decision of the Court of Appeal. KVP's appeal was dismissed.[14]

Several months later the company, undaunted, sought an order from the Supreme Court of Canada allowing it to apply to the High Court of Justice for a further suspension of the injunction if it were able to show special grounds. The Supreme Court, again, refused to make such order.[15] All in all, the case seemed a great legal victory for the gradually growing number of individuals who were calling for limitations on industrial pollution.

Yet the American owners of the mill, knowing something of the levers of power, were not ready to give up yet. Though some of the plaintiffs' solicitors, under tremendous community pressure, publicly stated that no application would be made to the courts to have the injunction enforced, the company threatened to close its plant on 4 April 1950 unless the injunction were lifted. It also enlisted political support. Delegations from Espanola travelled south to meet Premier Leslie Frost and leaders of the opposition parties in the legislature. Including municipal officials, representatives of the various political parties, at least two different labour unions, fishing and game associations, and groups of residents—merchants, doctors, clergy, farmers, guides—the delegations brought word that the company had taken corrective measures to cease its pollution of the Spanish River and that these had already gone a very long way to dealing successfully with the problem. A petition, signed by some 2,000 residents of Espanola and vicinity, added further weight to KVP's cause, emphasizing that the company was doing everything possible to prevent undue pollution of the Spanish River and calling for repeal of the injunction.[16]

KVP's efforts and those of its supporters to overturn McRuer's injunction attracted the sympathetic attention of the provincial government. Concerned about the severe economic consequences that a closure of KVP's Espanola plant would entail, Premier Frost set out the government's position in a speech to the legislature on 24 February 1950. In words that were forceful if not eloquent, he explained: "We do not regard lightly the matter of pollution of our streams. Indeed, we think it is a very serious matter and we have already taken action in this House and outside of this House to emphasize the fact that we think the pollution of our streams is an extremely serious matter which we on this side of the House do not hold lightly. We do not hold lightly the rights of individuals to protect their interests in the courts of this land. That is, in itself, a very important matter which we in no way hold lightly. We also regard as a matter of high importance the employment of our people and we do recognize that in these days of industrialization and the expansion of industry and the increase of population in areas of the province that we are bound to get a certain amount of pollution in our lakes and streams. At the same time, we are determined to hold that to the least possible limit."

Frost then noted that the government had decided to enlist the expertise of the Ontario Research Council—an agency, funded jointly by the provincial government and the private sector, that assisted the industrial and agricultural sectors in the development of the province's natural resources. The ORC, Frost said, would have the responsibility of "examining into the situation to assure that every reasonable step, scientific and otherwise, is now taken, and will be taken in the future by the company so that pollution will be reduced consistent with reasonable practice. The Ontario Research Council will be given unlimited powers, not only to investigate this special problem but also to consult authorities in other countries as to the most advanced practices in dealing with the problems of pulp mill waste. The Council will be asked to advise in the light of their inquiries and investigation into this whole matter as to what additional measures are required to reduce pollution by the company in this area.

"I can assure you of this, that we have no intention of putting people of that community out of employment, we intend to keep employment going. At the same time, we intend to protect to the fullest extent that we are able the interests of the people of the province of Ontario."[17]

The following month, on 21 March, Attorney-General Dana Porter introduced a bill that dissolved "every injunction heretofore granted against The KVP Company Limited... restraining the Company from polluting the waters of the Spanish River." So as not to run entirely roughshod over the interests of those who had sought to stop KVP's pollution, the bill preserved the right of citizens to any damages already awarded against the company for pollution as well as their right to bring future actions against it. Moreover, the company was statutorily obliged to submit to arbitration any allegations of damage arising from its pollution of the river. The bill's most innovative feature was found in section 4, which applied "the polluter pays" principle and pioneered an approach that, had it been vigorously pursued, could have become a blueprint for resolving many similar problems. As Premier Frost had promised, the bill stipulated that the Ontario Research Council "shall endeavour to develop methods that, if applied by the Company, would abate or lessen the pollution of the waters of the Spanish River by the Company." Then, having given the ORC a statutory responsibility to develop the technology and methods needed to abate the mill's pollution of the river, the bill added: "The cost of carrying out its duties ... shall be deemed to be a debt due by the Company to the Research Council of Ontario." Significantly, there was no limit on the amount the ORC could spend on this project.

The KVP bill received second reading in the legislature on 23 March.

The next week, on 29 March, the House went into committee of the whole, where an amendment was added to give the parties (still locked in dispute over the matter) the right to arbitration, and set out procedures on how such arbitration should proceed. On the afternoon of 30 March, the bill passed third reading; royal assent was given the next day. McRuer's injunction against KVP had been dissolved.[18]

Although McRuer was bitterly disappointed by this development, his ruling in the KVP case certainly enhanced his reputation among those who were concerned with environmental issues. Thirty years later, on 28 April 1979, McRuer delivered a lecture on "Judicial Review of Administrative Action" to the faculty of law at the University of Victoria. The faculty's first-year curriculum began with a one-month introductory program which featured the case of *McKie* v. *K.V.P.* as the vehicle for introducing students to the nature of the legal process and the role of the judiciary. It would not be an overstatement to say that McRuer had become the class's judicial hero.

After the lecture, at a barbecue at the home of Professor Frank Borowicz, a number of law students formed themselves into a choir to provide entertainment for their distinguished visitor from Ontario. To McRuer's surprise and delight, they sang an appreciative "Ode to McRuer and the KVP Case" to the tune of Davy Crocket:

> Pollution on the Spanish River
> Folks in arms
> The KVP is creating
> Lots of harm
> So they went off to court
> To have their stay heard
> And this is our rendition
> Of the judge's famous words
>
> Judge, Judge McRuer
> Took on the KVP
>
> He spoke of rights riparian
> And saw they were ignored
> He said all of this effluent
> We really can't afford
> So he issued an injunction

To keep the fish from dying
To tidy up the scenery
And keep things smelling fine

Judge, Judge McRuer
Took on the KVP

The Upper Courts of Canada
Approved of his decision
On appeal and in the Supreme Court
He met with no derision
But KVP would not give up
They had one final chance
A private bill they all believed
Might yet their cause advance

Judge, Judge McRuer
Took on the KVP

So they passed another statute
And the fish began to die
We'll compensate your sorry loss
Your happiness we'll buy
The KVP had won the day
And so our rights are fewer
Despite the mighty efforts
Of Chief Justice McRuer

Judge, Judge McRuer
Took on the KVP

McRuer likewise handled a number of controversial cases involving air pollution. He found such cases especially intriguing since great care was required in evaluating scientific information and technical reports in order to establish guilt or liability. He also believed that the relatively new problem of air pollution could be readily dealt with in the context of long-established legal traditions. Ultimately, these cases confirmed his belief in the resilience of the common law, but they also reminded him how his own authority as a judge was decidedly limited.

The first air pollution case to come before McRuer was *Walker* v. *McKinnon Industries Limited*. William Wallace Walker, a florist, owned a nursery in the city of St. Catharines where he specialized in growing flowers, particularly orchids, for the market. In 1936 McKinnon Industries purchased the property adjacent to Walker's operation and erected a plant to manufacture steel and iron products. The factory included a forge-ship and four cupolas which emitted gases some 400 and 600 feet respectively from Walker's property. The cupolas were fired by coke with combustion accelerated by a forced up-draft of 8,700 cubic feet per minute.

Walker was extremely concerned about the industrial activities of his new neighbour, and he soon started making complaints. At first he dealt directly with the management of McKinnon Industries. After much acrimonious discussion, the company agreed to compensate Walker for some of his losses, and in January 1942 the latter received a lump-sum payment of $1,225 from McKinnon in full satisfaction of all claims and demands that he had advanced to that date. Walker, for his part, granted an easement to McKinnon Industries allowing it to continue the activities complained of until 31 December 1944 in exchange for a sum of $600 annually.

Walker continued to collect his annual compensation, but over time he noticed a progressive deterioration in the condition of his plants. His profits, of course, were also declining with the quality of his orchids. By 1945 Walker was desperate, and in 1946 he sought a remedy in court, hiring Arthur Slaght, R.I. Ferguson (Slaght's partner and later one of McRuer's fellow judges on the High Court), and R.K. Ross to represent him. His action claimed damages for the period since 31 December 1944 and asked for an injunction to stop McKinnon from continuing to pollute the air. McKinnon Industries retained J.L.G. Keogh and J.L. Pound to represent it.

Walker's lawyers presented a case that impressed McRuer as both creative and comprehensive. Scientists had been commissioned to keep detailed records on the state of Walker's plants under various weather conditions, with readings correlated to emissions from the McKinnon factory. McRuer was especially interested in evidence that excessive emissions of sulphur dioxide gas from the McKinnon operation were substantially damaging plants on Walker's property. Once he had satisfied himself that McKinnon was indeed responsible for damaging and polluting Walker's property and plants (as well as the area generally), he had little difficulty in formulating his judgment; English legal tradition, incorporated in common law applicable to Canada, was clear about actionable nuisance.

Again reflecting his belief that fundamental and time-proven legal principles were the best source of justice for new problems, McRuer noted, in giving his judgment, that the law to be applied to these findings of fact had been discussed at great length in numerous cases and by many textbook writers, and that he did "not feel that [he could] add anything to the jurisprudence by a discussion of it, more than to make some reference to the legal considerations that ... guided [him] in coming to a decision." McRuer imposed an injunction on McKinnon Industries directing it to stop its pollution of the air, and he referred the task of assessing the amount of Walker's damages to a county court judge. In granting the injunction, McRuer's order again followed the balanced or reasonable approach he had taken in the KVP case, giving the polluting company a clearly fixed time to remedy matters so that ideally pollution could be stopped without endangering jobs: the injunction would be suspended until 1 November 1949 to permit McKinnon Industries to make alterations in its plant. McRuer believed that his judgment offered justice to all concerned.[19]

Yet, as in cases involving water pollution, *Walker* v. *McKinnon* did not end with McRuer's initial judgment. His decision was appealed to the Ontario Court of Appeal[20] and from there, somewhat unusually, directly to the Judicial Committee of the Privy Council in London.[21] (This was one of the last Canadian cases to go to the Privy Council.) At every level, McRuer's decision was sustained with only slight variations, and all the courts on appeal, despite granting temporary suspensions of McRuer's injunction, stipulated that the pollution must come to an end. Indeed, the Privy Council's decision stated: "Their Lordships will say at once that so far from being satisfied that the learned Judge wrongly exercised his discretion, they are well satisfied, having read his careful and exhaustive judgment, that he exercised it properly and that in the words of the Court of Appeal this was eminently a proper case for the granting of an injunction."[22] Still, McKinnon did not stop polluting the air around Walker's property. Effectively, McRuer's judgment was upheld in law but the nuisance continued in reality. Ultimately, however, the dispute was definitively concluded—not by the enforcement of court decisions but by the power of money: McKinnon Industries simply bought Walker's property from him and continued its polluting. The news galled McRuer.

The 1951 case of *Russell Transport Limited et al.* v. *The Ontario Malleable Iron Company Limited* had a more reassuring outcome. Russell Transport, located in Oshawa, Ontario, operated next door to the foundry of the Ontario Malleable Iron Company and was engaged in the business of transporting new automobiles from the manufacturer, principally General Motors, to the distributor. The transport company had a marshalling-yard at its premises in which new cars were parked pending their transportation. Trouble arose in 1951 when dealers receiving cars from Russell Transport's yard began complaining that the finish on the cars was defective. In some cases, metallic particles were even found embedded in the finish of shiny new cars.

Russell Transport brought an action for nuisance and sought an injunction restraining Ontario Malleable from discharging any substances likely to cause or continue the damage that Russell Transport had been suffering. Its lawyer gathered a body of evidence to prove that Ontario Malleable was emitting corrosive iron particles which damaged cars held in the yard by Russell Transport. Tests determined that the problem was not the result of defects in the original finish: steel panels finished in the same manner as those of cars were placed in different locations in Oshawa where they were subjected to emissions from different foundries, but none became pitted or corroded. To McRuer, the "irresistible conclusion" of these experiments was that the defendant's foundry was emitting fine iron particles of a corrosive nature, and he granted an injunction restraining the emissions from Ontario Malleable. In his reasons for judgment, McRuer commented on emission-control devices: "The evidence shows that insofar as the emissions from the cupola are responsible for the injury to the plaintiffs, and I think they are in large measure responsible for the injury complained of, the defendant has adopted no method of modern smoke or fume control. The cupola is an open stack with a conical shelter over it which arrests some solid particles and deflects them to the roof of the defendant's plant but permits the remainder to escape into the atmosphere. Mr. Beaumont, a witness called for the plaintiffs, gave evidence that there are in operation in the United States of America commercial devices for the control of smoke and fumes by a water-wash system which is at least 80 per cent efficient in arresting solid matter and 100 per cent efficient in arresting injurious gases. The defendant has considered the installation of a fume-control system in the cupola but has refrained from doing anything pending the outcome of this action. Some dust-arresters for the purpose of controlling other emissions from the plant have been installed in recent years. These arresters are designed chiefly to purify the air within the plant and it is not clear that they afford much protection to the surrounding property."

McRuer again relied on the established jurisprudence, referring to his earlier examination of the applicable case law in *Walker* v. *McKinnon Industries Ltd.*[23]

McRuer ordered that the operation of the injunction be suspended until 1 January 1953, some six months after his judgment of 24 June 1952. Ontario Malleable procrastinated but did not launch an appeal. The chief justice waited to see what would happen, remembering the futility of some of his earlier environmental judgments. Months passed, but then came some pleasing news. Ontario Malleable had invested considerable sums of money to seek a solution to the problem. By redesigning its plant, the company found that it could continue operations without polluting the environment. At last McRuer had seen real progress on an environmental issue.

Such is a sampling of the environmental cases that Jim McRuer tried in the course of his judicial career. In all of them, he was attentive in applying and reinterpreting common law so as to ensure that the rights of those suffering the bad effects of pollution would be respected. Yet, in seeking a remedy within the common law for those who had come to his court, he was relying on a body of law that itself was about to be submerged by larger events. As the pace of industrialization quickened in the 1950s, the rate of contamination accelerated also, affecting water, air, and soil. At the same time, government came under increasing pressure not to take action against polluters that would put jobs and prosperity at risk, and, in response, government itself embraced an ethic of "progress" that ensured economic growth and hence the maintenance of a solid tax base. More and more, the few people who continued to seek legal remedies for pollution in the courts found themselves confronting an infinitely more powerful government-industry coalition.

Against this background, McRuer's decision in the KVP case was one of the last attempts to respond to pollution by effectively enforcing "riparian" rights—the rights of people who live along the shore of a river or lake to continued and undisturbed use of clean water—through the courts. Five years later, in 1955, this same scenario was played out again. First, judge Charles Douglas Stewart issued an injunction to close the sewage treatment plant in Richmond Hill, Ontario, on the grounds that it had polluted the Don River and thereby violated the riparian rights of a Mrs. Stephens, who lived downstream. As with McRuer's KVP decision, Stewart's ruling was appealed and upheld.[24] Next, the provincial government responded in 1956 by overturning the court order.[25] What is more, the government also brought in at this time the Ontario Water

Resources Commission Act, which effectively superseded riparian rights by making government the primary authority responsible for protection of the environment.[26]

This shift of power in the mid-1950s from the courts to government—as represented by the KVP and Richmond Hill cases—undercut citizen action. It meant that people would now complain to government regulators about environmental problems rather than turn to the courts, and that riparian rights were a thing of the past. It did not mean, however, that Jim McRuer would not have other chances to examine the issue of how a citizen could assert his or her rights to property and a clean environment, for a decade and a half later he was given an opportunity to scrutinize the Ontario Water Resources Commission and other such bodies to determine whether they operated in the public interest. He would live and remain active long enough to see such matters resolved, and to have his own approach vindicated. That approach seemed radical in the 1950s but in fact he was simply ahead of his time in recognizing the primacy of the environment and the value of private citizens' ancient property rights.

ANOTHER ANCIENT RIGHT was the one belonging to Canada's first peoples to hunt and fish in order to live. The contemporary meaning of this right came before Chief Justice McRuer in the context of *R. v. Calvin William George*. At the heart of this case was the effort by aboriginal peoples to cope with rules which had been developed by legislatures beyond their power but which nevertheless affected their daily lives.

The George case involved issues dating back many years. In 1916, responding to demands by conservationists that the Canadian government take action to halt the slaughter of wildlife, the Government of Canada entered into a treaty with the United States that placed limits on the hunting of migratory birds. The following year parliament passed the Migratory Birds Convention Act, which gave legal effect to the international treaty within Canada.[27] Implementing the act raised major problems, however, one of which concerned the hunting practices and legal rights of Canada's native peoples.

In 1919 a major conference in Ottawa reviewed issues arising out of the act and its administration. Duncan Campbell Scott, deputy superintendent general of Indian Affairs, delivered a paper at this conference on the subject of the natives' relationship to wildlife. Pleading for a sympathetic understanding of the interests of natives, the "original fur hunters," Scott said that, because so many companies and individuals were competing for furs and there were so many game-hunting restrictions throughout the country, natives were finding it increasingly difficult to support themselves. His department was endeavouring to control native tribes and bring them under provincial game laws and Scott believed that its efforts were proving successful.

These arguments aroused a heated debate. Fred Bradshaw, Saskatchewan's game guardian (who considered the Migratory Birds Convention Act the best legislation ever enacted for game conservation), claimed that natives in his province ignored the game laws and that there were frequent complaints about their "wanton slaughter" of big game animals. "I may be wrong," Bradshaw concluded, "but the attitude of the Indian Department seems to be, that, while they are extremely sorry that such things are happening—the poor Indian must be fed, and presumably in the cheapest possible manner." He accused government Indian agents of encouraging, rather than discouraging, the illegal killing of game in order to keep departmental costs down, and he believed that such practices were supported by the department itself. "Is the Indian Department in sympathy with the enforcement of our Provincial Laws?" he asked Scott. Scott replied that the policy of his department was to assist provincial officials in any way it could, but that the law-making power and the enforcement of the law was in the hands of the provinces. "If the provincial delegates can make any suggestion at any time as to action that might be taken by the Indian Department," he said, "we shall be delighted to co-operate." At the end of the conference, the suggestion was made by provincial government representatives that the Canadian government use Mounted Police officers to enforce provincial game laws. This suggestion was subsequently acted upon, and over the subsequent decades it led to numerous charges, many of which were laid against natives hunting on their own reserves.[28]

One of those natives was Calvin William George. On 5 September 1962, George, an Ojibwa on the Kettle Point Reserve in southwestern Ontario, left his house to go hunting. He returned later in the day with two ducks, but, before he and his family could enjoy their meal, police arrived and charged George with unlawfully hunting a migratory bird out of season, in violation of the migratory bird regulations.

When George appeared in court, magistrate J.C. Dunlap had little sympathy for the defendant but he also realized that he had a difficult case on his hands. It all came down to which law should apply—George's treaty rights to hunt, or the Migratory Birds Convention Act, which pro-

hibited hunting at that time of year. To decide that issue, it was necessary to interpret a section of the Indian Act (section 87) which had
been drafted to try to balance native treaty rights against the laws of the
broader Canadian society.

Section 87 was one of those marvellous legal clauses that served to
postpone decisions until a specific problem actually arose, so that a
judge could then sort it all out according to the facts of the case, the
relevant treaty rights, and what seemed to be the most just result in the
circumstances. The actual wording of section 87 of the Indian Act was
as follows: "Subject to the terms of any treaty and any other Act of the
Parliament of Canada, all laws of general application from time to time
in force in any province are applicable to and in respect of Indians in the
province, except to the extent that such laws are inconsistent with this
Act or any order, rule, regulation or by-law made thereunder, and except
to the extent that such laws make provision for any matter for which
provision is made by or under this Act."

Although magistrate Dunlap held that section 87 of the Indian Act
made laws of general application applicable to Indians, he also ruled that
such laws were subject to the terms of any treaties and that the treaty
made by the crown with the Ojibwa on 10 July 1827 reserved to them
the right to hunt at any time on lands reserved under the treaty. His conclusion was therefore that the Migratory Birds Convention Act did not
apply to the accused; the charge against George was dismissed. At the
request of counsel for the attorney-general of Canada, Dunlap prepared
a statement giving his finding of fact and his interpretation of the law and
asking whether he was right in so holding. In this fashion, the appeal of
Dunlap's decision arrived, by way of a "stated case," before Chief Justice
McRuer of the High Court.[29]

When McRuer learned that he would be hearing this case, he suddenly
became painfully aware that, like most other Canadians, he knew next
to nothing of native history and law. Determined to remedy his lack of
knowledge, he searched the Osgoode Hall library for books, articles, and
prior cases, sifting through the rights of natives as defined by the white
man since the reign of King George III (1760–1820). He studied early
maps of the area in question and read the original treaty of 1827. From
cases such as St. Catharines Milling and Lumber Co. v. The Queen (1885)[30]
and Dominion of Canada v. Province of Ontario (1910),[31] he learned of
the natives' attachment to the land. In a recently published book on the
Caughnawaga Indians and the St. Lawrence Seaway, he discovered that
on no occasion had native title been extinguished on Canadian terri-

tory by any process other than that of the revision of an old treaty or the making of a new one. Finally, he read all the cases involving hunting laws made by white men for white men.

McRuer then stepped through the door into the courtroom to encounter two contending forces—the movement for wildlife conservation, and the struggle to assert native rights—which seemed irreconcilable. This battle of values, interests, and perceptions took many forms, and the law, rather than providing a definitive framework within which to resolve the conflict, resembled nothing more than grist thrown between these two grinding stones.

McRuer recognized the Migratory Birds Convention Act, under which George had been charged, as a valid attempt to curb the white man's seemingly insatiable urge to kill wildlife whether or not it was needed for food. (As an example, McRuer cited passenger pigeons, which once numbered in the billions in Canada but had been rendered extinct by 1914.) McRuer did not, however, see any justice in ruling that such an act could be applied to a native seeking sustenance on the very land on which his forbears had hunted since time immemorial and which had been reserved to him by both the Royal Proclamation of 1763 and the treaty of 10 July 1827. Rather, there would need to be clear and direct legislative language to extinguish George's right to hunt on this land.

In his thoroughly reasoned judgment, delivered on 29 May 1963, McRuer seized upon the paramountcy of the treaty. This was the solemn, written pact between the crown and the chiefs of the Ojibwa—in effect, an international treaty between heads of state. McRuer was singularly unimpressed by the arguments advanced in the name of the crown by the attorney-general of Canada, that subsequent parliamentary enactments, or, worse still, orders-in-council and regulations made under those acts, could limit or eliminate entirely the rights given in the treaty. He had no trouble with section 87 of the Indian Act, since it began with the very words "subject to the terms of any treaty." And he was disdainful of limp, technical arguments resting on the Interpretation Act, which provided that "every Act of the Parliament of Canada, unless the contrary intention appears, applies to the whole of Canada."[32] As he put it, "It would take much more than the provisions of the Interpretation Act to affect the rights claimed by the Indians in this case." The same reasoning applied to the Migratory Birds Convention Act.

McRuer lined up the act in his sights, like a duck in a shooting gallery, and fired a couple of rounds of case law at it—*R. v. Wesley* (1932), in which the Alberta Court of Appeal, basing its arguments on the treaty rights of natives, held that the Migratory Birds Convention Act did not take away the right of natives to hunt for food on unoccupied crown lands or other lands to which they had access[33]; and *R. v. Sikyea* (1962), in which the Migratory Birds Convention Act was held not to apply to natives hunting for food in the Northwest Territories because "there are no express words or necessary intendment or implication in the Migratory Birds Convention Act abrogating, abridging, or infringing upon the hunting rights of the Indians."[34] Then, to finish off the act once and for all, McRuer went even further: "Since the Proclamation of 1763 has the force of a statute, I am satisfied that whatever power the Parliament of Canada may have to interfere with the treaty rights of the Indians, the rights conferred on them by the Proclamation cannot in any case be abrogated, abridged or infringed upon by an Order in Council passed under the Migratory Birds Convention Act." The crown's appeal of George's acquittal was dismissed.

In rendering his judgment, McRuer made it clear that he was not called upon to decide, nor would he decide, whether parliament could pass legislation specifically applicable to natives that abrogated their rights to hunt for food on the Kettle Point Reserve. Yet he did note that "there is much to support an argument that Parliament does not have such power." He then added: "There may be cases where such legislation, properly framed, might be considered necessary in the public interest but a very strong case would have to be made out that would not be a breach of our national honour."[35]

It was a solid decision, and McRuer felt satisfied that the matter had been properly laid to rest. The Government of Canada, however, intent on "clarifying" the law about hunting game on Indian reserves in a way that coincided with its own interpretation, took McRuer's decision in the George case to the Ontario Court of Appeal. On 24 June 1964 Appeal Court justices W.D. Roach and J.L. McLennan agreed with McRuer and with magistrate Dunlap that the migratory bird regulations did not apply to hunting by Indians for food on reserves. Justice J.A. Gibson dissented, on the grounds that the question of hunting and fishing rights was not dealt with or considered under the treaty of 1827.[36]

McRuer's ruling was then appealed to the Supreme Court of Canada, which, in the meantime (on 6 October 1964), had reversed the lower court decisions in the *R. v. Sikyea*, one of the cases on which McRuer had based his judgment. In due course McRuer's decision was overturned as well, by a majority of six to one. The lone dissenting voice was that of Mr. Justice Cartwright, who wrote a lengthy and closely reasoned judgment.

For the majority, Justice Ronald Martland wrote but a page and a half in which, without even stating them, he cited the reasons given by the Supreme Court in *R.* v. *Sikyea*. His judgment claimed that "it was not the purpose of section 87 to make any legislation of the Parliament of Canada subject to the terms of any treaty" and that nothing in section 87 of the Indian Act rendered the provisions of the Migratory Birds Convention Act subordinate to the 1827 treaty; consequently, the provisions of the act overrode the hunting rights "guaranteed" by the treaty. The laws of parliament would apply to natives as to everyone else, and that was that. In reversing magistrate Dunlap's original decision, the Supreme Court fined George $10 for unlawful hunting.[37]

McRuer felt personally that the Supreme Court's decision was, all at once, an unfortunate turn of events for George, a blow to native rights, and a denial of justice. In his mind, the Supreme Court of Canada had shown itself willing to override time-honoured law.

McRuer would remember the lessons he learned from the trial of *R.* v. *George* when he was called upon to recommend reforms to the laws of Ontario, but, in the interval, he could only resign himself to this reversal. Years later he offered the following reflection on the George case: "I rather think that the philosophy of the Supreme Court decision was unfortunate because all of western Ontario had been reserved as hunting grounds for Indians and the territory was gradually acquired from them either by treaty or purchase. Their reserves were only the remnant of their hunting grounds in that part of Ontario. I never had that objection satisfactorily answered."

FROM THE VARIOUS ENVIRONMENTAL CASES that he tried, McRuer learned the limits of his power as a judge. He tasted the bitter reality that reason and justice alone could not change the world, because the contending forces appearing before him in the courtroom could also defend their interests in corporate boardrooms and in the legislative arena. Despite his frustrations, however, McRuer found great intellectual stimulation in environmental law. Reinterpreting venerable legal doctrines in the light of modern conditions very much appealed to his progressive brand of traditionalism. He viewed the law as majestic, a body of principles fashioned over centuries by the practical experience of wise people seeking justice in difficult circumstances. Judges had a duty to adapt the law to new realities, and, in McRuer's eyes, this challenge was particularly pressing in the area of the environment. Fundamentally, then, his decisions were inspired not by his attachment to the land, though that was real enough, but by a devotion to the law. As he later explained: "I came from the country and I liked pure air and pure water, but that didn't colour my decisions. It only helped me to understand the law that I was enforcing."

For McRuer, the George case posed special challenges because, on the surface at least, it pitted the rights of native people against the cause of environmental conservation. His decision in this case rested partly on his commitment to property rights—native people, after all, had such rights too—partly on his conviction that treaties with native peoples embodied law no less fundamental than any subsequent legislation passed by parliament, and partly on his instinctive sympathy for the oppressed. Still another reason for the conclusions McRuer reached in this case was the fact that, notwithstanding the claims of some conservationists, Calvin George's action in shooting a couple of ducks did not pose a serious threat to the environment. The Migratory Birds Convention Act had been passed to deal with the very real problem of overhunting; George had violated the letter of the law, but not its intent—he, and other natives like him, hunted only to survive. For McRuer, laws had to be applied with a sense of fairness and with compassion. Punishing natives such as George did little to protect the environment and did not further the ends of justice. In fact, the very reverse was true: McRuer, throughout his life, held to the view that the Supreme Court's ruling in the George case was a victory of narrow legalism over common sense and justice, a clear instance where the legal system failed in its obligations to society's disadvantaged.

This chief justice of the High Court was the same person as the young law student whose oft-read poem about "justice" portrayed greedy businessmen and politicians going their merry way, their excesses and crimes ignored, while the poor man was jailed for selling substandard eggs. What struck Jim McRuer as injustice had not changed in the intervening years. All that differed was the subject matter—as downstream farmers and fishing-lodge operators contested with mill owners and unions and chambers of commerce, or an Indian with two ducks encountered the RCMP and another civilization's game laws.

12

WOMEN, CHILDREN, AND WORKERS

DURING HIS TWENTY YEARS ON THE BENCH, Jim McRuer heard many cases about the rights of people who had been discriminated against or simply ignored. His judgments in these cases, in terms of the rights of the individuals concerned, were consistent in their commitment to justice; however, they were not uniform either on points of detail or in matters of substance because of the variety of human situations involved.

As a judge, McRuer defended the rights of those who could not always speak for themselves, vulnerable people who were not well served by the law. For example, he was committed to the equality of women under the law and in Canadian society generally, and he did what he could in his career as a judge to put this idea into practice; indeed, in one notable instance he was sixteen years ahead of the Supreme Court of Canada. Similarly, though he had a rather distant relationship with his own children, McRuer had strong views on the needs of the young, and again and again he acted as their champion. For him, there was "no such thing as an illegitimate child."

McRuer's decisions on the rights of another vulnerable group, workers, were a distinctive combination of consistency and flexibility. McRuer was generally favourable to the cause of labour, and in his term as chief justice he handed down several judgments that were highly progressive in their support of workers and unions. Still, whenever a strike interfered with other people's rights or threatened to lead to social disorder, he did not hesitate to place limits on workers' rights. At the same time, deeply distrustful of excessive power wielded arbitrarily, McRuer frequently overruled decisions of the Ontario Labour Relations Board (OLRB), a body whose purpose included reducing industrial strife by acting as an impartial referee in conflicts between employers and employees.

In all these cases, as in others, McRuer mapped his own course, relying on tradition but never afraid to break with it when new directions seemed necessary. A study of his judgments in cases concerning women, children, and workers, as well as those involving the OLRB, reveals his grasp of the law and his passion for justice while also illuminating the central elements of his judicial thinking.

McRUER'S FEELINGS about the position of women and children were evident as much off the bench as on it. For more than a decade, from 1946 to 1957, McRuer served as president of the Canadian division of the British-based Save the Children Fund. In this capacity he organized fundraising campaigns, helped the staff in policy matters, and gave radio broadcasts publicizing the Fund's various activities—especially its adoption program. On another but related front, from June 1945 to June 1946, McRuer chaired the United Church's Commission on Christian Marriage and the Christian Home. The purpose of this commission was to examine the state of the Canadian family in a rapidly changing society and to consider measures that would assist families as they tried to cope with the pressures caused by secularism and materialism, rural depopulation, urbanization and industrialization, the entry of women into the workforce, the expanding role of the state, and the growing popularity of divorce.

The commission's report, presented in September 1946, bore McRuer's imprint in a number of areas and deployed a masterly and unusual blend of theology and statistics (on birthrates, divorce rates, infant mortality, and mixed marriages), of history and sociology, of scripture and poetry, and of canon law and civil law. Based on this comprehensive view of the human condition, the commission's recommendations dealing with children were far-sighted. Those on the subject of women did not explicitly endorse equality between the sexes, but that principle was certainly implicit in the commission's approach. Instead of rejecting social change, the commissioners proposed ways in which church and state could help families survive in the midst of it. Stressing the central importance of the family to society, and the role of religious values in promoting stable family life, the report recommended, among other things, that each of the provinces make provision for civil marriages; that the church offer more services in the area of pre-marital and marriage counselling; and, revealing the church's less progressive side, that mixed marriages and divorce be discouraged.[1] It also proposed a variety of measures to protect the rights of children in divorce cases. Where neither the mother nor the father was a fit parent, the commission recommended that the child or children be committed to the custody of a children's aid society. It also recommended the appointment by the government of an officer charged with guarding the interests of children in all custody cases.[2]

The issues that McRuer addressed in his work with the Save the Children Fund and the United Church commission on the family also came before Ontario's courts. As chief justice, McRuer's commitment to the equality of men and women before the law was clearly on display in the case of *Freedman* v. *Mason*, which gained national attention when he tried it in 1956. His decision was reversed on appeal to the Ontario Court of Appeal in 1957, a reversal upheld by the Supreme Court of Canada the following year. Nevertheless, McRuer never changed his mind about the case, evidence of being "ahead of his time." Not only "the particular terms of the contract in question" need to be heeded, read the Chief Justice's decision, "but also the development of the independent rights of a married woman during the last century."

In the Mason case, Mr. and Mrs. Mason, owners of a farm in Scarborough Township, were sued by Sidney Freedman for breach of contract. Mr. Mason had listed the family farm for sale and received an offer of $136,000 from Freedman. Influenced by a real estate agent whose tactics McRuer described as "rather high pressure," Mr. Mason signed the necessary legal documents without his wife's consent, even though she had an inchoate right of dower with respect to the property. When Mrs. Mason refused to accept the sale, it fell through and Freedman brought suit against the couple, alleging that they had colluded in a scheme to extricate themselves from their commitment to sell.

After hearing the evidence, McRuer found that Mrs. Mason had worked as an equal partner with her husband in building up their family farm over the years. The price she and her husband were offered was obviously low, and McRuer noted that Mrs. Mason had consulted a lawyer who advised not to sell. "She worked with her husband on the farm and I knew what it meant for someone to be a farmer's wife," McRuer later recalled. "Farming was always a collective enterprise and she had a great interest in the land which her husband could not sell without her consent." Mr. Mason, McRuer concluded, had been taken in by a very smooth real estate operator, and his wife's only motive was her desire to protect her interest in a property that was as much hers as her husband's. In short, there had been no collusion between Mr. Mason and his wife, and so Freedman could not get the court to order performance on the specific terms that had been signed. Mr. Mason simply could not be allowed to sell out his wife's interest in the farm without her consent.

In overturning McRuer's judgment, both the Court of Appeal and then the Supreme Court of Canada ruled that Mrs. Mason did not have rights in the farm equal to those of her husband. Justice Wilfred Judson, writing for the majority on the Supreme Court, noted that Mr. Mason had not even tried, as was his obligation, to get his wife's consent to the sale. In the court's opinion, it was immaterial whether the Masons had acted independently of one another (McRuer's view) or had acted in concert to obtain better terms (the Ontario Court of Appeal's view). The Masons were forced to sell their farm. Freedman received title to the farm, although his deed to the land remained encumbered by Mrs. Mason's inchoate dower right. Part of the amount he paid to purchase the land was put on deposit with the court. This was to cover a possible future claim by Mrs. Mason to her dower interest, which she could still be entitled to if her husband died before she did. Freedman and his associates went on to turn a massive profit on a small investment; today, the Mason farm is the site of a multi-million-dollar subdivision.[3]

When McRuer's decision was overturned, he felt quite upset about the "shortcomings" of judicial procedures at the appellate level. While sitting on the Ontario Court of Appeal, he had been troubled by the realization that the original trial judge inevitably knew more about the special circumstances of any given case because of his direct contact with the individuals involved. Now, in the Mason case, McRuer was convinced that the judgment of the appellate judges had been distorted by the fact that they had not met the Masons themselves. No one who knew them, he believed, could doubt their honesty and sincerity. If the learned justices of the Supreme Court had been able to see the Masons and hear their testimony, they would surely have found in their favour. As it was, they were able to examine only the sterile legal documents generated by the suit; the result, McRuer lamented, was that justice had been thwarted.

McRuer vowed that he would work to ensure an end to such injustices, and, when serving in later years on the Ontario Law Reform Commission, he would refer a number of times to *Freedman* v. *Mason* when recommending changes to provincial laws. He never completely recovered from his disappointment over the Mason case. "I still grieve for that farming couple," he said towards the end of his life, "She made up her mind that she wouldn't sign and she didn't. How could the law compel her to sell, to sign her life's work away?"

McRuer had more success in defending women's rights in cases involving marital breakdown. In 1930 the Supreme Court of Ontario was given jurisdiction over divorces in the province—previously, a divorce could be granted only by a special act of parliament—and from that point on Ontario divorce cases were tried in the High Court of Justice.[4] Divorces remained difficult to get, however; the only legally recognized ground for divorce was adultery. That situation did not change until the Divorce Act of 1968.[5] Under this legislation, provisions were made for placing the married woman in a position equivalent to that of her husband for the purpose of obtaining a valid decree of divorce both in Canada and abroad, and grounds for divorce were extended to include not only adultery but also sodomy, bestiality, rape, homosexual acts, bigamy, physical or mental cruelty as well as marriage breakdown caused by imprisonment, drug or alcohol addiction, desertion, non-consummation, or three to five years' separation.[6] After his retirement from the bench in 1964, McRuer played an important role in effecting the reforms of 1968. While still chief justice, he was of course obliged to work within the framework of the existing law, but to his credit, he was determined to explore the limits of that framework. As a result, some of his judgments laid the foundations for a more progressive approach to divorce.

In approaching this area of matrimonial relations, McRuer remembered that an earlier chief justice of Ontario, William Meredith, had complained that a man could make his wife's life a hell on earth but if she was physically strong enough to stand it she had to stay with him and had no right of recourse.[7] That was the law at the time Meredith complained of it, and it was still the law during McRuer's time on the bench. In 1946 McRuer tried a case in which a woman was suing her former husband for alimony on the grounds that he was guilty of extreme mental cruelty towards her during the years of their marriage. In passing judgment, McRuer indicated that the High Court's decision in *Hawn* v. *Hawn* (1944), which dismissed claims for alimony in cases where clear physical cruelty had not been proved,[8] was binding law and prevented him from ruling in favour of the plaintiff. Still, deeply moved by the woman's plight, he openly criticized that earlier decision, noting, "One cannot escape the conclusion that the principles of law still applicable to these cases were expounded when the rights of a married woman were generally considered to be very inferior to those of a man."[9]

A hallmark of McRuer's judicial approach was that he sought the answer to current problems in the lessons of history and the time-tested (but often overlooked) common law. In this way he sometimes ended up applying ancient remedies to present-day ailments—if they could lead to a just result. Some of his colleagues were startled, for example, when McRuer used the principle of "alienation of affection"—an old legal doctrine that was seldom used and that has since been discarded—to help a woman whose husband had left her to live with another woman. McRuer's reason for dusting off this old common law doctrine as a remedy was that a wife had no cause of action against her husband for "criminal conversation." (Criminal conversation in law meant seduction of another man's wife, considered as an actionable injury to the husband.) This made no sense to McRuer, who saw marriage as a relationship of legal equality between a man and a woman. In the case in question, McRuer's views on the sanctity of marriage—and his resourcefulness as a judge—came through clearly. Eyebrows were raised by McRuer's judgment that "the other woman" should pay the wife for damages and loss of income—for a total of $7,500, a significant amount in 1945—but no appeal was made.[10]

By the same token, McRuer knew how to balance traditional common sense with strict legal propriety. In the 1957 case of *Alspector* v. *Alspector*, for instance, McRuer made it clear that he valued the spirit of the law more than its letter. Morris Alspector was an elderly and successful businessman who, on the death of his first wife, had married a widow, Mrs. Noodleman. The marriage ceremony was conducted according to strict Jewish custom, but the celebrants neglected to obtain a marriage licence from the Province of Ontario. The couple lived happily together, and, as the elderly gentleman's health declined, his second wife nursed him with selfless devotion. In his will Alspector left most of his assets to his second wife, but this provision was contested after his death by the children of his first marriage, who alleged that the marriage could not be considered valid since no one had purchased a marriage licence. Mrs. Alspector sought a declaration that her marriage was valid.

McRuer pondered the matter deeply, since marriage was to him one of the essential pillars of society and his ruling would have to respect the requirements of this key institution. Satisfied that Jewish ritual had been properly observed, he concluded that the union had been consecrated before God. He also noted (and here lay the real reasons for his decision) that the second wife had devoted herself to her husband while the children by the first marriage had ignored the wealthy old man until after his death, when they hoped to collect from his bountiful estate. In issuing a declaration that the marriage was valid, McRuer could barely disguise his disgust with the children. Alspector's widow had proven herself to be a true and loyal wife and should not be denied the gifts he had willed her. As for the children, McRuer later recounted, "they had done nothing for him during his lifetime, but they thought it was all right for her to look after him in his old age and then to leave her with nothing." Justice in the Alspector case was tempered by compassion, for McRuer would not see this woman wronged.[11]

An issue in divorce law that really angered McRuer was the practice of fabricating evidence. Given the narrow grounds on which Canadian law allowed couples to seek divorce during McRuer's years on the bench, many married couples agreed to simulate an adulterous affair in order to obtain release from their wedding vows. McRuer found this practice abhorrent and, when he had no choice but to grant divorces in such cases, he often made his views known in passing judgment. On at least two occasions, however, he used his judicial authority to have cases of this kind investigated, once by the queen's proctor and once by the attorney-general.[12] In a great many other instances, he refused to grant a divorce in the face of evidence of collusion. In *Scott* v. *Scott* (1947), he stated that, if a court turned a blind eye to collusion, its action would be "improper and contrary to the public interest."[13] The following year, in *McLean* v. *McLean*, he emphasized: "The Courts exist for the purpose of hearing honest actions ... Where, in bringing an action for divorce, the plaintiff and defendant act in agreement the Court is largely deprived of the sources of information which should be available in ascertaining the whole truth with respect to all the matters requiring consideration."[14]

Subsequently, McRuer insisted that "it was a corruption of the courts for the parties to make some arrangement whereby the wife would tell her husband to make some convenient arrangement with another woman ... 'She's a nice girl,' the wife might say. 'Take her away for a weekend and we will send a private detective to find you and then we will go to court about it.'" McRuer explained that "one of the reasons I sought a reform of the divorce laws was to put an end to this charade." When honest citizens and conscientious judges were forced to ignore the truth because of a law that had no bearing on the realities of life, McRuer concluded, it was time to reform the law. By refusing to grant some divorces, and by making loud noises in those instances when he did grant divorces, McRuer hoped to put pressure on parliament to change the Divorce Act.

The current situation meant that the government was asking judges to corrupt the courts by turning a blind eye to collusion.

With regard to children, McRuer's approach as a jurist was conditioned by a fundamental intellectual distinction. In his view, equal rights did not imply equal status, and equality before the law did not necessarily mean that uniform procedures should be followed in all cases. Indeed, it was the duty of the courts to make accurate distinctions between individuals in order to ensure that all parties to a suit received equal treatment and that justice was done. So, a child must be afforded considerations that were not appropriate to a sane adult, and an insane or mentally handicapped adult must be regarded in a different light than an adult without mental disability. Only by this approach could equality before the law be guaranteed.

Looking back on his career as a lawyer, McRuer often claimed that the most important case in which he was ever involved concerned a boy charged with murder. Initially the case had come before a magistrate of the juvenile court, but that judge ordered the boy to stand trial in the ordinary courts. At this stage McRuer became the boy's defence counsel. The preliminary hearing had not begun, and McRuer apprised the original magistrate of his right to reverse his decision and to try the case himself in the juvenile court. McRuer stressed the grave necessity of reversing this decision, for if the boy were tried before a jury and found guilty the only sentence would be death by hanging. Though the youngster was charged with a serious crime, McRuer asserted, society owed him a second chance. In the end the magistrate agreed to hear the case himself. On behalf of the boy, McRuer entered a plea of guilty to juvenile delinquency, and arrangements were made for his future. The boy was placed on probation, taken out of the broken home from which he came, and housed with a caring relative. Sent to school and given an opportunity to better himself, he emerged in time as a model citizen and family man.[15]

When McRuer mounted the bench, he drew on this experience to deal with many cases involving juveniles. One such case was R. v. *Yensen* (1961), which came before him on 19 June 1961. In this instance McRuer was conducting the second trial of a youth from Capreol who was charged with murder. The boy, Anthony Wayne Yensen, about fourteen years old at the time of the trial, had been arrested on 26 September 1960 after the stabbed body of a family friend, Mrs. Rose Kennedy, age twenty-four, was found in her home by her husband. The boy was moderately retarded. When he asked to be allowed to see his mother, the police officer replied: "You come along with me and I will see about that."

After receiving a caution (which, McRuer later ruled, the boy could not possibly have understood), he confessed his guilt. In the boy's first trial Mr. Justice G.T. Walsh admitted the boy's confession, the only evidence against him. The youngster was convicted of murder and sentenced to hang on 18 April 1961. Before the execution could take place, the Court of Appeal ordered a new trial on the ground that the trial judge had misdirected the jury. McRuer then held a special session of the Supreme Court to expedite the retrial.

The boy's treatment at the hands of the police affronted McRuer's sense of justice; he was also shocked by the manner in which the press had dealt with the boy's first trial, the "confession" having been printed in full in the Sudbury *Daily Star* and other newspapers.[16] When the boy's second trial came before him, then, McRuer barred the press from the courtroom on the grounds that the accused was merely a juvenile. The lad had a right to the presumption of innocence, and his future might be ruined by further flaunting of the case in the media. Freedom of the press, said McRuer, did not include a licence to deprive a youngster of his right to a fair trial.

Yensen's second trial began on 19 June but did not last long. McRuer ruled the boy's confession inadmissible since the crown had failed to establish that it was voluntary. Because there was no other evidence linking the boy to the crime, the prosecution's case collapsed and on 20 June McRuer directed the jury to return a verdict of acquittal. After this verdict was delivered, McRuer observed: "A great deal of publicity has been given this case—much more than should have been given." He later recounted that "I was strict with the police because of their handling of a young boy... The whole circumstances seemed to me unfair, where the boy could have been convicted on a statement made with no opportunity to have anyone else present and under a sort of overpowering intimidation." The press, which had been excluded from the courtroom by McRuer's order, was highly critical of the chief justice's verdict. The boy went free and the case was not again appealed.[17]

Not all the juvenile cases McRuer tried were matters of life and death, but, keenly aware that a child's future could be ruined by the actions of the courts, he treated them all with equal solicitude. An example of his approach was the trial of *Bird* v. *The Town of Fort Frances* (1949). In May 1946 a twelve-year-old boy was playing "cops and robbers" with his young friends in Fort Francis in northern Ontario when he discovered a cache of money amounting to about $1,500 hidden underneath the floor supports of the local pool hail. The boy gave most of the money to his mother, who had been deserted by her husband and was barely able to make ends meet. She hid the money under a cushion on the sofa in her parlour, but the boy began to spend his share with some panache. Within a few days local merchants had drawn the attention of the police to the spendthrift boy, who told the whole story when questioned by the town's chief constable. The mother then surrendered the money without objection to the police and in December 1946 the money was deposited to the account of the town of Fort Francis. It seemed that the mother and her boy were to be deprived of their unexpected windfall.

Then a well-known lawyer in the community approached the mother, telling her that the municipality had no right to the money and offering to take the matter to court. The case came before the chief justice of the High Court of Ontario. Fascinated by its implications, McRuer later confessed that "it was a lovely case to try. I enjoyed it." His reading of English law told him that, if the owner of the pool hall came forward to claim the money, he would likely be bound to find in the owner's favour. However, since no claim by such a third party was made, McRuer concluded that the cache was likely the take from a robbery or fraud of some kind. More critical, however, was the fact that under the law of the day the mother, since she was still legally married, had no right whatsoever to bring an action against the municipality to recover the money. Almost incredibly, only the husband, who had long ago abandoned his family, was legally entitled to make a claim. McRuer wrestled with his conscience, but decided to keep silent. He would leave it up to the municipality's lawyer to raise the point.

To his everlasting relief, the matter was not raised. McRuer quietly watched as counsel for the municipality presented one of the weakest cases he had ever witnessed. When all the arguments were closed, he ordered that the money be handed over to the mother and her boy. His verdict was not appealed; McRuer knew that he had been able to do some good for the struggling mother and son, even if he had had to bend the rules somewhat to ensure that justice was done.[18] This episode shows that McRuer, who in many cases was harshly outspoken in his remarks to lawyers about their presentation of the law, could in other instances hold his tongue if his sense of justice convinced him that such discretion was necessary.

Among cases involving minors, McRuer was particularly interested in those that concerned the rights of adopted children. He was, after all, as the Canadian leader of the Save the Children Fund, more than mildly interested in their well being. Perhaps the most contentious case that he tried in the field of adopted children's rights was *R.* v. *Blackwell and Toronto General Trusts Corp* (1959), or as the press dubbed it, "The Case of Linda Silverspoon." It certainly was a high-stakes affair.

Linda was the adopted daughter of a rich Toronto heiress, Mary Elizabeth Hambly O'Brien. The father of Linda's adoptive mother, Charles Seward Blackwell, had established a fund for the life interest of his daughter. This fund had accrued to an amount well over $1 million, and in his will Blackwell had stipulated that on the death of Linda's adoptive mother the fund should pass into the hands of either her "issue" or, in the event that she died childless, the Toronto General Hospital and the Toronto Sick Children's Hospital.

Linda's adoptive mother, who was diagnosed as having terminal cancer, had no children other than Linda, whom she had adopted in 1940. While she was still fighting for her life, the hospitals, sensing a golden opportunity, launched a suit seeking to ensure that Linda would be deprived of the inheritance. As an adopted child, the hospitals argued, Linda could not be considered a true daughter, and therefore all the money should be awarded to the hospitals after the death of the adoptive mother. A few years before, in 1954, the Ontario legislature had passed the Child Welfare Act, which gave adopted children all the rights of inheritance of naturally born children.[19] This law was not explicitly retroactive, however, and so counsel for the hospitals argued that, since Linda's adoptive grandfather had made his will in 1932, it could fairly be assumed that he had never intended that any benefit should pass to an adopted granddaughter.

The case came before McRuer in 1959. He heard testimony that the adoptive mother had given clear indication from her deathbed that she was appalled by the hospital's avarice, that she loved Linda more than anything else in her life, and that she earnestly wanted her to receive the inheritance. McRuer found in favour of the adopted child, and he did so by simply ruling that the day that the new act came into effect all adopted children enjoyed the legal right of inheritance. "Linda Silverspoon" received the inheritance that her adoptive mother had hoped to pass on to her, and the hospitals, having fumbled the operation, did not appeal.[20]

The matter did not completely end with McRuer's verdict. In a similar case that arose in 1961, Mr. Justice Wishart Spence delivered a verdict modelled on McRuer's "Silverspoon" judgment but his ruling was later overturned on appeal.[21] This setback ignited a fire under Ontario's legislators, and in 1965 the Child Welfare Act was amended to stipulate that "any reference to 'child,' 'children' or 'issue' in a will or other document, whether heretofore or hereafter made, shall be deemed to include an adopted child."[22] In the end, therefore, McRuer's views in favour of adopted children triumphed.

McRuer also had the opportunity—though it was seldom a pleasant one for him—to demonstrate his concern for the rights of children in a number of custody cases. Whenever matters of this kind came before him, he took the position that the judge should act as an advocate for the child, and he worked closely with the local children's aid societies and other competent authorities to ensure that the child's rights were protected. Often he was forced to make difficult and painful decisions. One of these cases occurred in 1947. It began when he received an application from the natural mother of a child to have the child restored to her custody. Two years had passed since she had signed away all rights under the Adoption Act, and the child was happily living in a new family setting. McRuer examined the situation closely, found that the child was now "with excellent parents, of better means than the natural mother," and so rejected the application on the ground that in every case of child custody the best interests of the child must be placed before the wishes of other parties.[23]

The range of child-abuse cases that came before McRuer was wide, and even included instances of murder. In one case he encountered a man who, on returning from a tavern, beat his five-year-old son to death with a belt—at least 113 strikes were inflicted—because he had wet his bed. After the man had been convicted of manslaughter, McRuer sentenced him to life imprisonment, stating, "You should not be at large... You might do the same thing to another child... I must confine you for the rest of your natural life so you do not inflict injury on others."[24] McRuer's reputation as a tough judge was based on cases such as this one. The *Toronto Telegram*'s widely read and respected columnist Frank Tumpane, in reference to McRuer's "You should not be at large" statement, described the chief justice's words as "the most heartening quote of the week," adding that "this fellow got what he deserved and what happened to him is in vivid contrast to some of the cream-puff sentences handed out lately in other courts for other vicious crimes."[25]

LIKE HIS DECISIONS concerning women and children, McRuer's judgments in cases involving the rights of workers revealed a strong sympathy for the underdog. Yet these judgments also had some distinguishing features. One was that the workers were usually represented by unions—and so the legal issues were cast as questions involving union powers, labour relations, and the jurisdiction of the Ontario Labour Relations Board. Another was McRuer's recognition, displayed earlier in his support of the War Measures Act, that rights are not absolute but rather have to be interpreted in such a manner that does not allow one individual or group to infringe the freedom of others or to harm the interests of the larger community. Of course, this perspective sometimes meant that, in order to protect the rights of some, McRuer had to curtail the rights of others. This is the hard dilemma of any judge, who has to serve society by deciding where the line between competing interests and conflicting rights is to be drawn. A third distinguishing aspect of McRuer's judgments in labour law was a deep and abiding distrust of the role of administrative tribunals in the regulation of labour-management relations.

As with most other cases that he tried, McRuer's record in labour cases was marked by frequent criticisms of counsel who, in his view, had put too little effort into their work. "The material in this case is not as satisfactory as it should be," said McRuer on 14 November 1960, looking down on H.B. Noble, counsel for Century Engineering Company, which sought to continue a labour injunction. "After all, I think that plaintiffs are to be discouraged, particularly in these labour disputes, from rushing to Court with loose material and asking the Court to intervene to grant an injunction against a number of defendants who are not shown by any of the material to have been doing anything wrong." True, "some of these defendants may have been on the picket lines when some of the violence that is referred to in the evidence may have occurred, but that is not sufficient. The Court does not make assumptions and grant orders against individuals without something definite to go on."[26]

In 1963, towards the end of his career on the bench, McRuer tried a dramatic case that combined the intrigue of a murder trial with the perplexities of a labour dispute. The case arose out of a conflict at Cochrane, in northern Ontario, between farmers working in the bush to bring out pulpwood logs and unionized loggers who had the exclusive right to load logs on the trains that would haul them to the mill. Normally, the farmers brought their logs to the railway station in Cochrane, where unionized loggers would load them. But when the union went out on strike, the farmers, fearing for their livelihood, banded together and decided to load the trains themselves.

Tension mounted in the community as news circulated of the farmers' intention to break the union's strike, and finally, on one terrible night, the small town exploded into violence. The farmers, armed with rifles, arrived at the railway station and began to load their logs onto the railway cars. Meanwhile, across town, about 500 union supporters, many of whom were also armed, were meeting to decide on a course of action. After some impassioned speeches, the unionists formed a parade of cars and headed off for a confrontation with the farmers. At the station shots were fired, and when the ensuing mêlée was finally broken up, a unionist was found dead on the ground with a farmer's bullet in his head.

The case came to McRuer's attention in weekly court in Toronto, where he was informed that twenty armed men had been arrested at the scene of the Cochrane riot and all were being held without bail, charged with murder. After considering a motion to quash the committal for trial of these men on the ground that there was insufficient evidence to sustain such a committal of any one of the twenty, McRuer concluded that to quash the case might only lead to further trouble in the divided town. After all, a man was dead and someone at the scene had fired the fatal shot. McRuer packed his bags and, announcing that he would preside over the matter himself, headed north.

In Cochrane, a grand jury was sworn to decide whether the trial of the twenty men should proceed. A mass trial of this sort was unprecedented in Canadian legal history, and McRuer took great pains in charging the grand jury. The theory of the crown attorney who was prosecuting the case was that, if it were proven that an agreement had been made among the farmers to commit an unlawful act by unlawful means by which a death might result, it made no difference who fired the fatal shot; all of those who willingly participated in the unlawful act were equally guilty of murder, and all should hang. In response, the defence contended that, if the agreement was not to commit an unlawful act but to resist force by reasonable force, then it would be necessary to identify the specific individual who fired the fatal shot. To this McRuer added that, if the grand jury saw no proof of an unlawful purpose in the assembly, it must identify the individual who fired the fatal shot. If this was not possible, the jurors must find no bill of indictment since there was no justification for proceeding with the trial of the men.

The grand jury reached a negative finding and their verdict was "no bill." All of the farmers then pleaded guilty to lesser charges; each paid a fine of $100 for unlawfully carrying firearms. Several union men were also charged with unlawful assembly, and they were fined $200 each. All in all, some may wonder whether justice was done in this case, but few would disagree that a sort of rough justice had been achieved since the dead unionist had contributed in some measure to his own death by participating in the riot. However, David Lewis, counsel for the union (and, years later, leader of the New Democratic Party), was less than pleased with the outcome.[27]

One of McRuer's best-known judgments in labour law became standard textbook material, concerning as it did a union member's right to strike without the risk of peremptory dismissal. Known as *R.* v. *Canadian Pacific Railway*, the case originated in 1961 when CPR's unionized hotel employees became engaged in a bitter but legal strike. The company sought to break the deadlock by simply dismissing its unionized workers and replacing them with non-unionized substitutes, an action that led the crown to lay charges against it under the Labour Relations Act. When the CPR was acquitted on these charges, the crown appealed to the High Court.

At this time, several agencies in Ontario, specializing in hiring so-called "security guards," were turning a handsome profit by providing strike-bound firms with replacement workers (known to unionists as "scabs"). McRuer felt that this practice of using professional strike-breakers was extremely unfair to workers on a lawful strike. He made his view clearly known in the CPR case. After hearing the evidence, McRuer ruled that the company's attempt to punish its employees for exercising their right to strike was illegal. He allowed the appeal and ordered a new trial. Shortly afterwards, his decision was affirmed both the Ontario Court of Appeal and the Supreme Court of Canada.[28]

There were other cases in which McRuer sided with striking workers. In *General Dry Batteries of Canada Ltd.* v. *Brigenshaw* (1951), he surprised many observers by ruling that "peaceful picketing" was not rendered unlawful by the fact that the picketers were engaged in an unlawful strike. Even if the employees had broken a collective bargaining agreement, reasoned McRuer, they still had a right under the common law to inform others peacefully that they were on strike.[29] Similarly, in the case of *Hersees of Woodstock Ltd.* v. *Goldstein* (1963), he dismissed an application of a retail merchant for an injunction restraining secondary picketing (by the workers of one of the applicant's suppliers) on the ground that there was no evidence of trespass or interference with the applicant's business.[30] Although the Ontario Court of Appeal reversed McRuer's decision, it did so on the ground that the secondary picketing was designed to induce the retail merchant to break his contract with the picketers' employer, and that this picketing did in fact interfere with the applicant's business.[31]

Yet McRuer also believed that limits had to be placed on the rights of strikers. In another case involving a strike by CPR hotel employees, *Hotel and Club Employees* v. *C.P.R.*, McRuer severely restricted the picketing activities of the workers. Two of Toronto's historic landmarks, Union Station and the Royal York Hotel, are linked by a pedestrian tunnel beneath Front Street. Workers in the hotel, which is owned by CPR, went out on strike and attempted to block the tunnel with pickets. CPR removed the pickets, claiming that it owned the tunnel, but the strikers, represented by David Lewis, went to court claiming that the tunnel actually belonged to the city. When the case came before the chief justice, many observers anticipated a long and complex battle to determine the ownership of the tunnel. McRuer, however, had a surprise for everyone involved in the dispute: he refused to rule on the status of the tunnel, and instead simply decided that CPR had a right to ban the picketers from the tunnel, since in order to reach the tunnel the strikers had to cross CPR property, either through the station or the hotel. In short, the workers' picketing rights in this rather unique situation were limited by the law of trespass.[32]

On other occasions, McRuer cited different reasons for limiting the picketing activities of strikers. In the 1958 case of *Wilson Court Apartments Ltd.* v. *Genovese*, he decided to continue an interim injunction restraining a union from picketing because a subcontractor employed non-union workers.[33] That same year, McRuer heard the case of *Canadian Overseas Shipping Ltd.* v. *Kake*, in which shipowners filed suit against a pilots' association that was picketing the port at Kingston. In this instance, McRuer again continued an interim injunction granted by a local judge restraining picketing on the Kingston docks because he believed that the real purpose of the picketing was not to inform the sailing masters of the dispute but to prevent shipowners from getting pilots and to induce the pilots themselves to violate their statutory duties. McRuer said that the shipping companies could enjoin such picketing because it was activity intended to deprive them of their right to have pilots according to the terms of the Canada Shipping Act.[34] In the trial of *Century Engineering Co.* v. *Greto* (1961), he delivered a similar ruling because of evidence that there had been unwarranted violence on the picket line.[35] Finally, in a 1962 case, strikers at a northern Ontario mine had brought in picketers from outside to disrupt the company's operations. McRuer then issued an injunction limiting the number of picketers to four, arguing that four picketers were enough to make it clear to anyone entering the company's property that the union was on strike.[36]

From this sampling of his decisions involving workers' rights, it is obvious that McRuer sometimes supported, and other times curtailed, strike activity. Although recognizing and supporting the right of workers to organize and strike, McRuer never believed that workers had the right to take the law into their own hands. Generally speaking, moreover, he did not see picketing as a useful method of achieving settlements in labour disputes; he believed that uncontrolled picketing could lead to civil disturbances and so threaten society. In McRuer's understanding of the world, the maintenance of social peace was in the best interests of employers and employees alike.

When it came to determining the role of administrative tribunals in labour disputes, however, McRuer reached conclusions that, superficially at least, contradicted his professed love of order. During the years 1944 and 1945 Ontario's newly elected Conservative government embarked on an ambitious program of social reform. Besides improving the bargaining rights of workers (Rights of Labour Act, 1944) and introducing the eight-hour workday and paid vacations (Hours of Work and Vacation with Pay Act, 1944), the government of George Drew established a labour relations board with loosely defined powers to arbitrate in labour disputes (Labour Relations Board Act, 1944). Several cases involving the extent of the Labour Relation Board's power came before McRuer. In two of these cases, he supported the board: in *Canadian Textile Council v. Ontario Labour Relations Board* he refused to quash a decision of the board concerning the bargaining agents for the employees of Harding Carpets[37]; and in *R. v. Ontario Labour Relations Board, ex parte Taylor* (1964) he approved a union certification order made by the board.[38] Yet in far more cases he either overrode the board's decisions or declared it incapable of intervening in disputes.

McRuer's position regarding the OLRB was set out in several cases. For instance, in *General Dry Batteries of Canada Ltd.* v. *Brigenshaw*, cited above, McRuer explicitly stated that the OLRB's authority did not supersede the jurisdiction of the courts, which must stand ready to protect the rights of both employers and employees in all proper cases. As he put it: "A forum [the board] has been provided under The Labour Relations Act to deal with labour relations, and my own personal view is that, as far as possible, these problems should be solved by those who are particularly skilled in the adjustment of labour matters. However, the Courts are always here to protect personal and property rights."[39]

Similarly, in *Re Grottoli* v. *Lock & Son Ltd.* (1963), McRuer held that section 34 (1) of the Labour Relations Act did not abrogate the right of an employee to seek redress for grievances in the courts. In this case, a worker sought a court order directing his employer, Lock & Son Ltd, to pay him the full amount of his vacation pay. The company's defence was that, in compliance with section 34 (1) of the Labour Relations Act, the collective agreement between the parties stipulated that the OLRB should arbitrate such cases and, therefore, the courts had no jurisdiction. McRuer decided in the employee's favour: he could not "believe" that the Labour Relations Act was meant to limit the rights that an individual had under the common law by requiring that disputes be resolved only through arbitration. No collective agreement, McRuer decreed, could deprive Grottoli of his right to seek justice in the courts.[40]

Another case in which the chief justice limited the OLRB's authority involved Harold "Hal" Banks, the ruthless leader of the Seafarers' International Union in Canada. In 1950 Banks's attempt to expand his union's jurisdiction to represent mates and engineers brought him into conflict with other unions and ultimately with the Canadian Labour Congress. The OLRB had ordered the Gulf and Lake Navigation Company to bargain with the National Association of Marine Engineers of Canada as the certified bargaining agent of its employees, but Banks and his associates wanted the order quashed. When the dispute reached the High Court, McRuer annulled the order on the grounds that the board lacked jurisdiction in the case.[41] This was at the time, coincidentally, that Banks was tacitly supported by the Canadian government as someone who could "clean up" several of the shipping unions on the Great Lakes that were considered to be Communist-infiltrated.

In another labour case, R. v. Ontario Labour Relations Board; Ex parte Hall (1963), McRuer dealt with a conflict of interest on the OLRB. David Archer, a member of the board, was also the president of one of the unions involved in a certification dispute being considered by the board. The dispute pitted two union locals against each other; one local belonged to the Ontario Federation of Labour (OFL), the other did not. Archer was president of the OFL and had taken an oath which, among other things, bound him faithfully to support the constitution, principles, and policies of the OFL and the Canadian Labour Congress. McRuer judged that Archer had no business deliberating on this matter. He ruled that, when a member of the Labour Relations Board was the chief executive officer of a central labour body and proceedings involving the interest of that central body come before the OLRB, that member should disqualify himself from participating in the board's deliberations. If he did not, he would be forced to do so by the courts. In McRuer's mind, this case clearly showed why judicial review of administrative tribunals such as the OLRB was necessary.[42]

One labour case that seemed made in heaven for McRuer's benefit concerned a conflict between the OLRB and a union whose constitution required its members to uphold "Christian and social principles as taught in the Bible." In this case, the board denied certification to local 52 of the Trenton Construction Workers Association, claiming that the union discriminated on the basis of religion and so was not a union at all but rather a religious body. The union filed a court action, arguing that the OLRB had exceeded its jurisdiction in dealing with matters of religion. McRuer took jurisdiction over the case and on 2 May 1963 quashed the board's order, stating that he found no evidence of discrimination that would justify denial of certification.[43]

A similar case involved the Christian Labour Association of Canada (CLAC), which was denied certification on the ground that its constitution made reference to Christian principles and so was discriminatory. In considering this case, McRuer was concerned not only with the interpretation of the written words of the CLAC's constitution but also with the functional operation of the organization itself. Essentially McRuer looked at two dimensions of the union's activities—the conduct of its business meetings and the admission of members to the union—in order to determine whether there was any evidence of discrimination. Six witnesses testified that the annual conventions of the union opened with a scripture reading, prayer, and a hymn, but in their experience no prospective member had ever been asked if he were a Christian nor had any member been excluded from membership because he was not a Christian. There was, at the end of it all, no evidence that the union in practice was discriminating against any person because of his creed. "It cannot be said that in law a requirement that the meetings of a trade union must be opened with prayer makes the trade union discriminatory within the meaning of s. 10 of the Labour Relation Act or s. 4 of the Fair Employment Practices Act," McRuer concluded. He continued: "Prayer is a supplication for divine guidance. It is true that it is a recognition of a supreme being. However, the Legislature that passed the Labour Relations Act opened its sessions the day the Act was passed with prayer. Likewise, the Parliament of Canada opens its daily sessions with prayer. The British National Anthem, used as the Canadian National Anthem, is a prayer. The Canadian Bill of Rights, 1960 (Can.), c. 44, affirms 'that the Canadian Nation is founded upon principles that acknowledge the supremacy of God.' The oaths of allegiance and the prescribed oaths of office of Her Majesty's Judges and Ministers together with the oaths of office of all public officials, all acknowledge the supremacy of God. Prayer is not a subscription to any creed in the sense that the word is used in the relevant statutes nor is the practice of signing hymns and psalms at the meetings of the union a subscription to a creed. Psalms as sung, and hymns, are merely poetry set to music and for the most part they are prayers. If I supported the Board's refusal to certify the union on the ground that its members engage in prayer, read passages from the Bible and sing psalms and hymns at their meetings, the result would be that a union that required no standards of ethical or moral conduct and opened its meetings by reading from Karl Marx and signing the Red International might be certified but one that permits the practices here in question could not be."

The other broad issue involved in the CLAC case—whether the courts should interfere in the workings of an administrative agency such as the Labour Relations Board—was always sensitive, as McRuer well knew. On this point, he stated that the power of provincial legislatures to confer judicial functions on administrative tribunals was limited by the constitution of Canada. He also quoted Lord Justice Denning of the English Court of Appeal who, he said, had "set out, with great clarity, the function of a judge in an application such as this." According to Denning, "the Court of King's Bench has an inherent jurisdiction to control all inferior tribunals, not in an appellate capacity, but in a supervisory capacity. This control extends not only to seeing that the inferior tribunals keep within their jurisdiction, but also to seeing that they observe the law. The control is exercised by means of a power to quash any determination by the tribunal which, on the face of it, offends against the law. The King's Bench does not substitute its own views for those of the tribunal, as a Court of Appeal would do. It leaves it to the tribunal to hear the case again, and in a proper case may command it to do so. When the King's Bench exercises its control over tribunals in this way, it is not usurping a jurisdiction which does not belong to it. It is only exercising a jurisdiction which it has always had."

Following this line of reasoning, McRuer had no difficulty justifying in law his "supervisory" role over the Labour Relations Board. He quashed the order of the board that had denied certification to the CLAC. Contrary to the board's finding, he found no evidence that the union had discriminated on the basis of creed.[44]

Another McRuer decision quashing the order of an administrative tribunal, in *Canadian Pittsburgh Industries Ltd.* v. *Orliffe,* came in 1961.

The previous year, the provincial government had created—under the Labour Relations Act—the Jurisdictional Disputes Commission to deal with disputes between unions regarding the right to do particular work. When one of the commission's decisions was challenged in court, McRuer, always keen to wade into the controversial realm of judicial review of a labour tribunal's work, took the case himself. At issue was the commission's authority to order an employer to have work done by members of a union other than the union that represented that employer's workers. McRuer ruled that the commission had no jurisdiction to make such an order under the Labour Relations Act. "If it was the intention of the Legislature to give the Jurisdictional Dispute Commission such wide powers to interfere with the peaceful relations between the employer and his employees concerning which neither had made a complaint," said McRuer, "much clearer language would be necessary" than that used in the Labour Relations Act. He added that "the Commission by a wrong exercise of its jurisdiction could not give the Labour Relations Board jurisdiction."[45] In 1966 the Jurisdictional Disputes Commission was disbanded, and the OLRB was vested with authority to resolve jurisdictional conflict—but under the watchful eye of the courts.

The reasons for McRuer's many judgments against the OLRB were complex. They are worth noting, however, for they foreshadowed—and in many respects were preparation for—his work in the area of civil rights and the far-reaching changes he would help bring about in the functioning of all tribunals in Ontario.

Philosophically, McRuer was suspicious of non-judicial tribunals, which, in his view, wielded too much power and failed to meet the rigorous standards of evidence and procedure observed in the courtroom. Yet, in passing judgment in cases involving the Labour Relations Board, McRuer said that his personal feelings were irrelevant—he simply applied the law as he understood it. In the case of the OLRB, the law establishing this body was widely considered ambiguous and inadequate, and so McRuer relied on the long-established principles of the common law (even though they were much less solicitous of workers' interests than the statutory rules administered by the Labour Relations Board). Those common-law principles, in his view, placed strict limits on the power of administrative tribunals, and the courts were therefore entitled—and indeed obliged—to ensure that such limits were not transgressed. To critics such as Bora Laskin, who argued that he was not allowing the OLRB the wide-ranging powers which its creators had intended it to exercise,[46] McRuer had a ready reply: he was merely defending the full measure of the inviolable rights guaranteed to every individual by British legal tradition, and these rights could be eliminated or circumscribed only by express and clear enactments of the legislature. This answer was somewhat irrelevant, however, given that Britain did not have anything similar to Canada's statutory regime and labour-relations bodies.

In the end, McRuer's decisions limiting the power of the Labour Relations Board revolved around the issue of workers' rights, and his own views about them.[47] McRuer, as a good liberal, believed profoundly that each individual has rights, and he was equally convinced that it is the responsibility of the courts to ensure the protection of those rights. At the same time, McRuer realized that one person's rights could not be allowed to infringe those of another—at least not without some valid process to determine where one person's rights end and another's begin. Balancing rights, then, was a large part of the judge's role.

Sometimes, as with cases involving women and children, McRuer could affirm the rights of the disadvantaged without worrying that the rights of others were being limited. Yet on most occasions, and particularly when the rights of striking workers were involved, the scales of justice had to weigh the competing rights of different individuals and groups. Although such cases were never easy to decide, McRuer invariably reached decisions that were sensibly grounded in law. Other cases, specifically those involving the Labour Relations Board, fell into a different category because of the involvement of unions and a tribunal—but again, the question of rights was ultimately central. Here, in McRuer's mind, an unaccountable tribunal with "malignant powers" threatened the rights both of employers and employees and ignored the jurisdiction of the courts.

This view encountered considerable criticism, but, as the smoke cleared, most observers came to recognize the progressive thrust of McRuer's labour decisions. His support of the underdog was certainly evident in *Hersees* and in *Canadian Pacific Railway*, and it underlay his substantive ruling in *General Dry Batteries*. Seen in this context, McRuer's judgments in OLRB cases stand as instances where his general predisposition to employ legal principles sensitively and equitably gave way to his profound distrust of administrative agencies.

13

IN PURSUIT OF JUSTICE

THE LIFE OF JIM MCRUEr, like that of anyone else, did not fall neatly into compartments. He pursued different interests and activities simultaneously. The last few chapters have detailed McRuer's judicial decisions in the period from 1944, when he was appointed to the Ontario Court of Appeal, to 1964, when he resigned as chief justice. During these same years, however, McRuer's career as a judge was paralleled by a variety of other professional activities, and to know about them is to learn more about the character of the man himself. From 1945 to 1946 he was vice-president of the Canadian Bar Association, and from 1946 to 1947 he served as the association's president. In the following decade, McRuer chaired two royal commissions: one studied the law regarding insanity as a defence in criminal cases, and the other investigated the law's treatment of sexual psychopaths. Finally, in the midst of his career as a judge and his work on royal commissions, McRuer somehow found time to publish books.

These activities demonstrated McRuer's capacity for hard work and his ability to juggle different interests and tasks at the same time. In addition, as with his career as a lawyer and his decisions as a judge, McRuer's leadership of the CBA, his chairmanship of royal commissions on insanity and sexual psychopaths, and his published writings reveal a man deeply engaged by the law and unwavering in his dedication to justice. Jim McRuer travelled many roads at once, but, wherever those roads took him, he always remained the same person.

DESPITE A LONG INVOLVEMENT in the Canadian Bar Association dating to the 1930s, McRuer's election as vice-president of the organization in 1945, and then as its president in 1946, was unusual. Indeed, many people, both inside and outside the legal profession, were scandalized that a judge should accept leadership positions in the CBA, partly because of the organization's reputation as a self-serving lobby for well-heeled lawyers and also because of a belief that McRuer's association with the CBA compromised his impartiality as a judge. Not for the first time, however, McRuer saw things differently.

Towards the end of the Second World War, McRuer had become convinced that a new world order was in the making and that one of its foundations would be an international system of justice. This belief was similar to the one he held at the conclusion of the First World War, but it now reflected his experiences over the intervening decades. After the war's end, he set out his view of the new international order in his 1946 "New Year's Message" as CBA president. In this address, which was published in the *Canadian Bar Review*, McRuer stressed that "on the lawyers and jurists of Canada lies a grave responsibility to do their full share in creating a world public opinion, *not for peace, but for justice* under the law." He explained that international cooperation between organized bodies of lawyers was the key to the future. "We have in the Canadian Bar Association a medium through which the whole legal profession of Canada can exercise a united influence not only at home but abroad," McRuer said. "In the past we have made some contribution to the development of international legal process. Avenues are opening up through which we may make a much greater contribution." He concluded: "As the curtain rises again in 1947 and we view the confused scene of international affairs, there is more than a faint glimmer of hope that the rule of law, *with power to exercise its authority*, will someday be established throughout the world."[1]

Given his views on the responsibilities of the legal profession in creating a new, better world, McRuer saw no impropriety in his acceptance of a leadership role in the CBA; on the contrary, he strongly believed that he had an obligation to assume such a role in order to ensure that the CBA—and the entire Canadian legal profession—played its part in the development of an international system of justice and the maintenance of world peace.

Even before the war was over, McRuer demonstrated the strength of his convictions by helping to create a special CBA committee to consider the legal obstacles standing in the way of an international organization for peace. Founded in August 1944, this "Peace Committee," as it was known, was chaired by Chief Justice W.B. Farris of British Columbia; McRuer served as vice-chairman of the national body as well as chairman of its Ontario branch. The Peace Committee worked closely with other legal bodies throughout the world to formulate policies and rally support for an international organization dedicated to collective security and peace and for a world court.

As part of the planning that preceded the formation of these bodies, the Peace Committee held a conference in Toronto in February 1945 to debate such questions as the responsibilities of a world court and its relationship to the new international organization. Afterwards, McRuer concluded that the "weight of the meeting" favoured an organic link between the world court and the international organization; that the court should be known as The Permanent Court of International Justice and be seated in The Hague; and that the court should have "the widest possible compulsory jurisdiction over nations." Finally, noted McRuer, who himself was in complete agreement with all these ideas, "It was realized that the world needs a comprehensive code of international law, universal in its application, and this should no longer be left to intermittent growth by treaties limited in application to their signatories. This code of law should be created by legislators and not jurists."[2]

In furthering these ideas, McRuer was instrumental in establishing a formal liaison between the CBA's Peace Committee and a similar committee of the American Bar Association. Later, with the creation of the new United Nations and the establishment of the International Court of Justice after the end of the war, McRuer was even more hopeful that a new era of international peace and justice had dawned. As CBA president he worked tirelessly to ensure that his dreams became a reality, conducting an extensive correspondence with lawyers, judges, and legal associations all around the world. He saw such contacts as an essential component in building up the new international legal system.

Alongside these grand projects on the international stage were, inevitably, many more mundane matters. When McRuer became president of the CBA at the end of August 1946, he soon realized that his most pressing task was to reform the association from within. At this time, the CBA could not claim to represent much more than 40 per cent of Canada's lawyers, and the association laboured under a deficit of more than eight thousand dollars. McRuer and his associates on the CBA attacked both problems simultaneously. The entire deficit was wiped out through skilful salesmanship and administrative restructuring, and a low-key but effective membership campaign between December 1946 and July 1947 attracted roughly two hundred new lawyers into the organization.

During his year as president, McRuer visited every province in the country, meeting with local bar associations and promoting the national association's purposes. Wherever he went he dwelt on his cherished dream: the lawyers of the world must organize in strong bodies to promote a new international rule of law. McRuer did not hesitate to back up his idealistic speeches with some hard-nosed political dealings, and he frequently became deeply involved in efforts to have like-minded men elected to key CBA committees.

A matter of particular concern and interest to McRuer was the improvement of the CBA's journal, the *Canadian Bar Review*. The depression of the 1930s and the Second World War had taken a dramatic toll on young people entering the legal profession, and when McRuer came to the helm of the CBA the ranks of the association were dangerously top-heavy with well-established lawyers who saw no advantage in devoting their time to reading or publishing in the *Canadian Bar Review*. As a result, the CBR was of mediocre quality, to put it mildly, and few lawyers even bothered to read it. McRuer made it one of his central goals to rescue the journal by turning it into a high-quality and effectively promoted journal of legal opinion and knowledge. In his view, such a journal would appeal to a broad spectrum of readers ranging from the educated lay person to the chief justice of the Supreme Court of Canada. It would create increased interest in the law, and this in turn would result in increased respect for the law's principles.

McRuer was not alone in his view that the CBR should be improved. During the war years, young Bora Laskin emerged as a keen promoter of the *Review*, and in 1945 he offered to edit it when it seemed that no issue could be published. Certain powerful members of the CBA were uneasy about the appointment of a Jew to the staff of the CBR, but McRuer backed Laskin fully and the edition appeared. Later in 1945, while McRuer was vice-president of the CBA, G.V.V. Nicholls became the *Review*'s editor. He shared McRuer's vision of the CBR, and they worked closely together in formulating a new direction for the publication.

During 1946 and 1947, McRuer and Nicholls created a four-pronged policy for the promotion of the CBR. First, they sought to develop new interest in the journal by providing more detail in each issue about the daily operations of the CBA and its committees. Secondly, they solicited articles from key figures in the law, both in Canada and internationally.

Thirdly, they reached out to other professional publications, such as the *Canadian Medical Association Journal*, in an effort to encourage more exchanges between experts in related fields. Finally, they attempted to raise the quality of all inclusions in the cbr by adopting a more rigorous approach to editing. These innovations did not change the fortunes of the *Canadian Bar Review* overnight, but the editorial policy developed by McRuer and Nicholls set the *Review* on the path to considerable achievements in the coming decades. McRuer himself, although maintaining an extremely heavy workload in his years as a judge, contributed several articles to the cbr.[3]

As president of the cba, McRuer was particularly attentive to proposals for reform of the divorce laws. In the policy sessions of the cba convention that elected McRuer to the post of president, a strong resolution had called for modification of Canadian divorce laws to recognize the equal rights of women and to protect the best interests of children. Following the convention, McRuer wrote to every provincial attorney-general asking for support of these principles. He stated that "the Bench and the Bar of those provinces where divorce is granted through the Courts all feel very strongly that the interests of infant children are not now adequately presented to the Courts ... Frequently, applications are made for custody and little evidence is produced to indicate what would be in the best interests of the child. In other cases, no request is made for custody and the child is left without supervision under circumstances that are obviously detrimental to its welfare." McRuer's letter expressed his strong belief that the attorney-general in each province should be "charged with the responsibility of presenting the interests of the infant child to the Court" in these cases.[4]

Perhaps the most contentious issue considered by the cba while McRuer was president involved labour relations. In the immediate postwar years, the labour scene was chaotic, with unionized workers feuding with non-unionized workers, rival unions competing violently, and management doing battle with everyone else. Responding to these conditions, the cba, at its annual meeting in 1946, formed a special committee on industrial relations and labour law. The following year, the federal government introduced a bill that created new tribunals with a mandate to mediate in labour disputes. This bill raised the ire of the cba because, at the instigation of the trade union movement, the government included a clause severely limiting the right of lawyers to represent parties to a dispute brought before the new tribunals.

The cba's committee on industrial relations and labour law was chaired by McRuer's protégé, Andrew Brewin, and co-chaired by J.J. Robinette, who by 1946 was beginning to acquire his national reputation as an outstanding counsel. The committee quickly developed a detailed critique of the proposed legislation which rested both on its concern about the powers of extra-judicial tribunals and on its belief that the prohibition of counsel in hearings of these tribunals was a scandalous limitation of civil rights. McRuer presented the committee's brief to the government, whose initial response was decidedly lukewarm. Minister of Justice J.L. Ilsley expressed sympathy with the CBA's position but implied that employers' wealth allowed them to hire better lawyers than workers could afford to retain. He promised McRuer that he would "attempt to have the matter re-considered," but he did not hold out much hope for a change in the legislation.[5]

Yet McRuer and his colleagues on the CBA were not to be deterred. For some CBA stalwarts, the issue involved the association's mandate to protect the professional interests of its members, including their ability to earn fees; but for those of progressive views and a sure sense of the importance of due legal process, such as Robinette, Brewin, and McRuer, the issue transcended monetary considerations. Eventually enough pressure was brought to bear upon the government that the bill was withdrawn, a development that McRuer saw as one of his great achievements as CBA president. In his address to the association's 1947 annual meeting, he warned that lawyers must remain vigilant against this type of legislation. If lawyers were suspected of improprieties, he argued, the profession must subject itself to a critical sell-examination and ensure that no abuses occurred. Beyond that, members of the legal profession must raise their standards to keep pace with the changing times. To do less would be to betray the principles of justice.

During his years at the helm of the CBA McRuer also devoted much time and energy to improving legal education. Since his days as an instructor at Osgoode Law School, he had agitated for the comprehensive restructuring of legal education in Canada, and he now took advantage of his position as CBA president to advance his views further. From his perspective, the legal profession had to diversify to cope with such matters as the new international legal code, changes in family law, and the proliferating quasi-judicial tribunals, and at the same time individual lawyers ought to specialize in order to provide better services in particular fields. Training in specialized areas should be provided both through formal academic programs and through regularized post-graduate apprenticeships affording practical experience. Lawyers who completed these programs should be granted some special distinction, and should, within carefully defined limits, be allowed to advertise the fact that they have acquired these qualifications. All of this, McRuer believed, would tremendously enhance the public's access to the specific type of legal expertise which it would require in the post-war era. Once again, however, McRuer's ideas were ahead of their time. Another CBA president, Yves Fortier, promoted the same ideas in 1983, but only now, in the 1990s, is designated specialization in the practice of law becoming a reality—for the benefit of the legal profession and the general public alike.

In outlining his vision of a revamped system of legal training to the CBA's 1947 annual meeting, McRuer called on Canadian universities to assume some leadership in developing new programs in post-graduate legal education. In the preceding two years, he pointed out, the Canadian Bar Association had awarded scholarships to three students to pursue post-graduate legal studies from a fund established by the late R.B. Bennett, the former Conservative prime minister, but because no appropriate program of study was available in Canada all three students had found it necessary to study in the United States. This, McRuer maintained, was a national disgrace. Foreseeing (correctly, as it turned out) significantly higher numbers of people entering the profession, he exhorted members of the association to work together to create better educational opportunities for young people hoping pursue a career in the law.

Of all the events during his year as CBA president, the one that McRuer valued most was the association's annual meeting in Ottawa from 3 to 5 September 1947. McRuer was determined to ensure that this meeting went well, and he spent hours fussing over the tiniest details. For instance, he took great care in arranging the seating plan at the dinners so that wives (not yet spouses) would feel welcome and comfortable, looked after special requests for hotel accommodation, and arranged for a private rail car for the use of two special guests—the lord chancellor of Britain, Viscount Jowitt, and his wife—during their stay in Canada. Naturally, the CBA's administrative staff assisted him in all these preparations, but McRuer assumed personal responsibility for every aspect of the convention—just as he had, in the 1920s, planned each step of the raid on the Nash-Simington organization. In large things as in small, McRuer was fastidious; he understood that, ultimately, his reputation was on the line.[6]

Apart from the business sessions, the convention's highlights were two formal dinners at which Sir Norman Birkett, a judge on England's

Court of King's Bench, and Lord Jowitt delivered keynote addresses. McRuer's choice of these two speakers reflected his view that, in legal matters, England was the fountain-head for all of Canada. As on many other occasions, however, his fervent commitment to an idea blinded him somewhat to the side-effects. In this case, some French-Canadian members of the CBA felt that the program was unbalanced.

In his own presidential address, McRuer made it clear that his philosophy of law, with its unyielding commitment to justice, was firmly rooted in religious faith. Speaking as if from a pulpit, McRuer blended law and religion, justice and faith. "A true sense of justice is the vitality of all law," he said. "It is a spiritual force that grows with the spiritual development of mankind." He continued: "The function of the members of the legal profession, be they lawyers or judges, is to seek to regulate human relations so that within our all too narrow limitations God's justice may be done throughout the world. Fellow members of the legal profession, we are humble artisans laying the foundation of a temple of justice, the grandeur of which is known only to the Great Architect who holds in His hands the plans that show the proportions, the substructures and the elevations of the edifice to be erected on the foundations we lay. Minute are the details that come to our hands when viewed as part of the omnipotent plan, but our part is always to apply our minds and hearts to each of those details, however trifling they may seem, with a devout purpose that justice may be done between men."

Such remarks show that McRuer, the farm boy from Ayr who had given up the ministry in favour of a career in the law, had actually pursued both vocations at once, sublimating theology into legal philosophy and integrating spiritual endeavour with the administration of justice.

The man with the grand blueprint also was capable of gracious gestures. As a parting courtesy to Lord Jowitt and Sir Norman Birkett, McRuer arranged, through a series of telegrams to a New York City provisioner, to have tins of Canadian ham—"Maple Leaf Tendersweet"— placed in their staterooms before their ocean liner left New York for the return voyage to England. Since food rationing continued in Britain for a long time after the war, the hams were genuinely appreciated.

More than anyone, McRuer had injected new vitality into the CBA in the years just after the Second World War. This accomplishment did not go unnoticed by others. In the weeks following the CBA's 1947 convention, hundreds of letters—including one from Prime Minister Mackenzie King, who had attended the dinner where Lord Jowitt had spoken, sitting with McRuer at the head table—poured into McRuer's office praising the meeting and the role he had played in organizing it. Savouring these accolades, McRuer ended his term of office on the CBA's executive, but he still remained involved with the organization's work. For years the presidents of the CBA and their counterparts in the American Bar Association had attended each other's annual meetings, and in late September McRuer was present at the ABA's meeting in Cleveland, where he delivered an address entitled "The Judicial System as an Essential Part of Government." In subsequent years, he continued to support the causes he had espoused as CBA president, speaking on these issues before such organizations as county law associations, the Toronto Lawyers' Club, the Canadian Medical Association, the graduating class of Ontario Ladies' College in Whitby, Ontario, and the Canadian Save the Children Fund.[7] As in all other areas of his life, McRuer's efforts on behalf of the CBA showed that, when he believed strongly in something, he would spare no effort in promoting it. The CBA was the instrument through which he was working to create a new kind of lawyer (better educated, specialized), a new kind of society (based not on the power of governments but on the rights of individuals), and a new international order (characterized by justice and cooperation). Underlying all of this was McRuer's burning desire to allow "God's justice to be done through the world."

ON THE AFTERNOON of 25 June 1948 Chief Justice McRuer, addressing the annual meeting of the Canadian Medical Association in Toronto, set out his thoughts on the subject of "Insanity as a Legal Defence." This speech, as it turned out, marked the opening of yet another chapter in his career.

Since becoming a judge, McRuer had grown acutely aware of the difficulties involved in passing judgment on individuals who claimed that they were insane at the time of the crime for which they were standing trial. The Criminal Code of Canada contained certain general provisions guiding the courts in such cases, but much was left to the discretion of the judge and the crown's prosecuting officers. Psychologists and psychiatrists were unhappy with this situation and were calling for changes to the law. While McRuer was troubled by the conflicting theories and some of the recommendations that were being proposed, he came to believe by the late 1940s that insanity as a legal defence urgently required review in light of new psychological theories. It was time to give the issue an airing, to "crack it open and see what's there."

In addressing the Canadian Medical Association in 1948, McRuer pointed out that every plea of insanity as a defence in a criminal case was considered according to principles laid down by English judges in 1843 and known as the "McNaughton Rules." These rules were developed after a certain McNaughton, while labouring under a delusion that Prime Minister Sir Robert Peel had injured him, mistook a chap named Drummond for Sir Robert, and shot him dead with a pistol. McNaughton was eventually acquitted of murder after the jury found that because of the force of his delusion he was unable to understand that he was doing wrong at the time of the killing. The McNaughton Rules were formulated by the House of Lords during the controversy that followed McNaughton's acquittal, and they were later simplified and embodied in section 19 of the Canadian Criminal Code.

McRuer gave his listeners an abbreviated summary of the rules. The first rule, he said, stipulated that "no person shall be convicted of an offence by reason of an act done or omitted by him when labouring under natural imbecility, or disease of the mind, to such an extent as to render him incapable of appreciating the nature and quality of the act or omission, and of knowing that such an act or omission was wrong." The second rule added that "a person labouring under specific delusions, but in other respects sane, shall not be acquitted on the ground of insanity, under the provisions hereinafter contained, unless the delusions caused him to believe in the existence of some state of things which, if it existed, would justify or excuse his act or omission." A third rule stated that "everyone shall be presumed to be sane at the time of doing or omitting to do any act until the contrary is proved."[8]

Though the McNaughton Rules, McRuer said, had served very well . for the last century, "the real difficulty arises where the accused is suffering from some mental disease but the requirements of the McNaughton rules as codified by the Canadian Criminal Code cannot be proved." The McNaughton Rules only considered the intellectual state of the accused and did not take into account the power of emotional impulses, he observed, yet legal, medical, and scientific authorities increasingly seemed to accept the assumption that individuals may often fall victim to the urges of an "uncontrollable or irresistible impulse."

McRuer then carefully reviewed the arguments in favour of introducing the so-called "doctrine of the uncontrollable impulse" into the law on insanity as a legal defence, but in the end he came down strongly against it. "I have real fear that the introduction of the doctrine of the uncontrollable impulse into our criminal law would create such a confused state of the law that the result would be that in all cases where the defence of insanity is raised, a wide field of investigation would be opened up, the boundaries of which would be incapable of delineation." He told the Canadian doctors that "I have never forgotten a colourful phrase used by the late and much respected Dr. Behmer in an insanity case in which I was engaged. In answer to a question on cross-examination he said, 'It is very difficult to tell where the twilight ends and the dark begins.'"

To McRuer, it was hard to conceive how a court could arrive at a conclusion with any degree of certainty as to whether an accused acted under an "uncontrollable" impulse because of mental disease. He also noted that, "If we had no capital punishment in Canada the subject I am now discussing would not likely have a place on your programme." The idea that a person might hang for committing a crime while suffering from a disease of the mind was repugnant; on the other hand, use of the defence of insanity to get a murderer acquitted had provoked much anger among Canadians, many of whom believed that the weight given to psychiatrists' testimony was eroding the necessary firmness of the criminal justice system.

McRuer took pains to reassure his audience that many safeguards protected the interests both of the accused and of society at large. Within ten days of the imposition of a death sentence, he explained, every judge was required to submit a comprehensive report on the circumstances of the case to the secretary of state for the information of the minister of justice. A complete copy of the records of the trial, including all evidence and the judge's charge to the jury, also had to be sent to the authorities in Ottawa. If a defence of insanity had been offered, a full report had to be sent to the minister of justice. In cases of doubt, the minister of justice normally sought further psychiatric opinion before deciding whether or not to grant executive clemency to the prisoner. As McRuer reminded his audience, "The royal prerogative of mercy is just as much a part of the criminal law of Canada as Section 19 of the Criminal Code."

In closing his address, McRuer, often known for his bold statements calling for sweeping reform of Canadian law, displayed uncharacteristic caution. He was this way with anything pertaining—directly or indirectly—to the death penalty. Apparently he was uncomfortable in striking a balance between the opposing views on this subject, and so he chose to be almost mute on the issue of capital punishment and extremely wary on the question on the defence of insanity (which, as he noted, was primarily of interest as a barrier to the gallows).

McRuer did not advocate major changes in the law on insanity but suggested instead that the medical and legal professions should work more closely together to improve the administration of the time-tested law as it stood. "Before any change is made in the law dealing with insanity as a defence in criminal cases," he said, "it is of first importance to be clearly convinced that the condition of the body politic of Canada will be better under the new law than it has been under the old. In a matter of this fundamental importance, there is no room for experiment. Before we change the prescription we must be certain that the new formula will not produce other illnesses which will be worse than those from which we now suffer."

McRuer's speech, printed in the *Canadian Medical Association Journal* in November 1949,[9] attracted much interest across the country and abroad. People in places as diverse as South Africa and California sought McRuer's advice on the issue of insanity as a legal defence, and a joint committee of members of the Canadian Medical Association and the Canadian Bar Association was formed to study the matter. By the early 1950s the issue was being actively debated in parliament, and this debate soon led to McRuer's involvement in two more royal commissions.

In 1953 a special committee of the House of Commons recommended the creation of a royal commission to consider whether changes should be made in the law respecting a strange mixture of three controversial criminal justice issues: the defence of insanity, lotteries, and the imposition of corporal and capital punishment. The Liberal government of Louis St. Laurent was not itself prepared to tackle these questions, but it felt that a study of the defence of insanity coupled with the issue of sexual crime might be of use in demonstrating the need for law reform. Given his track record on these issues, McRuer seemed the ideal man to head the investigation. Early in 1954 Minister of Justice Stuart Carson asked McRuer to serve as the chairman of a new royal commission to study the law relating to the defence of insanity and to sexual psychopaths.

McRuer considered Carson's proposal, weighed his various commitments, and then telephoned Ottawa with a counter-offer. As always, McRuer was willing to make room in his hectic schedule for worthwhile public service, and he welcomed the opportunity to apply his expertise to the study of these pressing legal problems; indeed, he had already addressed the problem of sexual psychopaths twenty years earlier during the Archambault commission, and he was now willing to take a "second kick at the can." Still, he wanted to establish his own ground rules before accepting the new assignment. First, McRuer informed Carson that he would accept a place on a royal commission only if the work of the commission did not interfere with his duties as chief justice. The commission could hold hearings only during the summer recess of the courts, and its report would have to be written only during hours that McRuer could spare from his judicial responsibilities. Secondly, McRuer refused to accept any remuneration for his services on the commission beyond his actual living and travel expenses. A judge must not be seen to be receiving special favours from the government, and, in any event, McRuer was still mindful of criticisms of his government fees levelled during the 1935 election campaign. Finally, McRuer stipulated that two distinct royal commissions be established. The question of the defence of insanity struck McRuer's legalistic mind as being quite separate from the issue of sexual psychopathy, and he did not want these matters to become confused. At the same time, McRuer volunteered to chair both commissions simultaneously, and he suggested that the commissions could be run economically by holding meetings in tandem and by appointing an overlapping membership of commissioners and a common administrative staff.

Carson took McRuer's proposals back to the cabinet and in due course they were accepted. On 2 March 1954 McRuer was appointed chairman of the Royal Commission on the Law of Insanity As a Defence in Criminal Cases, and a little more than three weeks later, on 25 March 1954, he was also appointed chairman of the Royal Commission on the Criminal Law Relating to Criminal Sexual Psychopaths.

The Commission on the Law of Insanity was composed of four commissioners besides McRuer: Dr. Gustave Desrochers, the assistant superintendent of the Hôpital St. Michel in Quebec City; Judge Helen Kinnear, county court judge for Haldimand County, Ontario, and at the time the only female judge in Canada; Dr. Robert O. Jones, professor of psychiatry at Dalhousie University in Halifax; and Joseph Harris, a prominent Winnipeg businessman. McRuer arranged for one his former law students, James Worrall, to become commission counsel.[10] The commissioners were also assisted by Edouard Martel, associate counsel; and R. Noel Dickson, secretary. The Commission on Sexual Psychopaths, for its part, comprised commissioners McRuer, Desrochers, and Kinnear, along with Worrall, Martel, and Dickson in their respective administrative capacities. In addition, Dr. Frank Robert Wake acted as a research consultant.

As McRuer arranged matters, both commissions conducted their hearings in all the provincial capitals as well as in Montreal, Ottawa, and Vancouver. In any given city, the Commission on the Law of Insanity conducted its hearings first. Then Jones and Harris would withdraw, and McRuer, Desrochers, and Kinnear would reconvene as the Commission on Sexual Psychopaths. Scores of organizations and individuals presented briefs to the commissions in public meetings and many other private citizens and members of the judiciary were heard in camera. By the time the commissions' work was concluded, McRuer was satisfied that most competent parties wishing to make representations had been heard in full.

The Commission on the Law of Insanity was the first of the commissions to publish its findings. Its report, submitted to the government on 25 October 1956, was decidedly cautious. The commissioners' sixteen major recommendations amounted to a detailed elaboration of the points that McRuer had emphasized in his address to the Canadian Medical Association over eight years before; they included no significant calls for reform of the law. Two of the commissioners, Kinnear and Jones, dissented on several critical points. For example, between the time of McRuer's address to the CMA and the release of the commission's report, section 19 of the Criminal Code had been replaced by a new section 16 which employed slightly different language to convey essentially the same ideas.[11] Kinnear and Jones found the new terminology even more ambiguous than the previous wording, but the other commissioners felt that any ambiguity would be resolved through the interpretation of responsible judges. Normally, Chief Justice McRuer was a real stickler for clear and precise wording in statutes, and on just about any other subject he might have written the dissent himself. Yet, as a trial judge, he genuinely believed that, in a matter such as this, you "had to be there"— that is, in the courtroom—and so he favoured judicial latitude and discretion. The commission recommended no immediate change to section 16 of the Canadian Criminal Code.

The Commission on the Law of Insanity also gave serious consideration to recommending that Canada adopt the procedures of the State of New Hampshire and the District of Columbia in the United States, which required that those accused of capital crimes be kept under lengthy psychiatric observation before their trials. In the end, however, McRuer and the majority of his commissioners concluded that this "would not make for a better administration of justice in Canada." Kinnear and Jones again dissented.

All of the commissioners agreed that lower courts should retain their right to try cases involving accused individuals claiming the defence of insanity, that no change in the law should be made with regard to the procedure in determining criminal responsibility, and that the burden of proof in pleas of insanity ought to remain as it was. McRuer's commission was not entirely devoted to the *status quo*, however. It recommended that psychiatric services be extended to all individuals brought before the courts, and that a board of review consisting of three psychiatrists evaluate all prisoners condemned to death. Another change urged by the commission was the adoption of a standard charge to the jury for all murder trials in which the accused pleads "not guilty by reason of insanity."[12]

In effect, McRuer's commission recommended little more than the extension of psychiatric services to accused and convicted individuals within the framework of the existing law. Such conservative findings were something of a shock to those who knew him only by the reputation he had acquired through the press. Those who knew him well, however, took a different view of the matter, realizing that McRuer's advocacy of legal reform had always been rooted in a mixture of elements—a commitment to the rights of the individual, a belief in personal responsibility and the necessity of punishing the guilty, and a respect for legal tradition. The idea of "change for the sake of change" was anathema to his understanding of the world. Having carefully considered all the alternatives in the use of insanity as a defence, McRuer concluded that the best protection of individual rights and society in general lay in the judicious application of proven legal procedures.

Long after the report of his commission, McRuer continued to be interested in proposals for the reform of the law on insanity. In 1967, for example, he was called to testify before the House of Commons standing committee on justice and legal affairs about amendments to the law on insanity proposed by his long-time friend and former law partner Andrew Brewin, MP.[13] Judges, psychiatrists, and other authorities also contacted him seeking advice about the problem on a more or less regular basis throughout the 1960s and 1970s. During all these years, McRuer continued to defend the conservative approach taken by his royal commission. Though recognizing the need for periodic reviews of this area of the law, he insisted that any reforms be grounded in solid legal tradition. Too much was at stake to allow rapidly shifting fashions in legal and medical opinion to exercise undue influence in the administration of justice.[14]

The Commission on Sexual Psychopaths, in contrast, took a much more activist approach to the law than its sister commission on insanity. Its report, presented to the minister of justice in John Diefenbaker's government, E. Davie Fulton, on 21 March 1958, reviewed the law as it stood in Canada and six other countries and made numerous suggestions for reform. Three of the lengthiest chapters dealt exclusively with criticisms of Canadian law and legal procedures, and the report's tone was reflected in the title of another chapter, "The Insufficiency of the Law." The commissioners drew twenty major conclusions and presented seventeen principal recommendations, the sum of which amounted to a call not only for the reform of the law but also for a radical change in society's attitudes about sexual crimes.

McRuer's commission had been established primarily to evaluate the system of preventive detention, a new legal sanction introduced in 1948. As established that year and amended in 1953, Part XXI of the Criminal Code of Canada provided for the classification of certain convicts as either "habitual criminals" or "criminal sexual psychopaths." Convicts classified this way were subject not only to a definite period of detention in a penitentiary for committing the crime that had brought them before the courts, but also to an indefinite period of detention thereafter, Indeed, anyone classified as an habitual criminal or a criminal sexual psychopath could expect to spend most of the rest of his life in prison. The classification could never be withdrawn, and release from prison could occur only on the basis of a licence issued by the minister of justice. The licence could be revoked at any time, with or without cause. In addition, habitual criminals and sexual psychopaths were held in ordinary penitentiaries, where no therapy or rehabilitation programs were available.

McRuer's commission made a detailed study of the operation and effectiveness of the system of preventive detention, and found the system grossly inadequate. In the view of the commissioners, the law did not adequately distinguish between various types of individuals convicted of sexual crime, insufficient legal safeguards were provided for the convict, and the detention system offered little prospect of rehabilitation. If anything, the 1948 system threatened to make matters worse, for it was founded on many assumptions which ran contrary to the accepted traditions of British justice.

The McRuer commissioners began by recommending that the term "criminal sexual psychopath" be removed from the law. They concluded that sexual crimes should be treated no differently from other crimes, and they recommended that those convicted of sexual crimes should be known simply as "sexual offenders." Yet the commissioners also maintained that a distinction should be made between "common sexual offenders" and "dangerous sexual offenders." The former class of criminals comprised all those who committed acts of sexual crime while being essentially of sane mind, while the dangerous offender was "a person who, by his conduct in sexual matters, has shown a failure to control his sexual impulses and who is likely to cause injury, pain or other evil to any person through failure in the future to control his sexual impulses."

The McRuer commissioners believed that the courts should take great pains to determine whether a sexual offender was indeed "dangerous" in this technical sense. In a hearing before the trial judge, a minimum number of independent expert witnesses should assist in arriving at such a decision. The attorney-general should review all relevant evidence, and the offender should have a right of appeal. Once designated a "dangerous sexual offender," the individual in question should have his case automatically reviewed on a regular basis, and provisions should also be made, the commissioners argued, for the unconditional release of the offender when there was sufficient evidence of his rehabilitation.

Rehabilitation of the designated "dangerous sexual offender," the commissioners argued, should become the sole justification of his continued detention. The dangerous sexual offender should serve no definite term for his crime, since the courts had determined that he was not responsible for his actions at the time of the offence. Nor should the offender be held in a penitentiary. Instead, special institutions should be established to detain and treat this class of offender. New research and teaching programs should be inaugurated in Canadian universities to discover more about the treatment of sexual offenders and to produce qualified staff for the rehabilitation centres. Only by adopting this radical approach to the problem of sexual crime, McRuer and his colleagues believed, could society protect itself from this scourge.

The commissioners rejected several other possible innovations. They turned down suggestions that it should be made more difficult for the crown to prove that a sexual offender was legally classifiable as "dangerous," for example, and they also totally opposed the introduction of harsher punishments. They were particularly emphatic in rejecting the use of castration either as punishment or as treatment, for experience abroad indicated that the procedure was not only barbaric but also completely ineffective. In their eyes, only a humane and scientific system of detention and rehabilitation could be justified.[15]

Although the commission's report was submitted to the government in March 1938, it was not released to the public for more than a year—a delay that caused McRuer considerable embarrassment and frustration because the press held him and the other commissioners responsible. When the report finally did appear, *Toronto Telegram* columnist Frank Tumpane issued a public apology to McRuer and his colleagues on the commission, admitting that he had been mistaken in harshly blaming the delay on them rather than on the government.[16] McRuer was satisfied with this apology, but of greater significance to him was the press's reaction to the report itself.

Most newspapers, though not all, gave the report a warm reception. McRuer was particularly pleased by the reaction of the *Toronto Telegram* and the *Toronto Daily Star*, both of which printed lead editorials on the report on 20 April 1959. The *Telegram* praised the report's major recommendations as a "constructive contribution towards an understanding of the problem of sex crimes." The report made it clear, the *Telegram* asserted, that "Canada is still on the threshold of the judicial, penal and remedial approaches to the problem" and urgent action was needed. The *Star* echoed these remarks and called for the implementation of the report's recommendations: "We have reason to be grateful, then, for the long and careful study given this problem by the royal commission headed by Chief Justice McRuer of Ontario. Their report, just issued, displays a progressive and enlightened attitude, yet is realistic enough to reveal the difficulties frankly. It cannot be accused of lulling the public against inherent dangers."

When McRuer submitted his report on sexual psychopaths he reflected somewhat sadly that much of its contents were based on the findings of the Archambault commission of two decades before. Still, as the years passed, many of his specific recommendations were put into place. McRuer hoped that one day Canadian society, and its political leaders, would awaken to the need for a comprehensive reform of the penal system.

IN 1956 McRUER agreed to inaugurate the W.M. Martin Lectures at the University of Saskatchewan Law School with a series of three addresses entitled "The Evolution of the Judicial Process." Both the vastness of the topic and the approach he took in preparing his talks were typical of his *modus operandi* as a public speaker.

All through his adult life McRuer made several speeches a year. In preparing such speeches, he would write numerous drafts, starting with a handwritten text and afterwards revising several typed versions. Then, when he spoke, it was in fact a public reading, not oratory; he read his text line by line and seldom improvised or digressed. He sought to convert people to his position—whether it involved improvements to the prison system, law reform, or the rights of women and children—by close reasoning, not deep emotion. He was a man who "spoke for the record" rather than for the moment, and this predilection was both cause and effect of his rather austere and formal public persona.

In short, McRuer's public speeches were like the man himself: solid, correct, and formal. They were also ambitious in their scope. Wanting to "back up and take a good run at his subject," McRuer often treated his audiences to tours through Babylonian and Roman law, then the centuries-long evolution of English law, before getting to the Canadian story. One of his many listeners, Frank E. Lewis, described McRuer's address to a 1950 luncheon meeting of the Liberal Business Men's Club in downtown Toronto. The topic was the early history of Ontario and its government, and McRuer, when it was well past 2 p.m., was still going on in great detail about events and legislation. One by one his audience slipped away to return to their offices. As Lewis himself left, McRuer "was up to about 1841" and the end of the speech was not in sight.[17]

McRuer's inclusion of a wealth of historical detail in his speeches had a purpose: he wanted to make interesting and valuable comparisons between past and present legal systems. When evaluating the riparian rights of landowners downstream from a polluting pulp and paper mill on the Spanish River in northern Ontario, he would go back to Roman law; when assessing the rights of women in modern circumstances he would revitalize doctrines of the woman's right of dower and alienation of affection that other "contemporary" jurists would have been embarrassed even to mention for fear of sounding anachronistic. McRuer placed great emphasis on the importance of education, and for him, education required a comprehensive picture. In his W.M. Martin lectures, therefore, McRuer wanted to use the experience of the past to assess the problems of the future, and to achieve this goal he started at the beginning—in the ancient world. Following the completion of these lectures, the lectureship committee chairman, F.C. Cronkite, observed that McRuer's "great contribution lies in formulating by this method [of comparisons] a convincing and optimistic view of the future."[18]

McRuer's message in his lectures was just as distinctive as his approach. This message was that human society, if guided by good laws and the proper administration of justice, could evolve to a higher order.

Throughout his lecture series ran a deep respect for the rule of law and for individuals who "are prepared to ... bring to a reality the visions of those who have dreamed of a temple where the spirit of ... justice will be enshrined, before whose altar all men will worship and at whose gates the weak and the oppressed may find justice dispensed by those who 'do justly, love mercy and walk humbly' before their God."[19] In a practical vein, McRuer recognized that his lectures on the evolution of the judicial process could be neither a detailed catalogue nor a comprehensive history. Yet he hoped that, by providing a glimpse of history and communicating some knowledge of contemporary legal systems in other countries, he could foster an increased appreciation of the importance of the judicial process in regulating both domestic and international affairs.

McRuer began his lectures by stating his fundamental premise: law was essentially spiritual in nature. According to him, "there probably never was any organized body of human beings that has not had some sort of judicial procedure in relation to some form of government. But in all forms of government not based on the arbitrary power of force there is a concept of justice, and although the concept of justice is something that has been evolutionary in character it has had an anchorage in definite and eternal moral principles, without which it would be an empty bark drifting on an uncertain sea of political expediency. Historically in all states of civilization there has been some recognition or theory at least that there is a natural law of Divine dictation, and justice has been administered as an expression of the Divine will. This idea has been common both to those acknowledging one God and to those who believe in many gods."[20]

McRuer then traced "the evolution of the jural process devised to do justice between men."[21] Declaring that the roots of Canada's legal system lie in Babylon and Israel, he examined the Code of Hammurabi and the Mosaic law before moving on to the mediaeval English concept of trial by ordeal, which he considered a triumph of superstition over proper concepts of justice, and the later evolution of a judicial process founded on moral and spiritual principles. This was followed by a review of the establishment and development of England's court system and trial by jury. After expounding upon the degradation of the English courts, particularly under the Stuarts, and the beginnings of court reform in 1830, McRuer asserted that the evolution of the Court of Chancery "reflected the development of moral concepts born of an inherent spiritual desire in the human heart for righteousness in judgment rather than judgment according to rigid technical rules of law applied to proved facts."[22]

McRuer articulated in his lecture series a belief about the importance of the judge's role that he implemented in his career as chief justice of Ontario's High Court. He was speaking, after all, not as a legal theoretician, but as a man of power and influence—a trial judge who made decisions that affected people's lives, a royal commissioner whose recommendations had an impact on Canadian public policy and the administration of justice.

McRuer argued that "the most significant and distinctive feature of the evolution of the judicial process of England has been the manner in which the function of the judge and the dignity of his office have developed and increased." To McRuer, the administration of the law was of "paramount importance."[23] He warned that the "legal profession should be vigilant to expose and resist legislation which gives to governmental boards jurisdiction to decide cases between their employer, the government, and the Queen's subjects, with no adequate right of review in the courts." The independence of the judiciary was the bulwark protecting the citizen from the arbitrary and capricious exercise of power by even the most democratic state. Of course, he recognized that it behooved "the courts to conduct their affairs in such a manner that recourse to them" might be simple and their decisions "equitable and just, devoid of that technicality which denies justice."[24]

Having so thoroughly researched and prepared his lecture notes, McRuer wanted desperately to have them published as a book. So, gathering up his typed text, and with a neophyte author's self-assurance, he pressed himself upon his friend and neighbour Bill Clarke, president of the Toronto publishing firm Clarke, Irwin. McRuer rightly pointed out that the wide scope of his book, both in historical reach and the number of countries mentioned in its analysis, would certainly add to its broad appeal. He also stressed that he had tried, to the fullest extent of his talents, to present the story in an interesting and concise fashion. These features would make the book especially valuable in reaching, and educating, many people who would never otherwise hold a legal book of any kind in their hands.

After some initial reluctance, Clarke relented. Clarke, Irwin published the 113-page *The Evolution of the Judicial Process* in 1957. In doing so, it gained McRuer's appreciation, but lost money. As for the author himself, his publishing contract provided (as a sweetener for the doubtful Clarke) no royalties on the first 1,000 copies sold, and from 1958 to 1963 his accumulated royalties amounted to exactly $79.80.

Shortly after the appearance of his first book, McRuer became involved in another writing project. Many years earlier, in his days as a struggling young lawyer, he had produced a short manuscript about the legal aspects of the trial of Jesus Christ. It was another manifestation of his two main interests—law and religion. As a Christian and a lawyer, what could be more natural than to wonder if Jesus had received a fair trial? This question may have interested other lawyers through the ages, but only McRuer was industrious enough to turn his speculation on the subject into a major research project.

Over the years McRuer revised his manuscript again and again, and by September 1959 he had completed a 100-page, double-spaced typescript entitled "The Trial of Christ." This manuscript related Christ's trial, along with the relevant events that preceded it, to the political and religious affairs of the time as well as to the procedures of the Roman and Jewish legal systems. In writing it, McRuer aimed to produce not a dry legal treatise or religious tract but a compelling narrative that would hold the attention of Christians and non-Christians alike. Although he sought to evaluate the trial and condemnation of Jesus in strictly legal terms, he presented his account in words that he felt would bring the events of Holy Week alive for the average reader.

Manuscript in hand, McRuer began looking for a publisher. When he failed in his attempts to find one that would publish his book internationally, McRuer again turned to Clarke, Irwin. The Canadian publisher then subjected McRuer's manuscript to a review process that, to the author's chagrin, was to last more than four years. In late 1959, however, McRuer had no idea of what the future held for "The Trial of Christ"; indeed, far from being anxious, he felt certain that publication of his manuscript was imminent and so turned his attention to another matter—a trip to the Middle East that he and his wife and been planning for many years and that now, after years of anticipation, was finally to take place.

This trip lasted two months, through December 1959 and January 1960, and took the McRuers to Israel, Egypt, Syria, Lebanon, and, on the return leg, Cyprus, Turkey, and Greece. In addition to meeting a host of prominent people—judges, lawyers, journalists, business people, scholars—McRuer found time to discuss his ideas about Christ's trial with a number of Jewish intellectuals, who offered many suggestions for further reading. He and Mary also had time to do a lot of sightseeing, and their reactions to what they saw were mixed. Though distressed by the intrusions of the modern world into the Holy Land, and particularly by the commercialization of such hallowed places as Bethlehem, they nonetheless were often profoundly moved when they visited places described in the Old Testament and, even more so, when they walked in the footsteps of Christ and the apostles. As for the current state of the Holy Land, McRuer was deeply saddened by the plight of the Palestinians and appalled by the cycle of terror and suffering which he saw developing. Over the course of his trip he became convinced that peace could be achieved only through the imposition of international principles of justice and, specifically, the creation of a secular Palestinian state that recognized the equal rights of all citizens regardless of religion.

By the time of the McRuers' return to Canada, reviews of "The Trial of Christ" had been submitted to Clarke, Irwin by outside specialists. They were less than enthusiastic. In response to these critiques, and to follow up on ideas of his own that he had developed during his trip to the Middle East, McRuer again revised his manuscript over the course of 1960. By the autumn Clarke, Irwin was ready to commission another review, this one by Professor Sherwin-White of Oxford. R.W. Robertson, an editor at Clarke, Irwin, confidently told McRuer that Sherwin-White was "the very top man in his field." To McRuer's dismay, Sherwin-White, while recognizing the potential value of McRuer's project, recommended that the entire treatise be rewritten before being considered for publication.

In the summer of 1961 McRuer, with all the mixed emotions of a struggling author, began work on his treatise yet again. Taking the criticisms of his work as a challenge, he was determined to see his many years of effort in writing this book bear fruit. He also started planning a second trip to the Middle East, scheduled for December 1961 and January 1962, to examine again the scenes mentioned in his manuscript. While there, he intended to meet with more legal experts, Biblical scholars, and other authorities who might help him in coming to terms with his prospective book. Elaborate preparations were made for this journey, but a sudden death in the McRuer family forced the cancellation of the trip at the last moment. His daughter Mary Louise's husband, Dr. John R. Gaby, died of leukaemia after three days in hospital, leaving five children between the ages of eight and fourteen. McRuer was distraught and it took all his emotional strength to be his daughter's "everlasting backup," to use her words.

McRuer pressed on with his writing in any spare hours he could find. Finally, after years of further effort, his book was accepted for publication by Clarke, Irwin and appeared in 1964. Entitled *The Trial of Jesus,* and carrying the dedication "to my wife," the book was intended to be a sort of handbook for the lay person. It was divided into eleven crisp chapters plus a foreword, preface, epilogue, notes, and index, and its argument was clear and straightforward: Jesus's execution was the greatest miscarriage of justice in history.

Although McRuer's interpretation of Jesus's last days was not original, it again revealed how outraged he could be when, in his eyes, justice was violated. According to him, Jesus was the victim partly of the intolerance of the Jewish religious, commercial, and legal elite, which saw him as a threat to the established order, and of Roman authorities who were both weak and capricious in dealing with this "prophet." Working from the assumption that the gospel accounts of Christ's final days were essentially accurate, McRuer traced events as they unfolded through six major stages: Jesus's arrest in the Garden of Gethsemane; his interrogation before the high priests Annas and Caiaphas; his trial before the Great Sanhedrin, the Jewish High Court, which convicted him on a charge of blasphemy; his trial on a yet another charge, sedition, before Pontius Pilate, whose approval was necessary for all death sentences; his acquittal on the sedition charge, followed by a third trial, this time before Herod Antipas, Tetrarch of Galilee; and his last trial, again before Pilate, who turned Jesus over to the mob. Throughout these proceedings, McRuer argued, the aim of the Jewish authorities was to give the "destruction of Jesus" a "cloak of respectability," and "some form of judicial procedure was to be the cloak, no matter how stained and saturated with illegality."[25] The interrogation before Annas and Caiaphas was "illegal from beginning to end according to the Hebraic law," and the trial of the Great Sanhedrin was similarly a "mockery of judicial procedure throughout."[26] The trial before Herod was no less farcical, and, when Pilate finally washed his hands of Jesus, he set a precedent of sorts: "In all the annals of legal history," said McRuer, "it would be difficult to find another case in which a prisoner who had been declared not guilty by a court of competent jurisdiction was delivered to the executioner by the judge who had acquitted him."[27]

The appearance of *The Trial of Jesus* caused a small sensation. McRuer received letters of support and criticism from all over Canada, and reviews were published in the popular press and learned journals. International attention to the work was also enhanced when Blandford Press of London, England, issued hardcover and paperback editions on 1 March 1965.

The letters that McRuer received in reaction to *The Trial of Jesus* ranged from the reverent to the rude, the scholarly to the bizarre. Ministers, lawyers, and lay people wrote to congratulate him on producing such a helpful exposition of the events of Holy Week, to ask for autographs and copies of the book, and to praise him for testifying to the strength of his Christian commitment. For example, Charlotte Whitton, mayor of Ottawa, wrote McRuer on 5 June 1964, asking him to autograph a copy of the book "for 'auld lang syne's sake' and our association of thirty years ago in the Federal Royal Commission Report on Penal Reform." Others—both Christians and non-Christians—accused McRuer of sacrilege, blatant prejudice against the Jews, and even ignorance of the law. One individual tried to use his admiration, feigned or otherwise, of the book to obtain support for his application to become a magistrate. Another, a self-styled Christian, hounded McRuer for several years with lengthy and nearly incomprehensible letters and constant requests for a private interview, his goal being to convert the chief justice to the "true faith."

The published notices were equally diverse. Some of the headlines on newspaper reviews illustrate the interest stirred by McRuer's book: "A miscarriage of justice" (*Globe and Mail*); "If Jewish law had prevailed Jesus would have been freed" (*Toronto Telegram*); "Caiaphas: he violated court law" (*Hamilton Spectator*); "A mockery of a trial" (*Montreal Gazette*); "Pilate a milksop" (*Peterborough Examiner*); "Justice misdone" (*Birmingham Post*); "The trial of Jesus": judicial murder" (*Toronto Star*). As for the reviews themselves, many columnists praised McRuer for producing a concise, readable text which made complex issues understandable to the average reader. Others bitterly attacked him for allegedly stirring up anti-semitic prejudice.[28] In the May 1964 issue of *Saturday Night* magazine, William Nicholls, writing in the "Religion" column, used the publication of McRuer's book to ask, "Is anti-Semitism coming once more to be regarded as permissible by the public?" He went on to conclude that "in view of the present resurgence of anti-Semitism, I am inclined to believe that Chief Justice James C. McRuer's recent book ... is at least ill-timed."

After many years in the courtroom, McRuer was neither surprised nor upset by the variety of ways in which the press treated his book. He was more concerned, however, when scholarly reviews began to appear. Several notices by Christian biblicists were extremely favourable,[29] but McRuer was perturbed when he read a lengthy and critical review written by his old friend Haim Cohn, a justice on Israel's Supreme Court who had entertained Jim and his wife during their visit to the Middle East a few years earlier. Published in the *Israel Law Review* in 1967, Cohn's review drew on his extensive knowledge of Jewish legal traditions, and it approached the trial of Jesus by turning McRuer's basic assumption on its head. Cohn dismissed as nonsense McRuer's premise that the gospel accounts of Jesus's trial were essentially accurate. The gospels, he observed, were compiled many years after the death of Christ and "were written with tendentious religious purposes." Going farther, just as McRuer had accepted the veracity of the gospels, Cohn assumed the integrity of the Jewish authorities and legal system. Assuming that the Jewish authorities acted in accordance with the laws of their society, Cohn concluded that the "trial" of Jesus before them was in fact only a preliminary hearing. Both "the trial and the execution of Jesus were exclusively Roman," Cohn argued, and the Jews had been blamed for Jesus's death by malicious Christian propagandists.[30]

Although McRuer could see the logic of this analysis, he considered it specious. He spent much time in analyzing Cohn's text, and the two judges, although they remained on good terms personally, exchanged critical letters about the matter. Ultimately, McRuer considered it prudent not to reply to Cohn in print. His son, John, comments on this episode: "Note the difference in approach ... Father took the gospels as evidence—all the evidence there is. Cohn was speculating. Father had no patience for speculation."[31] What is curious, however, is that McRuer himself did not take many parts of the bible at face value, was skeptical about most of the "miracles," and simply placed no stock in several biblical stories—from Jonah and the whale to the Virgin Birth. Why, then, should he accept the "evidence" of the gospels? The answer may be that he had been working at this project so long, and had invested so much of his energy and spirit in it, that he relentlessly pushed ahead even as he was repeatedly told by some biblical scholars that he was on shaky ground. He did not personally doubt the accuracy of what he had written; the differences between him and Cohn were, at the end of the day, matters of interpretation.

Another colleague who reviewed McRuer's book, some years after it first appeared, was H. Aubrey Fraser, the director of legal education at the Norman Manley Law School in Kingston, Jamaica, in a May 1979 issue of the *West Indian Law Journal*. Commenting both on McRuer's book and Cohn's review, Fraser weighed one against the other and came down on the side of Cohn.[32] Again, however, McRuer decided to make no public response.

In the years that followed publication of his book, McRuer received invitations from many churches, service clubs, and the like to set out his views on the trial of Jesus. Such invitations reassured him that all his labour on the book was not in vain, and, eager to have his views reach a broad audience, he accepted them whenever his schedule allowed. On one occasion, however, his views were in fact popularized in a way that angered McRuer enough to make him consider legal action. In April 1972, one Ernest O. Hauser published an article in *Readers' Digest* entitled "The Man Who Sentenced Christ to Death." McRuer's friend J. Douglas Wilson considered this article a piece of blatant plagiarism, and McRuer and his publishers agreed. Greatly angered, McRuer pondered how the charge of plagiarism could be proved in court, but he eventually decided to let the matter pass.

Instead, McRuer stepped up his efforts around this time to find an American distributor for a new edition. With the consent of his Canadian publishers, McRuer began circulating copies of his book to prospective publishers, American churchmen, and other influential individuals, seeking their support for an American edition. Polite letters came back in reply, praising the treatise but also rejecting McRuer's proposal that it be republished. This cycle of optimism and disappointment continued for the rest of McRuer's life. He was pleased, however, when Clarke, Irwin agreed to print a paperback edition in 1978, under the title *This Man Was Innocent: The Trial of Jesus*. This reprint did not create the same interest as the original edition, but McRuer was gratified to see that the book would not be forgotten.

The Trial of Jesus was not the success that McRuer had hoped it would be. Still, it remains a powerful reflection of two themes that ran through his life—faith and justice. On the surface, Jesus's story was an odd choice of subject for a judge not particularly well versed in biblical scholarship. Yet McRuer was no ordinary judge. The trial and crucifixion of Jesus were events that lay at the heart of his Christian faith, shaping both his philosophy of life and the way in which he fulfilled his responsibilities first as a lawyer and then a judge. What is more, because these same events raised important legal issues, McRuer was drawn to them on intellectual grounds. Jesus's fate, in his eyes, was not merely a religious matter; it also stood as history's pre-eminent example of injustice. In sum, the trial and execution of Jesus spoke both to his religious faith and to his vision of the law. The depth of his commitment to the subject explains why he worked so many years writing and then revising his manuscript, and why he found harsh reviews by academic critics so wounding. He had put a lot of himself into this book; indeed few writers have said more about their view of the world, and their place in it, in such a modest volume.

The Trial of Jesus also stands as a symbol of McRuer's wide-ranging interests. As a judge, McRuer saw issues of justice and injustice everywhere, and his views were expressed with great force and logic not only in his courtroom decisions but in his leadership of the Canadian Bar Association, his chairmanship of royal commissions, and his books, speeches, and articles. The variety of his activities during his years on the bench emphasizes the point that McRuer was more than a legal technician; his reflections on everything from the Criminal Code to the trial of Jesus revealed a judge with an uncommon breadth of interests and a legal vision that reached beyond the courtroom to the wider world. The very fact that he would drive himself emotionally as well as intellectually to write such a book as The Trial of Jesus is eloquent testimony to his broad vision of justice. Together with his many other extra-judicial assignments, Jim McRuer's single-minded pursuit of justice left a legacy in many forms and forums.

14

CIVIL RIGHTS AND THE STATE

In 1964 Jim McRuer turned seventy-four. Most people are long retired by that age, but, for McRuer, retirement was unthinkable. As vigorous as ever, and with an undiminished appetite for hard work, he was entitled to remain on the bench for one more year before retirement became mandatory. Yet the idea of staying on as chief justice held less and less appeal for him. Thinking back on the extraordinary range of cases he had tried over the last twenty years—cases that involved everything from murder to pollution of Ontario rivers, from international espionage to the rights of women and children—he was proud of his judgments and of the mark he had made on the country's legal system. Still, despite his achievements and the continuing importance of his work as chief justice, McRuer was beginning to feel restive again. He was ready for a change—and for something that would engage his interests after he was forced to resign from the bench.

As often happened in his life, fate intervened with impeccable timing. In the spring of 1964 Ontario's Conservative government, now led by Premier John P. Robarts, asked McRuer if he would conduct a major inquiry into civil rights in Ontario. In reply, McRuer, always the hard bargainer, made a counter-offer of his own: he would agree to head the inquiry on civil rights if he was also named chairman of a proposed new commission on law reform. The premier agreed and McRuer stepped down as chief justice, ending a career on the bench that had spanned two decades.

As it turned out, McRuer's leadership of the civil rights inquiry from its beginning in 1964 to its conclusion in 1971, along with his long and simultaneous involvement with the Ontario Law Reform Commission, represented not an anti-climax but the true and logical culmination of his extraordinary career. His work on these commissions (traced separately in this and the following chapter) reflected his fervent belief in the importance of protecting individual rights and adapting the law to changing social conditions, and his legacy was a fundamental transformation in Ontario's governmental and legal system. That is why John Robarts, when asked to cite his greatest achievement as premier, gruffly replied with a one-word answer: "McRuer."[1]

McRUER'S INQUIRY INTO CIVIL RIGHTS had its genesis in a truly monumental political blunder involving the Ontario government's response to the problem of organized crime. In November 1961, one month after Robarts had succeeded Leslie Frost at the helm of the Conservative Party, Liberal leader John Wintermeyer unveiled major allegations about organized crime in Ontario. Wintermeyer claimed that social clubs used for syndicate gambling had received provincial government charters and that the illegal gambling proceeds from these clubs were financing legitimate businesses. In short, Wintermeyer charged that organized crime was operating in Ontario right under the government's nose. Robarts immediately established a royal commission, chaired by Mr. Justice Wilfred Roach, to investigate. In December 1962, following weeks of hearings that filled the media with talk of mob activities, the Roach commission concluded that Wintermeyer's allegations could not be substantiated.[2] That seemed to defuse the issue, and the official position of the provincial government continued to be that there was no organized crime in Ontario.

The next chapter in the saga bordered on the bizarre. In the very first session of the legislature following the election of October 1963, in which Robarts's Conservatives won a substantial majority, Attorney-General Fred Cass introduced major legislation dealing with police powers. Among other things, Bill 99 included a Section 14 that proposed giving the Ontario Police Commission the authority to force anyone to give evidence in secret or be jailed indefinitely if they refused. If there was no problem with organized crime, why had the Robarts government introduced such a measure? Two views promptly emerged about Bill 99. One held that the bill was really just a housekeeping measure, a reflection of the attorney-general's desire to have the province's legislature confirm and clarify powers that Ontario police already exercised. People of this view urged everyone to relax. The second view maintained that Bill 99 contained extraordinary new powers of a draconian nature, qualifying it for the epithet "police state bill."

Paradoxically, it was Attorney-General Cass himself who initially generated public alarm about his own legislation. In the annals of self-inflicted political wounds, Cass won top ranking when he emerged from the legislative chamber, paused to light up his pipe, and then, amidst a swirl of heavy smoke that symbolically obscured him from the television cameras, declaimed, "It's drastic and it's dangerous and it's new and it's terrible legislation in an English common law country."

It was downhill from there. The debate that erupted in and outside the legislature went on for days, with Premier Robarts himself among those at first trying to defend the measure. Outside Queen's Park, demonstrations by outraged citizens occurred daily, while the news media gave sensational play to the controversy. The issue had been blown into an attack on fundamental freedoms, and Robarts could hear the unpleasant sounds of his young government crumbling around him. A number of his own members, led by Toronto MPP Allan Lawrence, had begun to break ranks, publicly denouncing Bill 99 as intolerable. Finally, Robarts retreated. Fred Cass was sacrificed, and the infamous Bill 99 was promptly dispatched to the legal bills committee "for further study." The legislature then unanimously approved a motion of NDP leader Donald MacDonald calling for deletion of Section 14 from the bill. The vote was not a motion of confidence and so the Robarts government survived, but it was humiliated and discredited by the whole affair.[3]

To extricate himself from the mess, Robarts realized that he needed two things: a new attorney-general who could regain the public's confidence and trust, and a plan of action to deal with the issues that the controversy over Bill 99 had brought into sharp focus—crime, police power, and civil rights. He found a two-in-one solution: Arthur A. Wishart. A northern Ontario lawyer born on a farm near Chipman, New Brunswick, Wishart sat as the new backbench MPP for Sault Ste. Marie—in the very end seat, in the very last row. On 25 March 1964, when Robarts plucked Wishart from this obscure location to succeed Cass as attorney-general, just six months after his election to the legislature, most political observers assumed that he would hold the post only until Robarts could properly shuffle his cabinet. Yet Robarts knew Wishart well, the two of them having served with Charles MacNaughton as fellow members of the Ontario Water Resources Commission. The three had become good friends while working on the commission, and when Robarts became premier he promptly put MacNaughton in charge of the province's finances as treasurer of Ontario. It was only a matter of time before he would find a chance to clear out some of the political holdovers from the Frost government and bring Arthur Wishart into his cabinet too. The dynamite ignited by the "police state bill" gave the embattled premier the opportunity he needed.

Ontario's new attorney-general, escaping the crowd of reporters outside his large office at the west end of the Legislative Buildings, ensconced himself throughout that weekend in his room at the Park Plaza Hotel just north of Queen's Park. There he prepared the desperately needed plan of action for the Robarts government. His proposals, written out in Wishart's distinctive longhand on a pad of lawyer's yellow foolscap, called for the introduction of a new, milder version of Bill 99 and the creation of an inquiry into civil rights.

At this juncture, the thoughts of both Robarts and Wishart turned to Chief Justice McRuer. To their minds, he was the ideal candidate to take charge of the civil rights inquiry. Not only was he Ontario's top jurist, but he had unmatched experience as a royal commissioner and, given his ties to the Liberal Party, no one could suggest that he was in any way the creature of the Progressive Conservative government at Queen's Park. As Wishart expressed it, Robarts "knew that the importance of what we were undertaking merited picking the best man, wherever he could be found or whoever he was. Mr. McRuer was pre-eminent. The finger just pointed at him if we were looking for the best man."[4]

While these plans were being hatched, McRuer was in California investigating that state's procedures in dealing with medical evidence. He and deputy attorney-general William B. Common had been appointed by Attorney-General Cass in February 1963 as a committee of two to report on possible reforms in the way medical evidence was presented in civil cases. On returning home, he found a message from the premier awaiting him. Calling back, McRuer was told by the secretary that "Mr. Robarts would like to meet with you tomorrow morning at 9:00 a.m., if you can." No mention was made of what the meeting would be about.

When McRuer arrived at the Legislative Buildings the next morning, he was ushered directly into the premier's quiet office, its thick carpets and heavy curtains muffling the sounds of the steady traffic circling Queen's Park Crescent outside. Robarts, his black hair and moustache now accentuated by dark circles under his eyes, smiled warmly in welcoming the chief justice, thanked him for coming on short notice, and introduced him to the only other person present, Ontario's new attorney-general, Arthur Wishart. It was the first time McRuer had met the Sault Ste. Marie lawyer, a fellow veteran of the First World War. On the premier's desk lay an order-in-council, already signed. It was a document appointing James Chalmers McRuer as a one-man royal commission to inquire into the state of civil liberties in Ontario.

McRuer was astonished. He had actually expected, and certainly hoped, to be named chairman not of a civil rights inquiry but of a new law reform commission; he had been advocating the creation of such a body for a long time, and just recently he had discussed the matter in some detail with the new deputy attorney-general, Rendall Dick. When Robarts asked the chief justice whether he was willing to assume the chairmanship of the civil rights commission, McRuer characteristically sought assurances that he would be allowed a free hand in conducting the inquiry. These assurances were offered; the premier keenly wanted him. When McRuer then raised the stakes by asking for the chairmanship of the proposed commission on law reform, neither the premier nor the attorney-general batted an eye; no doubt they were swayed by McRuer's argument that "it would be very embarrassing if these two commissions got at loggerheads between them because they will both be engaged in law reform. It is going to be very difficult for them to sort out their work." McRuer had appraised the problem accurately and chosen his words well: if there was one thing Robarts wanted to avoid on the civil rights front, it was any more embarrassment. So the meeting concluded, with agreement all around. The course of McRuer's professional life for the next decade and a half was now set.[5] McRuer never regretted this decision. He realized that the inquiry into civil rights and the law reform commission offered him a unique opportunity to implement his life-long ideals, and that heading such inquiries would keep him active in a position of major influence for much longer than the two years left to him as chief justice.

On 1 May Premier Robarts, speaking in the legislature, announced the creation of the royal commission on civil rights, to be headed by Chief Justice J.C. McRuer. In explaining the reasons for his government's selection of McRuer, Robarts described the chief justice as "a jurist of distinction, who has established an enviable reputation in the position he occupies, particularly with respect to judgments he has delivered from time to time emphasizing the importance of protecting and safeguarding human rights and civil liberties."[6] The premier also announced that McRuer had been asked to chair the proposed Ontario Law Reform Commission, the enabling legislation for which was then before the legislature.

Most observers agreed with Robarts's assessment of McRuer's qualifications, but some doubted whether one man should head two commissions. A few months after the commissions were created, the *Globe* reported that there had been "some objection to the fact that Mr. McRuer has been appointed to head both the civil rights commission and the law reform commission," in particular from Vernon Singer, Liberal MPP for Downsview.[7] McRuer countered such concerns by again noting the overlap between the two commissions, which meant that much of the research and many of the subjects would be interchangeable.

Following Robarts's announcement in the legislature, McRuer indicated his intention to resign from the High Court as of 1 July 1964. A few days prior to that date, he gave an interview to the *Globe Magazine* in which he said that the commission on civil rights was "the most important royal commission appointed in my time. I doubt there has been anything similar in the English-speaking world."[8]

THE ROYAL COMMISSION INQUIRY INTO CIVIL RIGHTS, officially established by an order-in-council dated 21 May 1964 under the Public Inquiries Act and effective from 1 May, had extremely broad terms of reference. McRuer was to "examine, study and inquire into the laws of Ontario" which in any way affected the personal freedoms, rights, and liberties of Canadian citizens and others resident in Ontario, for the purpose of "determining how far there may be unjustified encroachment on those freedoms, rights and liberties by the Legislature, the Government, its officers and servants, divisions of Provincial Public Service, boards, commissions, committees, other emanations of government or bodies exercising authority under or administering the laws in Ontario." McRuer was also instructed "to recommend such changes in the law, procedures and processes as in the opinion of the commission are necessary and desirable to safeguard the fundamental and basic rights, liberties and freedoms of the individual from infringement by the State or any other body."[9]

Taking over some office space at Queen's Park, McRuer eagerly settled into his new quarters and began planning the organization of his inquiry into civil rights. As one of Canada's most seasoned royal commissioners, he realized that the success of his undertaking would hinge upon the calibre of his staff, and so he began his work by recruiting an impressive coterie of advisers and assistants. Professor David W. Mundell of Osgoode Hall Law School and Professor Robert S. Mackay of the Faculty of Law of the University of Western Ontario agreed to act as assistants; James A. Cory, then principal of Queen's University, and John D. Arnup, treasurer of the Law Society of Upper Canada, became consultants to the commission; John W. Morden was brought on board as commission counsel, and Carol M. Creighton was appointed chief research assistant. Additional appointments included Paul S.A. Lamek, Paul C. Weiler, and Barry B. Swadron, all of whom were engaged to do research for the inquiry. Stephen Borins joined Morden as counsel in 1966. The talents of these people and others were fully utilized by McRuer, who showed great administrative ability in delegating work to the staff and then overseeing its completion.

Once he had his team assembled, the systematic McRuer began a methodical study of hundreds of statutes and regulations and developed a detailed agenda of subjects to be considered. The inquiry's terms of reference, along with invitations to speak before it, were sent to about 7,000 individuals and organizations, including members of the Ontario legislature, Ontario MPs in the federal parliament, some thirty-two trade unions, boards of trade and chambers of commerce, universities, newspapers and radio stations, every lawyer in the province, and a large and varied group of organizations that included the Association of Mayors and Reeves, the John Howard Society, and the Elizabeth Fry Society. Public hearings were then convened between 7 December 1964 and 5 October 1965 in Toronto, Ottawa, Kingston, Windsor, London, Hamilton, Sudbury, Sault Ste. Marie, and Port Arthur.[10] All in all, thousands of letters and formal briefs were received and hundreds of witnesses interviewed.

Nothing quite like McRuer's inquiry into civil rights had been seen in Canada before. In a sense, it became a great work of constitutional reform—an attempt to give meaning, within the laws and legal procedures of the province, both to the civil rights acquired through the common-law tradition and to the other "inalienable rights" that Canadians enjoyed. In pursuing these goals, the inquiry had to overcome obstacles of various kinds. During its very first week of hearings, numerous witnesses appeared before McRuer seeking redress of purely personal grievances rather than discussing the complexities of the law. As one journalist, Albert Warson of the *Globe and Mail*, described the situation: "If this week's public hearings are a preview of what is to come, the public contribution to the Royal Commission Inquiry into Civil Rights will be disappointingly feeble. The 24 men and women who appeared before the commission covered many of the obvious civil rights issues ... About half of the witnesses submitted oral and written observations which will be of some use to the commission. But the others were aggrieved because of some personal transaction, or felt themselves to be persecuted, or just wanted to ramble on about their general beliefs." To the surprise of Warson, McRuer treated these individuals with respect. "If Mr. McRuer had a reputation for being severe on the bench," Warson said, "he certainly did not live up to it in the opening days of the hearings. His patience with some of the more emotionally charged witnesses was inspirational."[11]

Warson was not alone in his view that the commission should avoiding wasting its time considering irrelevant submissions. On 31 December 1964 a *Globe* editorial with the headline "A Misuse of Mr. McRuer" claimed that many of the submissions to the inquiry were "of dubious value. Some were by persons who clearly were mentally deranged and others by persons who carried some grievance which obsessed them. Their interests seemed to lie less in the structure of the law than in the need for someone to talk to who might understand their problems, real or supposed." Once again McRuer's unfailing patience was noted. The *Globe* said that "McRuer explained patiently at the beginning of the hearings that he was not there as an Ombudsman, but these people were not deterred. With all of them he was entirely polite and kind, even with those who came before him seeking little except personal publicity, and many left the hearing convinced that at last they had found someone in the confusing world of authority who cared enough about them to listen." Still, the paper insisted that McRuer's task was too important to be sidetracked by such individuals, and it noted with satisfaction that McRuer had tightened up his commission's procedures: "This kind of therapy is not ... the responsibility of Mr. McRuer, and he has since ordered that all submissions must be made in writing at least seven days before they are heard, in order that the irrelevant ones can be discarded."

After this initiation, McRuer's public hearings proceeded efficiently, and he was satisfied that the public was having ample opportunity to make its views known to him. Yet his goal at this stage was not simply to acquire, through examining statutes and listening to people, a close-up view of civil rights in Ontario. He also sought to place his inquiry in a broader context, and so he began an intensive review of jurisprudence relating to the rights and freedoms of individuals and the nature of the state and democratic government. To the same end, in the summer of

1965 McRuer took his commission on a tour around the world in search of new perspectives. The tour began in Great Britain, where McRuer met Lord Parker of Waddington, the lord chief justice of England, and Lord Denning, master of the rolls, whose brilliant record in reinterpret-. ing the law to give contemporary meaning to British justice was legendary. Concerned particularly with the role and powers of tribunals that stood outside both the legislative and the judicial branches of government, he conferred with Lord Tenby, chairman of the Council of Tribunals, Sir William Fitzgerald, chairman of the Lands Tribunal, David B. Bogle, chairman of the Scottish Committee Council on Tribunals, and other officials in similar positions of authority. To probe the conceptual context of civil rights, he also had extended conversations with Professor W.A. Robson of the London School of Economics, Professor C.J. Hamson of Cambridge University, and Professor H.W.R. Wade of Oxford University. McRuer's purpose in these various encounters was to assess the proper limits of the powers of tribunals in a democracy. One other subject investigated in the course of his visit to Britain was the role of parliamentary commissioners, independent mediators charged with investigating complaints against government and other public authorities by private citizens.

McRuer continued his study-tour in Denmark and Sweden, where he paid particular attention to the role of the ombudsman—a Scandinavian term used to refer to officials similar to Britain's parliamentary commissioners. After leaving Sweden, McRuer took a short time away from his work on the inquiry for a vacation with his wife in Africa. These were the days when many African colonies were winning independence, and Jim and Mary wanted to witness for themselves the "winds of change"— British Prime Minister Harold Macmillan's description—that were sweeping the continent. Jim's hopeful impressions about democratic self-government from this trip would be conveyed in an address, entitled "An Awakened Africa," which he delivered on 19 February 1966 to his fellow alumni of the Ruskin Literary and Debating Society.

From Africa the McRuers flew to Australia and New Zealand. Jim viewed these countries as sister members of the Commonwealth, blessed with many of the same advantages as Canada but also beset by similar social problems. New Zealand, in McRuer's eyes, was an island of stability in the changing world of the 1960s. He delighted in observing the country's legal system first hand, and, pursuing what was by now a familiar interest, took a close look at the work of New Zealand's parliamentary commissioner. As for Australia, it was undergoing a process of legal reform not unlike what McRuer envisioned for Canada, and he was eager to learn all that he could from its experience. While in Australia, McRuer attended the Third Commonwealth and Empire Law Conference. He had been invited as one of the conference's principal speakers, and his address on "The Motor Car and the Law"—later printed in several legal publications—spoke of the need for no-fault insurance in order to clear the courtrooms of automobile accident cases and thereby enable them to deal with real justice issues, such as crime and infringements of civil rights.[12]

Returning to Canada in early September, McRuer reconvened the inquiry's public hearings, which continued until 5 October 1965. He and his staff then conducted a painstaking review of the evidence compiled by the inquiry and plunged deeper into their systematic study of Ontario's laws. This process lasted more than two years. Mundell, Mackay, Morden, and Borins wrote the report's draft chapters, which McRuer then reworked and polished. The results were made public with the release of the inquiry's first report on 7 February 1968. It was a massive, beautifully printed, three-volume work that ran to 1,331 pages and contained 559 recommendations.

The first volume dealt primarily with "the exercise and control of statutory powers in the administrative process." In his general introduction to this volume, McRuer provided a statement of first principles and explained his theoretical framework. The "two dominant purposes" guiding his deliberations had been "to do justice to the individuals who make up the State, and to promote the Rule of Law in the State." Much of his liberal philosophy was then encapsulated in this crucial, single sentence: "There is no place in a true democracy for a doctrine of the welfare of the corporate State as distinct from the welfare of the individuals who are its components." Elaborating on this view, so central to his report, McRuer asserted that: "Apart from providing protection against an invader, the sole purpose of the democratic state is to regulate and promote the mutual rights, freedoms and liberties of the individuals under its control. State power is something in the nature of a trust conferred by the people on all those in positions of authority. While the State is an attribute of sovereignty, it is not the warden of freedom but the guardian of the right to be free. Law as the expression of the power of the State, and its enforcement, are not weapons but shields serving to protect and regulate the respective rights, freedoms and liberties of individuals *inter se*, from whom the authority of the State is derived. Excessive or unnecessary power conferred on public authorities corrupts and destroys democratic institutions and gives life to all forms of tyranny—some petty and some extreme."

McRuer pursued these ideas in a discussion of "basic concepts and constitutional principles." Here, he explored the powers of the three branches of democratic government—the legislative, the executive, and the judicial—and applied this analysis to the realities of Canada.[13] Then followed an examination of "statutory powers" in Ontario. Dividing such powers into three categories—administrative and judicial powers, "subordinate" legislative powers, and powers of investigation or inquiry—this portion of the report covered some 437 pages and contained 208 major recommendations.

McRuer recommended, first of all, that laws should be stated in precise terms which clearly indicate the limits of their applicability. Secondly, using the term "tribunal" to denote any person or group exercising power conferred by statute, McRuer recommended that distinctions should be made between judicial tribunals, administrative tribunals, tribunals exercising both judicial and administrative powers, and exceptional tribunals to which the general principles governing tribunals may not be applicable. Judicial tribunals were the ones exercising power "where the decision is to be arrived at in accordance with governing rules of law," while administrative tribunals were seen as those exercising power where "the paramount considerations are matters of policy." To give effect to his proposals for controlling the exercise of power by tribunals, McRuer recommended that the province enact a statutory powers procedure act. This act would establish procedural rules for the operation of all tribunals and set out provisions governing appeals against—and reviews of—decisions made by such bodies.[14] For the individual, the proposed act would be a procedural "bill of rights" when dealing with tribunals.

McRuer then set out a series of recommendations designed to limit and regulate the exercise of so-called "subordinate legislative powers," an expression he used "to describe rule-making powers conferred by a statute on a person or persons outside the Legislature." He insisted that such powers should be strictly limited in scope: "Subordinate legislative power should not be conferred on persons or bodies independent of the control of properly elected and responsible ministers," and all subordinate legislative power should be both regulated by carefully defined procedures and subject to thorough review by the legislature and the courts.[15]

McRuer examined the powers of investigation or inquiry conferred on individuals or groups of individuals by statute. Addressing an issue that had been at the heart of the controversy over Bill 99, McRuer wrote that "arbitrary powers of investigation ought not to be conferred in any statute." His recommendations on this point reflected a keen sense of the need to protect the individual from arbitrary interference from the state. All powers of investigation, he said, should be based on precedent and clearly formulated in statute. Witnesses compelled to testify in any investigation should be entitled to a reasonable witness fee. Strict limits should be placed on the power of search and seizure as well as on the power to stop and detain, while "power to search the person ought not to be conferred under provincial law." At the same time, the rights of individuals to appeal against decisions of investigating officers should be defined and extended.[16]

In this volume McRuer also paid particular attention to the role of coroners. In the early history of Ontario, the legal position of the office of coroner was similar to that in England, where the coroner was an integral part of the administration of the criminal law and the coroner's court had jurisdiction not only to inquire into causes of death but to commit persons for trial for murder, manslaughter, and infanticide. With the enactment of the Canadian Criminal Code in 1892, however, the coroner's right to commit for trial was taken away, and what remained was a prescribed system of investigation into deaths by violence or in untoward circumstances. McRuer reviewed the problems associated with coroners' work by the 1960s. One of his fifteen recommendations was that "political considerations ought not to enter into the appointment of coroners." McRuer also proposed that the number of coroners be reduced, since many of them conducted hardly any inquiries over the course of a year. Yet, for the smaller group that would remain, McRuer called for improved training and for clear limitations on their powers. He also recommended that coroners be supervised more closely by the crown. These steps were necessary, he asserted, both to protect the rights of the individual and to enhance the coroner's effectiveness in law enforcement.[17]

The second volume of McRuer's first report, concentrating on the administration of civil and criminal justice in Ontario, contained a number of far-reaching recommendations which reflected his mature thoughts on the judicial system. It began with a blunt statement on the role of justices of the peace: "The whole system pertaining to the office of justice of the peace should be reorganized." McRuer called for the dismissal of all incumbent justices of the peace, advocated the establishment of a training program for all new candidates for the position, and urged that "men and women should be appointed to the office without discrimination, and qualification should be the only criterion for appointment."[18] In a society where sexual equality was frequently dismissed as the fantasy of "crackpots," and in a political world where the office of justice of the peace was seen as a legitimate patronage plum, these were bold and refreshing recommendations.

McRuer also advocated reform of the magistrates' courts, believing that they should be organized according to uniform standards and supervised by an advisory judicial council consisting of the chief justice of Ontario, the chief justice of the High Court, the chief judge of the county and district courts, and the treasurer of the Law Society of Upper Canada or his nominee. All magistrates should be qualified lawyers and should receive the same salary as county court judges. For this remuneration they would be expected to work full-time and be barred from outside employment. Pointedly, McRuer added, "only those with qualifications sufficient to command such salaries should be appointed to be magistrates." In addition, he recommended that all cases in the magistrates' courts should be prosecuted by qualified lawyers, and that the practice of assessing costs in those courts should be abolished. By these and other means, McRuer hoped to transform the magistrates' courts into truly effective components of the legal system.[19]

Juvenile and family courts were next on McRuer's agenda. Calling for a new recognition of the importance of these courts, McRuer recommended that a special rules committee—consisting of judges, social workers, lawyers, the attorney-general, and members of the public—formulate new procedures for their proceedings. Clear distinction should be made between the two types of courts, and the province should assume full financial responsibility for their operations. Typically, McRuer was also prepared to make radical proposals regarding the qualifications of court officials: a special training course should be established in at least one university to train students in all branches of the relevant law and social sciences; and completion of this course and five years experience as a probation officer in juvenile and family courts should be a statutory requirement for the appointment of a judge to such courts. McRuer, ever sensitive to the legal position of children, went on to recommend that the term "juvenile delinquent" be struck forever from the law and that greater protection be given to the legal rights of the child. The juvenile and family courts, he firmly believed, had to gain recognition as critically important arms of justice in contemporary society.[20]

McRuer then focused on the county and district courts of the province. He asserted that "the administration of justice, particularly in criminal cases, should be reorganized so that the trial of cases will be prompt and expeditious," and he suggested a number of means by which this goal could be achieved. Above all, he believed, the county and district courts should be so organized as to facilitate the effective dispensation of justice in the local community.[21] Next for consideration were the division courts, and, once again, McRuer was adamant about the need for sweeping reform: "The Province should assume the financial and administrative responsibility for the operation of the division courts and they should be completely re-organized." McRuer suggested that the division courts should be brought under the supervision of the county courts, procedures in the courts should be standardized, and higher standards should be demanded of all officers of the courts. He added that the courts should be organized in such a way as to maximize their accessibility to the public.[22]

Turning to the Supreme Court of Ontario, McRuer was essentially satisfied that the High Court of Justice performed well in its function as a superior trial court, but he asserted that "a comprehensive reorganization of the appellate jurisdiction of the courts should be undertaken." McRuer maintained that this reorganization was vital to ensure that Ontario's growing population would be adequately served by the courts in the future, and he insisted that "rights of appeal should be enlarged rather than curtailed, and the method of appeal should be simplified." In McRuer's view, all appeals to the Supreme Court of Ontario should be heard by at least five judges, but new provisions should be made as well for appeals to lower courts and a new appellate division of the High Court of Justice for Ontario should be created. By dividing the work of the appellate courts in this manner, McRuer believed, the province could ensure that more appeals would be heard by a greater number of competent authorities.[23] The reality of the appeal process, and its availability, were both vital in any system concerned with an individual's civil rights.

Following its call for a sweeping reorganization of Ontario's judiciary, the second volume proceeded to offer ninety-seven recommendations on judicial personnel and the machinery of justice. McRuer recommended, for instance, that the Province of Ontario should assume full financial responsibility for the machinery of justice in the province, that judges should not normally engage in extra-judicial employment, that powers of arrest should be strictly regulated, and that bail should be granted more equitably. Although McRuer believed that no new restrictions should be placed on the news media regarding publication of judicial proceedings, he proposed the creation of a self-governing press council to ensure fairness in all reporting. He also recommended that the grand jury system be abolished and its powers vested in local sheriffs and the Supreme Court, that appeal procedures be broadened and simplified, that the system of court reporting be standardized, and that there be more flexibility in determining the admissibility of statements made by witnesses to traffic accidents. With regard to the role of private citizens in the judicial system, McRuer recommended that compensation be granted to wrongfully convicted persons, and, in a major innovation, that victims of crime also be compensated. He suggested that both jurors and witnesses receive more than a nominal fee as compensation for their contributions to the legal process, and that crown attorneys be better paid. In a drive to consolidate responsibility and provide uniformity in the legal concepts and drafting, he proposed that the attorney-general's department be given full responsibility for preparing all government legislation according to standard procedures, and that all legal services of the provincial government be directed by properly trained officials under the supervision of the attorney-general. The duties and qualifications of the attorney-general should be specified in new legislation.[24] McRuer's purpose in these proposals was to create legal procedures that would protect the rights of the individual while promoting efficiency and fairness in the judiciary.

In volume three of the report, McRuer looked to the need for "safeguards against unjustified exercise of certain special powers." Among other things, this section examined expropriation procedures, various forms of licensing, the operation of the Family Benefits Act of 1966, Ontario's self-governing professions and occupations, admission to and detention in mental hospitals, and the administration of estates of patients. Altogether in this volume McRuer presented a further 163 recommendations.

Over fifty of the proposals for new safeguards dealt with expropriation procedures. Though acknowledging that expropriation was a necessary power of government, McRuer insisted that this power should be strictly controlled, and his first recommendation was therefore that "the right of an owner whose property has been expropriated to be paid compensation should be secured in the Constitution"—an early call for constitutional entrenchment of property rights. In all cases of expropriation, McRuer asserted, the decision should be made by an accountable political authority, and in most cases a public inquiry should be held beforehand. A lands tribunal "should be established with jurisdiction to determine compensation in all cases where the power of expropriation is exercised, and in those cases where statutory powers to acquire rights over land are exercised." Clear arbitration procedures should be established to ensure that no injustice occurs.[25]

McRuer took a similar approach to the question of licensing. The government's licensing powers should be clearly detailed in legislation, and bodies with power to confer or revoke licences—whether for the sale of liquor in a restaurant or the operation of a taxi cab—should be held accountable to the public. Hearings should be held when licences are denied or revoked, and the affected individual should have statutory rights of appeal.[26]

The Family Benefits Act of 1966, at that time the most recent version of Ontario's evolving welfare legislation, was scrutinized by McRuer according to his basic principles, an exercise that led to ten recommendations. McRuer asserted that those receiving benefits under the act should not be investigated without reasonable grounds, and all potential or actual recipients of benefits should have the right to appeal any decision refusing, suspending, or cancelling their entitlements. Boards of review should be created to oversee the administration of the act, but those affected by the decisions of these boards should have the right of appeal to the courts. McRuer showed the need for the language of the act to be revised to eliminate any misunderstandings.[27]

As for Ontario's twenty-two self-governing professions and occupations, McRuer acknowledged the value of such bodies as the Law Society of Upper Canada and the College of Physicians and Surgeons, but he advised that "the power of self-government should not be extended beyond the present limitations" except in unusual circumstances. Each self-governing body should develop a code of standards, and members of the affected profession should be protected from unreasonable disciplinary procedures. At all times, McRuer made clear, the primary concern of these bodies should be the protection of the public.[28]

The final concern of McRuer's first report was the detention of the mentally ill. He recommended that the Mental Health Act of 1967, considered quite progressive by many, be amended to state that mentally ill individuals should be detained only on reasonable grounds in the interests of their own safety or the safety of others. He proposed that the public trustee be appointed to administer the estate of any person detained under the provisions of the act, and that this official should be fully accountable to the legislature.[29]

McRuer's first report on civil rights was tabled in the legislature on Tuesday, 5 March 1968, with McRuer himself in the public gallery to witness the event. Premier Robarts promised prompt and thorough study of the document and assured the public that action would be taken to implement its recommendations. "We are starting forthwith upon an intensive study," Robarts said, "which will lead to the application of the principles and recommendations embodied in it." Describing the report as the most comprehensive study of civil rights ever made in Ontario, Robarts expressed his own belief that "as the complexities of our modern life increase, we must be more careful than ever that the rights of the individual do not become lost in the intricacies of all forms of social government."[30] Similar remarks were made by the opposition parties. Liberal Leader Robert Nixon declared that the report "obviously is going to be the cornerstone in the changing and development of the statutes of this Province."[31] MPP James Renwick, speaking for the New Democratic Party, remarked that the report was "a first-class beginning for protecting the average citizen against the executive power of government."[32]

That same afternoon, McRuer outlined his proposals in a lengthy Queen's Park news conference attended by media representatives not only from Ontario but across the country. As editors and reporters struggled to come to terms with the sweeping scope of McRuer's report and to distil its intricacies into comprehensible copy, the realization dawned on almost everyone that the inquiry into civil rights marked a turning-point in Ontario history. The report challenged the public and its elected representatives to clean house with a thoroughness that had never before been seen in Canada, and it provided the necessary tools to accomplish this goal.

The day after the report's release, the *Toronto Telegram* proclaimed: "The McRuer Royal Commission on Civil Rights comes ... as a welcome reaffirmation of the importance of the individual and a chart for government to follow in protecting and restoring his rights ... Mr. McRuer's recommendations reflect not only concern at the whittling away of civil liberties. They reflect the exalted position in which he holds the law. And his report is scathing in its criticism of abuses in the administration of laws ... Mr. McRuer has charted the course for government. His report must now be studied and legislation to correct abuses should be forthcoming as soon as possible.

Other newspapers were no less laudatory. The *Globe and Mail* declared: "The fearsome jungle that has grown up in Ontario—in Canada—to separate the citizen from his civil liberties has never been so devastatingly charted as by the man who would clear it away. By saying what must be done to correct the situation, former Chief Justice J.C. McRuer must leave both citizens and legislators gasping at how bad the situation has been allowed to become. What Mr. McRuer is attempting is the restoration of justice to the individual, who has lost a lot of it to a complex and indifferent society."[33]

Under the headline "Mr. McRuer strikes a blow for liberty," a *Toronto Daily Star* editorial stated: "Without endorsing his vast work in every detail, it is possible to say now that Mr. McRuer has done a great service to the people of Ontario. His report seems certain to lead to wider and more secure liberty than the individual enjoys today."[34] The *Montreal Star* voiced the general opinion that the report was a document of great significance for more than the province of Ontario. "The whole country could benefit from the study of the McRuer recommendations for reform of Ontario laws affecting the rights of the individual. For the problem his commission was asked to study is not confined to Ontario; it exists across the country."[35]

Support for the report also came from leading figures in the legal community. Bill Poole, prominent London lawyer, professor of law, and McRuer's colleague on the law reform commission, predicted that the influence of the report would "be felt for the next fifty years," for, by providing "a mould or pattern which will serve as a framework for legal thinking," it would affect "all laws initiated in this province."[36] Similarly, A.W.R. Carrothers, dean of law at the University of Western Ontario, announced his "unqualified acceptance" of McRuer's first report and added that Commissioner McRuer was a man "like Caesar's wife. He's above suspicion."[37]

Not everyone applauded. One of the strongest dissents to the McRuer report came from a lawyer, John Willis. A professor of law at the University of Toronto at the time, Willis would subsequently work with the Ontario Securities Commission and thereafter return to his native Nova Scotia and a position in the faculty of law at Dalhousie University in Halifax. His critique was no mere quibble about details or emphasis but rather a challenge to the entire ideological underpinning of the McRuer commission's work. First appearing as an article in the *University of Toronto Law Journal* in 1968, Willis's critique then circulated like an underground document among Queen's Park officials.

Willis, who saw the issue as a clash between "lawyers' values" and "civil servants' values," emphasized that McRuer's report should not be regarded "as if it were the Ten Commandments, engraved on tablets of stone and brought down by Moses himself from Mount Sinai." That reverential respect, he said, characterized "how the Toronto Globe and Mail, opposition members of the Ontario legislature, and, to my own personal knowledge, many lawyers" were treating the document. He sought to "warn" deputy ministers to study carefully the recommendations pertaining to their departments so as to grasp which ones they could live with, and which ones they could not. Especially he wished to "alert" those civil servants who were responsible for the development of legal policy (deputy attorneys-general, lawyers in the civil service, legal draftsmen, and the like) against "hamstringing the social policies of their non-lawyer confreres in obedience to the dictates of this monolithic document." As someone well versed in, and sympathetic towards, the ways of the civil service, Willis expressed an alternate view to that of McRuer, a view resting on different values and—as he saw it—less ideologically driven. Unlike McRuer, Willis—and those who thought like him—believed that flexibility, simplicity, and informality were essential to the success of modern government.[38]

On a different plateau from Willis's critique, groups specifically affected by McRuer's recommendations also reacted negatively. For instance, school boards, which were deeply involved in the largest school-building boom of the province's history, were disturbed by the limitations McRuer would have placed on their powers of expropriation, and more than one police official warned against the restrictions that McRuer would have imposed on their powers of search, seizure, and detention.[39]

Yet such reactions were to be expected—many individuals in positions of authority had much power and prestige to lose, or at least were faced with major changes in the way they did business, if McRuer's reforms were implemented. To its credit, the Robarts government remained essentially unmoved by the criticisms of those with a vested interest in the preservation of the *status quo*. Protests still were heard, but, as McRuer's inquiry continued its work, it did so with the full support of the Ontario government.

The first legislative steps implementing the recommendations of McRuer's report were taken within months of the report being received. In the 1968–9 session of the legislature, three important bills were enacted—the Expropriations Act, the Provincial Courts Act, and the Law Enforcement Compensation Act (which five years later was broadened and renamed the Compensation for Victims of Crime Act). Elements in each of these statutes were subsequently adopted by other provinces. Other McRuer recommendations, more far-reaching in nature, took somewhat longer to be digested and reworked by the Ontario political and legal communities. Shortly after receiving McRuer's report, the Robarts government, with the aim of provoking discussion and constructive criticism, made public two draft bills governing the actions of tribunals: the first, a sort of procedural "bill of rights" designed to provide new protections for the rights of individuals, established minimum uniform procedures for the operation of tribunals; the second addressed the issue of applications for judicial reviews of tribunal decisions, suggesting changes to the process that would make it simpler, more expeditious and effective, and less costly. After many months of review, debate, and consultation in the legislature and with members of the public, the judiciary, lawyers, academics, and the various tribunals that would be directly affected, Attorney-General Wishart introduced improved versions of both bills on 4 June 1971. More debate followed, and then the two bills were enacted as the Statutory Powers Procedures Act and the Judicial Review Procedure Act. Both came into force in early March 1972.

IN 1968 AND 1969 McRuer basked in the widespread approval for his report and in the interest it was generating not just in Ontario but across the country and internationally. At the same time, he continued to work hard, assisting the government's efforts to transform his recommendations into statutes, presiding over the daily workings of his commissions on civil rights and law reform, granting media interviews, and replying to countless letters (from grade school students to law professors, housewives to cabinet ministers).

McRuer was active in another way, too. The reports of his civil rights commission, like those of the law reform commission, proceeded in typical McRuer fashion: they began with an historical discussion of the issue, an examination and comparison with the situation in other countries, and a carefully detailed "root of title" traced through decades and centuries of laws. This comprehensive and detailed research, done by the McRuer team of academically inclined lawyers over many months (and reviewed, word by word, idea by idea, by McRuer himself) meant that the reports—if for no other reason than their sheer size—were educationally rewarding but not especially easy to read. McRuer himself realized that not everyone would be poring over each chapter and verse of his "new testament," and so he happily accepted many of the numerous invitations for speaking engagements that were arriving at his Queen's Park office. He did not mind at all having so many people interested in him and what he had to say; in fact, in his own restrained sort of way, he enjoyed it immensely.

In his speeches McRuer did his best to put complex legal ideas into non-technical language. On 18 April 1968, with the goal of describing the general philosophy underlying the first report of his inquiry into civil rights, he addressed the Empire Club of Canada on the topic "The State and the Individual." Beginning with his usual idealism, McRuer asserted that "the object of the Royal Commission, over which I have the honour to preside, is to strengthen the foundations and pillars of justice by drawing blueprints for improvement of the laws of Ontario as they express the power of the state in relation to the individual." McRuer stressed that "the strongest arm of law enforcement is the conscience of those who live under the protection of the law. The law cannot be efficiently enforced unless the vast majority of the people honour and respect it." In his view, this meant that the law must keep pace with changing social values. "Laws that are not based on modern concepts of justice," McRuer maintained, "may have to be obeyed but they will not be respected." McRuer saw his task as ensuring that Ontario's laws would be grounded in such sound principles of justice that they would command the respect of all informed citizens. In concluding his address, McRuer outlined the guiding principles of his inquiry into civil rights: "Laws are not an end but a means to an end. The end should be the recognition of every individual as an individual human being with a dignity to be respected, with rights to be safeguarded by law and, at the same time, with obligations to his fellow human beings to be observed and, where necessary, to be enforced by the authority of the law."

Soon afterwards, on 9 May 1968, McRuer addressed the Civil Liberties Union at McGill University's Faculty of Law in Montreal. A few excerpts reflect the tenor of his remarks: "Individual rights, liberties and freedoms without mutual obligations is an anarchic concept"; "A man may suffer grave injustice because the laws in themselves may be unjust or there may be no procedural rules by which they are to be administered or the administration of the laws may be in the hands of careless or inadequately qualified administrators or judges"; "The command of the majority to control and direct a minority does not form a sound philosophy of good law"; "If the courts are to maintain their rightful place as an ultimate guardian of the rights of the individual they must provide simple and expeditious procedures devoid of technicalities and within the financial grasp of the humblest individual"; "The acts of public men in their capacity as legislators, [and] the procedure by which law is administered should be under the critical scrutiny of public opinion."

In this address, then, McRuer repeatedly emphasized that there can be no true justice in a system where individual rights are violated, but he also underlined his understanding that each individual in society has a responsibility to defend civil liberties in accordance with the principles of democracy. In taking this stance, McRuer was reminding his young and left-leaning audience that successful social reform depends not only on effective legislation but also on the personal commitment of well-informed citizens. This was McRuer at his best: at once inspiring and disarming, straightforward and complex. The thrust of his speech that night in Montreal was wholly predictable, but he drove his message home in ways that many in his audience found surprising and unsettling.

A few months later, on 14 August 1968, McRuer took up these themes in a slightly different guise when he spoke before the annual convention of the Ontario Association of Municipalities. On this occasion, McRuer discussed "the essential features of the democratic process as a safeguard of the freedom of the individual," and some of his words addressed the assault on authority that was beginning to take its toll as the 1960s wore on: "We start with this. There is inherent in the nature of man a desire to be free—to be free from restraint imposed on him by others who are in a position to exercise authority over him. But without discipline and order freedom cannot long endure. The desire to be free and the love of power are in conflict, and as a result of that conflict the democratic process has evolved. The attack on the democratic process from without is becoming more menacing in this country." McRuer went on to describe the responsibilities of municipal officials to protect democracy and thus the freedom of the individual in modern Ontario. "I think the time has come," he asserted, "when it is necessary for us to do a great deal of self-examination and examination of our social attitudes toward law enforcement." He called on the municipal politicians gathered before him to do their utmost to promote civil liberties, and he suggested some concrete measures they could take to do so. Once again, McRuer presented his principles in terms that would be especially meaningful to his particular audience.

On 8 October 1968 McRuer had an opportunity to be more academic when he travelled east to deliver an address marking the official opening of the new faculty of law building at the University of New Brunswick. Again, however, his message was clear: "It is essential to have a positive philosophy of justice ... But justice, no matter how it is defined, is a term relative to a changing society—a sense of justice is a developing thing. It takes on new dimensions of meaning as man moves forward and upward on his course of evolution ... Laws and justice are not synonymous terms ... In your quest for justice as teachers, students, and lawyers your task will be to keep under constant examination the laws of the nation, and your province, to determine how far there may be unjustified encroachments on the rights of the individual and how far proper safeguards are provided for the rights of the individual in the administration of those laws."

At the same time as McRuer was giving speeches on the subject of the law and civil rights, he and his colleagues on the commission were preparing a second report. This document was submitted to the government on 15 September 1969 and tabled in the legislature on 28 October. Like the first report, the second was a well-developed statement of McRuer's progressive traditionalism: change must come, and should be encouraged, but it must be firmly grounded in the best values of the past. Containing thirty-seven recommendations under the heading of "general safeguards against unjustified encroachments or infringements on the rights of the individual," the second report again advocated major reforms. Perhaps the most important called for the appointment of an ombudsman, a recommendation based on observations during McRuer's world tour of 1965 and subsequent studies of ombudsmen and similar officials in Finland, Norway, and Hawaii as well as in the provinces of Alberta, New Brunswick, and Quebec. McRuer adamantly insisted that Ontario's ombudsman "should not be considered as a substitute for a proper legal framework which provides adequate substantive and procedural safeguards for the rights of the individual." He also warned against two dangers: giving the ombudsman any powers or authority that might subvert the province's traditional legal systems, and allowing the ombudsman's office to become the tool of special interests. True to form, while insisting that the limits of the ombudsman's role in Ontario's legal system be strictly defined, McRuer wanted the ombudsman to act with flexibility and informality.[40]

Pursuing this line of reasoning, McRuer made other recommendations. He advocated the creation of a special judicial council—composed of the chief justice of Ontario, the chief justice of the High Court of Ontario, the senior member of the Supreme Court of Ontario, the chief judge of the county and district courts, and a district or county court judge designated by the chief judge of the county and district courts. The purpose of this council would be to consider complaints about the workings of the courts or the actions of specific judges. In cases where the Judicial Council determined that a trial had been conducted poorly, for example, proper compensation should be awarded to the aggrieved party. The Judicial Council, then, would act as a sort of further court of appeal to consider cases of alleged maladministration of justice in the ·courts.[41]

Another topic carefully examined in McRuer's second report was that of the French administrative courts. These courts acted as advisory bodies to government and as adjudicators on claims against administrative bodies within the government. McRuer studied such courts at length, and while he admitted that such courts had some usefulness in the civil law system of France, he came down strongly against their establishment in Ontario. Instead, McRuer insisted that the traditional common law courts of Ontario should be strengthened and reformed to provide better safeguards for the citizen against the arbitrary actions of government.[42]

McRuer's second report also took up the advisability of enacting a bill of rights for Ontario. His discussion of this subject, among his most important pronouncements on the Canadian constitution and the proper relationship between the legislature and the courts in a democracy, presaged comments he would make when appearing before a parliamentary committee a decade later. The views he expressed may have surprised those who knew of his reputation as a strong champion of civil rights and therefore assumed that he would favour entrenchment of civil rights in the constitution. These views also contradicted the stated agenda of the new Liberal prime minister, Pierre Trudeau, a fact that puzzled some because both McRuer and Trudeau appeared to share the objective of strengthening civil rights against the power of the state. What complicated the matter even more was that Trudeau linked his charter of rights to patriation of the constitution, a goal that McRuer himself had long cherished. Over thirty years earlier, in his 1935 "Reform by Reformers" election platform as the Liberal candidate in High Park, he had included a specific pledge to work for "amendment of the British North America Act...to give to the Canadian Parliament the right to amend its own constitution." His commitment to patriation, however, did not entail support of an entrenched bill of rights, and Trudeau's linking of the two caused him great difficulty.

Although McRuer saw nothing wrong with the Bill of Rights passed by the Diefenbaker government in 1960—a measure that had no constitutional status (as an act of parliament, it could be routinely changed by another act) and that was being narrowly interpreted in the courts—he had a much more negative view of the entrenched charter envisioned by Trudeau. Inspired by a "deep sense of British justice," as someone had once described it, and by his veneration of the British legal system, McRuer believed that an entrenched bill of rights would be alien to Canada's legal and democratic traditions, and, even worse, could lead over time to the erosion of individual civil rights and democratic accountability. Reflecting on the experience of the United States, McRuer argued that the American Bill of Rights elevated the Supreme Court to an unwarranted position of power which threatened at all times to erode the fabric of democracy in that country. McRuer believed that laws, to be just, must be subject to evolving social conditions, and he insisted that any statement of rights must remain flexible in the changing world. An entrenched bill of rights was, by its very nature, anything but flexible, certainly in contrast to the prevailing Canadian (and British) approach under which an individual remained free to do anything unless it was expressly prohibited by law.

McRuer was prepared, reluctantly, to agree to an entrenched national bill of rights, but he set an important condition: in the second report of the civil rights inquiry he stated unequivocally that "the Province of Ontario ought not to consider agreeing to any entrenchment of a national Bill of Rights binding the legislative power of the Province in those fields committed to it" unless patriation and a satisfactory amending process had been agreed on beforehand. As for an Ontario bill of rights, he had three caveats. First, any provincial bill of rights "should be confined to the definition of the individual rights which themselves are the foundations of parliamentary democracy and these should be expressed in carefully qualified terms." Secondly, the bill of rights should be enacted as an ordinary statute—so as not to have constitutional status—and in this respect would be like the existing Bill of Rights at the federal level. That document guaranteed security of the person, freedom of religion, freedom of speech and of the press, and freedom of assembly and association. McRuer wanted any new bill of rights enacted by the province, if there should be one at all, to contain the following rights and freedoms: freedom of conscience and religion; freedom of thought, expression, and communication; freedom of assembly and association; security of the person and freedom of movement; the right of every adult citizen to vote, to be a candidate for election to elective public office, and to be eligible for appointment to appointive public office on the basis of personal qualifications; the right to fair, effective, and authoritative procedures, in accordance with principles of natural justice, both for the determination of rights and obligations under the law and for liability to imprisonment or other penalty; and the right to have the courts presided over by an independent judiciary.

Finally, McRuer repeatedly stressed that Ontario's bill of rights must neither be too detailed nor too vague; that it should be considered a set of guidelines rather than a catalogue of immutable truths; and that it should in no way be allowed to interfere with the natural evolution of social standards.[43] "A philosophy of government should not be adopted," cautioned McRuer, "which deprives the people of the ultimate right to determine their own social affairs through democratic processes and transfers the final power of decision in certain areas to appointed officials—the judges."[44] Although he agreed that the legislature, under the leadership of the cabinet, should have the power to overrule the courts, he simply did "not think it is consistent with a true concept of democracy for a court of appointed judges to be able to make a law with far-reaching effects touching the lives of everyone in the country with no power in Parliament to alter it."[45] It would, McRuer concluded, "be unwise for a government to lock itself into a constitutional straitjacket where the making of new laws to meet changing social conditions would be made almost impossible by reason of the difficulty in obtaining relief through amendment of the constitution."[46]

The final report of McRuer's inquiry was submitted to the government on 22 February 1971. This third report, tabled in the legislature on 15 April, applied broad principles to specific cases. The principle was that safeguards had to be provided to protect the civil rights of the individual from the exercise of power by government-created tribunals. McRuer considered twenty-two of the most important tribunals in Ontario—such bodies as the Farm Products Marketing Board, the Ontario Municipal Board, the Liquor Control Board of Ontario, and the Ontario Labour Relations Board. The safeguards he sought were as follows: tribunals should be held fully accountable to the public through responsible political officials; the powers of all tribunals should be strictly defined by statute; and citizens should always have the right to appeal the decisions of tribunals.[47]

McRuer's work in this area was actually quite detailed. A separate chapter devoted to each of Ontario's government-created tribunals described its purpose and activities, examined the existing remedies an individual could take if adversely affected by the tribunal's operations, and documented any case law which had considered the civil rights of citizens in relation to that body. The powers a tribunal had been granted to investigate, to set rates, to seize property, to expropriate land, to enter premises, or to delegate its power to do any of these things—all were painstakingly examined for each of the twenty-two government bodies in question. For example, McRuer found that the powers conferred on the Ontario Energy Board under several different statutes were greatly confused and contained inconsistencies with respect to procedure and rights of appeal; he recommended "a complete revision of the Energy Board's powers and procedures."[48] For the Ontario Police Commission, McRuer detailed eight changes needed in the Police Act, such as keeping judges from being appointed to police commissions, requiring all police board regulations to be approved by the commission and to be open for public inspection, and bringing fundamental rules of fairness to internal police force investigations and disciplinary proceedings.[49] As for the Workmen's Compensation Board, some twenty-six statutory changes were deemed essential to bring the functioning of this body into line with McRuer's standards for the proper respect of civil rights—such as setting out the procedure for considering claims under the Workmen's Compensation Act, and restricting disclosure of information obtained by the board in an inquiry.[50] In total, McRuer proposed 372 separate recommendations relating to statutory tribunals.

McRuer's personal scorn for many aspects of the existing legal system came through with cold clarity in the third report. Turning to the question of crown liability and crown privilege, he came face to face with a doctrine that he felt had no place in a democratic society—namely, the rule that the "crown can do no wrong" and therefore cannot be sued by an injured or aggrieved victim. McRuer cited a recent statute, the Proceedings Against the Crown Act (1962–3), which had been heralded by the attorney-general as a measure designed to put relations between government and individuals on a fairer footing. He documented how "the benefits for the individual purported to be conferred under that Act have been taken away by special statutory provisions."[51] Seven recommendations followed. One of these called for repeal of "all statutory provisions relieving officers and servants of the Crown from liability for tortious acts." Another stipulated that, even where it was considered just for government employees to be relieved of liability for damage caused by their wrongful acts, provision should be made to maintain the liability of the employer (be it the crown, a crown agent, or a crown corporation). In no case, McRuer emphasized, should the victim of wrongful acts of officers or servants of the crown be left without a remedy.[52]

The pattern was now predictable, the process unstoppable: Queen's Park churned out more statutes embodying reforms recommended by McRuer. On 15 April 1971 Robarts's successor as Conservative premier, William Davis, tabled in the legislature the third report of McRuer's inquiry into civil rights, noting that the people of Ontario "owe Mr. McRuer a very large debt of gratitude and, I know, will come to realize this more and more as the years pass by." Then, on 4 June 1971, Davis proudly announced that "the Government of Ontario is placing before the people of this Province "the most comprehensive programme for the development of individual rights that has been developed within Canada." He then introduced four new statutes, all based on recommendations in McRuer's third report: the Public Inquiries Act, the Civil Rights Statute Law Amendment Act, An Act Governing the Exercise of Statutory Power Granted Tribunals, and An Act on Judicial Review of Exercise or Failure to Exercise Statutory Power. "When these Bills are brought into force," Davis told the legislature, "they will bring to the people of Ontario a code of administrative law procedure that will be the first of its kind in the Commonwealth."[53]

The names of these statutes, and others that were presented at this time, were scarcely designed to stir the populace; they were accurate, legalistic, and very much in the McRuer mode. Yet their substance embraced a new philosophy about law and the way statutes in the province were to be written and enforced. The Public Inquiries Act, for example, defined in considerable detail the operating procedures for royal commissions and other investigative bodies, while also giving new procedural protections to people affected by such inquiries.[54] The Civil Rights Statute Law Amendment Act amended some ninety-one provincial statutes, clarifying in each the nature and scope of decision-making powers and procedures in terms of their effects on individual rights.[55] The Judicial Review Procedure Act established a court of appeal, to be called the Divisional Court of the High Court of Justice for Ontario, that would hear appeals from the province's dozens of tribunals.[56] All three statutes were interrelated and their provisions, noted Attorney-General Allan Lawrence, the very man who had deserted the government side years before over the issue of the infamous Bill 99, "constitute a complex mosaic." Believing that the new statutes were "among the most progressive in the world," Lawrence added that they represented "far-reaching and substantive changes in the law relating to the powers of provincial tribunals and inquiries as they affect the rights of citizens and society as a whole."[57]

A common thread clearly woven throughout each of these measures was procedural fairness to the people who come before tribunals. From now on, whenever a citizen appeared before a provincial government tribunal for a hearing and a decision, he or she could virtually always assert and insist on eight basic rights: the right to reasonable notice of the time and place of the hearing; the right to reasonable information of any allegations respecting the character, propriety of conduct, or competence of a party if such issues are relevant; the right to a public hearing unless public security or intimate financial or personal matters are involved; the right to be represented by a lawyer or an agent; the right to call and examine witnesses, and to cross-examine other witnesses; the right to protection against self-incrimination respecting the use of evidence in any subsequent criminal proceedings (as far as the province could grant this right, criminal law being federal jurisdiction); the right to reasonable adjournments of a hearing; and the right to a written decision, with reasons, on request.

Such provisions make it clear that McRuer's civil rights commission radically changed the orientation of government in Ontario. In place of the old emphasis on the organic nature of society, the collective interests of the community, and the broad social and economic purposes of government institutions, the McRuer commission substituted a new focus on the individual. Following its reports, individuals, armed with legal rights and represented by lawyers, gained new recognition and status in Ontario—a development that pleased McRuer greatly. Although he had never succeeded in getting elected to parliament, he finally had the satisfaction of seeing many of the fundamental tenets of his liberal philosophy made the law of the land.

BY THE TIME McRuer was finished with his unprecedented inquiry into civil rights, the three separate reports he had produced stretched to five volumes and 2,281 pages and contained some 976 specific recommendations. Together, the legislative measures that followed these reports affected almost every private undertaking regulated in some way by government. For example, Queen's Park could no longer suspend the licence of a used-car dealer, a mortgage broker, or a pest exterminator without a hearing. The acts strengthened the legal protection available to collection agencies, foster homes, day nurseries, the tourist industry, slaughter houses, employment agencies, ambulance operators, truckers, welfare recipients, and medical researchers.

McRuer's role in bringing these changes to pass was widely recognized and admired in legal circles. For example, Willard Z. Estey, then vice-president elect of the Canadian Bar Association, said in an interview with the *Toronto Star* that the legislative reforms stemming from McRuer's inquiry into civil rights "brought a new code of morality" to administrative law in Ontario.[58] Similarly, John Yaremko, an able lawyer and one of the most astute ministers in Robarts's cabinet, became an ardent admirer of McRuer as the civil rights commission matured. "You can talk about Magna Charta and habeas corpus," Yaremko pointed out, "but if a person running a restaurant or operating a taxi-cab can't get the little slip of paper—the permit, or licence, from government—on which his livelihood depends, then of what value are these more celebrated freedoms?" In conversation with friends, Yaremko stressed the position of the "little guy" who must confront the massive bureaucracy of government, with its complex rules and often intimidating procedures. "McRuer understood that need," Yaremko concluded, "and that in simple terms is what the Statutory Powers Procedure Act is really all about."[59]

Within the academic community, too, positive appraisals of the McRuer report emerged after the report's release, and they were followed by others in later years. For instance, a dean of one Canadian law school said of McRuer's civil rights work, "It is often referred to as a monument but I like to regard as a beacon."[60] Similarly, in September 1981 three professors from the department of political economy at the University of Toronto, George Heiman, John Hodgetts, and Glenda Patrick, appeared before a legislative committee to comment on legislation that would revise and extend the protection of human rights in Ontario. After noting that "the relationship between state, rights, and law" had been "admirably defined" by McRuer in his "monumental work," they drew heavily on McRuer's report for their own analysis and presentation. It was their view that, in "Canadian political literature," the McRuer report ranked with the seminal Rowell-Sirois report on federal-provincial relations four decades earlier.[61]

The analogy was perceptive. In their constitutional scope and political impact, McRuer's civil rights reports were indeed the equivalent of the report of the Rowell-Sirois Commission. Not only did McRuer's hundreds of recommendations generate fundamental statutory changes within Ontario, deeply altering what might be considered parts of the province's constitution, but they had a significant ripple effect on other parts of Canada. What is more, McRuer's inquiry into civil rights transformed the province's political culture over time, in much the same way that the Charter of Rights and Freedoms would, after 1982, remake the entire country's intellectual foundations by infusing public discourse with a rights-based and legally oriented perspective.

Through the three reports of McRuer's civil rights inquiry, the informing spirit and essential principle was that all people are equal before the law and, at the same time, no one is exempt from the law. The concept of "rule of law" is, of course, at the very heart of the body of public law that governs the relationship between individuals and the state. As formulated initially by the English jurist and scholar Albert Venn Dicey, the doctrine of the rule of law rests on two main propositions: first, "that no man is punishable or can be lawfully made to suffer in body or goods except for a distinct breach of law established in the ordinary legal manner before the ordinary courts of the land"; and secondly, "that no man is above the law, but that every man, whatever his rank or condition, is subject to the ordinary law of the realm and amenable to the jurisdiction of the ordinary tribunals."[62] Interwoven with these ideas was the maxim that, whatever the law was, judges and courts were responsible for giving it meaning. Central to the Dicey position, too, was the liberal assumption that "society as a whole was protected if individual rights were protected."[63]

McRuer's ideas about the rule of law and the rights of individuals were largely derived from Dicey, and so one lawyer, Robert Macaulay, has said that Dicey's views "became embedded in the law of Ontario through the medium of Chief Justice McRuer."[64] Yet this is only partly true. While McRuer was profoundly attracted to Dicey's position about "the rule of law," he was more than a blind disciple. Whereas Dicey accepted the statutes of parliament "only reluctantly, because they were not proclamations of the court,"[65] McRuer's reports were replete with references to the democratic accountability of elected representatives, the central law-making role of the legislature, and the pivotal responsibility of cabinet ministers. In this important respect McRuer adjusted Dicey's ideas so as to match them more harmoniously to the judicial-legislative balance appropriate to Ontario as a modern democratic state, and with his own deeply held views about the primacy of elected law-makers over appointed ones. To make this adjustment, McRuer drew on the more democratic philosophy elaborated by Sir Arthur Goodhart and Sir Ivor Jennings.

That being said, however, it is clear that McRuer's central doctrine— the rule of law—assumed that the public interest was largely identical with the protection of the individual, and that this protection was safe-guarded best by following procedures resembling those used by judges in court proceedings. In his first report McRuer noted that "the Rule of Law should be the paramount aim of every sound legal system as a pro-tection against any disposition on the part of those with power to exer-cise it arbitrarily or capriciously."[66] No one has any difficulty accepting this statement, observes Macaulay, "so long as one does not read into it that private rights are necessarily synonymous with the public good."[67] Macaulay, like John Willis, argues that McRuer's reports on civil rights led to the judicialization of administrative powers and procedures in Ontario, creating a system based on a judicial rather than a functional approach. As an alternative to McRuer's vision, Macaulay cites the idea of "curial deference," developed in Canadian labour law cases from 1945 to the late 1970s first by Chief Justice Bora Laskin and then by Chief Justice Brian Dickson. This idea maintains that courts should defer to and not overturn an agency decision unless it is "patently unreasonable." As Macaulay notes, Laskin and Dickson "extended to agencies greater latitude to determine matters of policy and law without interference or second guessing by the courts."[68]

In the end, McRuer chose an approach that was consistent with his own philosophy and experiences. His goal as head of the civil rights inquiry was a comprehensive program for the development and protec-tion of civil rights in Ontario, and no one would deny that he was suc-cessful in achieving just that. Thirty years later, some may claim that his "identification of the public interest with the rights of the individuals and the insistence on a judicial model" for the operation of government bod-ies "lies at the root of many of the problems faced by agencies today."[69] However, an equally potent source of this "problem"—if indeed it is a problem—is the constitutionally entrenched Charter of Rights and Free-doms, about which McRuer himself had grave misgivings. Furthermore, while there are admittedly difficulties in the present-day administrative operation of government in Ontario, some of these difficulties are no large price to pay for accountability in the exercise of power and for safe-guarding the rights of the individual from the might of the state in late-twentieth-century Canada.

In the midst of his ground-breaking inquiry into civil rights, McRuer experienced a heart-breaking personal tragedy. During the year 1966, Mary McRuer was dying of cancer. When the end finally came on 17 December, the man who always kept his feelings to himself broke down. Although he did not talk much to people about Mary's death, Jim's family and professional colleagues could see that he was "just overcome, devastated" by his loss.[70]

Mary McRuer was a woman who had gone her own way, and indeed in some respects she had been forced to be independent because of Jim's obsessive commitment to his career. They had successfully weathered the normal rough patches in a marriage and over time had fashioned a happy life together built on deep affection and mutual concern. Mary had been extremely supportive of Jim's work, and she proudly kept scrapbooks of newspaper articles recording the progress of his career. Jim, for his part, wrote her constantly while on his seemingly endless travels around Ontario, across Canada, and abroad, and these letters were full of tenderness and love.[71]

Mary's funeral service was a small, private affair held at home.[72] Although they had been pillars of the church, and Jim would make an endowment to Bloor Street United Church in Mary's name, he was too distraught for a large church service. Mary was buried at Ayr. The very next week, Jim put the house up for sale and moved into an apartment on Deer Park Crescent in the Yonge-St. Clair area of Toronto. In the months that followed he was at loose ends, but his state of mind improved considerably when he started seeing Robena Dow, Mary's first cousin. Jim, always mindful of his public reputation, asked the advice of family, friends, and colleagues, and then took the fateful step, marrying Robena in March 1968.[73] He told his daughter Katherine, "We'll put your mother's memory reverently away, but we won't forget her."

Through all the ups and downs, of course, McRuer had his work. When the civil rights inquiry concluded in 1971, he could turn his attention more fully to another major undertaking, the Ontario Law Reform Commission. His involvement with this body kept him busy throughout the 1960s and 1970s, and, like his work on the civil rights inquiry, was to result in major changes to Ontario's legal system. Reflecting on both commissions towards the end of his life, McRuer remarked, with a twinkle in his eye, that "I really did my best work after I turned 70!" This quip did not do justice to his achievements in earlier years, but there was more than a grain of truth in it all the same.

15

REFORMING THE LAW

JIM MCRUER was a fulfilled man in the 1960s and 1970s. Not only did his civil rights commission give him an opportunity to further a cherished cause—the protection and enhancement of individual liberty against those who wielded authority in the name of the state—but his contemporaneous chairmanship of the Ontario Law Reform Commission (OLRC) provided a vehicle through which he could pursue the other abiding passion of his life. In truth, not even a guardian angel could have written a job description more suited to Jim McRuer's interests, convictions, and talents than the one he obtained as head of the OLRC. He resolved to make the most of it. The incessant activity that characterized the commission's work during these decades was a direct measure of McRuer's determination to conduct a thorough overhaul of the laws of Ontario.

In contrast to the civil rights commission, which was operated as a one-man show, the law reform commission was a larger body directed by five commissioners including McRuer. Nevertheless, McRuer was undoubtedly the dominant figure on the commission. His interests largely shaped its agenda, and his leadership ability was one of the key reasons for its success. The people who worked with him on the commission were talented people in their own right, and they, too, deserve credit for the law reforms that flowed from their recommendations. Yet even they recognized that McRuer was their leader and that, without him, the commission (if it had existed at all) would have been a much different—and more cautious—body. They might even have admitted that a law reform commission without McRuer was inconceivable, so closely did he come to be identified with it. From the very first, the commission bore McRuer's personal stamp, and over the years its many reports reflected his distinctive vision of the law and of society. The Ontario Law Reform Commission was, in essence, the institutionalization of James Chalmers McRuer.

REFORMING AND CHANGING THE LAW so it would be "relevant" to people had, broadly speaking, been McRuer's bread and butter for most of his professional life. Through all his years in the law—as a lawyer, a judge, a teacher of police and law students, a key figure leader in the legal profession's associations, and, especially, a participant in over a dozen royal commissions and judicial inquiries—he had been calling for a more formalized and systematic approach to reviewing and revising laws.

This mission can be seen taking form as early as 1922. "A very elementary knowledge of history tells us that social problems of today ought not to be adjusted in light of conditions of the eighteenth and nineteenth centuries," asserted a thirty-one-year-old Jim McRuer in 1922. "It is neither just nor equitable that our Courts should be bound by precedents of English law, notwithstanding their age, or the customs and habits of life in vogue at the time the precedent was created." Stressing that "social conditions change with time," McRuer added his belief that a Canadian court's decision "must in every case be relative to the prevailing social conditions insofar as such decisions involve social or public problems."[1]

At this stage, McRuer was focusing on the role of individual judges in revamping legal doctrines in contemporary ways; he had not yet broadened the quest for systematic reform of the law beyond a liberal-minded exhortation to the judiciary. That would come later. Still, it is significant that, even in these early years, McRuer insisted on placing issues of legal reform in their broad social context. This approach was just as evident in a 1922 address to the Toronto Lawyers' Club. At that time, the lanky and earnest McRuer, a young crown attorney who had been married for only two years, decried the "archaism" in Canada's marriage laws, especially the law of alimony, a topic on which he had also published an article in the January 1922 issue of the *Canada Law Journal*. His call for "an extension of women's rights under the law" was not mere youthful idealism; it reflected an abiding conviction and was to become one of his familiar refrains in the years ahead.[2]

By 1938 a more seasoned McRuer had further developed his ideas about how laws should be modernized. It was no longer only a matter for a progressive judiciary. On 9 November 1938 McRuer wrote a letter to Ontario Attorney-General Gordon Conant, who was also interested in the matter of law reform. Emphasizing that "a large measure of kudos [would] come to the Government by reason of the appointment of a Royal Commissioner to investigate law reform," McRuer made two suggestions which anticipated to a remarkable degree what would actually come to pass a quarter-century later. The first was that the government's investigation of this issue be headed, not by a lawyer in active practice, but by someone more like a retiring judge; the second was that the process be "more formal" than Conant had proposed. "I think the general public will entirely agree with a desire to simplify procedure and reduce expense," McRuer noted. "Many things of vast importance could be dealt with and your hands would be strengthened by having the report of a man of outstanding ability who had made a careful investigation." McRuer and Conant met over lunch several times to discuss this subject, but, in the end, no formal investigation of law reform issues was conducted.

Apart from his general quest—which for the time being seemed to be getting nowhere—McRuer also raised specific issues of law reform with Conant. In the late 1930s a series of letters issued forth from the law offices of McRuer, Mason, Cameron, and Brewin counselling Conant on a wide range of topics. For example, while McRuer believed that grand juries should continue to operate, he proposed that they follow new procedures which would protect the interests of taxpayers and the accused alike. Similarly, he explained how the Criminal Code's provisions regarding traffic deaths should be reworded so as to achieve greater precision; specifically, these provisions should apply to those "in charge" of a motor vehicle rather than just those "having the care" of it, the object being to place criminal liability on the perpetrator. As McRuer said, "I do think it is important to use the most apt phraseology possible in framing the criminal law."[3]

Equally illustrative of McRuer's approach to law reform in this period was his position on the long-smouldering controversy surrounding financial payments on the loss of life. For years, judges and lawyers felt that the common law was unjust in refusing to recognize liability for damages in cases where one person had negligently killed another. It was true that damages could be recoverable under the Fatal Accidents Act, but, as a general principle of law, if one person killed another through negligence, he or she was ironically in a much better position than if the victim had been merely maimed. The situation was obviously absurd, and the judiciary's tendency increasingly had been to limit this doctrine of the common law. Where the deceased person lived for some time after sustaining injury, for example, judges came to recognize the victim's legal right to sue for out-of-pocket expenses, pain, and suffering. Then, early in 1938, a decision of the House of Lords (applicable in Canada) in the case of *Rose* v. *Ford* recognized a further right, namely, the right to sue for damages for the loss suffered by reason of the injury, notwithstanding that the victim had died. The implication of this decision disturbed many people in Ontario, and on 2 March 1938 MPP Ian Strachan introduced a private member's bill intended to limit again the recovery of damages for loss of life.

By this time, Jim McRuer had already given the matter of financial damages for loss of life "some study," prepared a substantial memorandum on the legal principles involved, and, just the month before, addressed fellow Toronto lawyers at considerable length on the topic. Learning from his morning newspaper on March 3rd that the attorney-general would face questions in the legislature about this issue, McRuer immediately wrote Conant that same day, urging a cautious but firm approach based partly on principle and partly on clear-eyed realism. McRuer could see the point of those who objected to what the House of Lords had decided, and he understood why Strachan proposed a statute-made law to deny Ontarians a new judge-made right, but he did not agree with them. "I think we should be careful," he advised the attorney-general, "in flying to legislation to take away from the King's subjects a right of action that is so reasonable." He was also unimpressed by the suggestion quoted in the press that this right to sue for damages "tends to ambulance chasing." "Surely subjects are not to be deprived of their just and legal rights because some lawyers may indulge in this practise," he retorted. McRuer's extensive practice in the 1930s dealing with automobile injury claims had shown him that there was something worse to be concerned about than the prospect of a few lawyers chasing ambulances to get legal business. "As against this it is well-known that many insurance companies ambulance chase in another way, that is, they pursue the injured person for the purpose of getting a settlement and a release before he has had an opportunity of having legal advice, this for the obvious purpose of depriving him of his just legal rights." In words that echoed the approach of his political hero, Mackenzie King, McRuer then advised Conant that the matter should "be permitted to develop in order that all the aspects of the situation become evident." Then, "if after they are all known some restrictive legislation is necessary in the interests of the people of the province as a whole," such legislation might be considered. In the meantime, however, "it would seem a bit hasty to proceed in advance of England from whence the decisions have emanated." That same week McRuer learned, not only that Conant found his legal memorandum "of great use," but that the attorney-general's views were identical to his own and that he was very glad to have McRuer's timely opinion on how to handle the situation politically.

McRuer's thoughts on this occasion revealed both his respect for judge-made law, especially when it represented a judicial effort to protect a citizen's rights by standing up to influential insurance companies, and his protective concern for the law itself. To his mind, laws should not be changed hastily or in piecemeal fashion or in response only to the demands of special-interest groups and those (such as Ian Strachan) who spoke for them. The law had to be protected from those who wanted to get moving even before they had plotted a course, and who might well panic and start hacking mindlessly at everything that obstructed their way. At the same time, government should also defend society against the exploitative designs of human predators eager to take advantage of people who had become lost in the legal maze. Still another danger that had to be taken into account was plain fatigue with the complexity of issues of law reform, for such fatigue could lead to hasty and ill-advised changes simply to be done with the matter. Inescapably, for McRuer, the controversy sparked by Strachan's bill highlighted all of these dangers and emphasized the need for a more formalized structure to deal with questions of law reform. "This brings home very forcibly the wisdom of the suggestion you made the other night," he told Conant, "to have the services of an unbiased committee to give a cross-section of views on these subjects of pure law." The idea was maturing.

Even during the war, when most people put such matters as law reform aside, McRuer persisted. After all, were Canadians not fighting Nazi Germany in order to save democracy and the rule of law? In a 1942 speech McRuer again called, this time publicly, for a royal commission on law reform.[4] He also continued to deal with the specific changes needed to improve the workings of the law. In this he was being pragmatic, for he realized that he could accomplish many things while waiting for the golden day of full-blown law reform.

When talking with police officers during his lectures at the police school during the war years, McRuer learned that a police officer would frequently be called upon to deal with a person who had become mentally ill and dangerous. Under the existing law, the officer had no power to take the ill person into custody. If the officer chose to proceed under the provisions of the Mental Hospitals Act, which necessarily contained safeguards to protect individuals from unwarranted confinement, the requisite delays and administrative procedures meant that, in the meantime, the mentally ill person could injure himself or others. In such cases, the police officers told McRuer, they would take the person into custody and then, to protect themselves, lay a charge of vagrancy. This deeply angered McRuer, who recognized the procedure as being "wrong and illegal." "A man is not a criminal because he has become mentally ill," McRuer asserted indignantly. He explained to the policemen in his class that the "alleged protection" the officers thought they were achieving with the vagrancy charge "is no protection at all because it is merely a sham." The officers then asked their instructor what they should do in the circumstances.

That was invitation enough to McRuer, who promptly launched himself into the task of providing an acceptable answer. To discuss the matter in both its practical and legal dimensions, he met with Bill Common and C.P. Hope of the attorney-general's department and with others responsible for policing and crown prosecutions. Eventually he reached the conclusion that there should be legislation permitting a police officer to take any person into protective custody under certain strict limits. True to form, McRuer followed this up with yet another letter, dated 19 March 1942, to Attorney-General Conant. In it he set out the specific amendment he believed necessary to cope with this civil liberties issue. The new statutory power would permit an officer to take into custody a person whom "he has reasonable and probable grounds to believe is mentally ill and likely to do injury to himself or any other person, with a supplemental provision that no person taken into custody shall be detained by the police officer longer than until noon the next day without taking proceedings under ... the Mental Hospitals Act." McRuer described his formulation as "a rough suggestion," but he assured Conant that some form of legislation along these lines would be an improvement over the "irregular and undesirable proceedings" that currently prevailed, particularly in the outlying districts of Ontario where an officer might have to travel some distance before he could get to a justice of the peace or deliver the ill person to a hospital. Legislation was then drafted to amend the Mental Hospitals Act in the way McRuer suggested.

McRuer's calls for law reform continued following his elevation to the bench; indeed, his feelings on the issue ran so deep that, even as a member of the normally discreet judiciary, he remained outspoken. His most detailed and eloquent statements on this subject came in the early 1960s, when his mounting annoyance with the *status quo* pushed him to mount a public campaign for law reform. As chief justice he certainly had a platform, and, nearing the mandatory retirement age of seventy-five, he felt that he could speak his mind with impunity. The first of these statements, on 7 January 1963, was, as one observer subsequently noted, "the genuine origin" of the Ontario Law Reform Commission. Speaking in the convocation room in Osgoode Hall after the "red mass" at St. Michael's Cathedral, a special service that inaugurates the opening of a new session of Ontario's courts, McRuer delivered a carefully prepared message which strained the conventional limits of what judges could safely say about public policy, and he did so before an assembly of legal and political luminaries that included Premier John Robarts and Mr. Justice Taschereau of the Supreme Court of Canada.

In his thin and high-pitched voice, McRuer invited those present to consider how far the courts of justice were "really accomplishing their purpose," and he pointed to the need to reform laws "that have never been good laws" and "laws that at one time served society well but with changing conditions have lost their social usefulness." Any thoughtful lawyers of experience, he contended, "could prepare quite a catalogue of laws and procedures that serve the ends of justice ill." Then, fixing his gaze directly upon Robarts, McRuer's voice rose slightly higher as he informed everyone that he wanted "to take advantage of this opportunity to make one or two constructive suggestions, particularly in view of the fact that we have present the Prime Minister of this Province, who is himself a lawyer." Robarts was not a man given to squirming, but at that moment he likely braced himself.

"All Governments and all Universities sponsor vast schemes of research into all branches of science," the chief justice began, laying out the arguments and evidence for the case he was about to make. "We have huge sums of money spent on research on how to make men live longer, and how to kill men quicker. We have research on how to get to the moon and research into the habits and customs of beetles, but I know of nowhere in Canada where there is any organized legal research directed to improve our laws and our legal procedures so that justice in its true sense may be better administered." McRuer deplored this state of affairs. He then noted how the attorney-general of Ontario had the benefit of a committee on the administration of justice which had worked well in suggesting improvements in the law, but McRuer asserted that this body was neither intended nor equipped for research work, consisting as it did of busy lawyers and judges. "Legal research to be effective must be organized, independent, and financed as all other research," said McRuer, in a restatement of his 1938 argument. "It should be so organized as to harness not only the experience and wisdom of judges and practising lawyers but the vast resources of academic scholarship that we have in Canada today."

Nine days later, on 16 January, McRuer returned to the same themes in an address delivered at Osgoode Hall to the York County Law Association. Asked in advance for his topic, the chief justice said tersely that he was going to speak about "bad laws." That sounded interesting. The word got around, and newspaper reporters were out in force when McRuer approached the podium. They were not disappointed. On this occasion, in contrast to his usual practice of reading a carefully prepared and lengthy text, McRuer came as clóse as he ever did to improvisation—the pages before him contained only some topic headings and a few typed extracts from old law reports. What was just as striking, and certainly refreshing for both the lawyers and journalists present, the chief justice seemed to have abandoned caution and was speaking instead with deep feeling.

McRuer's speech began with the assertion that "in every field of law and procedure there are old outworn laws that are quite inconsistent with the society in which we live, laws that are not founded on any modern concept of justice." He then proceeded to give a few examples of laws that were "unjust, outmoded, thoroughly bad, and lacking in common sense." The first was drawn from the law of wills and trusts and featured a lengthy treatment of "the rule against perpetuities." This rule is based on the common law principle that there must be certainty about just who is to receive bequests under someone's will in order to prevent heirs from appearing (that is, being born) without any time limit, or, in perpetuity. The need for such a rule arises when a will is unclear, naming a class of beneficiaries rather than specifically naming each child. In these cases, judges must interpret what the testator really meant by "constructing" the will. McRuer had done just that on many occasions, the most memorable example being the case of a little girl named Linda.

The case, argued before McRuer by J.J. Robinette, involved a will with a bequest for the children of the deceased and his grandchildren, with a residuary gift to his great-grandchildren. The inheritance for his great-grandchildren was intended for their education, and in this group the dead man had included a little girl called Linda because, as he had said, she was about the same age as his great-grandchildren. Robinette cited the rule against perpetuities to support his position that this bequest to little Linda was void. His clients, the children, did not want to see their inheritance reduced, and this was the legal gambit that best served their interests. The assumption of the common law was that a woman could give birth to a child even if she was a hundred years old, and Robinette therefore argued that this class of great-grandchildren was still (potentially) incomplete and so that portion of the will failed because of uncertainty about just who the recipients might be. It was being assumed that the granddaughters could still have children for years and years to come. That meant the gift failed, none of the great-grandchildren (or Linda) would get anything, and the inheritance of the grandchildren would accordingly be greater. McRuer had "no sympathy for this nonsense." He reached the judicial conclusion that the deceased clearly had in his mind a group that was composed of children who were already living and who would be living at his death, and not prospective children who might be born years afterwards. On this basis, McRuer got past the dreaded rule about perpetuities, upholding the entire will as valid. The great-grandchildren received their educational bequests, and so did little Linda.[5]

In his 1963 address to the York County Law Association, McRuer drew on this experience when he commented, in reference to the rule against perpetuities, that the law is often an "ass." The stupid assumption that a woman is able to bear children whatever her age—"9 or 90"—can prevent inheritances being received by the intended beneficiary. It had been questioned as long ago as 1832, McRuer noted, but it was still present in the law, denying fairness in the distribution of inheritances. "It's this sort of thing one loses patience with when we talk about what great laws we have," he chided.

Moving on to other examples, McRuer pointed out how a summary conviction, with a fine, could be taken to the Court of Appeal, while a *habeas corpus* application—such as an objection to extradition—could not. He explained how dogs under the common law had more rights than humans, because they were entitled to one bite. A child might be brutally attacked by a dog without redress unless it could be proven that the dog had bitten someone before. "The onus should be on the dog owner to prove the dog was not vicious," he argued. "The owner should get insurance, giving victims compensation." McRuer next described how intentional killing may sometimes be non-capital murder, but a person who accidently kills while committing robbery is guilty of capital murder. "That doesn't seem right," he concluded.

Following his speech, McRuer received a standing ovation and reporters swarmed around him to get more details about "bad laws" and his opinions about them. The next day, newspapers well beyond Toronto carried the story of this senior jurist's crusade for law reform. In addition to extensive news reports, numerous editorials endorsed both McRuer's quest for a solid program of law reform and his belief that lawyers themselves should be promoting this cause. In a lengthy and closely-reasoned editorial on 19 January, the *Globe and Mail* noted that it came as "something of a shock" to hear from the "eminent judge" about laws that seemed illogical or simply absurd. Analyzing several factors that gave rise to poor law, the *Globe* fully supported McRuer's position: "What is needed, as Chief Justice McRuer suggested, is an organized program of research to bring to light the laws which for one reason or another may be productive of injustice rather than justice." The next day the *Toronto Telegram* stated that it saw "much merit" in McRuer's appeal, noting that he had called for the establishment of organized legal research on the pattern of the American Law Institute or the Lord Chancellor's Committee of Britain, and it concluded that "if the lawyers take the lead as Chief Justice McRuer suggests, they should have no trouble getting support for such a great public project as a legal research institute." The day after, the *Toronto Star* joined in, stating that while there "may be a tendency to dismiss many of the chief justice's examples as legal curiosities," his criticisms "should not be shrugged off." They "come from a distinguished jurist of extensive experience," the *Star* said, and many of the unjust and "unright laws he cites are in common, everyday use." Neither should the legal profession dismiss McRuer's plea that it expose and seek to correct these unjust laws, instructed the *Star*'s editorialists, on the excuse that laws are drawn up by governments and so government should make sure the laws are sound and equitable. "While every legislature does have a legal department to help it draw up new statutes and revise old ones, it is in the courts that deficiencies and anomalies are brought to light." The profession was urged to "take up the chief justice's challenge."

McRuer's selection of "bad laws" shows that he had come to understand what got press. The *Star*'s headline "Dog Has More Rights Than Man" was mere trivia. Similarly, McRuer's example of a New Brunswick law that prescribed the death penalty for adulterers might have made interesting conversation, but it was a provision never used because, among other reasons, under the Canadian constitution only parliament could enact such an enforceable penalty. Given the many profound changes he sought in the law and the administration of justice, McRuer had run the risk of starting to sound like an old man who was losing perspective, even becoming slightly unhinged. Yet the publicity trick seemed to work. Public support for his cause was growing, as a flurry of correspondence as well as supportive editorials attested, and a number of lawyers—following the chief justice's precedent—began commenting on laws that required reforming.

One of the many interesting exchanges following the speech of 16 January took McRuer's mind back twenty-five years to the days of the Archambault commission. On 31 January Justice Joseph Archambault, just about to celebrate his eighty-fourth birthday, in good health except for some trouble with his legs, and still, as he said, "very much interested in legal problems," wrote McRuer a letter from his Drummond Street apartment in Montreal. Indicating that *La Presse* had reported McRuer's speech, Archambault expressed agreement that "some of our laws can be amended or corrected." He acknowledged McRuer's point about the robber being hanged for accidentally killing someone, but he observed that this was "according to the criminal law which is English" and suggested that it might "remain as it is, otherwise thieves would not abstain from murder." Then he turned to McRuer's example of the child who, after being bitten by a dog, has no recourse against the owner unless it can be proved that the dog had a history of biting people; in this instance, Archambault "entirely" agreed with McRuer's view that the onus should be on the dog's owner to prove that it is not vicious. He added, with pride, that "our Civil Code article 1055 states that 'the owner of an animal is responsible for the damage it causes, whether it is under his care or under that of his servant or has strayed or escaped from it.' You see that our law is different from yours."

McRuer replied on 1 February. "I am conducting an agitation to have some form of organized legal research in Ontario sponsored either by some foundation or by the government," he explained. Noting that Archambault's letter "points out how much benefit could be derived from research that would bring to the attention of the common law provinces some of the provisions of the Quebec Civil Code," McRuer considered the code's provisions regarding damage done by an animal to be "much more just than the common law which is affected by some of the early English traditions which have no doubt been influenced by the English-man's love of hunting."

Archambault was not the only prominent figure interested in McRuer's ideas in law reform. Apart from newspaper editors, a number of important players in Ontario's political and legal establishment had also reached the conclusion that the time was right for a thorough renovation of the province's legal edifice. McRuer's long crusade for the launching of a formal, structured campaign of law reform—now taken to new heights by his "red mass" and "bad laws" speeches—was finally on the verge of success.

OF ALL THE PEOPLE hearing McRuer's appeal for law reform, no one would be more affected than Premier John Robarts. Intrigued by McRuer's ideas, Robarts spoke with his attorney-general, Fred Cass, about responding to the chief justice's challenge. Yet the project began slowly, to say the least. It was fully a year later, very early in 1964, that the next step was taken. The occasion was a meeting of the committee Cass had set up to advise on legal problems requiring attention. McRuer came to the meeting at Cass's invitation, and there he heard a suggestion that the law regarding "dower"—the right of a married woman to claim, on the death of her husband, part of his property for her support and that of her children—should be abolished. The lawyer making this suggestion observed that no woman had ever asserted in modern times her right to dower, but the legal profession still required all these married women to sign dower-release documents, a waste of time and money which showed how the law was a slave to an outdated provision that should long ago have been scrapped.

McRuer was utterly appalled by what he was hearing. The proposal was another example of the kind of "law reform" that infuriated him. It was half-baked law reform, and McRuer always adhered to the maxim of an earlier chief justice of Ontario, Sir William Meredith, that "half-measures which mitigate but do not remove injustice are, in my judgement, to be avoided." Had nobody heard what he had said so plainly, on so many occasions, to so many people, including in his speech a year ago on the opening of the courts, about the need for systematic and well-researched law reform? "If you take away dower," he asked the lawyer pointedly, "what rights has a married woman got?" In a voice that barely concealed his rage, McRuer said firmly, "Don't take something away until you know what you're going to put in its place!" Then he sat back, his arms folded tightly, in stony and severe silence.[6]

Later that same day, deputy attorney-general Rendall Dick, who had been present at the committee meeting, showed McRuer a handwritten

draft of a proposal for a law reform body. It was a very loose draft, infor-
mally presented and, it seemed, hastily prepared. Scanning the proposal,
McRuer noticed that the body would be set up as a unit within the attorney-general's department. "No," he said without hesitation, "that's not
what you want at all. You want an independent body that will ..." Dick
interrupted: "Will have its own staff and appoint its own researchers and
so on?" "Yes, exactly," rejoined McRuer, a more cheerful tone reentering
his voice. "It should be an independent body away from the Attorney
General's Department, report to him, true, but set up so that it will operate independently as an independent commission."[7]

An act of the Ontario legislature would be needed to bring this law
reform commission into being, and Rendall Dick quickly took charge
of getting draft legislation together. To come up with the right statutory
framework for the new process of law reform, Dick and his colleagues
certainly enjoyed plenty of scope: there was no model in existence anywhere in the Commonwealth for a law reform commission. The only
example on hand in Ontario itself was the in-house attorney-general's
committee on the administration of justice, but its role had been to
make confidential advisory reports to the attorney-general, and even
then only on topics chosen by him. Neither of these features satisfied the
new demands for a process that would be both open and independent.
Besides, as McRuer himself had pointed out in his address of 7 January
1963, the committee was not a good model because it was not designed
to do research work. Even worse, it was not independent! Neighbour-
ing New York State's Law Revision Commission was briefly considered
by those framing the Ontario law reform commission act, but its narrow focus and limited role provided no helpful pattern either. Certainly
McRuer was looking for a body with a far broader mandate, perhaps, as
he had suggested in his speech of 7 January 1963, along the lines of the
American Law Institute, the American Judicature Society, and the lord
chancellor's law reform committee in Britain.

Meanwhile, as the drafting of the legislation was under way, McRuer
(as recounted in the previous chapter) met with Robarts and Attorney-
General Wishart and emerged from the premier's office with an agreement that he would be named chairman of two separate commissions:
the surprise one on civil rights and the one on law reform that he had
long dreamt of. Shortly afterwards, on 5 March 1964, the government
introduced the Ontario Law Reform Commission Act in the legislature.[8]

The act reflected McRuer's objectives and was in accordance both
with John Robarts's directive to find "made-in-Ontario solutions for

made-in-Ontario problems" and with his preference for brevity. A single page long, consisting of a mere three sections, the act established the law reform commission, stipulated that the commission could consist of three or more members, and authorized the hiring of staff. The money that the commission needed to operate would be voted by the legislature. As for the commission's functions, it was mandated to inquire into and consider any matter relating to reform of statute law, the common law, and judicial decisions; the administration of justice; and judicial or quasi-judicial procedures under any act. The OLRC could do any of these things on its own initiative, a remarkable degree of freedom and independence which was directly owing to McRuer's arguments. Additionally, it was directed to inquire into and consider any subject referred to it by the attorney-general. Significantly, there had been no effort to define or even limit the meaning of the word "reform" in the OLRC's statutory mandate.

The Ontario Law Reform Commission Act was approved by the legislature on 8 May, with not a single vote against. McRuer had been only one party in the establishment of the OLRC, and he would be only one participant in its proceedings, but the sense of satisfaction and excitement he felt this spring day was fully justified. Without him it would not have happened, certainly not in this way.

The next step in making McRuer's dream a reality was for the Robarts government to bring this new legal entity to life by appointing members to it. There was no doubt about who would be at the helm—James Chalmers McRuer. Appointed as vice-chairman was H. Allan Leal, a doctor of laws and a seasoned Ontario lawyer who was currently the dean at Osgoode Hall Law School (where students addressed him as "Dean Leal," or sometimes, out of earshot, "Lean Deal").

Over the next several years, McRuer and Leal would work together closely and effectively. Leal, a full generation younger, was the more outgoing and sociable of the two, always willing to live up to his reputation as an enthusiastic raconteur of legal stories. Yet they had a lot in common, too. Besides a voracious appetite for work, Leal and McRuer shared an interest in professional education and served on committees together (Leal had supported McRuer in his outspoken defence of dower and married women's property rights at that 1964 meeting of the attorney-general's advisory committee). In the unfolding work of the OLRC, it became clear that, while the other commissioners were inclined to focus on particular areas of the law, Leal and McRuer were keenly interested in *everything*. They would also tend to reach identical views on many of the issues they grappled with, because both were liberal-minded individuals who nevertheless understood and respected the law's traditions,

Jim McRuer had few real friends, since he kept just about everyone at a distance, but Allan Leal certainly became as close to him as anyone; One indication of McRuer's feelings towards his vice-chairman was provided when McRuer rewrote his will to name Leal, together with his daughter Mary Louise, as executor of his estate. This meant that Leal was entrusted with the most personal financial and family matters, and that, as one of McRuer's literary executors, he was responsible for his private and public papers as well as anything pertaining to books by or about him.

Perhaps even more revealing of the special relationship between the two men was McRuer's decision in the summer of 1966 to step down as chairman of the OLRC; he then became vice-chairman, and Leal assumed the chairmanship. McRuer positively loved work and delighted in showing everyone how he could run two commissions at the same time—just as he had done years earlier when chairing both the royal commission on the legal treatment of sexual psychopaths and the royal commission on insanity as a criminal defence. So what had changed?

At this time, the law school at Osgoode Hall, an operation of the Law Society of Upper Canada, was being transferred to the recently established York University, miles away at the very northern edge of metropolitan Toronto. This placed Allan Leal in a difficult position. He believed that the school should be moved instead to a new building on University Avenue in central Toronto where it would continue to have the three branches of the law—the courts, the practising legal profession, and the government—as well as the Law Society in its backyard. Moving out to York would gain the school a larger library (there was, after all, plenty of room in those open fields), but teaching law there would be like instructing medical students without a hospital nearby. Because Leal profoundly disagreed with the move, and because York University officials could not offer him the Osgoode deanship on a tenured basis, he believed, probably correctly, that he had no future at York.[9]

As McRuer became apprised of this problem, he recognized that Leal's stand—with which he agreed—would cost him dearly. He also realized, however, that Leal's status would be safeguarded by a timely move from the deanship of Osgoode Hall Law School to the chairmanship of the Ontario Law Reform Commission. Accordingly, he went straight to Premier Robarts and asked that Leal be made chairman. Robarts immediately agreed. Bill Poole, who had been appointed to the OLRC as a third commissioner and its representative from western Ontario, was not surprised by Robarts's action. "Robarts saw McRuer as a god," Poole says, and "with Robarts, McRuer always got his way." Poole was also one of the few who knew McRuer's real reason for resigning as chairman. "There was no need for you to be so generous other than these stark facts alone," Poole wrote McRuer from London, Ontario, after returning home on 3 August 1966 from the OLRC meeting where the chairman and vice-chairman exchanged positions. "I consider your act the finest thing I have ever seen. I know of no one else in this province who would do for Allan what you have done."[10]

Bill Poole, senior partner of the law firm Poole, Bell and Porter in London, Ontario, was a progressive-minded Tory and a confidant of Premier John Robarts. Educated at the University of Manitoba and McGill University, Poole served in the Canadian navy during the war, studied law at Osgoode Hall in the veterans' classes, and became a criminal lawyer. A dapper man with an outgoing personality, known among other things for the breadth of his knowledge and his love of fine cigars and good art, Poole could cut incisively to the heart of things in commission debates. He also could provoke thought along new lines, but in human terms it was his nature to be conciliatory. This quality became a valuable attribute at certain OLRC meetings when McRuer, in single-minded pursuit of a legal point, appeared oblivious to the raw feelings and bruised egos his style sometimes left in its wake. Poole invariably was on hand to clasp his arm around the shoulder of the walking wounded, bantering cheerfully as he took the victim out to lunch during the noon break or to a bar following an afternoon session.

The other two commissioners appointed to the OLRC were W. Gibson Gray and Richard A. Bell. Gray, a Toronto corporate lawyer with the large firm of Borden Elliot, had for years been an important figure in the Canadian Bar Association, especially in its labour-relations and civil-justice subsections. On 11 November 1964 Attorney-General Wishart offered Gray a position as a member of Ontario's new law reform commission, and Gray accepted. His specialties would help the OLRC in three areas. Having had considerable experience running the finances at Borden Elliot, Gray would work closely with McRuer in preparing the commission's annual budget. His expertise was also valuable in the preparation of OLRC studies on labour relations law and motor vehicle negligence litigation, as well as on any questions touching the Ontario legal profession itself. (During his time at the OLRC Gray also served for two years as treasurer of the Law Society and for six years as chairman of the Society's finance committee.) A third asset he brought to the commission was what McRuer described as a "common sense approach to things."[11]

Dick Bell, like Bill Poole, was a prominent lawyer with impeccable Tory credentials. A former national director of the Conservative Party, he also had served both as an MP for the riding of Carleton and as the minister of citizenship and immigration in the latter days of the Diefenbaker government. He possessed an instinct for organizational work but was just as effective in addressing policy questions, which he saw as being as important as good organization. These attributes, as well as his engaging personality and boundless energy, served Bell well in his work at the OLRC, where many of the policy issues the commission considered involved the organization and administrative "machinery" of justice as well as substantive provisions of the law itself.

The OLRC, of course, consisted of more than its commission members. One whose presence at the OLRC proved critically important was William B. Common. Common, who had been appointed deputy attorney-general in 1956, was a friend and colleague of McRuer, the two having worked together on many committees and also in numerous trials and investigations over several decades. When Arthur Wishart became attorney-general in 1964 and Rendall Dick moved up to replace Common as the new deputy minister, Premier Robarts promptly received a request from McRuer that the retiring Common be named counsel to the law reform commission. There were many good reasons why this should happen. "I thought it was so important that the commission be aware of the protocols of government and not inadvertently tread on toes or offend people when no offence was intended," McRuer told his vice-chairman, Allan Leal, in explaining why he wanted Common on board the OLRC. Despite his years of running the courts as chief justice, his many experiences with royal commissions, and his earlier dealings with governments in Ottawa and Toronto, McRuer recognized that he was like a babe-in-the-woods when it came to the protocols of government in Ontario in the 1960s. For detailed knowledge of the provincial government and its ways, not to mention shrewd understanding of its principal players (who to see first, who to avoid), very few came close to rivalling Bill Common. As counsel to the commission, he could interpret and advise with the best interests of all in mind, and his role at McRuer's right hand would be instrumental in the OLRC's successful launching and smooth sailing in the crucial formative years. He was to remain in this post until 1967.

Another key employee, of whom it would come to be said that "she knows more about the Ontario Law Reform Commission than anyone else," was Aileen F. Chute. A single woman, Chute lived for her work and devoted herself with selfless dedication to assisting McRuer in his legal career. She had served as McRuer's secretary while he was a judge, and when he moved to the civil rights and law reform commissions, she went with him. "Miss Chute," as she was universally known, was one of the reasons Jim McRuer could so smoothly accomplish his very large workload. She regularly remained at the office until about 10 o'clock at night, using the quiet evening hours to clear up the volume of correspondence, reports, speech texts, scheduling arrangements, and other items of business that swirled around McRuer. She could hold her own with anyone, from a rude delivery boy to a learned law professor, from an inquisitive journalist to a superior court judge.

McRuer, for his part, was always concerned about Aileen. Often including her in formal McRuer family occasions, he respected Aileen Chute so much that he always tried to get more money for her. Whenever salary increases were under discussion, and sometimes even when they weren't, he promoted her cause with the officials administering the highly discriminatory employment categories of the public service. "If she was a man," McRuer asserted, "she'd be paid not as a secretary but as an administrator."

For the first two years, the OLRC operated out of offices in the Legislative Buildings at Queen's Park, which was immensely convenient for McRuer since that was also where his civil rights commission was housed. From time to time as he walked between the two offices, McRuer would run into Robarts, and the two would exchange pleasantries and occasionally chat. "How is your work going?" the premier would inquire, adding, "not that I'm trying to rush you or anything."[12] There were other encounters, too. The OLRC's rooms were on the fourth floor, east end, of the Legislative Buildings, and along the same corridor was an office where Joseph Salsberg, once the "red blot" on the legislature, the Communist Party member for the Toronto riding of St. Andrew until his defeat in 1955, was working on some project or other. He often strolled into McRuer's office to engage him in debate. Although McRuer could easily get rid of most people, usually by intimidating them, he met his match in Salsberg. It was a scene from a movie: the stiff, hard-working Presbyterian Liberal visibly annoyed at being interrupted by the engaging, hard-talking Communist Jew eager to have his left-wing views influence the course of law reform. They had nothing in common, except determination.

In 1966, when Allan Leal became chairman of the OLRC, the enterprise was relocated to more spacious quarters on the 10th floor at 18 King Street East, the same downtown Toronto office building where the attorney-general's department was situated. But, wherever it was located, what exactly did the OLRC do? How did "law reform" work in practice? The lack of any definition of the term in the commission's governing statute meant that its members had plenty of scope, but they still had to decide the kind of reforms the OLRC should contemplate. To understand the decisions they did make, some appreciation is needed of the larger context within which the five commissioners were operating.

The paradoxes inherent in the elusive and imprecise elements of law reform may explain why McRuer could sometimes describe this cause as "a hackneyed business" and yet still view his work on the OLRC as his "most important contribution" and greatest achievement. Although the term "law reform" has become a familiar one, the concept itself is fundamentally ambiguous. After all, legislatures and judges engage in law reform when they modify an existing law or replace one law with another. While judges normally deal with the laws in piecemeal fashion, legislators alter the law in more fundamental and comprehensive ways— a reasonably good partnership and division of labour. In this partnership, Canadian judges have traditionally assumed a relatively narrow role, deferring to the legislatures as the primary law-making agency in a democratic society. From the latter part of the nineteenth century, as J.H. Farrar notes, "the inherent tendency of the courts to develop the law" has been accelerated by increased legislative intervention.[13] Still, they are the same two partners dancing, just to faster music. The pace of such "law reform" has increased, but the practice has not changed much.

Then there is the problem of differing perceptions of the law reform process. Some people see urgent need for changes in the institutions of the legal system and perhaps even alterations in the very form of the law (as distinct from reform of the law's substance). They might, as a result, suggest constitutional changes, or radical organizational restructuring, or perhaps both of these and more. In contrast, other people are innately conservative. They choose almost intuitively to adapt themselves to existing ways, including the current legal order whose norms have largely become their own. Reinforcing this tendency is the fact that many individuals and commercial enterprises rely for their livelihood on the prevailing set of legal relationships; not least among them, of course, are lawyers, whose careers rest on their knowledge of existing laws. To these people, "law reform" is just another term for earthquake. In its aftermath comes troublesome and costly rebuilding—the psychological hurdle of new learning, and the non-remunerative hassle of retraining. So, for them, prevention becomes the order of the day, achieved by maintaining the *status quo*. This instinctive social bias against law reform has an even further dimension as far as the legal profession is concerned: lawyers' education is largely a process of socialization, a way of coming to accept certain thought patterns. One of the most fundamental of these patterns is the drive to seek out, and often be governed by, precedent. If someone has taken the step before, then it must be the route to follow; if no one has ever gone that way, there must be something wrong with it.

A further difficulty with law reform, which the OLRC had to grapple with, is the conceptual challenge presented by the relationship between law and society. The laws by which a society chooses to govern itself are themselves products of that society. Yet, as McRuer had been stressing for years, societies evolve over time and some laws that were appropriate for one era grow out of step with new conditions. These fossilized laws cannot be seen as reflective of peoples' real wishes or current needs, but still they survive. Thus the past rules the present, and it does so disjointedly, ineffectively, without any purpose. In truth, of course, it is no great accomplishment to change or reform a remnant law, or the legal concept behind that law, when it has grown hopelessly out of date; it is just a matter of getting around to doing it. If the law is a particularly bothersome anachronism, public pressure will soon enough generate the requisite political initiative to do the deed.

The real challenge in law reform is to deal with an issue that divides people, some still favouring the existing law and others fervently agitating for change. At what juncture does the law reformer stride boldly onto this stage and deal with drug laws, economic regulation, women's property rights in marriage, abortion, genetic engineering, or minority language rights? "There is nothing more difficult to take in hand," observed no less an authority on the workings of power than Machiavelli, "nothing more perilous to conduct, or more uncertain in its success, than to take the lead in the introduction of a new order of things. The innovator has for enemies all those who have done well under the old conditions, and lukewarm defenders in those who may do well under the new."

Traditionally, courts and legislatures provided a diffused focus for the cause of law reform. This meant that, when an issue became too controversial, those with the power to change laws could avoid doing so. When neither the legal institutions nor the political institutions could cope, moreover, the issue could always be dealt with in other ways—through a royal commission if the object was to buy time and diffuse the crisis, or through a plebiscite if one wanted to bring the issue to a head and have the people themselves confront and resolve it. This was the Canadian pattern, but it was disrupted by the emergence in 1964 of the Ontario Law Reform Commission, a completely independent body whose exclusive mandate was the renovation of existing laws. True, the OLRC would be only recommending reforms, not actually implementing them; it would still be up to the political institutions to deal with the commission's proposals. Yet now gone were the days when law reform could take place behind the scenes. Unlike earlier "advisory committees," which had made confidential and discreet reports to justice ministers, the OLRC addressed law reform issues in a hard-hitting and highly public way.

Such were the broad realities of the system which Jim McRuer and his colleagues on the commission confronted. More particularly, what they faced was an entrenched system consisting of many individuals and moving parts, each one having a life of its own. Picture this imaginary scene from the 1960s. A law professor, with a strong personal interest in one corner of the law, is conducting research and publishing his findings in a scholarly article, with the hope that his idea for up-dating the law might gradually take hold. Meanwhile, a group representing a particular industry is meeting behind closed doors with departmental officials seeking from the government a change in some law or regulation. On another front, the government has just created a royal commission to investigate a particular problem—is it the mining industry this time? or automobiles and highway safety?—and its recommendations could lead to a new law or revision of existing laws. Simultaneously, a committee of MPPs is looking at laws in foreign jurisdictions—for workers' compensation, or human rights, or liability for agricultural land-drainage systems, or legal entitlements to public housing and other social benefits—and this committee may conclude that such measures are a good fit locally, more or less bought off the rack with just a few alterations.

The scene has other players, too. An alert lawyer has just discovered some anomaly in the law and brought it to the government's attention—perhaps by using the loophole to his client's advantage and the government's temporary chagrin, or perhaps by a timely letter written as a good deed in the public interest (not necessarily to be overlooked in future considerations from the government). Another lawyer with a strong political bent is drafting a new legislative proposal designed to be one of her party's planks—"A better legal deal for Ontarians" is the rallying cry she favours—in the coming provincial election. While this is happening, interest groups are lobbying for far-reaching changes to the province's laws. All the while, judges, in their role of resolving legal conflicts, may create a bit of new law, or smooth away the rough edge of some statute that had been enacted by the legislature. At the same time, a cabinet minister is ready to reform one of his department's practices, and he directs his legal officers to draft changes to the regulations which he in turn gets cabinet to approve. Nor is even that the end of it. Already at work across Canada are "uniformity commissioners" (Allan Leal and Bill Common were two of them), who seek to achieve uniformity in laws from one common-law province to another by developing a model of the best legislation available.

As new players in this extraordinarily complex and multidimensional process, the five OLRC commissioners recognized that—in the view of many Ontarians—the prevailing system for changing laws worked tolerably well. In this context, the question was, should the commissioners focus on "black letter law"—the specific words printed on paper which carried clear legal meaning in precise situations—and clear up problems in this area, maintaining a low-profile, highly technical approach that would keep them busy with what many would call "lawyers' law"? Or should they take advantage of their unique resources—time, money, and access to the legal talent in the province's six law schools—to tackle the bigger questions no one else really could, such as a comprehensive review of family law and the legal status of women in marriage, or the vast body of law governing trusts? In fact, they decided, it should be a bit of both: technical or narrowly focused law reform, and broader reforms of social policy, legal practices, and legal institutions.

By deciding to walk on both these legs, the OLRC avoided the public criticism that would have been aroused if only one approach or the other had been adopted. More positively, the OLRC's decision meant that the interests of the five commissioners could be combined, fulfilling both views of the commission's role and allowing a "see as we go along," common-sense approach. Furthermore, the decision showed the commissioners' recognition that the OLRC was not going to become the sole source of law reform. All the other players in the existing system would still remain active, too; the commission was simply to be a catalyst in that complex process, clarifying the nature of specific law reforms and speeding up the work of bringing them about. No one understood this better than McRuer who, for all his insistence on the need for a more structured process for law reform, possessed a deep appreciation of just how intricate, varied, and culture-driven the operation could be: "The greatest law reformers were Gilbert and Sullivan who ridiculed law in their operettas, and Charles Dickens and Thomas Macaulay who exposed the human plight of bad laws in their books," McRuer once wryly observed.

IN THE EARLY DAYS OF THE COMMISSION, before all five of its members were appointed, McRuer and Leal were understandably anxious to get things moving. They met with Attorney-General Wishart, and the three men discussed the commission's work and plans. McRuer urged that the commission's first project be the subject of married women's property rights. He explained that, while dower was badly outdated, it currently was the only property right a woman had, except for the right to apply under the Dependent's Relief Act or perhaps, in other circumstances, to bring a lawsuit for alimony. McRuer spoke quietly, but with passion, about the injustices he had seen women suffer over the years because of the harsh workings of a legal system crafted by men. A woman had no right to leave her husband for cruelty, he recalled, if she was physically strong enough to take the abuse; she could get a divorce only through an act of parliament. Although McRuer saw the family as society's vital unit and deeply regretted broken homes, he believed that the laws governing divorce were still unduly harsh and that the humiliation of having one's divorce proceedings based on fabricated evidence was something no citizen should have to endure. McRuer explained that a law reform project on women's property rights would involve a lot of work by the commission, because both the law and human relationships were so complex. Yet that was precisely why he had urged the creation of an ongoing body in the first place, so it could conduct the thorough study necessary and then recommend comprehensive reform. He knew that the law reform commission could "only lay the framework on which the legislature could build," but he expressed his deep conviction that "this area is crying out for change." McRuer—having confronted that lawyer who suggested abolishing dower with the sharp demand, "What are you going to replace it with?"—now wanted to answer his own question.

Arthur Wishart had fixed his gaze intently on McRuer all the while. Nodding, he told McRuer, "Go ahead. I'll back you up all the way." That was the understanding that marked the beginning of significant changes to the whole area of family law in Ontario.[14] Taking more than a decade to complete, and coinciding with a growing movement in society for women's equality, the project was destined to become, in legal terms, more a revolution than a reform.

While this ambitious project was taking shape, another item made its way onto the OLRC's agenda. McRuer resolved early on that the commission would deal with the rule against perpetuities, and it did. Dr. Cecil Augustus Wright, "Caesar" Wright to most, dean of law at the University of Toronto and a towering figure within the legal community, was probably the most knowledgeable person in Canada on the subject of perpetuities. He had supported McRuer's efforts to have a law reform commission established, and so he was pleased to be asked to prepare an OLRC report on the rule against perpetuities. This report was presented to the commission in January 1965. No one even considered—or dared, given Wright's imposing status—changing a word; they just voted to adopt it as their first report, signed and dated it, and presented it to Arthur Wishart. Score one for "black letter" law reform. After the report had circulated a few months, some letters and briefs in response had been received by Wishart, who passed them on to McRuer with a request for OLRC answers on each point raised. McRuer, in turn, forwarded them to Wright. A few months later Wright once more appeared before the commissioners, having made several changes to his own report. The commissioners, again adjusting not a word, submitted their supplementary report on the rule against perpetuities on 1 March 1966.

That year the Ontario legislature enacted the Perpetuities Act, the first actual change in law generated by the OLRC. The subject was hardly the stuff to galvanize the interest of Ontarians; one MPP, who had a low view of lawyers and little natural sympathy for the OLRC, said sarcastically in the legislature about the rule against perpetuities, "Why, my constituents talk of nothing else!"[15] Nevertheless, the exercise set a good precedent. A topic clearly researched and a recommendation convincingly made had resulted, reasonably quickly, in new legislation. There had been wisdom in starting with something small and specific (as other law reform commissions, such as the Law Reform Commission of Canada, would subsequently discover when they sought to tackle massive subjects that eventually led to academically interesting reports, but not legislative enactment). The OLRC understood this point well, and, as the years unfolded, it would achieve a high success rate in the implementation of its proposals.

Two other law reform reports appeared in 1965. On 3 March the commission presented its findings relating to problems with the assignment of workers' wages (which resulted, after a longer delay this time, in amendments to the Wages Act in 1968), and on 28 March it released a report on personal property security legislation. The latter report is a perfect example of how the OLRC was only one of many players in the law reform process. Its focus was a draft bill on the subject of personal property security legislation that had been prepared by the Canadian Bar Association (the CBA's interest in this issue was long-standing). The commissioners suggested amendments to the bill and recommended that it be introduced into the legislature. This was done, more comments were received, and in 1966 the OLRC released a supplementary report on the subject. The following year the legislature passed the Personal Property Security Act.[16]

The main purpose of the Personal Property Security Act was to introduce into the law of Ontario the legal concept of a security "interest" in goods, fixtures, documents of title, instruments, securities, chattel paper or intangibles, where the interest is given by the buyer or reserved by the seller in order to secure payment of money or performance of an obligation. Until that time, this area of the law had been covered by many different statutes—such as the Bills of Sale and Chattel Mortgages Act, the Conditional Sales Act, and the Corporation Securities Registration Act. Confusion had abounded when it came to giving a security interest in personal property under these various statutes, and the situation was made even worse by the technicalities of registration of documents and the movement of personal property from one county to another. For instance, a car might be subject to a conditional sale agreement which was registered in Carleton County, but, if it was driven to Essex County and sold, the purchaser would have great difficulty knowing where to search for encumbrances that may legally exist on the car he or she has just bought. The two main features of the new Personal Property Security Act provided for uniform methods of creating security interests (the older acts mentioned being repealed) and a central registry system with branch offices throughout Ontario in which anyone could search to see if personal property situated anywhere in the province had been charged to secure an obligation. As Gibson Gray remarked to McRuer when they dug into this field of law reform, "You can't have the law dragging along away behind the commercial community."

Meanwhile, initiated by the commission or by the attorney-general, work was under way at the OLRC on a range of topics both broad and narrow: provisions in the law of evidence (especially dealing with the admissibility of business records in court), mechanics' liens, the question of extending a guarantor's liability on construction bonds, exemption of certain goods from seizure under the Execution Act, the newly developing law of condominium, and the basis for compensation when the government expropriates property. Each of these topics became the subject of a separate OLRC report during 1966 and 1967.

The report on condominiums was typical of how the OLRC addressed discrete areas of the law. In the 1960s there was a growing demand in Ontario for condominium development, which was seen to provide the amenities of apartment living on a shared-cost basis with the advantages of home ownership. Alberta and British Columbia had already followed other jurisdictions in enacting legislation to make this system of property ownership easier, but nothing similar existed in Ontario. The OLRC initiated a project to see whether condominium legislation was needed for Ontario, engaged Professor R.C.B. Risk of the University of Toronto's faculty of law to study the question, and, in March 1967, presented Attorney-General Wishart with a report recommending such legislation and providing a fully drafted statute. Later that year the legislature passed the Condominium Act. The way was paved for a "condo" building boom across Ontario, which, combined with the later introduction of province-wide rent controls, prompted developers to pull out of the construction of apartment buildings and to move instead into the new area of private-ownership, high-rise living. Who said law reform was only a matter of importance for lawyers?

The OLRC was scoring well with its other reports, too. The 1966 report on the admissibility of business records led to the Evidence Amendment Act, 1966; the report on mechanics' liens that same year resulted in the Mechanics' Lien Act, 1968-9; and the report, also in 1966, on the exemption of goods from seizure led to the Execution Amendment Act, 1967. This was the pattern that tended to be repeated year after year. Some reports received only partial implementation; for example, the 1969 report on the limitation of actions produced changes in three statutes—the Highway Traffic Act, the Fatal Accidents Act, and the Trustee Act—rather than the proposed across-the-board set of limitation periods for lawsuits. Some were delayed a few years before reaching the statute books; thus, while the OLRC issued its report on the proposed extension of guarantor's liability on construction bonds in 1966, it was not until 1975 that the government responded with three pieces of legislation—the Mechanics' Lien Amendment Act, the Ministry of Transportation and Communications Creditors Payment Act, and the Public Works Creditor's Payment Repeal Act. Yet the overwhelming body of the OLRC's work in the 1960s—in everything from family law to courts administration, from the coroner system to land registration—generated massive and far-reaching law reform. Chairman Allan Leal, on reviewing OLRC reports and subsequent legislation, calculated that they achieved an 80 per cent success rate—"not bad for a budget of less than one million dollars."

The commission's offices in these years were a formal, solemn place, and the commissioners, all older males, set the tone of correctness. They were not aloof, but the staff (both lawyers and non-legal) operated in an environment of "them" and "us"; in general, they saw the commissioners as demanding but cordial. At first there were just a few people on staff, since to a large extent the OLRC had its research work done by outside teams of academic lawyers. McRuer had always seen the presence of so many law schools in the province as a treasured resource to be tapped.

Gradually legal staff was built up within the commission as well, which was especially important in helping to develop policy options in-house. The lawyers on staff felt privileged to be there, given the significance of the work and the challenge of working for such distinguished figures in the Ontario legal profession. They consisted of academics and lawyers who preferred the scholarly side of law to legal practice.

The OLRC's *modus operandi* mirrored McRuer's serious-minded and intense approach to work, in the way that all institutions inevitably reflect the influence of their founders. Each month, the high point to which all activity built was the meeting of the commissioners. A full-scale, two-day event, this was a command performance. The staff worked all month developing policy papers for the meeting, and a formal, fixed agenda was drawn up in advance and sent, along with binders of reports, to the commissioners. On the fateful day, the out-of-town commissioners, Poole and Bell, would arrive, joining Torontonians McRuer, Leal, and Gray. In the commission's first years, the legal staff was excluded from these monthly meetings, unless specifically involved in the item under discussion. In time, however, they all met together, which proved much better for the work of the OLRC because the staff could hear the discussion by the commissioners (rather than just read minutes of it after the fact) and participate in the exchange of ideas. Each staff person would be ready to speak to the agenda items, with academics called in as needed, or to defend a research paper they had been commissioned to write. "Defend" was often the operative word, too, in the same way a doctoral student has to defend a thesis before an imposing panel of professors.

The proceedings began with chairman McRuer calling the meeting to order. Then the minutes of the previous meeting—thirty, forty, or even fifty pages of them—were reviewed and discussed, often at great length. Next McRuer directed the members through the scheduled work, item by item. For each topic, huge binders had been prepared, with tabs marking the various issues involved. McRuer directed a round-table discussion, followed by a recorded vote on the issue at hand. As soon as one issue was decided, the next was brought forward. McRuer drove ahead, methodically and relentlessly, intently focused. Most people smoked, and a bluish-grey haze filled the room. Time was valuable and was used so as to get "sixty seconds worth of distance run" from every minute. The meetings started sharp at 9 a.m. and ran until noon. There was one hour off for lunch (the commissioners, after the move to King Street in 1966, walked across the street to the basement cafeteria at the King Edward Hotel, while the staff either sought out a better restaurant or skipped lunch to work up a policy memo needed for the afternoon session). They then continued working to 5 p.m. It was the same both days, every month, every year.

Although Jim McRuer thrived on this nine-to-five job, he certainly did not treat it as piece-work employment. Requiring that law reform proposals be thoroughly thought out, he never rushed a discussion of any legal concept or policy issue, or indeed a choice of a single word. For his part, he was always prepared for a meeting. He had read everything in the thick binders as well as additional memos and correspondence, underlining passages and writing notes in the margins. He was ready with questions; in fact, he had something to say on every topic, delving into its minutiae and lingering over a single point for so long that Bill Poole would finally urge with cordial exasperation that they "get on." Through it all, the tone was serious and formal; the staff addressed each commissioner as "Mr.", the commissioners returned the compliment, and all questions by staff were directed through the chair. McRuer's values were those of old Ontario, and they prevailed in all OLRC meetings.

The OLRC never lobbied to get its recommendations implemented, not because of indifference but as the result of a clear and deliberate decision. Early on, McRuer and his commissioners discussed whether they should push and prod the government, and Dick Bell, as a former cabinet minister, presented informed views on the pros and cons of doing so. They considered three separate issues: Would they have opportunities to lobby government? Did they have a responsibility to undertake such lobbying? And, if they did lobby, what were the risks? Their eventual decision was that the OLRC ought not to lobby the government. Instead, they would take their very best shot in each report presented to the government on a law reform topic, and then let it fail or succeed on the merits of their recommendations and the supporting text. They asked only that the government be fair about bringing their reports to the public's attention. This is indeed what happened. Attorney-General Wishart rose time and time again in the legislature, after the OLRC really got rolling, typically to say, "Mr. Speaker, I have in hand yet another report from the Ontario Law Reform Commission. I have not yet had a chance to read it, nor even to read the executive summary, but so that there will be no delay I am tabling it the legislature today in the hope that honourable members and the general public will soon be able to read and comment on it."

In the OLRC's early days, there was a feeling among some at the commission that the pace of their work was too slow, that reports on major legal issues should be delivered to the attorney-general as quickly as possible. McRuer, however, never felt this way. A report would go to the government when he was ready to sign it, and he would not do so until he was satisfied with every detail. His methodical approach even contributed to the departure of commission counsel Lyle Fairbairn. Fairbairn, who assumed the position in 1973, worked diligently, functioning not only as legal counsel but as an executive director. He oversaw general operations, devoted much effort to questions of policy, and, like his predecessors (Bill Common, Richard Gosse, and Edward Ryan), acted as liaison between the five commissioners and the OLRC staff. To Fairbairn's dismay, material that he carefully prepared on one of the commission's major projects, a study of support obligations, was demolished by McRuer at meeting after meeting. Sometimes it seemed that the commissioners existed only to grill their researchers, The project appeared to be going nowhere, and Fairbairn quit in frustration in July 1976.

His replacement as counsel came as a surprise to many. Patricia Richardson, who had worked as a law clerk at the Supreme Court of Ontario for one year, seemed to have two strikes against her—age (she was only twenty-nine) and sex. If most of the commissioners could have had their way, they would not have given her a second thought: she would be in over her head because she had never done enough "outside" work (meaning experience other than academic study and legal research). They wanted as counsel someone more senior, an active legal practitioner and, though no one ever said so directly, a man. Yet McRuer thought that Richardson could do the job. Moreover, he believed it was time for a woman, and not just any woman but one who could probably do the job better than most males. So he set about persuading the other commissioners, and on i December 1976 Patricia Richardson was appointed OLRC counsel, a position she would successfully occupy for more than a dozen years.

When beginning their work in the mid-1960s, the OLRC members had decided to work closely with the universities and draw upon their academic staff for assistance. At no time, however, did McRuer let the commission's relationship with the universities endanger its treasured independence; the OLRC was to remain in charge. At an early meeting with the deans of law from the University of Ottawa, Queen's University, York University, the University of Toronto, the University of Western Ontario, and the University of Windsor, McRuer explained how the OLRC would operate and indicated the services it would provide. Specifically, he said, "If members of your staff work on projects with us, they will be better professors and be able to teach better when they are through the project than they were when they started. And we will have the benefit of their assistance and their learning." There was little doubt in McRuer's mind about the mutual benefits involved, but his attitude conveyed clearly who was in the driver's seat. Or so he thought. Shortly afterwards, as the OLRC began its monumental family law project, McRuer had a confrontation with two of the deans. Angered that the commission had appointed the project's director and staff without consulting them, these deans protested vociferously and insisted that they be involved in the hiring of any professors from their faculty. McRuer hit back firmly. "No," he told them. "The Law Reform Commission is going to decide and we are not handing over any of our responsibilities to any individuals or anyone, not even to the Attorney General to whom we report."[17]

McRuer's tough-mindedness was also evident in his dealings with legal scholars. When the OLRC began its work there was not a great deal of legal writing around, and so it decided to produce such writing itself by commissioning legal scholars to write research papers on a wide variety of subjects. Typically a project director would make a proposal for law reform research to the commissioners, suggesting names of people who might do the work and setting the fee, which was usually low and sometimes non-existent. (McRuer prevailed upon John Honsberger to prepare a study on limitation periods without charge, as his "duty to the profession.") If the proposal was accepted, the project director would then recruit the scholar and give him precise instructions on what was needed. In this fashion, for example, Jacob Ziegel prepared a full report on the sale of goods, Stephen Waddams on products liability, and Donovan Watters on the law of trusts. On completion of the study, the commissioners would analyze it in round-table discussions. Further research work would be commissioned, as needed, and the OLRC legal staff would also rework the material. Ultimately, if the research work of outside scholars could withstand the scrutiny of McRuer and his fellow commissioners, it would become incorporated as an important part of a commission report, providing background information, legal analysis, and justification for particular recommendations.

When the academic who had prepared his paper came to the commission meeting for its review, the discussion sometimes became frustrating and tense for all concerned. Professors tended to be offended by questions that they regarded as ill-informed but that the commissioners themselves saw as perfectly legitimate. McRuer would certainly argue a point fiercely with a professor. On one celebrated occasion, he almost lunged across the table at Jacob Ziegel. At another meeting, devoted to the OLRC's "change of name project," Patricia Richardson was the victim. In this project, McRuer sought to clarify and restate the common law right of women to keep their own names after marriage, but he had real difficulty with proposals regarding children's family names. Gradually and reluctantly he was persuaded by Richardson that children should be able to use hyphenated names to identify both parents in cases where the mother kept her maiden name. Yet when she pressed her argument even farther, suggesting that children should be given the option to choose the name of whichever parent they wished, that was just too much. Her idea amounted to nothing less than gross interference with the integrity of the family unit, McRuer cried, as he came across the table at her. That boardroom table served other purposes than holding overflowing ashtrays and heavy binders. It often protected those in attendance from McRuer's famous rages.

For McRuer, however, these were intellectual battles only. He loved the "game" of debating ideas and also knew that such exchanges were necessary if the commission was to understand fully the important issues involved. The stakes were much higher than a law professor's bruised vanity. Yet it was a two-way street. While McRuer was extremely aggressive in debate, he would not stick to his position as a matter of pride if he could be convinced that he was wrong (or his opponent was right). At these meetings, recounts Patricia Richardson, he apparently had no concern that he would be made to look foolish on a point. He would concede. Richardson considered him "very combative, but fair."

McRuer's no-nonsense manner was evident not only in the commission's monthly meetings but also in smaller settings. Typical were the sessions in his office dealing with the project on the law of evidence, a project that culminated with the commission's report in March 1976.

Professor Allen W. Mewett of Osgoode Hall Law School (subsequently of the University of Toronto Law School), who had written the basic research document for the OLRC, joined commission counsel Patricia Richardson and staff lawyer Carol Creighton in McRuer's office at 9:30 a.m. They worked steadily, with absolutely no interruptions, no calls, no coffee, until 12 noon. McRuer then arose and left for lunch, usually eating by himself—he disliked making small talk. They never worked through lunch; the McRuer regimen called for sensible eating. They would reassemble in his office at 1:30 and continue working for three more hours. At 4:30 p.m. it was time to go and McRuer would simply get up and leave. The next day would be the same. When a break was required, for instance to check an important fact, Mewett, Richardson, and Creighton sometimes went out for a cup of coffee; McRuer had a glass of milk brought in. Despite their working side by side day after day, McRuer did not get very close to any of the staff, nor they to him. His austere bearing and reserved manner guaranteed that. McRuer was kind toward the staff, recalls Richardson, but he "just wasn't there" in human terms. She also remembers that "life never seemed to be any trouble for him. He always turned up on time and exquisitely dressed, right down to his dapper bow tie. While others had to leave a meeting to make personal telephone calls, never him. He was disciplined, and always unruffled."

Another lawyer working closely with McRuer at the OLRC was Mel Springman. Joining the commission in 1974, Springman later became responsible for directing all legal research and eventually was made general counsel. As a research lawyer assigned to the project on landlord and tenant law, Springman handed McRuer draft material on a daily basis, and every day McRuer would revise it, word for word. "He was a working vice-chairman, taking part in all the projects," Springman recalls. "The government really got good value for its money, and he earned it all." McRuer was, for Springman, "intellectually astute and very smart." He was also "great to work to work with. He could get a bit ornery, as old people do, and he was not always on the mark, but given his age ...!" Like a good Presbyterian, McRuer had a firm sense of what was morally right and wrong, and he carried it into his work. "He was not wishy-washy," says Springman. He "listened, made decisions, and then moved on. He was a real CEO. He was respected by those of us working with him, because, at the end of the day, he *was* J.C. McRuer."

Springman also observed, working closely with McRuer over these years, that "he was an intellectual person ... he was interested in anything that would pass his desk—and anything that didn't pass his desk!

He was constantly inquiring, questioning about things. In terms of law, there wasn't any question he did not ask, and he'd ask it himself, going to the library and doing the work." He was "intellectually curious, at least within the four corners of the law. He seemed widely read, and within the scope of law reform, there would be *nothing* he wasn't aware of. You couldn't get anything past McRuer!" At meetings, Springman and others took a deep breath when they heard McRuer say "Now just one minute!" They knew that they were in for a long, long day.

One person on the OLRC staff who had a more easy-going relationship with McRuer was legal research officer Catherine H. MacLean. As a young lawyer who joined the OLRC in 1974, she immensely enjoyed working with McRuer. Rather than being intimidated by him, she acted just as naturally as she might have with any other older and special person, like a grandfather or great uncle. A bundle of life, always laughing, she would actually tease McRuer—and he loved it, chuckling, his eyes twinkling. He delighted in Catherine's lack of formality—she would just walk into his office and comment on something, or engage in quick-witted banter that challenged him and instantly broke the McRuer ice—and yet she was always respectful of him and would never cross that invisible line. Somehow she had recognized that behind the mask of formality lived a shy and sensitive man. They became quite good friends, and Catherine, accompanied by her fiancé, Ronald Chang, often visited him and Robena at their Deer Park Crescent apartment.

McRuer's workload on the OLRC, which was combined with his duties on the civil rights commission, certainly did not diminish in the late 1960s and early 1970s. In 1968 the OLRC released over half a dozen reports, the range of which could not have been broader. One report examined a major policy area that touched just about everyone's life, the protection of individual privacy; another dealt with the limitation period for actions under the Sandwich, Windsor and Amherstburg Railway Act of 1930. A third report treated certain aspects of the new divorce legislation proposed by the Government of Canada, while a fourth considered the proposed adoption in Ontario of the Uniform Wills Act. Three other reports in 1968 covered insurance, the trade sale of new houses, and residential tenancies under the Landlord and Tenant Act. And so Ontarians interested in their privacy, their wills, their insurance, their apartments, or their divorces certainly had reason to see the Ontario Law Reform Commission as relevant to their lives.

The report on the reform of the law governing new house sales is another example of how the OLRC's agenda reflected McRuer's own concerns. In 1966 he told Gib Gray that it was "absolutely terrible that you can buy something that is worth $100 and you get a great big fancy warranty, but on the other hand you buy a house and put all your life savings into it and it is *caveat emptor*" ("let the buyer beware")—a legal principle meaning that, in the absence of a clearly stated warranty and apart from fraud or mistake, a purchaser assumes the full risk for whatever he or she buys. The following year, the OLRC initiated a study of the law concerning defects of quality and workmanship in houses sold in the province. The report that followed in October 1968 called for legislation that would both broaden and make stricter the prospective liability of those engaged in the business of building or selling new houses for profit. The commission's recommendations on this point were not implemented right away—protests from the construction industry and the homebuilders association had to be accommodated—but it was really just a matter of time. In 1971 the Davis government sponsored, and the legislature enacted, the Ontario New Home Warranties Plan.

The next year saw McRuer and his commission unveil reports on limitation of actions (how much time could go by before a person lost the right to sue somebody else), the age of majority (how old Ontarians had to be before they could make contracts, vote, drink, or drive), the status of adopted children (the commission recommended that adopted children should have the same legal rights within a family as children naturally born to that family), and, on 4 November 1969, the first of a series of reports on family law—the immense project initiated after McRuer's meeting with Attorney-General Wishart in 1964. In total, there were to be five family-law reports, concluding in 1975 with the OLRC's report on support obligations.

Wishart had come to appreciate the depth of McRuer's interest in family law during the course of their meeting, and it was not long before OLRC staff did so as well. Patricia Richardson, who spent all her time in her first year at the OLRC studying policy questions arising from the commission's family law project, recalls that McRuer was "dead keen on family law." She is right. Just as his years on the bench had been marked by a number of judgments in which he set out his view that marriage was a partnership between equals, McRuer made it one of his missions at the OLRC to develop legal concepts and new laws that reflected the equality of husbands and wives. This would mean, for instance, equal property rights for both spouses and an equal division of all matrimonial property (including a husband's business assets) in the regrettable event of marriage break-up through divorce—a radical idea at the time.

McRuer also believed, given the family's central role in society, that the state should get involved if need be to support and defend it—for example, by chasing after a disappearing husband and father for payment of his support obligations.

These beliefs provided the intellectual underpinning of the OLRC's family law project, a project that had as its goal the creation of a "detailed design" for a "law reform program which, if implemented, would bring the laws affecting all those in the family relations into closer consonance with the needs and expectations of contemporary society."[18] The goal was achieved as the OLRC's recommendations on family law were transformed into government legislation, most notably the Children's Maintenance Act, the Infants Act, the Deserted Wives' and Children's Maintenance Act, the Child Welfare Act, and the Matrimonial Causes Act. At the federal level, the Divorce Act of 1968 also reflected the OLRC's philosophical assumptions and reformist convictions. Taken together, these measures heralded a genuine revolution in the legal ordering of family relationships. It was a revolution that McRuer himself had longed for during the years as a judge, when he had presided over so many painfully tragic cases involving family law.

Another of McRuer's abiding interests that attracted the OLRC's attention was the issue of automobile accidents. McRuer had vivid memories of the time he first saw a car; he was ten years old and was working on the family farm when a car sped past with a resounding put-put-put, leaving a swirl of dust in its wake. In later life, as a lawyer in the 1930s, his practice included a growing number of highway accident cases. His son, John, remembers visiting his office as a young boy and seeing two model cars on his desk. When he asked what they were for, his father told him that they were used in court to explain to judges how an accident had occurred.

McRuer drove a car until the age of fifty-six, when he suffered a seizure. Frightened that another one could strike while he was driving, he gave up his licence and henceforth either took public transit or had others, including his wife and daughters, do the driving for him. This act of self-denial, prompted by a sense of responsibility to himself, others, and the judiciary over which he presided, was matched by the personal courage McRuer displayed in thereafter performing all his public functions against the background fear that another seizure might occur.

Cars, however—or rather, accidents involving them—continued to hold his close attention. During his years on the bench he became increasingly concerned about different aspects of automobile law. He

was appalled by the light sentences often handed out to drunk driv-
ers—he believed that they should be dealt with severely under the Criminal Code, whether or not they were involved in accidents. He was also
greatly perturbed by the vast amount of automobile-accident litigation
in the courts. Holding, as he did, a high view of the rule of law and the
administration of justice, McRuer lamented the debasing of the courts
into a forum for settling compensation between insurers of automobile
owners and accident victims. He had a similarly negative view of legal
efforts to assess liability in automobile accidents, and he felt that these
trials, which were often lengthy, frequently delayed the resolution of
other, more deserving, cases.

Over the course of the 1950s McRuer reached the view that the best
way for dealing with automobile accidents was through the creation of
a liability-without-fault scheme modelled on the Workmen's Compensation Board. As noted in the preceding chapter, he set out a detailed public defence of this proposal in his 1965 address to a legal conference in
Sydney, Australia, and, as OLRC chairman, he launched a study of the
same subject. The result was a 1973 report in which the commission
concluded that the existing system of automobile-accident compensation was fragmented, inconsistent, inadequate, slow, and expensive. It
recommended instead an integrated no-fault scheme and the creation of
a system specifically concerned with accident victim compensation. In
doing so, the commission's primary goal was an efficient and fair system
of compensation, which in turn would have the positive effect of unclog-
ging the courts.

The Conservative government, faced with vociferous protests from
several special-interest groups and a politically mobilized insurance
industry, decided not to take action on the OLRC's report, and subsequent
calls for no-fault insurance—by McRuer and others—were similarly
ignored for another two decades. In the early 1990s, first the Liberal government of David Peterson and then the NDP government of Bob Rae
moved again to establish a liability-without-fault-insurance plan that,
in certain essentials, would address the concerns and reflect the recommendations of McRuer and the OLRC.

McRUER STEPPED DOWN as vice-chairman of the OLRC on 8 February
1977, but he remained a full-time member of the commission until that
June. Even afterwards, he stayed at the OLRC to work on studies of the
law of trusts and of the law governing the enforcement of judgment

debts.[19] It was not until four years later, on 1 June 1982, that he submitted his final resignation. As the tributes began flowing in, McRuer remarked, "It seems a bit like the curtain coming down."

Throughout his life, Jim McRuer's sense of justice was shaped by the interplay of his fervent desire for reform and his passionate attachment to traditional institutions, and in the OLRC he saw the fulfilment of his dreams. McRuer felt comfortable with the paradox that reform could be directed by an elite. Unlike the Law Reform Commission of Canada, which saw its function principally in terms of raising public conscious-ness of legal issues, the OLRC operated largely behind closed doors; it did not consult through public hearings[20] and, in McRuer's day, never pub-lished working papers. This Ontario enterprise was results-oriented law reform, conducted by progressive members of the legal profession and backed up by good staff work and the advice of outside legal specialists.

Results there certainly were. Over the 1960s and 1970s the OLRC contributed substantially to the fundamental reshaping of laws touch-ing virtually every area of Ontario life, from divorce to debts, child wel-fare to wills, insurance to individual privacy. Its influence also spread beyond Ontario's borders, not only to other Canadian provinces but also abroad.[21] Success is never absolute in such a massive, and often amor-phous, undertaking as law reform; there are always other laws requiring attention, and sometimes those that have been fixed need fixing once again. Yet, on the whole, there can be no doubt that the OLRC was a remarkably productive body and that the reforms that followed its rec-ommendations changed Ontario for the better. McRuer, never one to be easily pleased, certainly believed that this was the case. By the time he left the commission for good in 1982, he was satisfied that he had done all he could in the area of law reform. The torch could now be passed to others.

Through the 1980s and early 1990s, the OLRC has continued its work, building upon the achievements of McRuer and his fellow pioneer com-missioners. Yet no one would ever claim that it is the same kind of insti-tution.[22] McRuer's commission, certainly during his period as chairman and even afterwards, was unique, a product of one extraordinary man. He shaped the early OLRC in his image, and, at the end of the day, the commission's legacy was also his own.

16

ONE MAN AND THE LAW

IN SOME RESPECTS, Jim McRuer was most influential during the last decade and a half of his life. Though he was now elderly—he turned eighty in 1970—people of many different backgrounds listened to him as they had rarely done before. He had become an elder statesman of the law, commanding increasing respect from his legal colleagues, governments, and the population at large.

At the beginning of the 1970s, while he was immersed both in the ongoing work of the law reform commission and in completing the last report of the civil rights inquiry, McRuer's professional achievements were recognized in a special way. On 29 April 1970 all lawyers of the Ontario legislature, including Premier Robarts and Attorney-General Wishart, hosted a reception and dinner in his honour. Amid sustained applause, McRuer received a large silver tray bearing the engraved signatures of each of the twenty-three lawyer-MPPs at Queen's Park and an inscription expressing their esteem for his "labours in the realm of Civil Rights." McRuer was deeply moved, as any member of the legal profession would be, by this gesture. In time he would proudly donate the tray to the Legislative Library for permanent display.

The address he delivered that evening was vintage McRuer. Step by step, he went through the guiding principles behind his inquiry into civil rights, and he challenged his listeners—in words that were obviously heartfelt—to remind themselves continuously of their solemn responsibility as legislators and as private citizens. The heritage of the past and the hope of the future was in their hands, McRuer affirmed, not merely by virtue of their professional calling, but also because of the example they were obliged to set as leading members of society. It was a theme to which McRuer would return time and time again in his numerous public appearances after 1970.

Being honoured by all the lawyer-MPPs in Ontario was not the only recognition that McRuer received for his years of service to the country. On 12 November 1968 he received the Medal of Service in the Order of Canada, and in 1972 he became an officer of the order. On 31 May 1973 he received the Civic Award of Merit from the City of Toronto. Years before, in 1947, McRuer had been granted an honorary doctorate from Laval University, and now further honorary doctorates followed from the University of Toronto (23 November 1962), Trent University (31 May 1968), the University of Windsor (25 September 1970), and Queen's University (5 June 1971). These degrees mattered greatly to McRuer, whose commitment to education had been evident since his days in the 1930s as a founder of the Ontario Police College and as an instructor at Osgoode Hall Law School. The importance he attached to academic life continued to be evident after 1970, and indeed, because he now had more free time, he increasingly could be found on Ontario campuses sharing his knowledge and experiences with students and professors. He taught a seminar course at the University of Toronto Law School from 1969 to 1977, and he also made a gift to the law school of "The McRuer Scholarship in Administrative Law," to be awarded annually to the student with the highest marks in administrative law. He was frequently invited to participate in public forums, such as the University of Toronto conferences on law and contemporary affairs on 1 February 1975 and 3 February 1978, as principal speaker. And he delivered guest lectures hither and yon, such as at the University of Windsor (25 September 1970), the University of Western Ontario (1 April 1971), Queen's University (5 June 1971), Trent University (24 January 1974), the University of Victoria (20 April 1974), and York University (4 April 1975). Quite often these lectures were subsequently reprinted in books and law journals. For example, his lecture at the University of Toronto in 1962, on the occasion of his receiving an honorary doctorate, was published in the 1963 book *Changing-Legal Perspectives*. Entitled "Liability without Fault in the Law of Tort," it was widely circulated in revised form because the Ontario government was then considering no-fault automobile insurance—the main focus of McRuer's lecture and his chapter in the book.[1]

Through all these years, McRuer continued, as he had done since the earliest days of his career, to contribute special articles to newspapers and other publications.² As something new for him, he also reached much larger audiences through television. In 1971 he participated with enthusiasm in a series of television programs on the law produced for use in high schools by the Ontario Educational Communications Authority. Five years later, TV Ontario filmed a four-part series on McRuer's life that was broadcast over four weeks in January 1977. It was compiled from over fourteen hours of interviews with McRuer conducted by Bill Davidson, a Toronto feature film producer. Claude Bissell, former president of the University of Toronto, assisted in putting the story together, and in the film he referred to McRuer as "the last of the great puritans," a statement intended to convey his respect for McRuer's dedication to work, his personal integrity, and his unflagging commitment to the principles that guided his life.³

Despite his age and his diverse obligations, McRuer still found time for travel. In the summer of 1972, for instance, he paid a twelve-day visit to China, accompanied by his wife Robena, his daughter Mary Louise, her friend Margaret Pope from Ottawa, and, inevitably, officials of the All China Travel Service. At the time, China was off the beaten track for tourists; it was still unrecognized by the international community and had just emerged, with physical and psychological scars, from the chaos of the Cultural Revolution. McRuer was therefore able to see what most other foreigners could only imagine, and he made the most of the opportunity, observing everything with a careful eye, listening attentively to whatever his hosts told him, and asking questions.

Throughout his China trip, it was clear to McRuer that he was more than a mere tourist. Indeed, because he was of some help to the regime in improving relations with the West, McRuer was treated by the Chinese officials as an exalted guest. Though he was feeling fine, his hosts constantly fussed over his health. They also agreed to his request to meet with law professors at Peking University. There, McRuer was curious to learn how much of the country's judicial system had been rebuilt following the Cultural Revolution. The professors, all elderly men themselves, gave him a sketch of the system of justice that was currently in the process of creation. Although this system was fundamentally different from the legal system of the West, McRuer was diplomatic enough not to criticize it but only to listen and learn. After his exchange with the professors, McRuer and his party toured the university library, where Robena, formerly a librarian, dove into the catalogue in search of the Canada section. She found a sheaf of index cards about two inches thick containing

several basic texts by Canadian authors on Canadian history and government, but not very much that had been written in recent years. On
their return to Canada, Jim—again following a familiar pattern of speaking about his experiences abroad in lectures—addressed the Toronto
Lawyers' Club on the subject of his trip. His message was that "when
you are in China, you are in another world, and when you have been in
China, you have a different view of the world."[4]

Even in these years, McRuer found it impossible to be separated from
work for long. In 1977 Premier Bill Davis established a commission on
freedom of information and individual privacy, and McRuer, just having resigned as vice-chairman of the OLRC, accepted with relish the post
of consultant to the new body. Over the next couple of years, McRuer's
work with this commission illustrated three of the main elements of his
legal career. The first was his ability to help define and raise issues and
get them on the public agenda; the second was his role in working assiduously with others to develop a reasonable and effective solution to a
given problem; the third was his view that there were certain limits to
what the law could accomplish.

The issues of freedom of information and individual privacy had long
been of interest to McRuer. In the 1960s he had observed with some dis-
quiet the growing accumulation of personal information in the hands of
government officials. Increasingly he realized that, when statutes authorizing the collection of personal information had been enacted, privacy
had seldom even been taken into account. As a result of his concern, the
OLRC reported to Attorney-General Wishart that "a grave threat is posed
to all free men and democratic institutions by modern technology and
well-intentioned government and commercial practices that expose the
individual to public and institutional scrutiny; that record and collate all
his transactions; and that treat him as an object to be manipulated in the
attainment of public, social and economic goals."[5]

With similar concerns being expressed in the newspapers, in parliament and the provincial legislatures, and at meetings of the Canadian Bar
Association, the OLRC initiated a study of the problems involved in protecting privacy in modern-day Ontario. Its report, released in September
1968, referred to practices that "both shock the conscience and intensify
the increasing apprehension that is felt in this province and in Canada
for the need for protection of the privacy of the individual."[6] The OLRC
recommended a royal commission or a specially constituted task force
to examine the problem and propose the necessary legislation.

When the Commission on Freedom of Information and Individual

Privacy was finally created in 1977, there were two views about govern-
ment-held information. One school of thought, arguing that government held the reins of control too tightly and shrouded public business
in unnecessary secrecy, sought "freedom of information." The other
school argued that individual privacy was under attack and wanted
guarantees that the extensive amounts of personal data in government
hands would remain confidential. The two views could readily be seen
as opposite sides of the same issue, and so the government wisely chose
to treat the question "in the round," or as one, in order that neither goal
would be achieved at the expense of the other. This balanced approach
clearly reflected McRuer's own view of the problem.

The commission, chaired by Dr. D. Carlton Williams, former president of the University of Western Ontario, set up its operations at 180
Dundas Street West in Toronto. The two other members of the commission were Dorothy J. Burgoyne and G.H.U. Bayly, while Bill Poole,
McRuer's OLRC colleague, acted as counsel, John D. McCamus as director of research, and Doris E. Wagg as registrar. As a consultant to the
commission, McRuer took an active interest in its work. He appeared
regularly at its offices, read every one of the briefs that were submitted,
and attended meetings for discussion of the research papers—all "in an
effort," he said, "to come to a wise conclusion, whatever it might be, in
due course." Fascinated by the issues and appreciating their complexities,
he described the challenge facing the commission as "a very comprehensive thing and very difficult but to some people, particularly editorial
writers, extremely simple." Bill Poole describes McRuer's contribution
to the commission as invaluable, noting that he had a "most incredible
grasp of all the statutes of Ontario, back to front." John McCamus agrees.
When McRuer attended commission meetings, McCamus states, "people had confidence in what he was saying, although he could get argu-
mentative if he saw something he didn't like. He was not tentative in the
expression of his views!"[7]

McRuer took advantage of every opportunity to publicize both the
work of the commission and his own belief that government should avoid
passing hasty, ill-conceived legislation that, in the long term, would create practical problems in the realm of government operations. He spoke
at public meetings and gave interviews to reporters, and, because of his
eminent reputation, his utterances carried great weight. The boy who
had grown up in an isolated farmhouse in the 1890s was now grappling
with a new world of satellite transmissions, electronic surveillance, and
computer data-banks.

Among McRuer's audiences was a group of some 900 municipal government representatives attending the Ontario annual conference of the Association of Municipalities at Toronto's Royal York Hotel on 22 August 1978. On this occasion McRuer spoke about an article published in *Municipal World* which recommended the opening of municipal government records "subject to specific exemptions" but did not explain what those exceptions should be. "May I suggest to you," he said in his polite yet stern fashion, "that you review your recommendations and supplement them with more precision." Knowing how extensively personal information was gathered by local governments and thus how relevant the policies and actions of the municipalities were in this area, McRuer gave his listeners several illustrations. One concerned an applicant for public assistance. In this case, he explained, the obviously conflicting interests include the right of the donor of the assistance to know all the circumstances giving rise to the application, the right of taxpayers to know how the money paid by them is spent, and the right of the applicant to have his family affairs kept private. It was in this sort of specific situation, McRuer explained, that broad or general words had to be found to respect all three needs if any legislation was to be enacted.

McRuer also took his message to the campus of the University of Toronto. As the keynote speaker at the conference on law and contemporary affairs in February 1978, he emphasized that free public discussion of public affairs—"the breath of life for parliamentary institutions"—must necessarily be based on information. Yet in this area, he added, "there are no absolutes. Just as it is important that the electors (in whom the final authority rests in our particular system) should have information concerning the basis for the exercise of the power of government, it is important that those having the power to govern have information, the release of which would destroy their power to govern." That was the central dilemma, and McRuer always insisted on emphasizing both sides, rather than simply making grand proclamations in favour of "freedom of information" or "the right to privacy."

McRuer was just as capable as anyone in discussing all the detailed aspects of the commission's work. His speech at the University of Toronto conference, in the methodical and comprehensive McRuer style, ranged over the 102 separate Ontario statutes imposing specific restraints on release of information, examined the "unparalleled" new abilities of government aided and abetted by computers "to intrude on an individual's privacy," and delved into many specific operations of government. Yet he always brought the discussion back to the basic conundrum—that is, because so many conflicting public interests were at work, giving legal shape to the principle of freedom of information was extraordinarily difficult. Indeed, McRuer held that "precise definition of these conflicting interests is not possible." Attempts to define or limit them by law had been made in other jurisdictions, "but it cannot be said with confidence that this has been done in such a manner that it produces satisfactory results." In his considered opinion, "complete freedom of information and complete protection of privacy cannot be reconciled in areas of the governmental process. Likewise, complete freedom of information in governmental processes, and the public right to an efficient operation of government in all its aspects are not easily reconciled." True, it "is not hard to prescribe legislative sedatives, but it is hard to find wise, workable solutions that will justly recognize the many areas of conflicting public interests."

It was McRuer's position, then, that legislation governing freedom of information and individual privacy needed to be drafted carefully and with a full recognition of the complexities involved. On this issue as on others involving competing rights, the best approach was a balanced, realistic one that made fairness its principal aim, avoided absolutes and theoretical purity at all costs, and kept open the possibility of creative improvisation. In the end, he thought that the provincial government steered a wise, moderate course in its Human Rights Act of 1978, which guaranteed freedom of information. A more ambitious measure, the Freedom of Information and Protection of Privacy Act—was not passed until 1987, two years after his death.

Following the University of Toronto conference, McRuer returned to Florida where he and Robena frequently wintered. On this particular vacation, he suffered a broken hip, but by late summer he was fully recovered. On 23 August he celebrated his eighty-eighth birthday with a game of golf at the Toronto Hunt Club, and, as further evidence of his good health, he was looking forward with great anticipation to an appearance before a Senate committee scheduled for 7 September 1978. This committee had been struck to consider the Trudeau government's ambitious plans for a new Canadian constitution as set out in Bill C-60. Thirty members strong, it was chaired by Senator Robert Stanbury.

On the day that he took his seat before the Senate committee, McRuer was in fine form: alert, nicely dressed in a light suit, his once-intimidating black moustache now faded to a friendlier grey. Eager to share his views with the committee, he told the senators that he regarded their constitutional deliberations as "one of the most important matters in which I have had an opportunity to participate in my lifetime." This was not just a diplomatic or politically tactful remark; McRuer had never been given to massaging other people's egos. He viewed his appearance before the committee as an opportunity to speak out as an elder statesman in ways that might be beneficial, and his presentation left no doubt that he saw Bill C-60 as a challenge to many of his deepest convictions.

McRuer began by expressing his fundamental belief that parliament should not be discussing the creation of a new constitution as long as it lacked "definite agreement as to how it may be amended." With regard to the Supreme Court of Canada, he objected to the proposal that the number of judges on the court be increased from nine to eleven or even fifteen, arguing that such a body would be unwieldy; he criticized the idea that the government be constitutionally obliged to select Supreme Court judges according to a regional formula ("What we should have is the best men and women available."); and he dismissed the complicated plans for nominations to the court as well as the suggestion that the overhauled Senate—to be called the House of the Federation—be given the authority of ratifying such appointments.

On the entrenchment of a bill of rights in the new constitution, McRuer repeated to the senators the arguments he had presented to the Ontario government in his inquiry's report on civil rights. Convinced that an entrenched bill would not enhance, but reduce, the rights and freedoms of the individual Canadian citizen, he declared forcefully: "Any bill of rights must consist of general words which have to be construed by the courts ... This gives the courts very wide legislative powers which the judges have no special qualifications to exercise and, in some cases, can be a denial of the protection of the rights of the individual." He then explained that "it has been the history of entrenched bills of rights that the courts have distorted the language of such a bill to give it entirely different meanings." That was certainly the case in the United States, where, for roughly thirty years, "the legislators were denied the right to legislate on hours of labour, on child labour, and on matters of that sort, because they interfered with the [Fourteenth] amendment—freedom of contract." McRuer, for his part, did not believe that "judges are the best interpreters for the purpose of legislating what is meant by general language. 'Freedom of religion'—what does that mean? To me, entrenchment does more harm to the rights of the individual than it does good." Moreover, McRuer argued, constitutionalizing rights ignored the fact that society was constantly evolving. As he explained, "We do not know what social conditions will be ten, fifteen, or twenty years hence. I have seen social conditions change a great deal, and I have seen public opinion change a great deal."

Senator Joe Greene challenged McRuer's negative assessment of the Bill of Rights in the United States, citing civil rights as an area where the Supreme Court's quasi-legislative role had helped reshape American society along progressive lines. But McRuer did not give any ground. "In the first place," he replied, "I think it is a very considerable reflection on our whole parliamentary system if we have to depend on those appointed to the bench to take leadership in the defence of human rights. I am not prepared to indict our parliamentary system in that way." To his mind, the protection of people's rights was best achieved by "the courts enforcing the legislation passed by the legislators and not attempting to legislate on their own behalf." He accepted the argument that the American system "has done a great deal of good in areas where there were political obstacles, but I think we have to find solutions for our political problems without asking the judges to solve them."

The final major topic McRuer addressed in his appearance before the Senate committee concerned the role of the monarchy. His remarks on this issue were cautious, complex, and nuanced. Though he was concerned that Bill C-60 did not adequately define the queen's constitutional role, he also took pains to emphasize that the monarchy's constitutional prerogatives should be left intact. "My concept of the monarchy in the Canadian democratic society is this," McRuer said. "The Queen is a living, visible manifestation of the sovereignty of the ideas of the people of Canada in whom the sovereign political power rests, and those engaged in all processes of government derive the powers they exercise from the constitutional right of the people to effectively express their ideas by voting." He noted that there existed in Canada "many unwritten prerogatives of the Crown" and that "some of these prerogative powers are exercised through elected representatives, some by the Governor General and some by judges of the superior courts." It was essential, he stressed, that "these prerogative powers are not disturbed by any provisions of a written constitution." Though he admitted that it was difficult to define "in any clear and simple statement all the attributes and meaning of the monarchy" in Canada's constitution, he thought it could and should be done. "It is no compliment to the Queen to keep in our written constitutional scheme words with little meaning."

Fundamental to McRuer's view of a stable Canadian society, where individuals enjoyed freedom under law, was the presence of a "constitutional head of state through which the rule of law is safeguarded and the ideas of the people are safeguarded against any form of the exercise of non-democratic power. That, in my view, is the true function of the monarchy." In defining the monarchy's role in modern Canada, McRuer said, constitution-makers should recognize that "we have hundreds of years of development of principles, traditions, customs and conventions" and that these should be "guarded with vigilance as part of our nation-hood." In short, McRuer believed that the new constitution should make it clear that "the Queen exercises no authority in her own right over the Government of Canada but, at the same time, is the manifestation of the sovereignty of the ideas of the people. This may be idealistic, but I think it is realistic."[8]

When the chairman's gavel signalled the end of the session, McRuer had spent over four hours before the committee. The positions he had set out were unequivocal: the current system of selecting judges was producing good results and so should not be changed; the rights of the individual should be protected, but legislators, not judges, should have the final say in defining and defending those rights; the monarchy's posi-tion in modern-day Canada should be defined clearly and succinctly, and in such a manner that none of the prerogatives it currently enjoyed would be touched. In explaining his views on these issues and others, McRuer performed impressively, fielding questions with skill and hold-ing his own in exchanges with the committee's members, including the redoubtable constitutional expert Eugene Forsey.

Taken together, McRuer's two main presentations in 1978—his address to the University of Toronto conference on law and contemporary affairs, and his remarks before the Senate committee on the constitution—shed additional light on some of the essential characteristics of his legal and political thought. Although he remained profoundly committed to equality under the law, the rights of the individual, and democracy itself, McRuer was more a realist than an ideologue. As he revealingly put it to the senators, he was an idealistic realist. He approached issues of public policy with clear ideas and convictions, but also with an understanding of what could be accomplished through government and the law and what could not. While taking a remarkably progressive stance on a host of issues, he never lost his keen sense of tradition and particularly his deep attachment to the common law and the British parliamentary sys-tem.

McRuer's realism was evident in his position on the issue of freedom of information versus individual privacy. He was convinced that any

attempt to give absolute, unchanging legal definition to these competing rights was bound to fail; in this area as in so many others, there
was no legislative panacea to the dilemmas that frequently faced governments and the courts. As for the Trudeau government's Bill C-60,
McRuer's realism again came into play: he thought that many of the
proposed constitutional arrangements were too cumbersome to work in
practice, and, besides, they were unnecessary—the *status quo* was working satisfactorily. Yet, in this instance, McRuer's traditionalism was no
less important than his realism in determining his position. To him, the
proposal for an entrenched bill of rights was deeply misguided because
it reflected American constitutional principles more than British ones.
McRuer was passionately proud of the British common-law tradition
and the parliamentary system, and he was adamantly opposed to Canada's discarding that heritage in favour of American practices. Reinforcing
this visceral attachment to tradition was McRuer's belief that Canada's
existing legal and political system was more effective than that of the
United States in protecting individual freedom.

Such were some of the ingredients of McRuer's philosophical vision.
The intellectual force of that vision—his liberalism balanced by realism, his commitment to individual rights tempered by an awareness
of the collective good, and his progressive instincts harmonized with a
deep respect for Canada's legal and political inheritance—moulded Jim
McRuer's many contributions to the law.

THIS BOOK has had much to say about McRuer's professional career from
its beginnings before the First World War to its close more than half a
century later. Yet what more can be said about McRuer the man? What
was he really like as a person?

To the end, McRuer was a man of puzzling contradictions. During the
Great War, he was a farm boy-turned-soldier with an interest in collecting fine bone china. Later, as a crusading crown attorney, he believed
that people needed to respect the law, but he also spent much of his
time enforcing prohibition—a cause that many viewed with contempt.
He was a civil libertarian who supported the curtailment of certain civil
liberties during the Second World War. As a judge, he took his court to
communities all across the province, but he also kept a courtroom of
people waiting for hours until completing the formality of having Canada's royal coat-of-arms hung. He could be moved to tears by the plight of
society's unfortunates, especially children, yet he had no compunction

about sending murderers to the gallows. He campaigned tirelessly for prison reform, but he sent convicted individuals to these same prisons with heavy sentences. Away from the bench, he was a committed democrat who, on being asked by his next-door neighbour how she should address him, stiffly replied, "Just call me 'Chief Justice McRuer.'" He was a champion of the "common man" who once upbraided the staff at his golf club for allowing his watch to be stolen and then later, for fear of losing his dignity, failed to apologize when he found the watch in his own locker—an insensitive act for which the club cancelled his membership.

Given his complexity, it is not surprising that perceptions of McRuer have always differed widely. For some, he was stern and unforgiving, a cranky, domineering figure with few, if any, redeeming virtues; for others, he was all sweetness and light, a gentle man who identified with the misfortunes of society's marginalized people and often displayed great compassion towards them. To a certain degree, these conflicting perceptions derive, not from any paradox in McRuer himself, but from the particular circumstances of those who came into contact with him. Defendants who appeared before McRuer and were sentenced to death did not perceive the same man as did the young girl who, on trial for the shooting of her abusive father, was acquitted in McRuer's court. The businessmen and officeholders whose careers were felled by McRuer as a crown prosecutor intent on punishing fraud saw him as an implacable, ruthless man entirely lacking in mercy; the many other people who were helped along the way by McRuer, such as the mother in northern Ontario who was allowed to keep money her small boy had found in the local pool hall, saw him as an angel of mercy.

The key to understanding the character of Jim McRuer lies in the statement of his son, John, that his father's greatest liability was his "excruciating shyness." Throughout his life, McRuer was an extremely private, reserved person whose profound shyness led him to keep his innermost feelings to himself. The result was that he often appeared aloof and emotionally difficult, intellectually talented but also cantankerous and incapable of human affection. He commanded wide respect but had few friends; hardly anyone knew him well enough to realize that his crusty demeanour was only a veneer, reflective not of meanness of spirit but of psychological vulnerability. Finding it difficult to relate to people, he erected emotional barriers around himself that were designed to keep the outside world at bay, and over time these barriers became an inseparable part of his character.

Because he cared about people and yet was too shy to form relationships with them, McRuer reached out to others through his work. As a lawyer, he could delve right into the heart of someone else's life, but from a safe distance. Later, as a judge, he could make decisions that profoundly affected other people's lives even as he maintained some measure of formal distance and objectivity. This was why he hated the "dry, boring" work of an appellate judge and loved the "human drama" that the trial judge encountered as daily fare. Particularly in murder cases, he found himself immersed in the human dimension of the story unfolding before him—so much so that, in the Evelyn Dick case, he effectively ceased to be a judge, asking too many questions from the bench, intimidating the jurors, even advising the crown attorney how to proceed. The Dick case was exceptional, but McRuer's deep engagement with the lives and problems of other people was similarly on display whenever vulnerable individuals—a child, a mentally retarded youth, an abused wife— found their future in his hands. When dealing with such people, he felt a profound empathy for their situation. The courtroom—his courtroom— was the place where he felt secure and able to reach out to other people and touch their lives, all under the protective cloak of judicial formalities.

The law was also useful to McRuer in that it gave him a vehicle through which he could express his views without fear of exposing his inner self. This point is illustrated by the contrasting ways in which he responded to two separate requests for newspaper articles in the 1960s. In 1969 the *Toronto Star* was doing a series on different people's versions of life in the city, and that September the paper's editor-in-chief, Peter C. Newman, asked McRuer for an article called "Judge McRuer's Toronto." After considering the request for almost two weeks, McRuer said no. "I would be quite unqualified to write such an article. I feel I do not know the city at all." This was a remarkable statement for a man whose life had centred on Toronto, and not in any marginal way, for more than sixty years. "In fact," he confessed, "I walked over to Osgoode Hall the other day and I was astonished to find so many old landmarks had been removed since I last walked along King Street West from Yonge to York Street." McRuer's unease with the demolition mania that hit Toronto in the 1960s was a plausible excuse for his not writing the article, but there was more to his decision than that. In reality, this shy man was not capable of sharing his personal world even with those who were close to him, let alone the anonymous readers of Canada's largest newspaper.

Yet Jim McRuer felt no reluctance in talking or writing about the law and the great personalities of his legal world. When William French of the *Globe and Mail* asked him for a review of H. Montgomery Hyde's biography of Lord Birkett—one of the guests at the CBA annual meeting in Ottawa the year of McRuer's presidency—McRuer agreed readily and wrote the piece while vacationing in florida. Ironically, it was through writing about Lord Birkett, whom he greatly admired, that McRuer revealed himself. "What stands out most in this absorbing book is not Birkett's success in the courts nor the large fees he earned," McRuer wrote, "but his passion for justice and his professional integrity." He certainly saw Birkett as a model for the entire legal profession, but perhaps he did not realize how much he mirrored this man in significant ways. Or, then again, perhaps his portrayal of Birkett was a shy man's subtle way of describing himself by writing about another. McRuer recommended Hyde's book because it showed "Birkett as a man dedicated to his profession with a high respect for law and its just administration which he regarded as the supreme test of any civilized society."[9]

Part of McRuer's problem in inter-personal relationships rested in the people around him. Bill Poole certainly respected McRuer, but he also had the fun-loving approach of many members of the criminal bar. "McRuer's reputation was such that nobody would disagree with him," says Poole. For his part, Poole was less reverential. He actually teased McRuer, and McRuer loved it. "Have you been down lately to see the women in the cages at Victoria Station?" Poole once asked, referring to the scantily clad exotic dancers at a Toronto club. McRuer laughed.[10] He liked this easy familiarity but seldom got it because most people were afraid of him. Poole and Catherine MacLean, his colleague at the OLRC, were two of the people with a rare gift for putting McRuer at his ease. Robena, his second wife, was another.

Regrettably, Mary, Jim's first wife, was not among this select company. While she and Jim were deeply fond of one another, she apparently was unable to nurture him emotionally, and he, for his part, was too shy to reach out to her—except in his letters. At home, says John McRuer, Jim wanted to be a beloved patriarch, but he "could never get close enough to his family to be more than a shadowy, severe presence—kind, well meaning, but generally inappropriate and rather trite." He was not much help with domestic problems. These were Mary's responsibility. She was no more emotionally equipped to face up to delicate situations with his children than his own father had been with him. John remembers his mother telling him that his father was "very sensitive," and he notes that, because of this side of his character, "you couldn't discuss anything with him. If you had something on your mind you spoke; he pronounced his advice; he would then be hurt because his advice was not heeded—usually because of inadequate understanding of the situation on his part. His shyness did him in. He was too shy, and too scared of ridicule to acknowledge bewilderment, other people's values, uncertainty of choice, or the communication of a touch. He must have been very lonely."

At the dinner table in the McRuer household, Jim "just talked on endlessly about his court cases," boring the children so much that one of them would follow Katherine's signal and "spill a glass of milk to create a distraction." John also recalls "as a small child being somewhat puzzled when my father kissed my mother with warmth and affection. It happened so rarely that each time was an event!" Another of his memories dates to his father's old age. "I went walking with him from his apartment, slowly, he with his cane. He talked as we walked about working on some thoughts about his [religious] beliefs. I didn't remember the details, but it was one of the few—very, very few moments when we were ever close."

Still, though he was not a particularly warm husband or father, there is no doubt that McRuer loved his family greatly. His love was expressed more in acts of kindness than in words and embraces, but it was no less real for that. On many occasions, he was a great father, taking his children on foreign vacations and, at the family's Stoney Lake cottage, teaching them how to clear away stones to make a flat area to play badminton, how to cut firewood, or how to pick raspberries faster by looping a tin cup on one's belt and keeping both hands free to work. Whenever the children were sick at home, Jim always brought them presents. He revelled in their successes—a good report card at school, an important role in a play—and he could sometimes do generous and unexpected things, such as buying Mary and daughters Katherine and Mary Louise expensive fur coats, or, on a trip to London, taking them to the silver vaults to buy a "worthwhile souvenir" of their visit. From time to time, he could even be an entertaining father, able to set work aside and concentrate on just enjoying himself. Mary Louise remembers one such occasion. When McRuer's three children were seven, five, and two years old, he took them camping. As Mary Louise puts it, Father, "leaving Mother behind for a well-earned rest, packed all the children and their equipment into the old Essex: a hugh bed roll on the fender, and a big white tent and folding wash basin, pots and bathing suits stuffed inside to the roof and outside on the running board." The children could hardly see out the car's windows, and Mary Louise, embarrassed by all the paraphernalia, desperately hoped that they would not be spotted by any of their friends.

Family was not the only pillar supporting McRuer's life; another was religion. According to John McRuer, his father's faith "was highly non-conformist, if not heretical. What he believed, or didn't believe, was never, at any time, discussed with me. But from things that weren't said, or small subtle hints, I believe he didn't take any of the fundamental tenets of Christianity any more literally than I do." John continues: "I don't think he believed in the virgin-birth, the miracles, or the resurrection... I don't think he ever thought about the Trinity, or took it any more seriously than words to describe a state of spirituality. This is conjecture, for he never talked much about the things he really cared about." In John's opinion, which is shared by his sister Katherine, Jim even "lost his faith" towards the end of his life; "he stopped going to church and took no interest in church affairs." John and Katherine may or may not be correct in claiming that their father's faith evaporated in his old age; there is no way of knowing for certain. What is clear, however, is that McRuer's faith was important to him for a very long time and the substance of that faith had little to do with traditional Christian dogma. Christianity, for McRuer, did not consist only of doctrines; it was as much a frame of mind as an intellectual system. He absorbed the Christian outlook at an early age, and in the years to come he could no more abandon it than shed his skin. His belief in the value of hard work, his determination to live a life of strict integrity and morality, his commitment to the idea that each man and woman should love their fellow human beings, his consciousness of human sinfulness and of the necessity to restrain and punish it—all of this was rooted in a Christian ethic that did much to shape the world in which McRuer himself came into maturity.

Remarkably, McRuer told strangers more about his religious views than he conveyed to his own family. On 5 May 1971, in an address to the Ontario Leadership Prayer Breakfast at the Royal York Hotel in Toronto, McRuer spoke openly about his disenchantment with dogma, his hostility to conformism, and his fundamental belief in the value of religious freedom. He also gave moving expression to the vision that lay at the heart of his faith. "It is hard," he said, "for the finite mind to know what his part may be in the infinite, just as it is hard for our finite minds to comprehend the infinity of the universe. But meaning it all has and man has a meaningful part in it all—a spiritual part ... It is the life of the spirit that measures the value of the one apart from the herd ..." Noting that "the glass through which we see is still dark but it is not as dark as when St. Paul looked through his glass," McRuer pointed to the many signs of hope that were visible in the world—everything from the widespread "concern to comfort the sick, to relieve suffering, hunger and destitution" to new laws designed to achieve a greater measure of social justice. All these were "rays of light that give us hope and a sure confidence that there is a purpose in all life; that there is a God 'who has a spiritual presence, in whom we live and move and have our being, whose name is love and whose temples are human hearts.'" McRuer concluded, "We now know only in part but we shall yet fully understand."[11]

Such a religious vision owed more to the liberal Christianity of McRuer's times than to the Calvinist tradition that formed the core of his Presbyterian inheritance. That said, however, the term Calvinism has slipped into popular usage to denote certain character traits—a love of work, a dislike of alcohol, strait-laced morality—and in this sense Jim McRuer was so Calvinist as to be stereotypical. In terms of his work habits, certainly, he was Calvinist to a fault. Throughout his adult life, he worked long, even brutal hours, completely immersed in the task at hand. The very fact that, at the age of seventy-three, he began a new career as a civil rights commissioner and law reformer speaks volumes about how much work meant to him. Indeed, for McRuer, work was not a way of life—it was his life. First as a lawyer, then as a judge, and finally in his last incarnation as a crusader for civil rights and law reform, McRuer lived and breathed the law; he was constantly thinking about the issues currently before him, and, as soon as he completed one assignment, he was off to another. He lived this way partly because of his own fascination with the law, but also because, in his view of the world, there was no other way to live. Fortunately, McRuer was blessed with the kind of constitution that allowed him to put his commitment to work into practice, and he also knew the importance of recharging his batteries at regular intervals. John McRuer recalls that his father "was a very high energy person always, but he knew how to husband this energy"; he "was very good at catnapping," John says, sleeping for fifteen minutes before dinner and, in his later years, an hour after lunch. These habits, in John's mind, "went a long way to extending his productive and healthy life."[12]

McRuer's Calvinist genes were also reflected in that familiar Scottish trait, frugality. McRuer always lived well, and, as his son points out, loved "fine china, good music, good art, and beautiful furniture and silver." Yet his fondness for "nice things" stemmed from an attraction to beauty, not from mere acquisitiveness. In many ways, indeed, he prided himself on living simply. Those after-lunch naps that he regularly took in his later years happened on a used chesterfield that he had found in a government warehouse; Public Works officials had wanted to supply him with new furniture—he was then conducting the civil rights inquiry and presiding over the law reform commission—but he found it, in John's words, "too expensive and too extravagant." More revealing still was McRuer's consistent refusal, after his appointment to the bench, to take advantage of the limousine service available to Court of Appeal and High Court justices. Instead he travelled on public transit, walking half a mile to the bus stop each way. Later, after his appointment to the civil rights and law reform commissions, he continued to take public transit despite his age; after all, he pointed out, tickets were cheaper for senior citizens! At home, even after he became financially successful, he still let Mary make her own clothes. This changed only when one of his law partners commented to Mary that Jim was making lots of money and so she no longer needed to be her own seamstress, From then on, Mary bought her dresses.

Like many strait-laced Presbyterians, Jim McRuer despised the ways in which alcohol could blight human lives, and for many years he was a strict abstainer—with the odd exception. On one memorable occasion, when his law firm held a party for the lawyers and their wives on the roof garden of the Royal York Hotel, one of the young lawyers got there early with a bottle of gin and spiked the fruit punch. Jim and Mary arrived, and he naturally avoided the bar, taking instead a glass of the innocent punch. As the evening wore on, no one could believe what fun Jim was having. That was a glimpse of possibilities.

Later in life, after Mary's death, Jim McRuer became a happier, more relaxed man. One reason for this transformation was his marriage to the vibrant Robena, who touched Jim in human ways and connected with his happier elements. Another was his new appreciation of the loosening effects of alcohol—something for which he was indebted to his colleague Gibson Gray, whom Katherine McRuer often introduced to other people as "the man who taught my father how to drink." One day at a fishing camp McRuer returned badly sunburned and very hot. "Gib, I'm really terribly thirsty," he said. "I would like a drink, not too alcoholic." So Gray brought in a cooling concoction that he called, appropriately enough, a Presbyterian"—"half an ounce of gin, a little bit of ginger ale, a little bit of tonic, and so on." Soon McRuer delivered his verdict: "Oh, it is very, very tasty." Then, Gray reported, he had three Presbyterians. The drink became quite a hit. At a mid-winter CBA meeting in Toronto, Gray received a phone call from Bill Poole. "Dammit,

Gib, come up here." When Gray arrived in the music room, he was told: "J.C. wants a Presbyterian and this Italian guy doesn't know how to make one." McRuer then joined them, directing Gray to the bartender with the words, "Talk to this man."[13] A "Presbyterian" was not the only alcoholic drink that McRuer came to enjoy. Another colleague, John Arnup, would later observe that the emergence of a more easy-going McRuer coincided with "his change from one dry sherry to two gin and tonics."[14]

Jim McRuer's discovery of "Presbyterians" helped him to become a less austere figure, but, even before, he was never so earnest as to be incapable of human warmth. His essential goodness was constantly on display in his courtroom, but it was also shown in his willingness to lend a helping hand to others in less public ways. Robena said of Jim that, most of all, "he was a kind man, a *kind* man," and his kindness often took the form not just of words but of concrete action. In the summer of 1953, after witnessing the coronation of Queen Elizabeth II in London, McRuer visited a Cansave clinic for amputee children in Italy. Deeply moved by children who had learned to paint by holding brushes with their toes, he then moved on to Austria, where he saw malnourished children being nursed back to health in another Cansave-supported clinic.

In a small Austrian hotel on that same visit, he met the head waiter, Otto Lenzer, who was complaining about the lack of opportunities in Austria. McRuer suggested that he immigrate to Canada, and later, back in Canada himself, he wrote Immigration Minister W.E. Harris on Lenzer's behalf. Owing largely to McRuer's help in cutting through the red tape of immigration procedures, Lenzer and his wife were accepted into Canada. He worked for five years at Winston's Restaurant in Toronto, and then disappeared from McRuer's sight until 1970. That year, McRuer, when stepping out of the elevator at the Skyline Restaurant in Niagara Falls, was given a bone-crushing bear-hug by a man who turned out to be the Austrian waiter he had helped enter Canada so many years ago. He was now a maitre d' and had a family and good home in Niagara Falls. "Lunch," Otto Lenzer declared enthusiastically to a beaming McRuer, would be "on the house."

On one occasion, McRuer's kindness had exceptional results. In the late 1940s, on one of his judicial visits as chief justice to Port Arthur in northern Ontario, McRuer accepted an invitation to a Sunday afternoon recital in the home of a friend, the performer being a young man from Saskatchewan named Jonathan Vickers. Although McRuer never thought of himself as a connoisseur of music, Vickers's voice deeply impressed him. McRuer asked what he was doing to further the development of his musical career and it turned out that the answer was nothing; he was simply working in Kresge's department store. When McRuer returned to Toronto, he spoke to Dr. George Lambert, then the baritone soloist in Bloor Street United Church and also a teacher of voice at the Royal Conservatory of Music in Toronto. He told Lambert about Jon Vickers and between them they arranged for the singer to come to Toronto for an audition. Lambert took him on as a pupil in 1950 and a scholarship was arranged for his continuing study at the Royal Conservatory. Vickers's professional career was soon launched and by the late 1950s he had become renowned throughout the operatic world. Years later he encountered McRuer at the Guelph Spring Festival and told him, "But for you, I would not be here."

Then there was the sad case of Fred McMahon. A friend of Jim's wife Mary, McMahon was a Port Hope lawyer who had invested heavily in the stock market and then lost everything in the crash of 1929. To make matters even worse, McMahon had used his clients' securities to the amount of about $5,000 to support the bank loan that had financed his stock market activity. The strain of making ends meet while also covering the trail of his financial transactions proved too much for him, and in 1933 he suffered a nervous breakdown. After two years in a psychiatric hospital, he experienced still more misfortunes: he was dismissed from a job with the Ontario Pension Board after an anonymous person leaked word of his financial dealings in Port Hope; he then was convicted and imprisoned for those same offences; and, after enlisting in the army in 1939, he suffered another nervous collapse and was discharged.

Through all of this, McRuer did everything he could to help Fred McMahon and his wife, Jean. He found both of them work, testified as a character witness at McMahon's trial, lobbied for his transfer from Kingston penitentiary to the more humane Collins Bay prison, secured his release after he had served one year of his two-year sentence, and finally, after his discharge from the armed forces, berated the military authorities for their insensitivity. In undertaking these efforts, McRuer showed how kind he truly was. Writing to Minister of Highways Leopold Macaulay on behalf of Jean McMahon, McRuer wrote, "I cannot conceive of any more deserving case for help." Later, when requesting McMahon's transfer from Kingston to Collins Bay, he stressed that—if the transfer failed to take place—"it would not take many months to break his mental condition down again...and I fear he would never recover." Then, towards the end of this tragic tale, he told military officials that "this is not the time to show injustice, especially to a man whose nervous system was no doubt undermined in his service in the last war."[15]

The McMahon episode graphically illustrates the lengths to which McRuer would go in assisting other people. It also, of course, brings us back to a subject at the centre of this book, the meaning of justice. For McRuer, the interests of justice often demanded that those guilty of crimes be punished with the full rigour of the law; on other occasions, however, he was equally convinced that justice needed to be tempered with compassion. In the case of Fred McMahon, McRuer believed that no one's interests would be served by imprisoning this unfortunate man; as he explained, if McMahon were jailed, "there will be no possibility of his creditors ever getting anything. My experience has taught me that once a man has served a term in prison, it is only in the rarest cases that he is ever given a chance to redeem the past."[16] The fact that McMahon was not only jailed but then denied a good job and later treated shabbily by the military struck McRuer as a perversion of justice. Punishing him so harshly meant both that he and his family suffered grievously for McMahon's offence, while his creditors lost any hope of ever seeing their money again. In short, if ever there were a case in which clemency was appropriate, this was it. Destroying McMahon had served no other cause than that of vengeance.

McRuer's views on justice were not merely part of his intellectual outlook; in a very real sense, they were at the core of his being, giving his life both purpose and direction and shaping the way he viewed the world. They were also closely linked to his Christian faith. McRuer once said that people "seek a spiritual quality in the administration of justice. Law, in its purest form, is a form of religion." That summed up his vision of the law. In his mind, law and religion were so interconnected as to be indistinguishable; the concept of justice was central to law; and justice itself derived from the precepts set out in the Gospels. McRuer often compared the law to a beautiful temple, and the temple he had in mind was taken right out of Scripture. Until the day he died, he kept a Little Bible Lesson card that had been given to him as a boy of nine. The card, dated 3 September 1899, showed a picture of the rebuilding of the temple in Jerusalem. "God's people went back to Jerusalem," said the printed text. "They built houses to live in. They made an altar for the worship of God. Then they got ready to build a new temple. They laid the stones for a foundation. When these were in place the priests blew trumpets and sang praise to God and everyone was very happy." The card also had written upon it an Old Testament message from Ezra: "The temple of

God is holy, which temple ye are." There was another message, too, from Ezekiel: "I will put my spirit within you." Jim believed deeply in these sayings and lived by them,

So McRuer the man cannot be understood unless his commitment to justice is appreciated. Yet one question still remains unanswered, and it too goes to the heart of McRuer's personality. Why was McRuer so unshakeably certain in his vision of the law? In our own times, when self-doubt and ideological relativism are fashionable, McRuer's self-assurance seems to betray his intellectual limitations, a sign, perhaps, not of breadth of vision but of rigidity and shallowness. To take this perspective, however, is to apply the standards of our age to a much different era. Like other men and women of his generation, McRuer came to maturity in a world where most people subscribed to a common set of assumptions and values. The First World War shattered the intellectual confidence of some of these people, but many more survived the war with their principal beliefs intact. It was to this group that McRuer belonged. Products of less ambiguous times, when the differences between right and wrong were more clearly etched, they were capable of quickly grasping the heart of any issue and then speaking forthrightly about it. They knew who they were and what they wanted; equally important, they believed that they knew what was best for society as a whole. Carrying themselves with dignity, and possessed of great inner strength, they lived their lives according to maxims they had learned as children. For them, the truth of these maxims was obvious. The self-questioning of later generations was as foreign to them as their absolute certainty is to us.

McRuer, like many others of his generation, was committed to changing the world for the better; he also was firmly convinced—and here again he was not unusual—that this better world was within our reach. To the end of his life, McRuer was an optimist about the human condition. Recognizing the depth of humanity's capacity for evil, and understanding only too well the limits of the possible, he nonetheless was certain that great things could be accomplished by men and women of good will and determination. This idealism was evident throughout his career in the law, and it also underlay his feelings about young people. In his later years, he delivered many speeches to young people, and he saw the activism of youth in the 1960s as a promising sign that the world was heading in the right direction.

His hopefulness was especially evident in an address he delivered on 10 June 1969 in Toronto to the graduating class of Branksome Hall, a class that included his granddaughter Shelagh. McRuer, now seventy-nine years of age, began by noting that "it is many years ago since I sat where you sit now, throwing off the restraining influences of the past and looking forward with considerable excitement to what seemed to me some of the freedoms of the future." Reminiscing about his life on the farm outside Ayr at the turn of the century, McRuer explained how different that world was from the present. "It had no radio, no television, no aeroplanes, few motorcars and a few telephones," he said, and the moon, instead of being visited by spaceships from earth, "was left alone to shine on clear nights in the romantic hearts of young lovers." Then, coming closer to the future his granddaughter and the other youthful graduates faced, he continued: "I have lived in, and we are now living in, a world in revolution, and whether you like it or not you are being caught up in it and you will be part of the revolution which sweeps over the world as unrelentingly as the tides of the sea."

McRuer called upon his audience to take an active and constructive role in shaping the revolutionary changes lying ahead, for, "with every freedom there is attached an obligation—an obligation to preserve and extend justice to all." Looking at the youthful faces before him, he urged them to attack the plagues of hunger and illiteracy and expressed his joy that young people were already doing so much good. In words that conveyed the crusading idealism characteristic of his own life, he declared: "I am one of those who are proud to see youth on the march, youth rebelling against much of the sham and hypocrisy of the past, youth that will no longer be satisfied with mere pious declarations of human rights, youth that is demanding that those declarations be put into action as a way of life."

This old man—who in his time had wrought justice out of injustice, created laws out of concepts, and lit a beacon of hope for the rights and dignity of the individual—was seeking, as ever, to work with God in the fulfilment of others' lives. The graduation was taking place at Metropolitan United Church, and, most appropriately, McRuer was speaking from the pulpit. His audience had grown silent in respectful awe. His granddaughter suddenly saw this familiar figure in a new light—not only as a pillar of strength who gave her a feeling of security, but also as a challenger who caused her to wonder if she would be able to live up to the standards he expected. That was precisely the same kind of unnerving impact that he had had on most of the people who encountered him during his long lIfetime.

Robena drove Jim home from his granddaughter's graduation—the kind of happy event marking personal accomplishment that invariably made him grow sentimental—to their Deer Park apartment with its fine art and one of Canada's largest private collections of law reports. There they no doubt enjoyed a glass of sherry together.

That day he had spoken of the graduates' youth, their rebellion against hypocrisy, their dissatisfaction with pious declarations, and their witness through action—but even as he had called out his challenge, this kindly old man looking at those youngsters was seeing something of himself in them. James Chalmers McRuer actually smiled. He knew that the spirit he had embodied—a passion for justice—would somehow go on in the lives of others.

A NOTE ON SOURCES

There are two principal sources of information for this book. One is the large collection of McRuer letters, documents, books, and other records—measuring about thirty feet in total—at the Archives of Ontario. The other is a collection of tape-recorded interviews, conducted by the author, with McRuer. The transcripts of these interviews, running to more than one thousand pages, are held by The Osgoode Society. Included in this collection are the extensive handwritten notes that the author made in preparation for the interviews.

Unless otherwise indicated, quotations and other material in this book are taken from the above two sources.

In 1975 TV Ontario taped some fourteen hours of conversation with McRuer for a four-part documentary film, which was broadcast in January 1977. Typed transcripts of these interviews are among the McRuer Papers at the Archives of Ontario.

During the seventeen years of researching and writing this book, I have also interviewed hundreds of people who knew McRuer—family members, fellow lawyers, judges, royal commissioners, government officials, students, friends, acquaintances—and the information gleaned from these interviews has been incorporated into the book.

Other sources used in the preparation of this book are: various collections of private papers (especially those of prime ministers, premiers, and attorneys-general) and government records at the Archives of Ontario, Library and Archives Canada, and the University of Toronto Archives;

interviews conducted for the Ontario Historical Studies Series (Archives of Ontario) and for the Legal History Project (Osgoode Society); reports of the many royal commissions and inquiries in which McRuer participated, as well as the reports of the Ontario Law Reform Commission; miscellaneous law journals; cases published in the law reports (primarily those argued and decided by McRuer); newspapers and magazines; and a wide range of secondary literature, including Osgoode Society publications.

Many of the political, governmental, and legal events (particularly those involving the Ontario Law Reform Commission) are ones of which the author has some direct personal knowledge.

McRuer arranged during the 1970s for many documents and records to be delivered to the Archives of Ontario and the province's law faculties. For instance, in 1973 he sent ten boxes of material from the files of the Royal Commission Inquiry into Civil Rights to the law library at the University of Windsor, and more to the University of Toronto's law library. He also deposited all his "bench books"—the red binders in which he wrote in longhand his judge's notes—with the University of Toronto law library. These cover more than 500 cases, and I have reviewed all of them. For those cases that McRuer decided and that were later reported, the citations given are from the law reports. For unreported cases, the citations usually refer to their chronological file number in the bench books (i.e.: *Canada Fishing Tackle* v. *Dawe* [1960], unreported, case #377).

NOTES

The following abbreviations are used in the notes section

AC	*Appeal Cases*
AO	Archives of Ontario
CCC	*Canadian Criminal Cases*
CR	*Criminal Reports*
DLR	*Dominion Law Reports*
JCM Papers	James Chalmers McRuer Papers
OCA	Ontario Court of Appeal
OHCJ	Ontario High Court of Justice
OLR	*Ontario Law Reports*
OR	*Ontario Reports*
OSC	Ontario Supreme Court
OWN	*Ontario Weekly Notes*
NA	National Archives (Library and Archives Canada)
PC	Privy Council
RSC	*Revised Statutes of Canada*
SC	*Statutes of Canada*
SCR	*Supreme Court Reports*
SO	*Statutes of Ontario*
WWR	*Western Weekly Reports*

1   AYR AND BEYOND

1 When the French word *chambre* became naturalized in Scotland, the "b" was dropped through the process known as elision. At the same time, an "l" was added to preserve the length of the "a" in pronunciation. No definite regulations governed the spelling of names when they were first developing, however, and so many different versions of the same name appear in early Scottish records. Among the more frequent forms this surname took in the early years were Chamber, de la Chambre, Chawmyr, and Chalmers. The most prevalent spelling by the time the family came to Canada was Chalmers. The "l" in the name is silent, the pronunciation of this consonant being considered a modern affectation.

2 Years later, on 8 June 1952, McRuer returned to Paris to address an audience celebrating the 100th anniversary of the incorporation of South Dumfries Township. On that occasion he told all assembled that "to Ida Tovell I owe more than to any other one person outside of my own family for any return that life has given me." He would say much the same thing in a speech of 22 Oct. 1973 to Windsor Rotarians.

3 *Ontario Star* (Paris), 23 Oct. 1975.

4 For a thorough history of Canada from the 1890s until the late 1910s, see Robert Craig Brown and Ramsay Cook, *Canada 1896–1922: A Nation Transformed* (Toronto: McClelland and Stewart 1974).

2   THE MAKING OF A LAWYER

1 AO, JCM Papers, McRuer to Dennis Reid, 28 July 1971. Eventually McRuer would donate these paintings to the McMichael Gallery in Kleinburg, Ontario.

2 Margaret Prang, *N.W. Rowell: Ontario Nationalist* (Toronto: University of Toronto Press 1975).

3 Years later David Croll, the first Jew to serve in the Ontario cabinet, answered "No" when asked if he thought that McRuer's attitude towards these Jewish land speculators was motivated by anti-semitism. McRuer's feelings, Croll noted, were "natural." He added: "This was something new, this coming in and buying. McRuer's people didn't do it, and people before them didn't do it that way ... you can

quite understand his reaction. But no one could ever convince me that the man had a dislike for anybody—a real dislike. He may not have cared for them. He may not have looked to them socially, but if he didn't like you he left you alone." Interview with author, 10 July 1990.

4 Mary Dow was the daughter of Dr. John Dow, who had practised medicine for many years at Bellwood (near Fergus, Ontario) before moving to Toronto for the sake of his children's education. He delighted young Jim McRuer with his many anecdotes about medical practice in rural Ontario—anecdotes that reminded Jim of the times he had spent with his brother handling medical emergencies in the remote areas outside Huntsville.

3 INTO EUROPE'S BLOODY MUD

1 Quoted in Desmond Morton and J.L. Granatstein, *Marching to Armageddon: Canadians and the Great War 1914–1919* (Toronto: Lester and Orpen Dennys 1989), 142.

2 During the last days of the war, McRuer recorded his experiences and thoughts in both letters home and diary entries. Excerpts from this material were later compiled by his daughter Katherine McIntyre and published in the *Globe and Mail* (11 Nov. 1986, 7).

4 ENFORCING THE LAW

1 McRuer set out the reasons for his decision in a letter to judge John Burridge, 6 Sept. 1977 (AO, JCM Papers).

2 On Raney, see Charles M. Johnston, *E.C. Drury: Agrarian Idealist* (Toronto: University of Toronto Press 1986); and Peter Oliver, *G. Howard Ferguson: Ontario Tory* (Toronto: University of Toronto Press 1977). For an overview of the history of temperance and prohibition, see Gerald A. Hallowell, *Prohibition in Ontario* (Toronto: Ontario Historical Society 1972).

3 Quoted in Peter Oliver, *Public and Private Persons: The Ontario Political Culture 1914–1934* (Toronto: Clarke, Irwin 1975), 78.

4 *Saturday Night*, 20 Nov. 1920.

5 Stephen Leacock, *Wet and Dry Humour* (1931), quoted in Oliver, *Public and Private Persons*, 82.

6 Ibid.
7 McRuer explained his views on prohibition in an interview with the author on 4 Aug. 1983. John McRuer remembers that his father "used to gloat over how much money he saved by not buying liquor" (interview with author).
8 *Toronto Star*, various issues; see JCM scrapbooks (AO), 20 April 1922, 8 August 1923, others n.d.
9 For a detailed account of the Jarvis-Smith affair, see Oliver, *Public and Private Persons*, 182–261.
10 Oliver, *G. Howard Ferguson*, 131.
11 Oliver, *Public and Private Persons*, 240.
12 Ibid., 244.
13 On the Home Bank case, see *R. v. Gough et al.* [1925] 57 OLR 426; 28 OWN 391 and 394; AO, RG 4, Series 4–32, File 2499/1923, vols. 1, 3, 4.
14 AO, RG 4, Series 4–32, File 2499/1923, vol. 1, McCarthy to Nickle, 6 Feb. 1925.
15 JCM Papers, McRuer to Colin Campbell, 19 June 1980.
16 Ibid., and interview with author, 4 Aug. 1983.
17 JCM Papers, William Price to McRuer, 27 May 1957.

5   LAWYER AT LARGE

1 *Investigation into Alleged Combine in the Distribution of Fruit and Vegetables, Report of Commissioner, February 18, 1925* (Ottawa: Department of Labour).
2 Quoted by McRuer in interview with author, 11 Aug. 1980. Murdock's statement also appears in McRuer's letter of 25 Jan. 1973 to Hamilton city solicitor K.A. Rouff (AO, JCM Papers).
3 Ibid.
4 *Rex v. Simington* [1926] 45 CCC 249. See also further discussion in *Report of Commissioner, October 31, 1939, under Combines Investigation Act, into an Alleged Combine of Wholesalers and Shippers of Fruits and Vegetables in Western Canada* (Ottawa: Department of Labour 1939). Also of interest is the *Morning Star* (Vancouver), February and March 1926 (and especially the editorial "Justice Done," 15 March 1926).
5 *Daily Express*, 15 March 1926.
6 The McRuers had sold their Armadale Avenue house in 1927. They lived in a rented house on Indian Trail while their home on Glenayr

Road was being constructed.

7 Interview with McRuer, 8 Sept. 1982.

8 *Proprietary Articles Trade Assn. v. A.G. Canada* [1931] *AC* 310.

9 *Rex v. Singer* [1931] *OR* 202.

10 [1942] *SCR* 147, affd. [1941] 3 *DLR* 145 (OCA), affd. [1940] 4 *DLR* 293 (OSC).

11 Interview with McRuer, 14 Sept. 1982.

12 See *Report of Commissioner, under the Combines Investigation Act, into an Alleged Combine in the Distribution of Tobacco Products in the Province of Alberta and Elsewhere in Canada* (Ottawa: Department of Labour, 31 Aug. 1938), especially J.A. Cony's discussion of W.C. Macdonald Inc., appendix I, The Law of Resale Price Maintenance in Canada (1937).

13 JCM Papers, McRuer to James R. Wilkinson, 30 Oct. 1934.

14 JCM Papers, Lougheed to McRuer, 14 April 1942. See also *The Policeman's Review* (Toronto) for this period; the Toronto *Globe*, 12 March 1935 and 28 Jan. 1936; and records of the Ontario Police College, Aylmer, Ont.

15 *Report of Royal Commission to Inquire into and Report upon the Events and Circumstances Connected to Arrest of Albert Dorland and William Toohey* (typescript, 1933, Ontario Legislative Library).

16 NA, MG 26 (WLM King Papers), Series J-1, vol. 184, r.C.-2304:131581-4, King to McRuer, 26 Jan. 1928, McRuer to King, 31 Jan. 1928.

17 Ibid., vol. 215, r.C-2320:151332, McRuer to King, 29 July 1930.

18 These letters to Lambert and Massey are in the JCM Papers. In one instance, McRuer declined to speak to the Hamilton Liberal Club when he learned of a "bitter feud" in its ranks. Instead he arranged to have fellow lawyer Arthur Slaght go in his place.

19 Interview with McRuer, 3 June 1982.

20 On Hepburn, see Neil McKenty, *Mitch Hepburn* (Toronto: McClelland and Stewart 1967); and, more recently, John T. Saywell's *"Just Call Me Mitch": The Life of Mitchell F. Hepburn* (Toronto: University of Toronto Press, 1991).

21 AO, MU 4913 (Hepburn Private Papers), Mulock to Hepburn, 15 March 1934, and Hepburn to Mulock, 22 March 1934.

22 Ibid., telegram from "WRW" to Jack Hambleton, 1 June 1934.

23 Interview with McRuer, 3 June 1982. McRuer admitted his awkwardness as a public speaker in a letter to Ian Outerbridge of the Law Society of Upper Canada on 8 Nov. 1978. In this letter McRuer, who had agreed to give an address to the Society, requested that he be

permitted to speak from notes as he had "never felt secure speaking extemporaneously" (JCM Papers).

24 AO, MU 4913, "Address to be given at McGregor's School," 9 April 1934.

25 AO, RG 3 (Hepburn Public Papers), Box 222, telegram, 19 June 1934.

26 McKenty, *Hepburn*, 57.

6   REFORM BY REFORMERS

1 For an account of this episode, see John T. Saywell, *"Just Call Me Mitch": The Life of Mitchell F. Hepburn* (Toronto: University of Toronto Press 1991), 98–9, 119–20 Henry's remark is quoted in Neil McKenty, *Mitch Hepburn* (Toronto: McClelland and Stewart 1967), 45.

2 AO, RG 18, B-89, Inquiry into the Hydro-Electric Power Commission, Box 1, transcript of proceedings.

3 McKenty, *Hepburn*, 62.

4 Interview with McRuer, 11 May 1983.

5 AO, RG 18, B-89, Inquiry into the Hydro-Electric Power Commission, Report.

6 AO, JCM Papers, McRuer to the Reverend Richard Roberts, 23 Nov. 1934.

7 Interview with author, 10 July 1990.

8 NA, MG 26 (WLM King Papers), Series J-1, vol . 208, r.C-3682:179003, McRuer to King, 5 Jan. 1935.

9 *Toronto Star*, 16 Feb. 1935.

10 See *Toronto Star*, 16 Feb. 1935; *Globe*, 16 Feb. 1935; *Silverthorne Examiner*, 20 Feb. 1935.

11 Margaret Stewart and Doris French, *Ask No Quarter: A Biography of Agnes Macphail* (Toronto: Longmans 1959), 200-1. More recent biographies are Doris Pennington, *Agnes Macphail: Reformer* (Toronto: Simon and Pierre 1989); and Terry Crowley, *Agnes Macphail: The Politics of Equality* (Toronto: Lorimer 1990).

12 On this episode, see Crowley, *Agnes Macphail*, 135–8; and Stewart and French, *Ask No Quarter*, 182–99.

13 NA, MG 27 (Macphail Papers), III-C4, vol. 1 (1935), Macphail to McRuer, 23 May 1935.

14 Stewart and French, *Ask No Quarter*, 198.

15 Toronto *Globe*, 31 May 1935.

16 NA, MG 27-111, C4, vol. 5, press clipping.

17 *Kingston Whig Standard*, 13 June 1935.

18 McRuer told this story to the author. It is also related in Stewart and French, *Ask No Quarter*, 196, and in Crowley, *Agnes Macphail*, 143.

19 Canada, Department of Justice, *Report of His Honour Judge E.J. Daly upon a Commission of Inquiry into Certain Allegations Respecting Kingston Penitentiary* (Ottawa: King's Printer 1935).

20 JCM Papers, Macphail to McRuer, 11 July 1935.

21 Stewart and French, *Ask No Quarter*, 196.

22 M.W. Rossie, editor of the *London Free Press*, was another prominent supporter of the cause of prison reform. For the involvement of the *Free Press*, the *Globe*, and *Maclean's* in this issue, see Crowley, *Agnes Macphail*, 135, and Pennington, *Agnes Macphail*, 164.

23 JCM Papers, Macphail to McRuer, 11 July 1935.

24 D. Owen Carrigan, *Canadian Party Platforms 1867–1968* (Toronto: Copp Clark 1968), 118.

25 On the election of 1935, see H. Blair Neatby, *William Lyon Mackenzie King: The Prism of Unity* (Toronto: University of Toronto Press 1976) 110-25.

26 NA, MG 26, Series J-1, vol. 208, r.C-3682:179005, McRuer to King, 1 Aug. 1935.

27 *Silverthorne Examiner*, 9 Oct. 1935.

28 *West Toronto Weekly*, 10 Oct. 1935.

29 *Globe*, 11 Oct. 1935.

30 Interview with McRuer, 6 June 1980. See also *Globe*, 5 Oct. 1935.

31 *Globe*, 8 Oct. 1935. The rival *Telegram* also denounced McRuer's candidacy. See *Telegram*, 9 Aug. 1935 ("Why Call in the Doctor Who Made Us Sick"?) and 9 Oct. 1935 ("McRuer Should be Content with One Foot in the Trough").

32 JCM Papers, *Frank Yeigh in Memoriam* (a printed booklet containing McRuer's funeral service address of 28 Oct. 1935 and his address of 2 Nov. 1936 on the opening of the Frank Yeigh Memorial Room).

33 *Report of the Royal Commission on the Textile Industry* (Ottawa: King's Printer 1938), 200.

34 *Hansard*, quoted in speech of J.S. Woodsworth, 22 June 1938, 4129.

35 Ibid.

36 *Financial Post*, 20 Feb. 1937.

37 *Report*, 205–6.

7 INSIDE CANADA'S PRISONS

1 *Report of the Royal Commission to Investigate the Penal System of Canada* (Ottawa: King's Printer 1938), v.
2 NA, MG 27 (Agnes Macphail Papers), III-C4, vol. 1 (1936), Macphail to Maurice B. Bodington, 23 June 1936.
3 This was a very shrewd bargain; very few lawyers earned $35 a day in 1936. Furthermore, by calling it "an expense allowance" the government made it tax-free. By the time the commission's work was completed, McRuer would receive $10,313 in allowances.
4 *Report*, 1.
5 NA, MG 27, III-C4, vol. 1 (1936), Macphail to Bodington, 23 June 1936.
6 *Report*, 1–4. The European trip took place in the summer of 1937. While crossing Canada, the commissioners had made detours to the United States to visit prisons in Minnesota and Illinois and on the Pacific coast. The survey of prisons in the eastern United States was conducted in October 1937.
7 Margaret Stewart and Doris French, *Ask No Quarter: A Biography of Agnes Macphail* (Toronto: Longmans 1959), 102.
8 Interview with McRuer, 8 June 1980.
9 *Winnipeg Free Press*, 5 June 1937.
10 *Report*, 28–9; also, interview with McRuer, 14 Sept. 1981.
11 *Report*, 44–8; also, interview with McRuer, 14 Sept. 1981.
12 Many years later McRuer suggested a similar scheme of volunteer visitors—perhaps members of service clubs—to teach vocational subjects in Canadian jails. This idea was rejected by the authorities, however, even though McRuer pointed out with exasperation that a Rotarian was unlikely to smuggle a knife into prison.
13 This was neither McRuer's first nor last holiday in Europe. In 1932 he and Mary had placed the three children in an English boarding-school and then travelled extensively through England, Scotland, and Wales; in July 1936 he argued a case before the Privy Council in England, and afterwards, accompanied by his wife, daughter Mary Louise, and father-in-law, he made a trip to Paris; and in 1939, after arguing another case before the Privy Council, Jim and Mary McRuer toured England, France, and Italy. On his 1936 trip, he expressly stayed away from the Berlin Olympics because he did not want to be where Hitler was "spouting off."

14 *Report*, 354.

15 *Report*, 51.

16 *Ottawa Journal*, "Just a Triumph for Tim Buck?," 18 June 1938.

17 *Report*, 345. See also 339–42.

18 Ibid., 342–3.

19 Ibid., 356.

20 Ibid.

21 Ibid., 357.

22 Ibid., 358; also, interview with McRuer.

23 *Report*, 148 and 316.

24 Ibid., 145.

25 Ibid., 145–8.

26 Ibid., 358, 227, 230–1.

27 Ibid., 259.

28 Ibid., 359–61.

29 The JCM Papers in the Archives of Ontario include scrapbooks. One of these is filled with several hundred newspaper articles and editorials from French- and English-language papers, daily and weekly, commenting on the *Report* from mid-June to mid-July 1938.

30 *Globe and Mail*, 30 June 1938.

31 *Windsor Star*, 2 July 1938; *Ottawa Evening Journal*, 30 June 1938; *Winnipeg Free Press*, 30 June 1938; *Canadian Forum*, July 1938.

32 NA, MG 26 (WLM King Papers), Series J-1, vol. 291, r.C-4571.

33 Ibid.

34 JCM Papers, scrapbook (see note 29).

35 J.C. McRuer, "Canada's Penal System is an Aid to Germany," *Saturday Night*, 16 Nov. 1940, 28. McRuer and *Saturday Night*'s editor, B.K. Sandwell, worked closely together during the war in the Toronto Civil Liberties Association (Sandwell was its president). Sandwell was also a strong advocate of prison reform. *Saturday Night*'s initial response to the Archambault report appeared on 25 June 1938, and Sandwell himself was the author of fifteen articles on the subject that appeared in the magazine from 1931 to 1940.

36 This address was delivered on 15 Jan. 1943.

37 JCM Papers, n.d., and 12 June 1942.

38 NA, RG 73 vol.42, file 1-20-11, pt. 5, "Recommendations of the Royal Commission of 1936 on the penal system of Canada which have been implemented."

39 Two subsequent commissions have studied the Canadian penal system. One, chaired by Gerald Fauteux, reported in 1956; another,

chaired by Roger Ouimet, reported in 1969. There have also been a series of reports on the subject by the justice committee of parliament. From these and other sources it is possible to extrapolate the extent to which the Archambault report's recommendations have been implemented.

40 One of these speeches was delivered on 22 February 1946 to the Big Brothers' Association of Hamilton (*Hamilton Spectator* and *Globe and Mail*, 23 Feb. 1946). The following year, McRuer, speaking in his dual role as chief justice and president of the Canadian Bar Association, called for prison reform in a speech to the Montreal Rotary Club (*Montreal Daily Star*, 25 March 1947). On still another occasion, he wrote a full-page article on prison reform for the *Financial Post* (17 Dec. 1949); and in 1953 he spoke on the same subject before a select committee of the Ontario legislature (*Kingston Whig-Standard*, 2 Sept. 1953).

8 LAW, POLITICS, AND WAR

1 McRuer made this comment in a speech to the Ottawa Women's Club, 28 April 1938.
2 *R v. O'Donnell* [1936], 2 *DLR* 517 (OCA).
3 *Windsor Star*, 1 Feb. 1938.
4 *R. v. Manchuk* [1937] *OR* 693.
5 *The King* v. *Manchuk* [1938] *OR* 385.
6 For a discussion of these various appeals, see John D. Arnup, *Middleton: The Beloved Judge* (Toronto: The Osgoode Society 1988), 177–81.
7 *Manchuk* v. *The King* [1938] *SCR* 341.
8 Interview with McRuer, October 1980; the case was unreported. See *Toronto Star*, 18, 19, 20 Nov. 1937.
9 [1934] *OR* 464, [1934] *OR* 472 (CA), [1936] *SCR* 127 (SCC), [1938] *AC* 247 (PC). Other sources for this account are an interview with McRuer and the *Globe*, 30 Oct. 1937.
10 *Maclean's*, 1 Sept. 1938; also, interview with McRuer, October 1980.
11 See, generally, *Report of the Royal Commission on the Bren Gun Machine Contract, Hon. Henry Hague Davis, Commissioner* (Ottawa: King's Printer 1939). Also of use in preparing this account were interviews with McRuer, October 1980 and June 1981.
12 H. Blair Neatby, *The Politics of Chaos: Canada in the Thirties* (Toronto: MacMillan 1972), 124. Hepburn's personal life is deftly portrayed in

John T. Saywell's *"Just Call Me Mitch": The Life of Mitchell F. Hepburn* (Toronto: University of Toronto Press 1991).

13 For a detailed account of Hepburn's response to the Oshawa strike, see Saywell, *"Just Call Me Mitch"*, 303–33.

14 Neil McKenty, *Mitch Hepburn* (Toronto: McClelland and Stewart 1967), 125.

15 Neatby, *The Politics of Chaos*, 139; McKenty, *Mitch Hepburn*, 149.

16 McKenty, *Mitch Hepburn*, 169.

17 For full details of this "Hepburn-Drew Axis," see Saywell, *"Just Call Me Mitch"*, 385–411.

18 NA, MG 26 (WLM King Papers), Series J-1, vol. 254, r.C-3736:216508-9 (copy in JCM Papers).

19 Ibid., 216510, King to McRuer, 29 Dec. 1938.

20 *The Mackenzie King Record*, vol. 1, 1939–44 (Toronto: University of Toronto Press 1960), 93.

21 Ibid., 23; also, interview with McRuer.

22 See McKenty, *Mitch Hepburn*, 171; NA, MG 26, Series J-1, vol. 254, r.C3736:216508-9 (copy in JCM Papers). McRuer also spoke about this meeting in an interview with the author, October 1980.

23 NA, MG 26, Series J-1, vol. 254, r.C-3736:216510, 29 Dec. 1938.

24 McKenty, *Mitch Hepburn*, 209.

25 Ibid., 209.

26 Ibid., 214–16.

27 Ibid., 217.

28 NA, MC 26, Series J-1, vol. 273, r.C-3746:231159, 26 March 1940.

29 Ibid., vol. 291, r.C-4511, 27 March 1940.

30 McKenty, *Hepburn*, 227.

31 Ibid., 229.

32 Ibid., 241.

33 NA, MG 26, Series J-1, vol. 329, r.C-6809:280493–4, 5 Feb. 1942.

34 JCM Papers, McRuer to Conant, 23 Oct. 1940.

35 Ibid., McRuer to Mulock, 23 Oct. 1940.

36 Interviews with McRuer, October 1980.

37 McRuer and B.K. Sandwell shared a common concern that the association was being infiltrated by Communists and others who wanted to impair the war effort.

9   ON THE BENCH

1   Gibson Gray notes that McRuer and Roberston had "a very strong dislike for each other." Osgoode Society, transcript of meeting at Campbell House, Toronto, 22 Jan. 1991, 42.
2   *Yachuk v. Oliver Blais Co. Ltd.* [1944] 3 *DLR* 615 (OHCJ).
3   *Yachuk v. Oliver Blais Co.* [1945] 1 *DLR* 210 (CA).
4   *Oliver Blais Co. v. Yachuk* [1946] 1 *DLR* 5.
5   *Yachuk v. Oliver Blais Co.* [1949] 3 *DLR* 1. The Supreme Court Act was amended in 1949 to end appeals to the Privy Council.
6   Interview with McRuer, 3 May 1983.
7   "Sentences," *Canadian Bar Review*, vol. 27 (November 1949), 1001.
8   Ibid., 1001–2.
9   Ibid., 1003.
10 Ibid., 1004.
11 Ibid., 1018.
12 Ibid., 1013.
13 Ibid., 1018.
14 Letter to author, 17 June 1989.
15 AO, JCM Papers, McRuer to Jowitt, 8 Feb. 1949.
16 *Windsor Star*, 27 Sept. 1950. McRuer's single-minded approach in the running of his court was also revealed in a case that he tried near the end of his time on the bench, *R v. Canadian Breweries Ltd.* This case, which came before him in early 1960, had been germinating for many years while the federal government endeavoured to determine whether Canadian Breweries' takeover of National Breweries was in violation of the Combines Act. At length, the government decided to prosecute, but in the subsequent trial McRuer acquitted the company. His judgment was significant, for it established the principle that a combine operates in violation of the law only when it does demonstrable harm to the public good. Just as important as his judgment, however, was the way he treated E.P. Taylor, one of the most powerful businessmen in the country and a key figure in Canadian Breweries. On the very first day of the trial, McRuer looked down on Taylor, who was sucking a lozenge for a sore throat. Thinking that he was in fact chewing gum, McRuer instructed a bailiff to tell Taylor to get rid of the gum immediately. See Richard Rohmer, *E.P. Taylor: The Biography of Edward Plunket Taylor* (Toronto: McClelland and Stewart 1978), 211–14.

17 *Kitchener-Waterloo Record,* 13 Feb. 1963.
18 Mackay was a Conservative in politics and would later serve as Ontario's lieutenant-governor.
19 JCM Papers, McRuer to Jowitt, 8 Feb. 1949.
20 *Globe Magazine,* 27 June 1964, 10.
21 Letter to author, 17 June 1989.
22 Ibid.
23 Address delivered at the unveiling of a portrait in bronze of McRuer, Osgoode Hall, 23 Sept. 1985. The commission to which Scott refers conducted its inquiry in 1958.
24 Speech delivered on 4 May 1960 to the Waterloo Historical Society, Kitchener. Printed in the *Kitchener-Waterloo Record,* 5 May 1960.
25 *Toronto Star,* 13 June 1964, 7.
26 *Globe Magazine,* 13 June 1964, 7.
27 Letter to author, August 1989.
28 McRuer's discussions with the attorney-general following the Schroeder incident resulted in a 1946 amendment (*SO* 1946, c.43, s.2) to the Judicature Act. That act granted judges the power to make arrangements for holding the courts and for deciding who was to transact the courts' business. The 1946 amendment empowered the chief justice to readjust or reassign sittings of the court already determined by the judges. This provision now appears in The Courts of Justice Act, RSO 1990, Ch. 43.
29 Interview with author, 20 March 1994.
30 *Toronto Star,* 17 April 1944, 6.
31 JCM Papers, McRuer to Robinette, 3 Dec. 1953.

10   SPIES AND MURDERERS

1 *Globe and Mail,* 21 March 1946.
2 *Winnipeg Free Press,* 11 April 1946.
3 House of Commons, *Debates,* 15 March 1946, 8.
4 Ibid., 16 March 1946, 138.
5 *R. v. Benning* [1947] *OR* 362 (CA); *R. v. Mazerall* [1946] *OR* 762 (CA); *R. v. Mazerall* [1946] 86 *CCC* 147 (OHCJ); *R v. Adams* [1946] *OR* 506 (OHCJ).
6 Robert Bothwell and J.L. Granatstein, eds., *The Gouzenko Transcripts* (Ottawa: Deneau n.d.), 14–15.
7 See chapter 14. Volume 4 of *The Report of the Royal Commission*

Inquiry into Civil Rights (Toronto: Queen's Printer 1969) deals with problems of self-incrimination.

8 The information regarding these proceedings is derived from interviews with McRuer conducted in September and October 1981; also, in the JCM Papers (AO) there is a long memorandum he wrote concerning the procedures to be followed at the Montebello hearings. For a general assessment, see Donald Creighton, *The Forked Road: Canada 1939–1957* (Toronto: McClelland and Stewart 1976), 109–13.

9 McRuer's fascination with murder trials stretched back to his childhood. In 1890, the year he was born, an unidentified body was found in the Blenheim swamp just ten miles down the road from the McRuer farm. Soon an Englishman named Reginald Birchall, who had previously masqueraded in Woodstock as "Lord Somerset," was charged with the crime. Evidence at the trial revealed that Birchall had placed an advertisement in the *Daily Telegraph* in London soliciting £500 from any young man who wanted a partnership in a Canadian farm. When Benwell, the victim who responded to the ad, became suspicious after they reached Canada, Birchall lured him into the swamp, where he shot him. The Birchall case brought together leading figures of the bar, including B.B. Osler, who prosecuted, and George Tate Blackstock, who led the defence. It attracted world-wide attention. The London newspapers covered the trial, and the talk and memory of it all made a deep impression on young Jim and every other child in the area for years to come. Even in the 1960s, in an address to the Medical Association in Toronto about the work of coroners, McRuer began with the Birchall case.

10 In 1944, the most recent death sentence for rape had been pronounced by Mr. Justice Robert Grant Fisher in Ontario the decade before.

11 A.J. Macleod, "Criminal Legislation," in W.T. McGrath, ed., *Crime and its Treatment in Canada* (Toronto: Macmillan 1967), 17–20.

12 In his criminal procedure lectures, McRuer discussed the power to grant pardons and to commute death sentences in the English common law. See his *Evolution of the Judicial Process* (Toronto: Clarke, Irwin 1957).

13 *R. v. Gach* [1943] *SCR* 250.

14 *R. v. Boudreau* [1949] *SCR* 262, 94 *CCC*.

15 In addition to the law reports of the Dick case, see Marjorie Freeman Campbell, *Torso: The Evelyn Dick Case* (Toronto: Signet 1974), 131.

16 *R. v. Dick* [1947] *OR* 105, 87, *CCC* 101, 2 *OR* 417; [1947] 2 *DLR* 213.

17 Ibid. See also Campbell, *Torso*, 174.

18 *R. v. Dick* [1947] *OR* 695.

19 Unreported. AO, JCM Papers, trial transcript and McRuer's jury charge; interview with McRuer.

20 98 *CCC* 22.

21 *Kingston Whig-Standard*, 22 Oct. and 17 Nov. 1950.

22 Unreported. JCM Papers, trial transcript and McRuer's jury charge; interview with McRuer.

23 *Ottawa Citizen*, 14 Feb. 1951, 21.

24 Unreported. JCM Papers, trial transcript and McRuer's jury charge; interview with McRuer.

25 See *Ottawa Journal*, 13 Feb. 1951; *Ottawa Evening Citizen*, 23 Feb. 1951; *Toronto Daily Star*, 14 Feb. 1951. As a judge, McRuer took an active interest in how the media reported his, and indeed all, cases. He felt that the media could serve an important role in educating the public about the legal process, but he was also distressed by journalistic sensationalism. In a letter written on 29 Nov. 1954 to Dr. Lena Lewis, he noted that he had "been engaged for some time in Ontario in an effort to prevent serious criminal trials becoming sort of press theatrical performances." He acknowledged that his efforts were not popular with "some elements of the press" but believed that other elements were just as anxious as he "to preserve the administration of justice from this sort of thing."

26 J.C. McRuer, "Criminal Contempt of Court Procedure: A Protection for the Rights of the Individual," *Canadian Bar Review* (March 1952), 225–41.

27 *R. v. Suchan and Jackson* [1952] 15 *CR* 310, 104 *CCC*, 193 at 196 (SCC).

28 At the Supreme Court, Mr. Justice Estey in chambers dismissed the application for leave to appeal.

29 *R v. Suchan and Jackson* [1952], 15 *CR* 310, 104 *CCC* 193 (SCC).

30 *Toronto Telegram*, 15 Dec. 1952, 1.

31 *Toronto Star*, 27 Feb. 1954, 1.

32 Unreported. JCM Papers, trial transcript and McRuer's jury charge; interview with McRuer.

33 *Balcombe v. The Queen* [1954] *SCR* 303, 110 *CCC* 146.

34 *Toronto Star*, 27 Feb. 1954, 13.

35 110 *CCC* 148.

36 Interview with author, 14 Sept. 1980.

37 Guy Favreau, Minister of Justice, *Capital Punishment: Material Relating to Its Purpose and Value* (Ottawa: Queen's Printer 1965), app. D.

38 Neil Boyd, *The Last Dance: Murder in Canada* (Toronto: Prentice Hall 1988), 39.
39 This statement was made in Fulton's "Memorandum for the Cabinet, Re. Criminal Code Amendment Bill, Department of Justice, Files Relating to the Criminal Law Amendment Act 1976," 20 Feb. 1961. Neil Boyd obtained a copy of this document under the Access to Information Act in September 1986, and he quotes it in *The Last Dance*, ch.2.
40 These amendments to the Criminal Code are now included in the consolidated *RSC*. For analysis, see David Chandler, *Capital Punishment in Canada* (Ottawa: Carleton Library 1976), 16–34.
41 Boyd, *The Last Dance*, 40.
42 The "gangland executions," as the newspapers styled the double murder, prompted a *Toronto Star* editorial on 20 Nov. 1961 that called on the Ontario government to appoint a royal commission on organized crime. A one-man commission (Mr. Justice W.D. Roach) was in fact established prior to Lucas's trial before McRuer.
43 Unreported. JCM Papers, trial transcript and McRuer's jury charge; interview with McRuer.
44 *R. v. Lucas* [1962] 38 *CR* 403, at 410 (CA).
45 *Lucas v. The Queen* [1963] 1 *CCC* 1, 39 *CR* 101 (SCC).
46 *Toronto Star*, 10 Dec. 1962, 1; *Toronto Telegram*, 11 Dec. 1962, 3.
47 *Telegram*, 10 Dec. 1962, 10.
48 Alan Hustak, *They Were Hanged* (Toronto: Lorimer 1987), 157.
49 *Toronto Star*, 10 Dec. 1962, 2.
50 Hustak, *They Were Hanged*, xvii.

11 LAW, THE ENVIRONMENT, AND NATIVE PEOPLE

1 *Canadian Westinghouse v. Corp. of the City of Hamilton* [1948] *OR* 144. See also *Hamilton Spectator*, 3 Nov. 1948 ("Chief Justice McRuer Goes Down the Drain").
2 *Gifford et al. v. City of Oshawa* [1951], unreported, case #203.
3 [1962], *OR* 1057, 35 *DLR* (2nd) 206.
4 [1877], *LR*, 2 *CP*, 239, at 243–4.
5 Unreported. AO, JCM Papers, trial transcript and jury charge; interview with McRuer.
6 [1948] *OR* 398, [1948] 3 *DLR* 201.
7 Ontario Legislative Assembly, *Debates*, 23rd Leg., 24 Feb. 1950, A-6.

8 [1948] *OR* 400

9 Ibid., 401.

10 Ibid., 411.

11 Ibid., 406.

12 Ibid., 418.

13 [1949] 1 *DLR* 38.

14 [1949] *SCR* 698.

15 [1950] *SCR* vii.

16 The debates in the Ontario legislature contain much of this story. See also *Globe and Mail* and *Sudbury Star*, 14 Dec. 1947 to 9 Jan. 1948. A McRuer memorandum entitled "Environmental Cases" and dated 21 Jan. 1977 is among the JCM papers. Also useful for this account were several interviews with McRuer.

17 *Debates*, 24 Feb. 1950, A-6.

18 K.V.P. Company Limited Act, 1950, *SO* 1950, c.33.

19 *Walker* v. *The McKinnon Industries Limited* [1949] *OR* 549, [1949] 4 *DLR* 739 (OHCJ).

20 [1950] 3 *DLR* 159.

21 [1951] 3 DLR 577.

22 Ibid., 579.

23 *Russell Transport Limited et al.* v. *The Ontario Malleable Iron Company Limited* [1952] *OR* 621, [1952] 4 *DLR* 719.

24 *Stephens* v. *Richmond Hill (Village)* [1955] *OR* 806, [1955] 4 *DLR* 572 (OHCJ); affd. with variation as to damages [1956] *OR* 88, 1 *DLR* (2nd) 569 (OCA).

25 *SO*, 1956, c.71. This act, which authorized the continued operation of the sewage treatment plant, was, ironically, an amendment to the Public Health Act. It directed the Ontario Department of Health to investigate the plant's practices and impose additional conditions as needed.

26 *SO* 1956, c.62. The act did not explicitly state that a citizen's riparian rights would be superseded by the operations and policies of the commission; however, this was in effect the result.

27 *RSC*, 1952, c.179.

28 For an account of this meeting, see Janet Foster, *Working for Wildlife: The Beginning of Preservation in Canada* (Toronto: University of Toronto Press 1978), 199–219.

29 The attorney-general for Canada requested magistrate Dunlap to prepare a written statement of both the facts of the case and the law as he interpreted it. Appeal by way of stated case, provided for in

the Criminal Code, was common. The magistrate's document would establish the basis of the case to be heard by McRuer.

30 [1885] 10 *OR* 196.

31 *AC* 637.

32 The Interpretation Act provides definitions and generic meanings to assist in the interpretation of ambiguously worded laws.

33 4 *DLR* 744, 58 *CCC* 269, [1932] 2 *WWR* 337.

34 40 *WWR*.

35 *R.* v. *George* [1964] 1 *OR* 240.

36 *A.G. Canada* v. *George* [1964] 2 OR 429.

37 [1966] *SCR* 267.

12   WOMEN, CHILDREN, AND WORKERS

1 On this point, McRuer was overruled by the commission's secretary, the Reverend James Mutchmor. Such an experience was rare for McRuer, but Mutchmor, who later became moderator of the United Church of Canada, was just as strong-willed as he was.

2 *Report of the Commission on Christian Marriage and the Christian Home* (Toronto: The United Church of Canada Board of Evangelism and Social Service, and Board of Christian Education 1946).

3 *Freedman* v. *Mason* [1956] *OR* 849, 4 *DLR* (2d) 576 (OHCJ); revd. on other grounds [1957] *OR* 441, 9 *DLR* (2d) 262; affd [1958] *SCR* 485, 14 *DLR* (2d) 529. McRuer's outlook on women's property rights first found expression at the Supreme Court of Canada in Bora Laskin's dissent from the *Murdoch* decision ([1975] 1 *SCR* 423), then in the majority decision three years later in *Rathwell and Rathwell* ([1978] 2 *SCR* 436).

4 *SC* 1930, cc. 14, 15.

5 Marriage and Divorce Act, *RSC* 1952, c.176, s.4.

6 *SC* 1967–8, c.24.

7 McRuer strongly believed that the law truly was "an ass" with respect to women, and he kept a file entitled "Canadian Cases—Material for Book" in which he wrote extensive observations about "Women and the Law." By this—as he said in notes for one of his frequent speeches to women's clubs—he did "not propose to have anything to say about women enjoying the practice of law but rather to say something of what has been practised on women in the name of the law."

8 [1944] 4 *DLR* 173 (OCA), [1944] *OR* 438.

9 *Brunton* v. *Brunton* [1946], unreported, case #108.

10 *Frampton* v. *Frampton and Whiteman* [1954], unreported, case #257.

11 *Alspector* v. *Alspector* [1957] 7 *DLR* (2d), 203; affd [1957] 9 *DLR* (2d) 670 (OCA).

12 *Barton* v. *Brandenburg* [1963], unreported, case #430; *Lem* v. *Lem* [1950], unreported, case #182.

13 *Scott* v. *Scott* [1947] 1 *DLR* 374, at 378.

14 [1948] 4 *DLR* 234.

15 Interview by author, 4 Aug. 1982.

16 After the trial, McRuer observed, "A great deal of publicity has been given this case, much more than should have been given." *Sudbury Daily Star*, 21 June 1961.

17 *R.* v. *Yensen* [1961] 29 *DLR* (2d) 314.

18 *Bird* v. *The Town of Fort Prances* [1949] *OR* 292.

19 *SO* 1954, c.8, ss.74, 75; re-en. 1958, c.11, s.3.

20 *Re. Blackwell and Toronto General Trusts Corp* [1959] *OR* 377, 20 *DLR* (2d) 107 (OHCJ).

21 *Re. Gage* [1961] *OR* 540 (OCA); affd. [1962] *SCR* 241.

22 *SO* 1965, c.14.

23 *Mary Laura Fex* [1947], unreported, case #142.

24 Interview by author, 20 Oct. 1980; also, *Toronto Telegram*, 6 and 7 Feb. 1958.

25 *Toronto Telegram*, Frank Tumpane's "Sincerely Yours" column, 9 Feb. 1958.

26 *Century Engineering Co.* v. *Greto* [1961] *OR* 91.

27 McRuer's recollection, however, was that Lewis was reconciled to the result. Interviews by author.

28 [1962] *OR* 108 (OHCJ); affd. [1962] *OR* 554 (OCM); affd [1962] *SCR* 609.

29 [1951] *OR* 522.

30 "Secondary" picketing is the public parading done by striking workers, not at the plant where they work, but rather at the premises of one of the suppliers, or one of the customers, of their employer.

31 [1963] 1 *OR* 36, [1963] 2 *OR* 81.

32 *Re. Hotel and Club Employees Union* v. *C.P.R.* [1961], unreported, case #384.

33 [1958] *OWN* 302, 14 *DLR* 758 (OHCJ).

34 [1958] *OWN* 300, 15 *DLR* (2d) 133 (OHCJ).

35 [1961] *OR* 85.

36 Interview with McRuer; also, author's correspondence with Professor

David Beatty, faculty of law, University of Toronto, October 1990.

37 *Re Canadian Textile Council* v. *Ontario Labour Relations Board* [1962], unreported, case #397,

38 [1964] 1 *OR* 173 (OHCJ); affd. [1964] 1 *OR* 270 (OCA).

39 [1951] *OR* 527.

40 [1963] 2 *OR* 254.

41 *Canada Labour Relations Board* v. *Hal C. Banks* [1959], unreported, case #349.

42 [1963] 2 *OR* 239.

43 *R.* v. *Ontario Labour Relations Board, ex parte Trenton Construction Workers Association, Local 52* [1963] 2 *OR* 376, 39 *DLR* (2d) 513.

44 *R.* v. *Ontario Labour Relations Board, Ex Parte Trenton Construction Workers Association, Local 52* [1963] 2 *OR* 376 (OHCJ).

45 [1961] *OWN* 233, 61; *CCC* 15, 373.

46 For a summary of the Laskin concept of judicial deference to the OLRB, see Robert Macaulay, *Directions: Report of the Review of Ontario's Regulatory Agencies* (Toronto: Queen's Printer 1989), especially chapter 4.

47 McRuer's views on administrative tribunals were also set out in his article "Control of Power," published in *Special Lectures of the Law Society of Upper Canada 1979—The Abuse of Power and the Role of an Independent Judicial System in its Regulation and Control* (Toronto: Richard de Boo 1979).

13 IN PURSUIT OF JUSTICE

1 "A New Year's Message," *Canadian Bar Review*, vol. 24, no. 10 (December 1946), 845–6.

2 AO, JCM Papers, "Confidential" twelve-page memorandum by the CBA's committee on legal problems of international organization for the maintenance of peace, 28 Feb. 1945.

3 In addition to his presidential address and his New Year's inaugural message, a representative sampling of McRuer's articles in the *Canadian Bar Review* would include "Sentences" (vol .27, November 1949, 1001–19), "Criminal Contempt of Court Procedure: A Protection for the Rights of the Individual" (vol. 30, March 1952, 225–44), and occasional book reviews.

4 These letters were sent to each attorney-general, 11 Sept. 1946.

5 AO, JCM Papers, J.L. Isley to McRuer, 22 May 1947; also, Prime Min-

ister King to McRuer, 26 June 1947, and Secretary of State for External Affairs Louis St. Laurent to McRuer, 17 May 1947.

6 McRuer's meticulousness was also evident in his private life. His
daughter Mary Louise states: "The same attention to detail led to
the success of his many travels abroad, beginning with our trip on
the Montrose when we three children were six, nine, and twelve and
ending with a trip to Hong Kong and Beijing in 1972. He took careful pains in the planning and building of our house on Glenayr Road,
spending many hours poring over the plans to make it more comfortable and charming."

7 One of the ideas that emerged in the CBA during McRuer's presidency came to fruition in 1949. That year, McRuer and twenty other
lawyers and judges were formed into a council to conduct a survey
of the legal profession in Canada. This was the first survey of its kind
and examined not only the number of lawyers in the country but
their location, incomes, and so on. See Charles P. McTague, "Survey of the Legal Profession in Canada," *Canadian Bar Review*, vol. 27
(1949), 951–7; and John P. Nelligan, "Lawyers in Canada: A Half-Cen-
tury Count," *Canadian Bar Review*, vol. 28 (1950), 727–49.

8 *RSC* 1927, c.36.

9 J.C. McRuer, "Insanity as a Legal Defence," *The Canadian Medical
Association Journal*, vol. 61 (November 1949), at 489.

10 Worrall, handsome, intelligent, and athletic (he had been on the
Canadian Olympic team in 1936), had grown close to Jim McRuer and
his family. Jim took an interest in Worrall, helping him to get started
in the law, and when McRuer's legal practice fell off in the Depression he paid Worrall to paint the family cottage at Stoney Lake. One
day Jim's daughter Katherine arrived at the cottage, looked at Worrall,
and exclaimed, "Ah, things are looking up around here!" Worrall, for
his part, grew devoted to McRuer. The two worked together closely
and well over many years.

11 *SC* 1953–4, c.51.

12 *Report of the Royal Commission on the Law of Insanity as a Defence in
Criminal Cases* (Hull, Que.: Queen's Printer, n.d.). See especially 6–8,
15–30, 38–41, and 46; for various dissents, see 48–70.

13 The purpose of Brewin's bill was to abolish the McNaughton rule
embodied in section 16 of the Canadian Criminal Code and substitute a rule more consistent with modern concepts of mental illness
and criminal responsibility (such as that adopted by the United States
Court of Appeals in 1954 in the case of *Durham* vs. *The United States*).

The chairman of this parliamentary committee was his erstwhile law partner and the successful Liberal candidate in his former riding of High Park, A.J.P. "Pat" Cameron.

14 As a judge, McRuer was known to be particularly skilled in charging a jury on the defence of insanity. In fact, the editors of the *Criminal Law Quarterly* published his 8 Jan. 1959 charge in *R. v. O.* (*Criminal Law Quarterly*, vol. 3 [1960–1], 151–65), contrary to their general policy not to report any jury charges, because the "direction in this case on the law of insanity was thought to be of such interest to the profession that it should be published in full."

15 *Report of the Royal Commission on the Law Relating to Sexual Psychopaths* (Hull, Que.: Queen's Printer 1959). See especially 7–11, 16–21, and 39–42.

16 *Toronto Telegram*, 21 April 1959.

17 In giving lengthy speeches, of course, McRuer kept some good company. When the prime minister of Ireland, John A. Costello, addressed a CBA luncheon in Montreal on 16 Sept. 1948, McRuer chaired the meeting. As Costello was entering the third hour of his discourse and the audience in the Windsor Hotel was rapidly dwindling, the chief justice interrupted the proceedings with his command to "lock the doors."

18 *The Evolution of the Judicial Process* (Toronto: Clarke, Irwin 1957), xi.

19 Ibid., 104.

20 Ibid., 4.

21 Ibid., 6.

22 Ibid., 36.

23 Ibid., 41.

24 Ibid., 20.

25 *The Trial of Jesus* (Toronto: Clarke, Irwin 1964), repr. as *This Man Was Innocent: The Trial of Jesus* (Toronto: Clarke, Irwin 1978), 42. See also 36, 39, and 40.

26 Ibid., 48.

27 Ibid., 72.

28 Reviews of *The Trial of Jesus* included: William Nicholls, "Religion," *Saturday Night*, May 1964, 40; John Marshall, *The Canadian Reader*, May 1964; Ian Burnett, "Thinking on These Things," *Ottawa Journal*, 21 March 1964; Kenneth McNaught, "Literature and Life," *Ottawa Journal*, 28 March 1964; David Green, *Kitchener-Waterloo Record*, 28 March 1964; *Times Literary Supplement*, 3 June 1965; *Hamilton Spectator*, 28 March 1964; Ralph Hancox, *Peterborough Examiner*, 28 March 1964; Douglas J. Wilson, *Montreal Star*, 28 March 1964; F.G. Rich-

ards, *Saanich Peninsula and Gulf Islands Review*, 8 April 1964; Roy St. George Stubbs, *Winnipeg Free Press*, 11 April 1964.

29 See review article by Rabbi Reuben Slonim, *Toronto Telegram*, 28 March 1964; S.B. Frost, *The Observer*, August 1964; Reginald Stackhouse, "A Miscarriage of Justice," *Globe and Mail Magazine*, 21 March 1964; F.F. Bruce, *Life of Laity* (London, England), 29 April 1965; A.B. Lovelace, *Sherbrooke Daily Record*, 20 June 1964; Donald MacLeod, *Princeton Seminary Bulletin*, February 1965, 65; *Catholic Book Review*, vol. 11, issue 1 (January 1965); Roland Potter, *Catholic Herald* (London, Ont.), 19 March 1965; Wilhelmina Gordon, *Echoes* (autumn 1964), 32; Paul Winter, *Anglican Theological Review* (Virginia, U.S.), spring 1965; *Evangelical Baptist*, April 1965; *Birmingham Post* (U.K.), 10 April 1965; Charles Wilkinson, *Toronto Daily Star*, 25 March 1967.

30 Haim H. Cohn, "Reflections on the Trial and Death of Jesus," *Israel Law Review*, 2 (1967), 332–79.

31 Cohn was not alone in criticizing McRuer's book on these grounds. The Reverend Reginald Stackhouse noted in a *Globe and Mail Magazine* review (21 March 1964), "In light of the recent debate over the Gospel record's accuracy, any writer on this subject must first establish his reasons for accepting that record as evidence."

32 H. Aubrey Fraser, *West Indian Law Journal*, May 1979, 60–3.

14   CIVIL RIGHTS AND THE STATE

1 Premier Robarts made this comment at York University following spring convocation, 1972 (Allan Leal, interview by author, 19 July 1980). This story was also told to the author by McRuer and others attending a retirement dinner in the premier's honour. His one-word reply, "McRuer," was taken by those present to mean the full implementation of the McRuer commission's recommendations and the changes this brought about.

2 An account of Wintermeyer's speech, his "scandal a day" campaign, and the proceedings of the Roach commission is found in Claire Hoy, *Bill Davis: A Biography* (Toronto: Methuen 1985), 42–4.

3 The main sources for the "Police State" bill controversy include interviews with Arthur Wishart, McRuer, Robert J. Boyer (the author's father and, at the time of the controversy, a Conservative MPP for Muskoka), and extensive newspaper clippings from the *Toronto Telegram*, the *Globe and Mail*, and the *Toronto Star*.

4 Osgoode Society, Ontario Legal History project, interviews with Arthur Wishart; also, several discussions between Wishart and author during 1970 and 1971.

   Not least among the many reasons for the selection of McRuer as head of the civil rights inquiry was his record on the bench. Over the years, McRuer had handed down a number of significant judgments in the area of civil rights, particularly the rights of the "little guy" when pitted against large organizations and powerful interests. See, for example, *Brawn* v. *Premier Trust Co. and Holmes* [1947] *OR* 50; *Gruen Watch Co. et al.* v. *Attorney-General of Canada* [1950] *OR* 429; Re. Martin [1951], unreported, case #213; *Ex Parte Robin* [1961] *OWN* 231; *Sparkhall* v. *Scarborough* [1961] *OWN* 219; *R.* v. *Board of Broadcast Governors ex parte Swift Current Telecasting Company* [1962] *OR* 190.

   In another category of cases, dealing with the fundamental civil right of voting, McRuer set the framework for municipal plebiscites by establishing what questions were legitimate and who could vote. See *Re Jones and Toronto* [1947] *OR* 20, [1947] 2 *DLR* 125; and *Freeman* v. *Farm Products Marketing Board* [1958] *OR* 349. For a discussion of how McRuer's decisions have affected democratic rights in Canada, see Patrick Boyer, *Lawmaking by the People* (Toronto: Butterworths 1982), 18–20; and Patrick Boyer, *Direct Democracy in Canada* (Toronto: Dundurn 1992), 162–3.

5 Interviews with McRuer and Arthur Wishart.

6 Ontario Legislative Assembly, *Debates*, 1 May 1964, 2694–7.

7 *Globe and Mail*, 3 Sept. 1964, 7.

8 *Globe Magazine*, 27 June 1964, 10.

9 Order-in-Council, 21 May 1964, pursuant to the Public Inquiries Act. The full text is reproduced in *Report of the Royal Commission Inquiry into Civil Rights* (Toronto: Queen's Printer 1968), vii–ix.

10 Albert Warson, "Civil Rights in Ontario and the Public's Attitude," in "Clippings ... Civil Rights" scrapbook, JCM Papers (AO).

11 *Globe and Mail*, 11 Dec. 1964.

12 McRuer's address was printed in *Osgoode Hall Law Journal* [1966] 4 OHLJ 54. An earlier discussion of the same subject was McRuer's lecture at the University of Toronto on 22 Nov. 1962, subsequently published as "Liability without Fault in the Law of Torts," in R.S.J. Macdonald, ed., *Changing Legal Perspectives* (Toronto: University of Toronto Press 1963) 37–70. For a further analysis of this issue, see chapter 15.

13 *Royal Commission Inquiry into Civil Rights, J.C. McRuer, Commis-*

sioner, Report No.1, 3 vols. (Toronto: Queen's Printer 1968), 1:2–3, 17–31.

14 Ibid., 338–55, esp. 212–13.

15 Ibid., 67–237, esp. 126.

16 Ibid., 383–462, esp. 426, 457.

17 Ibid., 482–97, esp. 496–7.

18 Ibid., 499–524, esp. 501, 524–5.

19 Ibid., 526–46, 543–4.

20 Ibid., 547–603, 569–70.

21 Ibid., 605–20, esp. 619–20.

22 Ibid., 621–48, esp. 644–6.

23 Ibid., 649–77, esp. 651–2, 669–71.

24 Ibid., 679–721, esp. 721–2. See also 892–955.

25 Ibid., 957–1083, esp. 1083.

26 Ibid., 1093–1132, esp. 1117, 1132.

27 Ibid., 1135–57, esp. 1156–7.

28 Ibid., 1159–1228, esp. 1209–11.

29 Ibid., 1229–52, esp. 1252–4.

30 *Debates*, 5 March 1968, 421.

31 Ibid., 421–2, and *Toronto Star*, 6 March 1968.

32 *Toronto Star*, 6 March 1968.

33 *Toronto Telegram* and *Globe and Mail*, 6 March 1968.

34 *Toronto Daily Star*, 7 March 1968.

35 *Montreal Star*, 8 March 1968.

36 *Globe and Mail*, 9 March 1968.

37 Ibid.

38 John Willis, "The McRuer Report: Lawyers' Values and Civil Servants' Values," *University of Toronto Law Journal*, vol. 18, no. 4 (1968), 351–60. See also John Willis. "Administrative Law in Canada." *Canadian Bar Review*, vol. 39 (1961), 251; "Trends in Administrative Law," *Canadian Bar Papers*, 1962, 1; and "Canadian Administrative Law in Retrospect," *University of Toronto Law Journal*, vol. 24 (1974), 225.

39 Copies of several submissions in response to the *Report*, made to the government and forwarded to the commission, are among the JCM Papers. See also *Toronto Daily Star*, 13 and 15 March 1968.

40 *Royal Commission Inquiry into Civil Rights, J.C. McRuer, Commissioner, Report No.2* (vol. 4) (Toronto: Queen's Printer 1969), 1339–83, esp. 1383.

41 Ibid., 1391–1405, esp. 1405.

42 Ibid., 1409–72, esp. 1472.

43 Ibid., 1475–1607, esp. 1595–1607.
44 Ibid., 1608.
45 Ibid., 1568.
46 Ibid., 1608.
47 *Royal Commission Inquiry into Civil Rights, J.C. McRuer, Commissioner, Report No. 3,* (vol. 5) (Toronto: Queen's Printer 1971), 1737–2215.
48 Ibid., 1945.
49 Ibid., 2139–40.
50 Ibid., 2191.
51 Ibid., 2197.
52 Ibid., 2215.
53 *Debates,* 15 April 1971, 430; 4 June 1971, 2374.
54 *SO* 1971, c.49.
55 *SO* 1971, c.50.
56 *SO* 1971, c.48.
57 Allan F. Lawrence, *New Civil Rights Protections for Ontario* (Toronto: Department of Attorney-General 1972), 13. See also D.W. Mundell, *Manual of Practice on Administrative Law and Procedure in Ontario* (Toronto: Department of Attorney-General 1972).
58 Quoted in Rae Corelli, "New laws open the way to civil rights revolution," *Toronto Star,* 13 May 1971.
59 Interview by author.
60 Quoted in a letter from McRuer to the Reverend Ernest Marshall Howse, moderator of the United Church, 11 June 1970 (AO, JCM Papers).
61 "Submission on Bill 7, An Act to Revise and Extend Protection of Human Rights in Ontario, by J.E. Hodgetts, George Heiman, and Glenda M. Patrick, Department of Political Economy, University of Toronto, September 10, 1981," 5.
62 A.V. Dicey, *The Law of the Constitution* (10th ed., 1961), ch. 4.
63 Robert Macaulay, *Directions: Report of the Review of Ontario's Regulatory Agencies* (Toronto: Queen's Printer 1989), ch. 4:1.
64 Macaulay, *Directions,* ch. 4:4.
65 Ibid.
66 *Report No. 1,* 1:58.
67 Macaulay, *Directions,* ch. 4:5.
68 Ibid., ch. 4:9. Passage of time and evolution of public administration in Ontario has provided new light for evaluating the McRuer-Willis debate over lawyers' values and civil service values. One of the most

comprehensive recent analyses is astutely rendered by authority on administrative law David J. Mullan, distinguished law professor and City of Toronto Integrity Commissioner, in "Willis v. McRuer: A Long-Overdue Replay with the Possibility of a Penalty Shoot-Out," in *UTLJ* 2005, 535–74.

69 Ibid., ch. 4:7.

70 Katherine McIntyre and Allan Leal, interviews by author, 8 and 12 March 1994.

71 One of Jim's most moving letters to Mary was written on 11 Nov. 1936 while he was working in Ottawa on the Archambault commission. After attending the Armistice Day service on Parliament Hill, Jim returned to his room in the Chateau Laurier and cast his mind back to the First World War. Then, taking up his pen, he told Mary that in 1918 "so much of my plans and hopes and dreams revolved around you." As he looked back over the years since their marriage, he could "truthfully say" that "you have been better than my fondest dreams and I never even hoped that we could be where we are today. We have both paid the price but the paying may help to bring us closer together as years go on." He finished the letter saying, "I still love you with a great abounding love. Some times—many times I fear—when nervously distraught my tongue has been very careless but my heart has never weakened for one moment. Love my dear forever. Jim."

72 By this time the McRuers were living on Silverwood Avenue in Toronto; their two earlier houses in the city, on Glenayr Road and Colstream Avenue, had been sold in the 1950s.

73 Robena was to outlive her husband. She died at a nursing home in Kitchener on 20 Dec. 1992, in her ninetieth year, and was buried in the Ayr cemetery alongside Jim and his first wife Mary.

15   REFORMING THE LAW

1 J.C. McRuer, "Modernizing the Law," address to the Lawyers' Club, Toronto, 25 April 1992. Copy in JCM Papers (AO).

2 J.C. McRuer, "Archaism in the Law of Alimony," *Canada Law Journal*, vol. 58 (January 1922), 1.

3 JCM Papers, Conant to McRuer, 1 March 1938; McRuer to Conant, 3 March 1938 (two letters); Conant to McRuer, 7 March 1938; McRuer to Conant, 9 Nov. 1938, 30 Aug. 1939, and 19 March 1942.

4 J.C. McRuer, "Constitutional Problems of Reconstruction in Canada,"

address to the Canadian Institute of International Affairs, 7 April 1942.

5 McRuer described this case in an interview with the author.

6 Interviews with McRuer and Allan Leal.

7 Interviews with McRuer and Rendall Dick.

8 *SO* 1964, c.78.

9 Interview with Bill Poole, 20 March 1994; also, discussions with Allan Leal and Brendan O'Brien, March and May 1994.

10 Ibid.

11 Osgoode Society, Ontario Legal History project, interview with Gibson Gray, 298.

12 Interview with McRuer.

13 J.H. Farrar, *Law Reform and the Law Commission* (London: Sweet and Maxwell 1974), 1.

14 Interviews with McRuer and Arthur Wishart.

15 Interview with Arthur Wishart.

16 *SO* 1967, c.72.

17 Interview with McRuer.

18 OLRC *Annual Report*, 1974, 12–13.

19 After a period of remarkable stability in its personnel over the first two decades, the OLRC now entered a phase of comparatively rapid turnover. Leal was replaced as chairman, when he left to become deputy attorney-general in 1977, by Derek Mendes da Costa. The latter left the OLRC for appointment to the bench in 1984 and was replaced by James R. Breithaupt. In 1991 Breithaupt was replaced by Rosalie S. Abella, and she in turn by John D. McCamus in 1993.

20 Any hearings the OLRC did hold were of a highly exclusive kind, such as its session with Court of Appeal judges on a Saturday morning in 1973 to discuss problems the commission was having in its project on the administration of the courts. However, McRuer and his OLRC colleagues did attend meetings organized by others. One of these was convened by Attorney-General Wishart to study major amendments to the Landlord and Tenant Act; another was an Osgoode Hall Law School meeting on personal property security legislation.

21 The OLRC's work in family law, particularly that relating to the division of property, was influential in the development of new matrimonial regimes in several provinces (William H. Hurlburt, *Law Reform Commissions in the United Kingdom, Australia, and Canada* [Edmonton: Juriliber 1986], 207). OLRC reports were especially influential in Atlantic Canada, where there were no law reform commissions.

Western Canadian law reform commissions also followed the work of the OLRC, just as the OLRC watched their efforts. Across Canada, the annual week-long gatherings of the uniformity commissioners reviewed the proposals of various law reform commissions, and, because the OLRC was the most senior of these bodies (with the largest budget, the most projects, and the best success rate in terms of legislative reforms), its reports received special attention. The OLRC also consulted with various law reform commissions outside Canada, particularly those in England, Australia, and New Zealand. The English commission was interested above all in McRuer's recommendation that special remedies (*mandamus, certiorari, quo warranto*) be abolished and replaced by a single judicial order under which a judge could grant a remedy sufficient for a given problem. That reform was developed by McRuer in his capacity as civil rights commissioner, not as leader of the OLRC. For foreigners, however, the distinction was irrelevant.

22 Another OLRC chairperson, Rosalie Abella, described the McRuer era as the commission's "golden years." Interview by author.

16   ONE MAN AND THE LAW

1 *Changing Legal Perspectives*, R.J.S. Macdonald, editor, was published by the University of Toronto Press.

2 See, for example, "Control of Power," in the March Lecture Series, Continuing Legal Education Program of the Law Society of Upper Canada, reprinted in *Abuse of Power* (Toronto: Law Society of Upper Canada 1979), 1–22; "The State and the Individual," an address to the Empire Club of Canada, Toronto, 18 April 1968, reprinted in *The Empire Club Addresses 1967–1968* (Toronto: Empire Club 1968), 412–25; "The Supreme Court as a National Institution," address at a symposium to inaugurate the Supreme Court Law Review, reprinted in *Supreme Court Law Review*, vol. 1 (1980), 467–72; "Modern Lawyers and Their Education," keynote address at a conference of law professors held at the faculty of law, University of Western Ontario, 30 Oct. 1969, reprinted in *Chitty's Law Journal*, May 1970; and "Malignant Powers Defy the Rule of Law," *Globe and Mail*, 4 April 1972.

3 This series, entitled "The Life and Times of J.C. McRuer," was broadcast on 2, 9, 16, and 23 Jan. 1977.

4 This address was delivered on 18 Oct. 1972.

5 OLRC to Attorney-General Wishart, 10 Sept. 1968.

6 Ontario Law Reform Commission, *Report on the Protection of Privacy in Ontario* (Toronto 1968).

7 Interviews with Bill Poole and John McCamus, 20 and 22 March 1994.

8 *Proceedings of the Special Senate Committee on the Constitution*, Hon. R.J. Stanbury, Chairman, issue no. 6, 7 Sept. 1978 (Ottawa: Senate of Canada), 6–50.

9 AO, JCM Papers, typescript of book review, subsequently published in the *Globe and Mail*.

10 Interview by author, 20 March 1994.

11 JCM Papers, "Address delivered at the Second Annual Ontario Leadership Prayer Breakfast, 5 May 1971, Royal York Hotel, Toronto," typescript. One aspect of McRuer's defence of religious freedom in this talk was challenged by the Reverend Alex Zeidman, director of the Scott Mission in Toronto, and lawyer John W. Younger. Both Zeidman and Younger took issue with McRuer's criticism of John Calvin for his role in the execution of the religious dissident Servetus. McRuer, however, had done his homework on this matter, and the most he was willing to concede was that Calvin preferred that Servetus "be executed by beheading rather than burning." See JCM Papers, McRuer to Zeidman, 11 June 1971.

12 For someone who was so delicate in his youth, McRuer certainly developed a hardy constitution in later years. In the late 1940s—he was then in his late fifties—he joined the Alpine Club of Canada and went on hikes in the Rockies. Speaking at the Ontario Ladies' College in Whitby, McRuer told the graduates that "you will find life a great deal like mountain climbing. For years I had opportunities from time to time to climb in the mountains but I never took advantage of them. I thought that was a sport for freaks and funny people. Later in life I got started and I realized then what I had missed. It was, alas, too late for me to take full advantage of the possibilities."

13 Osgoode Society, transcript of dinner meeting at Campbell House, Toronto, 11 Jan. 1991.

14 Ibid.

15 On the McMahon story, see the following letters in the JCM Papers: McRuer to Macaulay, 17 Jan. 1934, McRuer to M.F. Gallagher, 14 Nov. 1938, McRuer to H.R.S. Ryan, 20 Nov. 1937, McRuer to Norman Rogers, 5 June 1940.

16 JCM Papers, McRuer to H.R.S. Ryan, 20 Nov. 1937.

INDEX

CREDITS

MANY PEOPLE assisted in creating this book and I thank them all.

I am grateful for the cooperation of the McRuer family: J.C. McRuer and his wife Robena in their lifetimes, his son John, and his daughters Katherine and Mary Louise.

In addition to several hundred interviews and conversations I conducted over the years, Elizabeth Salter-Burt helped with the recorded interviews. Allistair Sweeney, Ralph Robinson, Sherry Henderson, Shaun Johnson, Kerry Badgley, Susan Biggar, Joan Hudson, Celia Hitch, Maryszka Clovis and my late father Robert J. Boyer assisted in various ways with the research and preparation.

Roy McMurtry, a unique friend, provided a constant source of encouragement for this project over the years. The late Peter N. Oliver, another friend of long standing who is much missed, helped keep the book moving forward and contributed indispensable observations both as historian and editor-in-chief of The Osgoode Society for Legal History.

I was happy to introduce Roy McMurtry to Peter Oliver and participate in the genesis of the Osgoode Society in the summer of 1978, a story now recounted by Roy McMurtry in his introduction to this paperback edition.

Marilyn MacFarlane, who assisted me by typing transcripts of the McRuer interviews even before The Osgoode Society came into being, and who has since become a mainstay of the Society, helped as well with arrangements for the original hardcover edition of this book through The Osgoode Society, for which I again thank her.

Many people read and commented on the manuscript through its evolution. For their time, interest and thoughtful critiques I especially thank Peter Oliver, Diana Daniels, William R. Young, J. Douglas Ewart, John McRuer, Katherine McIntyre, Mary Louise Gaby, Allan Leal, Rendall Dick, Allan Linden, Brendan O'Brien, John D. Honsberger, John W. Morden, Charles J. Phelan, Martin Friedland, John D. Arnup, David Beatty, and Gordon Bale.

Curtis Fahey brought considerable knowledge, skill, and experience to his role as editor for which I sincerely thank him.

Gary Long assisted with design of this paperback edition and its additional new features and I am grateful for his professional focus, technical skills, and friendship.

Corinne, my wife and close partner in all adventures until her death, carried the weight of this project from its first inception thirty years ago. She assisted with interviews of Mr. McRuer, commented on the manuscript, helped with publishing arrangements, earned money to help pay significant costs incurred during the book's preparation, and forewent many months of time we otherwise could have shared. The realization of this book was as much her achievement as mine and I am grateful she lived to see its first edition in print. Corinne's brightness was beacon for those who do not go where the path may lead, but instead "go where there is no path, and leave a trail."

ABOUT THE AUTHOR

J. PATRICK BOYER is a lawyer and historian who has written some seventeen books. His active involvement in democratic reform and the rule of law has led him into work as a journalist in Ontario, Saskatchewan and Quebec, as a Member of Parliament, and as president of such public policy organizations as the Couchiching Institute on Public Affairs and the Pugwash Commission in Nova Scotia. His initiatives on democratic renewal and parliamentary reform take place across Canada and overseas from Vietnam, Cambodia, and Thailand to Ukraine and Bulgaria.

He has been active in women's health issues, and was founding chair of the Corinne Boyer Fund for Ovarian Cancer Research and Treatment, today the National Ovarian Cancer Association.

Patrick founded Breakout Education Network as a not-for-profit educational organization ten years ago to help Canadian citizens break free from old patterns of thinking and action in relation to government, and today continues as the organization's chair of education.

Before election to the House of Commons he was a partner in the Toronto firm of Fraser & Beatty, today Fraser Milner Casgrain LLP, where he specialized in communications law, electoral law, and corporate law. He helped launch *Lawyer's Weekly*, was on its editorial board, and wrote a weekly column in the publication.

During his nine years in parliament Patrick chaired committees on electoral reform, equality rights, and the status of disabled persons. He was then parliamentary secretary for external affairs, and later for national defence.

Patrick Boyer holds a bachelor's degree in political science and economics from Carleton University, a master's degree in history from University of Toronto, and a doctor of laws from the Faculty of Law at University of Toronto. He also studied international law at the academy of the International Court of Justice in The Hague. At University of Toronto, he was a founder of the student international law society.

His designation as Queen's Council recognized his "major contribution to Canadian law" by authoring nine books on Canadian electoral law. These include *Political Rights, Lawmaking by the People, Money and Message, Election Law in Canada, Local Elections in Canada* from Butterworths, and *Boyer's Ontario Election Law* from Carswells.

He is a frequent commentator on CBC radio, a writer of newspaper columns and magazine features, and on-air host at *ichannel* Television.

ABOUT THIS BOOK

JIM MCRUER's resolute focus on justice changed the lives of married women with no property rights, children without legal protection, aboriginals caught in the whipsaw of traditional hunting practices and imposed game laws, and prisoners locked away and forgotten. Environmental degradation and those causing it, murderers, stock fraud artists, and Cold War spies all came within the ambit of J.C. McRuer's sharp legal mind and passion for justice as well. At age 75, McRuer embarked on his most important work of all, becoming Canada's greatest law reformer.

In *A Passion for Justice*, Patrick Boyer paints a sweeping portrait of James Chalmers McRuer, revealing the character, complexities, and personal dilemmas of one of Canada's outstanding jurists.

McRuer lived from 1890 to 1985. His active career of more than 50 years included periods as a crusading Crown prosecutor, service on the Archambault Royal Commission on Penal Reform (1936–8), chief justice of the Ontario High Court (1945–64), head of the one-man Royal Commission Inquiry into Civil Rights (1964–71), and leader of the Ontario Law Reform Commission (1964–77).

The law reform commission, the first such body in the British Commonwealth, was created largely through McRuer's relentless efforts. Its high success rate in major law reform recommendations implemented became McRuer's and the commission's most important legacy to future generations.

The driving spirit in McRuer was his passion for justice. He believed the justice system should serve the oppressed. He saw a need to adapt the law to better serve all people in the changed conditions of the 20th century. He possessed a sharp sensitivity to the often hidden injustices in an advanced industrial society and a bureaucratic state. In discerning the impulses that fuelled McRuer's career, Boyer equally shows the anomalies of this shy public man, committed to penal reform but known as "Hangin' Jim" for his readiness to send men to the gallows. Personal insensitivity curiously combined with legendary kindness.

In his many legal, political, judicial, governmental, and educational roles, McRuer articulated the philosophy of classic liberalism, expressed the power of individualism, and transubstantiated his deep religious conviction to the law. These values and works combined with James McRuer's tireless efforts remain today as part of his legacy, solidly embedded in contemporary law.